Developments in American Politics 5

Developments titles available from Palgrave

Maria Green Cowles and Desmond Dinan (eds)
DEVELOPMENTS IN THE EUROPEAN UNION 2

Patrick Dunleavy, Richard Heffernan, Philip Cowley and
Colin Hay (eds)
DEVELOPMENTS IN BRITISH POLITICS 8

Alistair Cole, Patrick Le Galès and Jonah Levy (eds)
DEVELOPMENTS IN FRENCH POLITICS 3

Paul M. Heywood, Erik Jones, Martin Rhodes and
Ulrich Sedelmeier (eds)
DEVELOPMENTS IN EUROPEAN POLITICS

Stephen Padgett, William E. Paterson and Gordon Smith (eds)
DEVELOPMENTS IN GERMAN POLITICS 3[*]

Gillian Peele, Christopher J. Bailey, Bruce Cain and B. Guy Peters (eds)
DEVELOPMENTS IN AMERICAN POLITICS 5

Stephen White, Judy Batt and Paul Lewis (eds)
DEVELOPMENTS IN CENTRAL AND EAST
EUROPEAN POLITICS 3[*]

Stephen White, Zvi Gitelman and Richard Sakwa (eds)
DEVELOPMENTS IN RUSSIAN POLITICS 6[*]

Of Related Interest

Ian Holliday, Andrew Gamble and Geraint Parry (eds)
FUNDAMENTALS IN BRITISH POLITICS

If you have any comments or suggestions regarding the
above or other possible *Developments* titles, please write to
Steven Kennedy, Palgrave Macmillan, Houndmills,
Basingstoke RG21 6XS, UK or e-mail s.kennedy@palgrave.com

[*] Rights world excluding North America

Developments in American Politics 5

Edited by

Gillian Peele

Christopher J. Bailey

Bruce Cain

and

B. Guy Peters

palgrave
macmillan

This new book is designed as a direct replacement for
Developments in American Politics 4 (2002)

First published 2006 by
PALGRAVE MACMILLAN
Houndmills, Basingstoke, Hampshire RG21 6XS and
175 Fifth Avenue, New York, N.Y. 10010
Companies and representatives throughout the world

PALGRAVE MACMILLAN is the new global academic imprint of the Palgrave Macmillan division of St. Martin's Press, LLC and of Palgrave Macmillan Ltd. Macmillan® is a registered trademark in the United States, United Kingdom and other countries. Palgrave is a registered trademark in the European Union and other countries.

ISBN-13: 978–1–4039–8705–1   hardback
ISBN-10: 1–4039–8705–X   hardback
ISBN-13: 978–1–4039–8706–8   paperback
ISBN-10: 1–4039–8706–8   paperback

This book is printed on paper suitable for recycling and made from fully managed and sustained forest sources.

A catalogue record for this book is available from the British Library.

A catalog record for this book is available from the Library of Congress.

10   9   8   7   6   5   4   3   2   1
15 14 13 12 11 10 09 08 07 06

Printed and bound in China

Contents

List of Figures and Tables

Figures

Tables

Preface

This is the fifth *Developments in American Politics*. It is the product of a team of authors drawn from the United Kingdom and the United States. All the chapters are original and analyze American politics and policy-making at the start of George W. Bush's second term of office. A book written at this stage of the George W. Bush presidency will inevitably devote a good deal of attention to the character of the 43rd president and his administration as well as to the relationship between the executive and the other key institutions of the American political system. But our authors also seek to put their topics into the wider context of changes in American society and political life.

We try to make the book as user-friendly as possible for students. The references to works cited in the text are collected together in a bibliography at the end of the book. There is also a short guide to further reading for each of the chapters and readers will also find there reference to relevant websites. In order to simplify usage we have used American spelling throughout the book.

The editors would like to thank Steven Kennedy, our publisher, for his help and encouragement. We also thank the anonymous referee for a series of useful suggestions for improving the manuscript. We thank our colleagues at the universities of Oxford, Keele, Berkeley and Pittsburgh for their intellectual support. Thanks are especially due also to Mrs Glynis Beckett, Tutors' Secretary at Lady Margaret Hall, Oxford, who cheerfully gave wide-ranging secretarial support, to Ben Bridle and his computing team at LMH, and to Kevin Sabet, who helped with checking and collating the manuscript.

GILLIAN PEELE
CHRISTOPHER J. BAILEY
BRUCE CAIN
B. GUY PETERS

Notes on the Contributors

Robert B. Albritton is Professor of Political Science at the University of Mississippi.

Christopher J. Bailey is Professor of American Politics at Keele University.

Chris W. Bonneau is Assistant Professor of Political Science at the University of Pittsburgh.

Bruce Cain is Robson Professor of Political Science and Director of the Institute of Governmental Studies, University of California at Berkeley, and the University of California, Washington Center.

Robert Darcy is Regents Professor of Political Science and Statistics at Oklahoma State University.

Ross English is Lecturer in Politics at the University of Reading.

Darshan J. Goux is a PhD candidate in the Institue of Governmental Studies, University of California at Berkeley.

Jonathan Herbert is Lecturer in American Studies at Keele University.

Baodong Liu is Associate Professor of Political Science at the University of Wisconsin-Oshkosh.

Robert Mason is Lecturer in History at the University of Edinburgh.

Gillian Peele is Fellow and Tutor in Politics at Lady Margaret Hall, Oxford.

B. Guy Peters is Maurice Falk Professor of American Government at the University of Pittsburgh.

John Sides is Assistant Professor of Political Science at George Washington University.

Tara W. Stricko-Neubauer is a PhD candidate in the Department of Political Science at the University of Pittsburgh.

Alex Waddan is Lecturer in Politics at the University of Leicester.

Graham K. Wilson is Professor of Political Science and Public Affairs at the University of Wisconsin-Madison.

Andrew Wroe is Lecturer in Politics at the University of Kent.

List of Abbreviations and Acronyms

AARP	American Association of Retired People
ABC	American Broadcasting Corporation
ABM	Anti-Ballistic Missile
ACT	Americans Coming Together
ADEA	Age Discrimination in Employment Act 1967
ADR	Americans for Divorce Reform
AFBF	American Farm Bureau Federation
AFDC	Aid to Families with Dependent Children
AFL-CIO	American Federation of Labor-Congress of Industrial Organizations
APSA	American Political Science Association
ARMPAC	Americans for a Republican Majority Political Action Committee
ATV	All-Terrain Vehicle
BCRA	Bipartisan Campaign Reform Act 2002
BIPAC	Business Industry Political Action Committee
BLM	Bureau of Land Management
BMI	Body Mass Index
BP	British Petroleum
CAFTA	Central American Free Trade Agreement
CBO	Congressional Budget Office
CBS	Columbia Broadcasting System
CCSL	Citizens' Conference on State Legislatures
CDC	Centers for Disease Control
CEA	Council of Economic Advisers
CFABA	Citizens for a Better America
CFC	Chlorofluorocarbons
CNN	Cable News Network
COPA	Child Online Protection Act 1998
COPE	Committee on Political Education
CPPA	Child Pornography Prevention Act 1996
CTEA	Copyright Term Extension Act 1998
DJIA	Dow Jones Industrial Average
DNC	Democratic National Committee
DNCC	Democratic National Campaign Committee

DOMA	Defense of Marriage Act 1996
DSCC	Democratic Senatorial Campaign Committee
EAC	Election Assistance Commission
EITC	Earned Income Tax Credit
EOP	Executive Office of the President
EPA	Environmental Protection Agency
ERISA	Employee Retirement Security Act 1974
ETS	Environmental Tobacco Smoke
FAIR	Fairness and Accuracy in Reporting
FAIR	Federation for American Immigration Reform
FBI	Federal Bureau of Investigation
FCC	Federal Communications Commission
FEC	Federal Election Commission
FECA	Federal Election Campaign Act 1971
FEMA	Federal Emergency Management Administration
FMA	Federal Marriage Amendment
FRC	Family Research Council
GDP	Gross Domestic Product
GOP	Grand Old Party
GOTV	Get out the Vote
HAVA	Help America Vote Act 2002
HEW	Department of Health, Education and Welfare (no longer existent)
HHS	Department of Health and Human Services
HIV/AIDS	Human Immuno Deficiency Virus/Acquired Immune Deficiency Syndrome
HMO	Health Maintenance Organization
HSA	Health Savings Account
HUD	Department of Housing and Urban Development
ICC	International Criminal Court
IMF	International Monetary Fund
INS	Immigration and Naturalization Services
IRS	Internal Revenue Service
MMA	Medicare Modernization Act 2003
MSNBC	Microsoft Network/National Broadcasting Corporation
NAACP	National Association for the Advancement of Colored People
NAFTA	North American Free Trade Agreement
NARAL	National Abortion and Reproduction Rights Action League
NASCAR	National Association for Stock Car Auto Racing
NASDAQ	National Association of Securities Dealers Automated Quotations
NATO	North Atlantic Treaty Organization

NBC	National Broadcasting Corporation
NCLB	No Child Left Behind Act 2001
NEP	National Election Pool
NFIB	National Federation of Independent Business
NHANES	National Health and Nutrition Examination Survey
NIH	National Institute of Health
NMD	National Missile Defense
NOW	National Organization for Women
NRA	National Rifle Association
NRCC	National Republican Congressional Committee
NRSC	National Republican Senatorial Committee
NSC	National Security Council
OASN	Old Age, Survivors and Disability Insurance
OECD	Organisation for European Co-operation and Development
OFBCI	Office of Faith-Based and Community Initiatives
OMB	Office of Management and Budget
Op-Ed	Opinion-Editorial
PA	Palestinian Authority
PAC	Political Action Committee
PFAW	People For The American Way
PhRMA	Pharmaceutical Research and Manufacturers of America
PIPA	Program on International Policy Attitudes
POW	Prisoner Of War
PRWORA	Personal Responsibility and Work Opportunity Reconciliation Act 1996
REP	Representative
RICO	Racketeer Influenced and Corrupt Organizations Act 1970
RNC	Republican National Committee
SCHIP	State Children's Health Insurance Program
TANF	Temporary Assistance to Needy Families
TRMPAC	Texans for a Republican Majority Political Action Committee
UAW	International Union, United Automobile, Aerospace and Agricultural Implement Workers of America
UN	United Nations
VAT	Value Added Tax
WASPs	White Anglo-Saxon Protestants
WHO	White House Office
WMD	Weapons of Mass Destruction
WTO	World Trade Organization

List of State Abbreviations

AK	Alaska	NE	Nebraska
AZ	Arizona	NV	Nevada
AR	Arkansas	NH	New Hampshire
CA	California	NJ	New Jersey
CO	Colorado	NM	New Mexico
CT	Connecticut	NY	New York
DE	Delaware	NC	North Carolina
DC	District of Columbia	ND	North Dakota
FL	Florida	OH	Ohio
GA	Georgia	OK	Oklahoma
HI	Hawaii	OR	Oregon
ID	Idaho	PA	Pennsylvania
IL	Illinois	RI	Rhode Island
IN	Indiana	SC	South Carolina
IA	Iowa	SD	South Dakota
KS	Kansas	TN	Tessessee
KY	Kentucky	TX	Texas
LA	Louisiana	UT	Utah
ME	Maine	VT	Vermont
MD	Maryland	VI	Virgin Islands
MA	Massachusetts	VA	Virginia
MI	Michigan	WA	Washington
MN	Minnesota	WV	West Virginia
MS	Mississippi	WI	Wisconsin
MO	Missouri	WY	Wyoming
MT	Montana		

The United States: States, state capitals and main cities

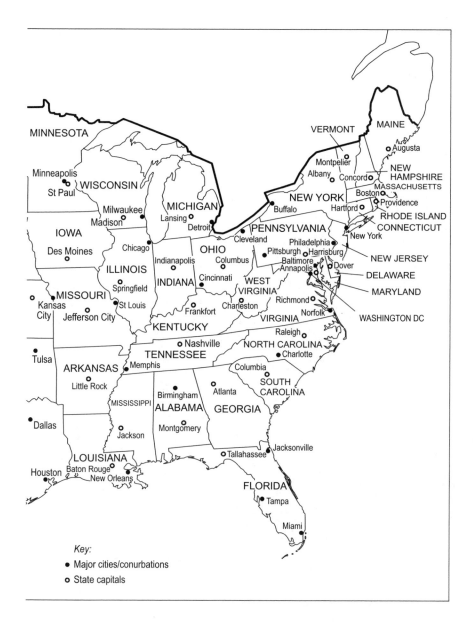

Key:
- Major cities/conurbations
- State capitals

Chapter 1

Introduction

Gillian Peele, Christopher J. Bailey, Bruce Cain
and B. Guy Peters

The period of George W. Bush's presidency – the opening years of the twenty-first century – has been a highly unusual one which has placed severe strain on the American political system but has also demonstrated the inherent flexibility and resilience of the country's institutions. The first term of the Bush presidency began in a mood of great political rancour following the bitterly contested election of 2000 which saw Bush capture the White House without a majority of the popular vote and only as the result of a highly controversial Supreme Court decision. Although the circumstances of the 2000 elections initially put Bush's legitimacy in doubt because of the absence of a mandate, the new President's strategy for governing did not reflect the slender nature of his victory. Rather Bush proceeded to try to shape a radical agenda focused for the most part on issues which had the support of the Republican Party and which reflected his own ideological instincts. Thus tax cuts, social security reform, strengthened defense, and greater reliance on faith-based communities in the field of social policy all figured prominently in his legislative program, as did the more bipartisan issue of educational reform. Although the terrorist attacks which hit New York and Washington DC in September 2001 transformed the political scene, allowing Bush to present himself as a strong and forceful leader and a unifying figure for a country which was faced with an unprecedented threat, he had already embarked on a governing strategy which in a sense defied political expectations.

The terrorist attacks turned George W. Bush's presidency into one where war, foreign policy and national security issues came to play a much greater part in his calculations than had been anticipated. Inevitably the crisis also allowed the executive more autonomy and played to Bush's preference for a presidency which could take policy decisions unilaterally. The fact that the wide-ranging Patriot Act of 2001 initially passed with such strong support from Congress, despite its implications for civil liberties, underlined the gravity of the perceived threat from Al Qaeda. Yet the Bush administration's decision to go to war against Iraq in 2003

1

destroyed much of the initial international sympathy for the United States and created deep divisions within America itself. And the discovery that the Bush administration had been engaging in unauthorized surveillance of American citizens caused the Senate to block renewal of the Patriot Act in December 2006.

Despite an increasing level of opposition to his policies at home and abroad George W. Bush won the 2004 presidential election, emerging the clear, if narrow, winner in both the popular vote and the Electoral College. This victory at first sight seemed to vindicate his personal handling of the presidency and to give him a mandate for further change. As Bush famously put it, he had earned "political capital" and he now intended to spend it. And because the 2004 elections slightly improved the Grand Old Party's (GOP) position in both the Senate and the House, it appeared likely that Bush would be able to deliver some significant part of a political agenda which had become increasingly radical. There was thus an optimistic sense on the right that the 2004 elections marked a turning point in American public policy and that the second term of the Bush presidency would enable progress on the President's program. At its most ambitious that program envisaged a new approach to public policy-making and a much more limited role for government in American society as well as radical reforms of the tax, legal and social security systems.

Just over a year later the prospects for the remaining part of the George W. Bush administration seemed much less promising. Whatever highs Bush's personal popularity had reached in the aftermath of 9/11, a series of natural disasters and political problems early in Bush's second term cast doubt on the President's leadership skills and on his capacity to deliver an ambitious agenda. The emphasis on going public and the strategic skill invested in handling the administration's public relations appeared increasingly ineffective as the administration was buffeted by a series of largely unforeseen events. Thus the devastation wrought by Hurricane Katrina, the forced withdrawal of Harriet Meiers as his second Supreme Court nominee and the indictment of Vice-President Cheney's chief of staff, Lewis "Scooter" Libby, on a perjury charge relating to the leaking of the name of a CIA operative saw Bush's approval ratings fall to their lowest level ever and the lowest ever recorded for a president. Although Bush's rating picked up briefly at the beginning of 2006, the opening of the new year also saw the danger that the reputation of the Bush administration would be tarnished by association with a new Capitol Hill lobbying scandal centered around Jack Abramoff which threatened a number of Republican politicians. The Bush presidency thus went quickly from looking triumphalist to being embattled, and there was talk of Bush having to refresh his personal staff to create a new image. Indeed there was even some discussion about whether Bush would see out his second term.

Explaining why the political strength – the "capital" – of the Bush presidency had eroded so quickly in the first year of his second term in the White House highlights the complex interweaving of long-, medium- and short-term factors which structure contemporary American politics and which will be explored in this book. Among the long-term factors are social, economic and demographic change as well as the logic of the country's constitutional arrangements. The medium-term factors are the shifting patterns within those longer-term forces: for example economic cycles and the balance of constitutional power within the constitutional system. Of course there are also important short-term factors which affect American politics, including the character of individual politicians and parties and the sequence of events.

Thus, however ambitious an individual president may be to shape the political agenda, he has to recognize the difficulty of moving public policy within the United States and the extent to which the system has its own in-built barriers to change, whether in the form of institutional checks and balances or in the form of competing interests and organizations. He has, in short, to recognize the peculiar difficulties of governance in the United States and the constraints put on executive power by the logic of the American Constitution. Certainly these constraints have faced President George W. Bush. Whatever Bush's hopes for a realignment in American politics that would create an enduring Republican majority, he has had to recognize the difficulty of building, let alone sustaining, consensus in a political system of diverse interests and multiple veto players. And he has had to accept the way in which his agenda has been blown off course by events not of his making, such as Hurricane Katrina, as well as by the unpredictable path of American involvement in Iraq. And as presidents well know, their ability to dominate the political system is crucially affected by their capacity to retain the public opinion support. In that battle communication is vital but, as Robert Mason shows in his chapter, technology has transformed the media making it more difficult for a president to exploit and create a range of divergent audiences.

Constitutional constraints

Although Americans naturally think that theirs is a system that exhibits majoritarian democracy, in fact the original design of the Founding Fathers has built in limits to majority power. The Madisonian philosophy of checks and balances was calculated to ensure that no single faction could dominate the polity and that minorities were protected. The two principles of constitutionalism and majoritarianism are thus juxtaposed, creating a dynamic which has shaped America's constitutional development. Today the tension between majoritarian values and concern for minorities is still apparent in many of the debates within American politics. It is also apparent in the working of many of America's key institutions where constitutional rules or political practice have ensured continued sensitivity to minority opinion. For example in the Senate the procedural device of the filibuster has long been the weapon which protected minorities on the left and the right of the political spectrum (Binder and Smith, 1997). Recently this device has become more prominent and has been under attack by a Republican president frustrated by its use to block controversial judicial and other appointees and to thwart legislative initiatives including the authorization of drilling in Alaska's wildlife reserves and the renewal of the Patriot Act.

The American Constitution is one which, while it gives a president flexible powers, also sets constraints on what the executive can do; and Congress can exert real influence over the detail of policy, forcing presidents even of their own party to compromise, frustrating their will and on occasion making policy less coherent. Although Congress was from 2002 firmly in Republican hands, it has not been an entirely docile body challenging Bush on key items of his programmes, including the tax cuts which were passed in 2001 and 2003 and the No Child Left Behind legislation which did not include, as Bush would have wished, support for school vouchers. At the same time, however, as Ross English shows in his chapter on Congress, the legislature itself experienced a series of procedural and substantive conflicts which cast doubt on its ability to respond to the nation's needs. Some of this conflict and frustration was the result of the closely balanced and highly partisan atmosphere that has marked the Bush presidency. Some of it reflected difficulties inside the parties themselves and a seemingly recurrent pattern of unethical or misjudged behavior on the part of senior politicians. Thus the Republican Party in Congress over the period 2001 to 2006 exhibited its own divisions, scandals and disagreements which have provided leadership problems in the House, where Majority Leader Tom DeLay was accused of money laundering and forced to withdraw from public life. In the Senate, the GOP had to adjust to a new leader after Majority Leader Trent Lott's resignation in the wake of leaked remarks at a party for veteran Senator Strom Thurmond.

The fact that the United States is a *federal* system imposes its own constraints on government. In a federal system there may be a diversity of policy and very different approaches to implementation. This diversity occurs between the several states and between the state and federal governments. For example the states have very different approaches to environmental regulation and indeed some states and cities have more stringent environmental regulations than the federal government: Seattle, for example, has attempted to abide by the Kyoto Treaty regardless of the Bush administration's rejection of it. As Robert Albritton points out in his chapter, however, the state level of government within the United States exhibits a degree of complexity which produces daunting problems of coordination. And that governmental diversity in turn reflects extensive differences in the geographic, demographic and economic character of the states themselves.

In addition to the checks imposed by federal government, the courts act as important constraints on government imposing their interpretation of what the constitution requires on the country's political institutions and citizens. The importance of the federal courts – and especially the Supreme Court – in developing the country's understanding of civil rights and liberties has of course given judges a highly contentious role in contemporary politics, as Chris Bonneau and Tara Stricko-Neubauer show in their chapter. This controversial role is especially obvious in the conflicts over the relative importance of civil liberties and public safety as underlined by the legal challenges to aspects of the President's handling of the war in Iraq and the treatment of prisoners in detention. From the period of the Reagan presidency there has been a systematic effort by conservatives to use the president's power of appointment to the federal bench to put a conservative stamp on the judiciary and, if possible, reverse some of the liberal decisions of the Supreme Court in the post-1945 era, especially the highly controversial *Roe* v. *Wade* decision which in 1973 gave women a constitutional right to abortion. Not surprisingly therefore, federal court appointments have been a major concern of George W. Bush, especially once it became apparent that with the vacancies caused by the retirement of Justice Sandra Day O'Connor and the death of Chief Justice William Rehnquist he would have the chance to remould the Court in his second term. The choice of John Roberts as Chief Justice to succeed Rehnquist and the nomination of Samuel Alito to the Court underlined the conservative values of the President himself but also the strategic problems of getting a nomination through the Senate. Although Alito has been confirmed, he was extensively questioned on his attitude to the litmus test issue of abortion and also on a wider range of constitutional issues including the scope of executive power.

It would, of course, be a mistake to see the constitutional constraints – the checks and balances of the system – as impediments to all change. Indeed the George W. Bush presidency underlines the extent to which informal forces and unusual events such as war can be exploited to overcome institutional opposition and move policy in radical new directions.The presidency of Franklin D. Roosevelt engineered a series of policy shifts which had profound political and constitutional consequences.Those shifts occurred as a result of a domestic crisis which gave a popular president extensive freedom of manoeuver. George W. Bush has sought to strengthen executive power in the wake of the war on terror, forging a theory of presidential authority which in many important respects is at odds with the traditional understanding of American constitutionalism. Yet, while shifts can and do occur in response to historically unusual events, the framework of constitutional government is strong and is likely to be reasserted once the crisis is past. Moreover, as many political scientists have pointed out, claims to enhanced political authority are heavily dependent on policy success; in the absence of that success a president's ambitions are unlikely to be fulfilled.

A diverse society

Part of the problem for the American courts (and indeed for the political system more generally) is the range of conflicting interests, values and preferences found within its boundaries and the extent to which America's democratic processes facilitate the translation of that diversity into political action. The system of checks and balances erected by the Founding Fathers was designed to prevent tyranny and it reflected the Framers' inherent suspicion of government. That trait has continued despite the enormously changed character of American society. Indeed it is one of the major achievements of the American system of government that it has managed to adapt to a society so different from that for which it was designed.

The Founding Fathers constructed their system of government for a society that was small and relatively homogenous: Americans at the beginning of the Republic were largely Protestants drawn from Britain and other parts of western Europe. They were, of course, white (although there was from the beginning the dilemma about how to include black slaves in the infant polity), and their primary employment was agriculture. The expansion of the US by immigration in the nineteenth century brought to its shores large numbers of immigrants keen to open the golden door of opportunity. The population of the United States, which was 76 million in 1900, had quadrupled in 2000 to a figure close to 281 million, a figure which has continued to rise dramatically even in the first decade of the twenty-first century. Indeed the years 2001 and 2002 saw the number of immigrants admitted to the United States top the million mark – a figure equalled in only nine previous years. However, security worries in the wake of 9/11 and subsequent tightening of immigration processes caused a drop in this figure thereafter.

Just how significant a factor immigration remains in the demographics of the United States is underlined by the fact that by 2003 some 11 per cent of the population was foreign born. Recent immigration to the United

States has been distinctive also in that it has come from very different sources from the countries whose emigrants shaped the United States until the 1950s. As late as the 1950s the majority of immigrants to the USA were of European background but increasingly today European immigrants are a small minority. Instead the new immigrants – and new Americans – are drawn from Latin America, Asia and the Caribbean, with substantial implications for the character of American society and, as Christopher Bailey, Bob Darcy and Baodong Liu show in their chapters, a major impact on the role of race in public policy.

The threat of global terrorism has inevitably had an effect on the way in which the United States handles immigration, making it more wary of granting amnesty to illegal and undocumented immigrants and producing enhanced efforts to secure America's borders through such plans as the Secure Border Initiative which entails stricter border controls, expanded detention facilities and more effective monitoring of the immigration laws. Such policies inevitably have had a particular impact in the areas most vulnerable to illegal migration – the states with a border with Mexico. Not surprisingly these initiatives have genereated a hostile response from Mexico and other Latin American countries.

Terrorism has also created a good deal of hostility to the increasingly important Muslim community within the United States. Although the precise figures for adherents of Islam in America is difficult to ascertain, the numbers are generally put at around 5 to 6 million. The vast majority (around 42%) of these Muslims are converts to Islam, which has proved popular among the African-American population. However, immigration to the United States is an important source of growth in the Islamic community.

The American population – refashioned in each generation by immigration – is thus now a mosaic of ethnic, religious and cultural identities. This diversity has reopened the question of what it means to be American. The initial assumption that the immigrants' different identities would be shed over time as Americans became absorbed into a new national whole was challenged in the second half of the twentieth century. Today there is much greater recognition given to the legitimacy of different cultural heritages within the United States and the melting pot metaphor made famous by Israel Zangwill has frequently seemed to be discarded in favour of the metaphors of the salad bowl or the great cultural mosaic. Yet race, as Baodong Liu and Bob Darcy argue, remains an ever-present issue in American politics even as governments seek to transcend it and to deracialize policy. And in the post-9/11 atmosphere of the United States new divisions have appeared which sometimes suggest an atmosphere of us and them not merely in relation to the international community but also inside the United States itself.

Although ethnicity and race have long played a prominent and often tragic part in the dynamics of American society, increasingly attention has recently turned also to the role of religion in society. Religion has always had a profound effect on American culture. The separation of church and state at the federal level provided a formula which could accommodate the diversity of sects and denominations (Ahlstrom, 2004). Official neutrality did not, however, mean indifference to religion: the United States – unlike much of Europe – is a country which retains an unusually widespread belief in a deity and an unusually high degree of religious observance (Wuthnow, 1998). The freedom of worship which the United States cherished from its origins had by the twentieth century created a rich diversity of religious organizations even if there was until the 1960s a subtle distinction between the churches in terms of their social and political appeal and acceptability. Today the religious variety of the United States is even more apparent than it was in 1960 when John Kennedy became the first Roman Catholic successfully to seek the presidency. As Diana Eck and others have argued, the US is now marked by a variety of religions outside the Judaeo-Christian tradition and these add a new dimension to the pluralism that is America (Eck, 2002). This new religious pluralism is marked by the physical appearance of Islamic mosques and Hindu and Buddhist temples across the United States.

Religious differences, of course, feed into cultural ones and shape what Robert Bellah called "habits of the heart" – the individual values which make America's national character distinctive and shape its public philosophy. Religion also has an impact on the key lifestyle issues which, as Christopher Bailey shows in his chapter, have become such an important component in American political debate. Indeed, as Bailey argues, lifestyle issues have become a new fissure in American politics, not merely pushing such issues as homosexual rights and reproductive rights up the political agenda but creating bitter battle lines and unusual alliances. Opponents of "Big Government" have championed increased public regulation of private activities, proponents of "states rights" have urged greater federal involvement in areas traditionally left to state and local governments, and the Christian right has occasionally joined with a liberal medical establishment to tell people how to live their lives.

The politics of diversity

These multiple divisions in part explain the difficulty of building consensus within the American political system. These divisions can be celebrated as pluralism but, as Graham Wilson suggests in his chapter, when they form the basis of pressure group activity they can also make the conduct of public policy much more complex and difficult. Ethnic, cultural and religious divisions also shape political identities and loyalties. The United States' system of party politics revolves around coalitions of groups which lean towards one party or the other. Perhaps these groups are not as solid or stable as they once were but discussion of the political scene in 2004 was suffused with images of a country deeply divided. Those divisions were symbolized by the colouring of political maps into red and blue states. The 2004 elections, like the 2000 presidential election before them, revealed a country with apparently clear fault-lines. Some of these divisions were geographic: the Republican strength was concentrated in the south and west and in the suburbs while Democrats found their support in the urban areas and the Northeast as well as in the California and Washington states. Yet a closer look at electoral preferences showed that the picture was altogether more complex with different counties revealing conflicting political allegiances so that instead of the stark red versus blue dichotomy much of the US appeared purple. The stark divisions conjured by the pundits were in large part a product of the Electoral College rather than social reality. However, in some respects there were stark divisions. Despite American reluctance to see politics through the lens of class, it was difficult to deny that the United States was deeply divided also on income lines. Indeed in the 2004 elections John Edwards, the Democratic vice-presidential candidate, depicted the United States as "two nations" separated by wealth and access to such benefits as health care and education. Evidence since the election has tended to confirm Edwards's analysis. Certainly in the aftermath of Hurricane Katrina there was widespread discussion of the inequalities of New Orleans where 28% of the residents were below the poverty line (84% of them black) and 100,000 had no car to allow them to escape the devastation (Frymer, Strolovich and Warren, 2005). More generally there is evidence that the benefits from America's economic growth are disproportionately enjoyed by a small sector of United States society – those who are college educated and in well-paid professions. Thus the top 20% of the population has more than half the country's income and the gap is becoming wider. And as far as poverty is concerned inequalities of health care, housing and income seem to be increasing, a development which is in part due to government policies.

The 2004 elections also underlined how far the country was divided on the interlocking grounds of religion, culture and to some extent gender. Indeed it was an important part of Bush's re-election strategy to solidify what was seen as a crucial part of his core vote – conservative religious voters who could be mobilized around the contentious issues of abortion and gay marriage. And while it was true that the Bush campaign had engaged in a partially successful strategy of trying to reach out to important ethnic minorities (notably Latinos and African Americans), racial divisions are still apparent in many aspects of American life, not least its politics. While it may be true the deepness of the political division at the electoral level may have been much less than at the level of elite politics (where Bruce Cain and Darshan Goux in Chapter 3 argue an atmosphere of intense partisanship has became the dominant motif), these divisions remain important, making it hard for an American president to build a durable consensus. A successful electoral strategy can thus fade as the results are called; the divisions endure.

These divisions in the American electorate are not, of course, new. They have been there for some time. Bush, however, managed to gain the advantage in 2004 by fighting a strategically more acute campaign, as John Sides shows in Chapter 2. Not only did Bush hold onto his core vote but he managed to ensure that the issues where he was the stronger, notably defense and security, dominated the campaign. The issues where his challenger Kerry had the advantage (such as the economy) were minimized in the campaign.

A successful electoral campaign and ultimate victory do not by themselves produce an ability to govern. That depends on a number of factors – the personal skills of a president, his vision of the office of the presidency, the strength and tactics of the many veto players, institutional and political, who flourish in the US scene and the complexity of the issues and events which face a president, as well as the clarity of the incumbent's ideological beliefs.

Ideology and the public policy agenda

Despite the doubts about his detailed grasp of public policy issues and concern about his relaxed decision-making style (to say nothing of his verbal infelicity), George W. Bush, as Gillian Peele shows in her essay on the presidency (Chapter 5), has clearly succeeded in putting together a tight-knit team and developing a leadership approach which suits him. Bush himself brought to the executive a vision of the presidency as an assertive institution; and one of his much-repeated claims, especially after 9/11, was his ability to provide strong leadership. Certainly one of the features which recur in Bush's conduct of the presidency is his willingness to use presidential power in a strategic manner and to maximize the authority of the White House within the political system. Some commentators have seen this resort to the many unilateral weapons available to the executive (the appointments power, the power to issue executive orders and the power to make recess appointments) as indicating a desire to implement an executive strategy of the kind explicitly formulated by Nixon (Aberbach, 2005b). Bush has also enunciated an ambitious agenda and indeed one of the most intriguing features of his presidency is the radical direction in which he would like to take American domestic and foreign policy. What needs to be asked therefore is what the ideological roots of this agenda are and whether it begins to address the public policy problems which confront the United States.

The United States' lack of ideological conflict has traditionally been seen as one of the features which distinguish it from other advanced democracies, perhaps even making it exceptional. While it is true that America has somehow remained remote from the great European cross-currents of ideological fire, ideas have always played an important role in American politics; no socialist party became powerful in the United States and American conservatism, at least until recently, remained a marginal movement. But ideas do matter in American politics and debates about the role of government, the nature of democracy, the relative values of individualism and equality, and the role of the state remain fierce.

Bush's ideology and that of the contemporary Republican Party have to be located within the context of a quarter century in which there has been a massive strengthening of conservative ideology, organization and activism (Peele, 1984). That revival of assertive conservatism which dates from the late 1970s fed into the modern Republican Party and has helped to polarize the parties. There are several strands to this new conservatism – the free-market and supply-side economic theories of Milton Friedman and others, the neo-conservatism of former Democrats such as Irving Kristol and Norman Podhoretz and the new right's emphasis on cultural conservatism and social issues. Even within the confines of the conservative movement, different politicians occupy different points on the spectrum and craft slightly different political messages. Bush's approach to the key issues confronting the United States was in many ways highly distinctive. Changing the relationship between church and state is an important part of Bush's agenda. The religious right is an increasingly important part of Bush's constituency, with Bush himself keen to rewrite the role of religion in American politics. The foundation of the new office of Faith-Based Initiatives inside the White House early in Bush's first term has been supplemented by presidential initatives designed to signal moral support for a range of conservative religious causes including opposition to abortion and stem cell research.

The Bush administration's conservative positions on a range of scientific and medical issues – including stem cell research but also environmental issues and reproductive health – inevitably incurred opposition from the scientific community which was outraged by the misuse of scientific evidence in the policy process and political manipulation of the web of advisory committees. In February 2004 a group of 80 senior scientists including Nobel Laureates signed a statement on the need to restore scientif integrity in government. A group (Union of Concerned Scientists) took up the statement and called for legislation and regulations to prevent the distortion of scientific inquiry for political ends and to restore objectivity and impartiality to the scientific advice given to government.

Although Bush's sympathy for cultural conservativism and his own religious convictions made him popular on the Republican right, some of his policies and priorities were in direct conflict with right-wing preferences. Thus, on education for example, his emphasis on improving educational standards by strengthening the power of federal government put him at odds with Republicans who for many years had urged the abolition of the Department of Education and for whom federal control of education was anathema. Nor were conservatives entirely happy with an economic strategy which, while it emphasized tax cuts, neglected the need to balance the budget. One interpretation of Bush's insistence on continuing tax cuts has been his determination to cut the capacity of federal government once and for all. The other has been the more positive belief that by cutting taxes and empowering individuals more money would be released for both investment and expenditure.

Policy issues

Bush's vision appears to be that of a strong state but one where a strong private sector and a vigorous voluntary sector support the government's role in the framing and delivery of social policy. Reducing the role of federal government has been a mantra of all conservative politicians for some time but this goal has frequently been difficult to reconcile with America's attachment to a number of its key social programs, especially social security. Yet, as Alex Waddan shows in Chapter 13 on social policy, Bush has been willing to "light the blue touch paper" to one of the most explosive issues in American politics: reform of the pensions programme. However, as Waddan notes, this theme was promoted after the election results and given relatively little coverage during the 2004 campaign itself. Also, Waddan notes, Bush's version of "compassionate conservatism" had produced some important first-term initiatives including the No Child Left Behind legislation and an expansion of federal medical provision of subsidized prescriptions for the elderly. These were hardly the actions of a small government conservative and indeed Bush has been happy to expand the role of federal government in selected areas: education, health care and, of course, defence. The stronger federal role in education was diametrically opposed to many Republicans' expectations about what the balance between federal and state government should be and ignored the utter opposition to the Department of Education in some conservative quarters. Nor indeed did Bush fear additional spending despite the implications for the budget.

One of the key items in George Bush's policy arsenal has been tax cuts. Andrew Wroe, in his analysis of the American economy (Chapter 12), shows that although the dominance of the world economy by the United States is such as to dwarf its competitors, the impact of the Bush administration on the economy has been debilitating: tax cuts plus increased expenditures have caused the deficit to rise, while the projected beneficial impact of the cuts on the economy have yet to be felt.

It is perhaps in the field of foreign policy that George Bush's administration has appeared most distinctive and where ideology has arguably played a crucial role. As shown by Jonathan Herbert's analysis of the themes running through Bush's approach to the international order, Bush has departed from the traditional approach of successive post-1945 presidents. Bush came to power exhibiting little interest in or knowledge of international affairs. Yet he surrounded himself with advisers whose beliefs and values were, if not hawkish, unafraid of the constructive use of American power. After 9/11 people like Donald Rumsfeld, Dick Cheney, Paul Wolfowitz and, in a slightly different way, Condoleeza Rice promoted a new American foreign policy which owed much to the attitudes of neo-conservatism. Its novelty was that it asserted the ability and the moral duty of the United States to act unilaterally to protect itself and it urged the promotion of American values throughout the world, even in areas where – as in the Middle East – the United States had traditionally sought stability. This radical twist to American foreign policy has widespread ramifications not least in relation to the anti-Americanism which has been unleashed throughout the world. Herbert detects a degree of movement in Bush's approach to foreign policy in his second term. This shift may be detected in the American government's renewed emphasis on diplomatic engagement and multilateralism as opposed to the unilateral pursuit of American interests and strategy. Yet, as Herbert acknowledges, if there is a movement towards a greater multilateralism, it is one which is very much tailored to American interests and policy preferences rather than to a genuine commitment to mutual decision-making. It is multilateralism when it suits the United States; when multilateralism becomes awkward it is likely to be abandoned. And, of course, as Herbert also notes, the continuing big issues of international politics, not least the future of the Middle East, remain perilous and less than amenable to the efforts of Washington's diplomats and politicians to make progress towards their solution.

One of the lessons which can be drawn, even thus far into the Bush administration, is how difficult it is for an American government to handle the problems of such a fragmented and dynamic society. Guy Peters, who in Chapter 15 addresses the general issue of governance, points out that neither stronger and more cohesive parties nor the absence of divided government have made the process of governing the United States less problematic. The failure of President Bush to get to grips with America's substantive policy dilemmas, despite strong Republican control of Congress, points to a deeper problem in the US system of governance. Indeed there seems to be a more general problem of governmental capacity in the United States which makes federal-level politics increasingly intractable. In order to get greater traction on the substantial policy problems of the United States, resort could be had to devolution (to the state or local government) or to a more administrative/bureaucratic style of decision-making. Yet neither are likely to be feasible in the context of today's highly competitive democracy. Instead we are likely to see a continuation of the paradoxes and conflicts which are so familiar to students of American politics and which in the end serve to guarantee the continuing vitality of the political system.

Peters is concerned with not only the problem of governance in the United States but also the wider issue of the country's style of democracy. He notes the conflict between the majoritarianism implicit in elections and the consensual assumptions built into much of its institutional structure and suggests that in many respects the United States is moving away from consensual democracy. Certainly there is much in contemporary American political life to support the view that the style of democracy which flourished for much of America's history is under strain, not least from a conservative populism which finds expression both in a new presidential assertiveness and in the frequent eruptions of popular sentiment in policy initiatives and referenda at the state level.

Perhaps these tensions are inevitable in a society as diverse, dynamic and fast-moving as that of the United States. It is even possible that the institutional arrangements which served the United States so well for so long are now dysfunctional and unable to handle the range of policy problems which confront the country. It is more likely, however, that the institutional structures will survive and adapt to the new demands placed on them in a manner which reflects the creativity and incrementalism of American political culture.

Chapter 2

Electoral Politics

John Sides

When George W. Bush was inaugurated as the 43rd President of the United States on January 20, 2001, almost 40 percent of the country and 70 percent of Democrats believed that Bush had not "won the election legitimately" according to a December *Los Angeles Times* poll. Protestors at the inauguration threw eggs at his limousine as it processed down Pennsylvania Avenue in Washington DC.

Barely ten months later, an ABC News poll conducted on October 8–9, 2001, recorded the highest job-approval rating ever obtained by a president in the age of survey research: 92 percent of respondents said they approved of the job that George W. Bush was doing as president. In a September *Los Angeles Times* poll, even 82 percent of Democrats approved of "the way President Bush [was] handling the terrorist attack and its aftermath."

Three years later, in the 2004 election, Bush emerged with the lowest fraction of the vote that any elected incumbent president had received since Woodrow Wilson. If approximately 60,000 votes in the state of Ohio had changed hands from Bush to his opponent, Senator John Kerry of Massachusetts – only about 1 percent of the total vote in that state – Kerry would have been elected the 44th President of the United States.

The events described above illustrate how much and how quickly the political and electoral circumstances in the US changed between the 2000 and 2004 elections. Bush won the 2000 election despite losing the popular vote, but saw his public standing skyrocket after the events of September 11. However, in the three years after that tragedy, traditional partisan politics reasserted itself, producing a tightly contested presidential race in 2004. Fundamentally, American politics remains closely divided, which in 2004 produced not just Bush's narrow victory but also a narrow Republican margin in the House and Senate. Thus, even though there were significant changes between the 2000 and 2004 elections – in the national agenda, in rules pertaining to campaigns, in campaign tactics, the outcome also reflected the "structural" features of American electoral politics – personal political loyalties, the advantages of incumbency – that tend to mitigate dramatic change and instead produce stability.

15

This chapter first traces the key events of Bush's first term in office and the 2004 campaign. I discuss how these events shaped the fundamental factors that influence presidential election outcomes, such as war and the economy. I also describe how these events shaped public opinion before the campaign got underway in 2004, and how the public's priorities worked to each party's advantage or disadvantage. I discuss as well changes in the "rules of the game," notably in campaign finance law, and how these changes affected candidate and party strategy. All of these topics constitute parameters within which the campaign operates.

I then discuss in more detail the chronology of the primary and general election campaigns, noting key events and explaining some of the novel strategies the candidates pursued in 2004, which de-emphasized traditional techniques like television advertising in favor of a more old-fashioned effort at voter mobilization. In addition to the presidential race, I discuss the consequences of other, sub-national elections in the 50 states and the implications those have for the overall interpretation of the election. Finally, I conclude by briefly evaluating the 2004 campaign on normative grounds, including such criteria as the level of participation.

From consensus to polarization

Despite the inauspicious beginnings of his presidency, Bush initially achieved several notable successes. Republicans had a workable majority in the House and, with Vice-President Dick Cheney's tie-breaking vote, a slim majority in the Senate. Bush was thus able to make good on his campaign promises as Congress passed a large tax cut and major education legislation. The latter, deemed "No Child Left Behind," drew the support of even liberal Democrats such as Senator Ted Kennedy of Massachusetts. Nevertheless, Bush's approval rating in this period was slightly lower than other presidents at the same point in their first terms. In a February 2001 poll by the Pew Center for the People and Press, Bush's approval rating was 53 percent, which was lower than Clinton's (56%), Bush Sr's (63%), Reagan's (55%), and Carter's (71%).

That changed with the terrorist attacks on September 11, 2001. Dramatic events, such as war and other threats to national security, typically lead citizens to "rally 'round the flag" and support the country's political leaders during the crisis. This "rally effect" is particularly notable when the President commands bipartisan support from other political leaders (Brody and Shapiro, 1989). Such was the case after the attacks on the World Trade Center and the Pentagon. Members of Congress from both parties publicly supported the president. On September 15, both houses voted nearly unanimously (98–0 in the Senate, 420–1 in the House) to authorise the president to use "all necessary and appropriate force" against anyone involved in the attacks. Bush described himself as personally transformed by these attacks and quickly moved to invade Afghanistan and overthrow the Taliban, the radical Islamic regime that had harbored Al Qaeda, including Osama bin Laden. On the domestic front, "homeland security" became the foremost priority; a new cabinet-level Department of Homeland Security was created in 2002.

The consensus that characterized the weeks immediately after the terrorist attacks was temporary. This return to politics-as-usual was not necessarily surprising in that "rally effects" typically prove short-lived. It was striking, however, how quickly an event that seemed to unify the country and, in some sense, the world gave way to one of the most polarized periods in recent political history. The specific events that produced this polarization are familiar, but can be summarized in brief. First, even the establishment of the Department of Homeland Security entailed some partisan wrangling over whether employees could be unionized. Second, though military action in Afghanistan was successful in deposing the Taliban, Osama bin Laden eluded capture and escaped, it is believed, to the mountainous region along the Afghan–Pakistani border. Third, the country's anguish following the terrorist attacks was accompanied by calls, initially resisted by the Bush administration, for an external commission to investigate the attacks and why the government failed to foresee them. Though the bipartisan "9/11 Commission" worked to remain above the fray, its deliberations and hearings inevitably provided grist for each party. Finally, and most importantly, the Bush administration prosecuted a war in Iraq that angered prominent allies and was controversial among Americans. Although American military forces marched to Baghdad, overthrew the regime of Saddam Hussein with considerable alacrity, and captured Hussein himself in December of 2003, a growing Iraqi insurgency has kept car bombings and civilian and military casualties on the front page. Moreover, American forces did not find any "weapons of mass destruction" – the presence of which was a key part of the Bush administration's case for the war.

The other major event of Bush's first term was an economic downturn. After several years of robust growth, the economy had showed signs of weakening during the last months of the Clinton administration. September 11 catalyzed a recession. Whereas in 1999 only 19 percent of respondents in a University of Michigan survey said that their financial situation had gotten worse in the past year, by the end of 2002, nearly twice as many (37 percent) of respondents expressed this view. The unemployment rate rose during this recession and, afterwards, began only a weak recovery. However, in the months leading up to the campaign, trends began to favor Bush: between January of 2003 and September of

Figure 2.1   *Approval rating of President George W. Bush (February 2001–October 2004)*

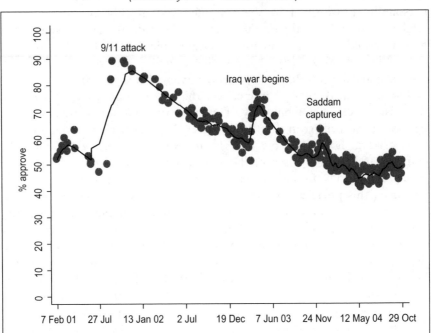

2004, the percentage of respondents saying their financial situation had improved increased from 37 percent to 49 percent.

The consequences of these events are visible in Figure 2.1, which tracks the job-approval rating of President Bush. Each dot represents an individual poll and the line represents the "smoothed" average of these polls. This figure shows the "rally" that occurred in September 2001 and its gradual ebbing away, with smaller rallies at the beginning of the Iraq war and when Saddam was captured. This overall decline in approval was accompanied by a striking polarization along partisan lines. In the first ten months of 2004, an average of about 90 percent of Republicans approved of Bush, whereas only 15 percent of Democrats did so. This gap of over 70 percentage points is the largest observed for any president beginning with the Eisenhower administration (Jacobson, 2005). Opinions about the Iraq war generated a similarly strong partisan disagreement. At the time of the 2004 election, over 80 percent of Republicans approved of the war, while only 20 percent of Democrats did so. This extent of polarization is greater than during any other major war, including the Vietnam and Persian Gulf Wars (Jacobson, 2005).

This pattern of polarization seems, on its face, to conform to the increasingly fashionable division of the United States into "red" and "blue" America, with "red" connoting Republican or conservative and "blue" connoting Democratic or liberal (Brooks, 2001). The red–blue distinction brings with it not only stereotypes about political preferences but also stereotypes about the consumer choices that allegedly accompany these preferences. Thus, Brooks (2001, 53), assuming the identity of a "blue" American, writes: "We sail; they powerboat. We cross-country ski; they snowmobile. We hike; they drive ATVs [all-terrain vehicles]. We have vineyard tours; they have tractor pulls." However, these descriptions amount to caricatures that are mostly false. Most American states and most American voters are not dogmatically red or blue, but instead a combination of the two – a shade of purple, as it were. This is to say, American states routinely vote for a presidential candidate of one party while simultaneously electing a senator or governor of the other party. American voters tend to have moderate viewpoints on most political issues, even divisive ones such as abortion (Fiorina, Abrams, and Pope, 2005). Thus, polarization in 2004 is not the result of immutable characteristics of states or of voters' preferences for cars, beer, or coffee. It is instead a reaction to a particular political moment and to the controversial policies of the Bush administration.

A well-known fact about American presidential elections is that their outcomes depend heavily on such factors as the incumbent's approval rating, the state of the economy, and whether the country is at war (Zaller, 2001). The conditions described above – a divided country, a weak economy, and a controversial war – did not on their face suggest an easy victory for Bush. However, among those political scientists and economists who use these conditions to develop models that forecast the outcome of the election, their unanimous opinion as of the early fall was that Bush would win, though in several such forecasts the race was quite close (Campbell, 2005). The conditions in the country in terms of these "fundamentals" were not so felicitous as to guarantee a victory for Bush, but neither were they so grim as to guarantee his defeat. These conditions, combined with the strong pattern of polarization noted above, provided all of the makings of a very competitive election.

The public's agenda

What issues did Americans consider most important as the 2004 campaign got underway? At the top of the agenda, unsurprisingly, were the economy, war, and national security. In a July 2004 Harris Poll, 42 percent of respondents named the economy or jobs as one of the "two most important issues for the government to address." Twenty-four percent cited the war in Iraq, 11 percent terrorism, and 11 percent national or homeland security. Several domestic issues garnered attention as well, including health care (17 percent) and education (9 percent).

On its face, this agenda tended to favor Republicans. Political parties in the United States accrue reputations over time that amount to "owner-ship" of particular issues (Petrocik, 1996). These reputations stem from the parties' attention to particular issues and their record of formulating policy to address these issues. Loosely speaking, the Democratic Party is thought to "own" domestic issues such as social security, health care, and education, while the Republican Party is thought to "own" issues such as national security and defense. For example, in an August 2003 *Washington Post* poll, voters were asked which party they trusted to handle "the war against terrorism at home and abroad." Fifty-four percent said they trusted the Republicans while only 25 percent said they trusted the Democrats (the remainder said both or neither). By contrast, the public's perceptions of which party was better able to handle the economy were more evenly split, with 47 percent trusting the Democrats and 37 percent the Republicans. Thus, the salience of the war in Iraq and national security concerns arguably benefited Republicans and in particular President Bush.

In considering the public's agenda, it is important also to differentiate the public and consider the specific agendas of particular sub-groups. Converse (1964) argues that the public can be conceptualized as an amalgam of individual "issue publics." Each issue public comprises the subset of the population that is attentive to that issue and likely to make choices based on it. In 2004, the "issue public" that garnered the most attention was religious conservatives. Although the visibility of religious conservatives had waned somewhat in the 1990s with the dissolution of its most visible interest group, the Christian Coalition, events during Bush's first term brought religious conservatives to the forefront once again.

Most notable was a series of events surrounding the issue of same-sex marriage. In February of 2004, the Massachusetts Supreme Court ruled that prohibitions on gay marriage were unconstitutional under the Massachusetts Constitution. The Mayor of San Francisco, Gavin Newsom, seized on that decision to begin issuing marriage licenses to gay men and women, in some circumstances performing the ceremony himself. City officials in several other communities, such as New Paltz, NY, and Portland, OR, did likewise. This produced a heated political debate, with President Bush himself endorsing an amendment to the US Constitution that would define marriage only in heterosexual terms. To be sure, despite this debate, few Americans ranked same-sex marriage as a top priority. In the aforementioned Harris Poll from July 2004, only 2 percent listed same-sex marriage as one of the two most important issues. However, this issue certainly animated many conservative Christian leaders and set the stage for a later debate over the role of conservative Christian voters in the election's outcome, to which I return below.

The "rules of the game"

As they formulate campaign strategies, candidates not only must grapple with fundamental conditions in the country, such as the economy, that are largely beyond their immediate control, but also must respond to important changes in the rules that govern the campaign. The 2004 election was the first conducted under a new set of rules that affected fundraising and spending in the campaign.

American campaigns are widely known to be long and expensive. The concern about the potentially corrupting role of money in elections is longstanding. It gave rise to the Federal Election Campaign Act of 1971 (FECA) and amendments to this act in 1974. FECA limited the amount that any individual donor could give to one candidate and all candidates as a whole. It also limited the amount of money that could be spent by the candidates. These contribution limits were upheld by the Supreme Court in 1976 (the *Buckley* v. *Valeo* decision), though the spending limits were struck down as an unconstitutional infringement on the free speech of candidates.

However, during the 1980s and 1990s, the Democratic and Republican Parties were able to take advantage of loopholes in FECA and circumvent these contribution limits by raising what was called "soft money." The parties could receive donations in *unlimited* amounts and spend it during the campaign as long as they did not coordinate their strategy with the candidates or specifically advocate for the election or defeat of a particular candidate using words such as "vote for" (which came to be known as the "magic words"). Critics argued that the parties were in essence participating in the same corrupt enterprise that existed before FECA and that this gave undue influence to corporations, labor unions, and others who could produce larger donations. They also argued that advertisements funded with soft money, while stopping short of the "magic words," were clearly partisan.

Finally, after years of efforts by its proponents, in 2002 the Bipartisan Campaign Reform Act (BCRA) – also known as "McCain–Feingold" for its two Senate sponsors, John McCain (R-AZ) and Russ Feingold (D-WI) – was passed by Congress and signed by President Bush. Its major effect was to ban the solicitation of soft money by the political parties. It also raised the limit on individual donations and instituted restrictions on when interest groups could advertise during the campaign. Its detractors challenged the BCRA in court, but ultimately the Supreme Court upheld these reforms in *McConnell v. Federal Election Commission* (2003).

How did the BCRA affect candidate and party strategy in 2004? Its opponents feared that it would leave the national party organizations without adequate funds for tasks such as voter mobilization. In actuality, the chief effect of BCRA was not to reduce the amount of money in elections, but to encourage the parties to innovate in how they raised money, in particular by capitalizing on the Internet to reach potential donors and allow them to give on-line. This, combined with the enthusiasm and passion surrounding this very competitive election, enabled the parties, as well as the candidates themselves, to raise much more money than they raised in 2000. In the 2004 elections, the Democratic Party raised $494 million (v. $300 million in 2000) and the Republican Party raised $657 million (v. $500 million).

The BCRA also had major consequences for interest groups, though the most important consequence was entirely unintended. Just as the political parties had been able to raise soft money because of loopholes in FECA, interest groups were able to do so because of a loophole in BCRA. As a result, many new groups were formed during Bush's first term, the most prominent of which strongly opposed his policies, and began to raise large sums of soft money. These groups became known as "527s" (the designation given to them under the tax code) and included groups such as MoveOn, Americans Coming Together (ACT), and the Media Fund. These groups raised money from citizens both rich and poor, but it was their large donations from rich individuals that drew the most attention. Most notorious among these individuals was the financier George Soros, who contributed approximately $27 million to several anti-Bush groups. Bush supporters reacted by setting up groups such as the Swift Boat Veterans for Truth. All combined, these groups spent over $500 million in the 2004 election.

The resources that these groups marshaled made them a significant player in the campaign in several respects. Though they could not spend soft money donations on advertisements that explicitly endorsed or opposed a candidate, they ran ads that clearly reflected a point of view, much as did soft money-funded party ads before BCRA. Furthermore, these groups could often air more strident or controversial messages that the parties or candidates would not. Most infamous were the advertisements aired by the Swift Boat Veterans for Truth, who criticized Kerry's record of service during the Vietnam War. Finally, these groups were also engaged in other important campaign activities, notably voter mobilization. The Democratic Party actually delegated most of its voter mobilization activities to groups like MoveOn and ACT, who organized volunteers to go out and contact voters.

At this point in time, it remains unclear whether 527 organizations will be allowed to raise soft money in later election cycles. Major proponents of campaign finance reform, such as McCain, want to close this loophole, and President Bush has expressed his willingness to do so. Whatever reforms are enacted in the next several years, the lessons of the BCRA suggest that, short of moving to a system of campaign finance that depends completely on tax revenue rather than private donations, money will continue to flow freely into the hands of candidates, parties, and interest groups. In the conclusion of this chapter, I discuss the normative consequences of money's role in elections.

A campaign chronology

The primary campaign

As the 2004 campaign got underway, the central question was who the Democratic Party would nominate to oppose Bush, who faced no opponent from within his own party. The Democratic field was wide-open, and nine major candidates came forward to run. Of these the initial front-runner was Governor Howard Dean of Vermont, whose quick rise to prominence surprised many observers. Though as governor Dean was not an ideologue – for example, he signed a bill allowing gay couples to form civil unions but opposed gun control laws – his message appealed to the left wing of the party because he was strongly opposed to the war in Iraq. The other more prominent candidates – Kerry, Senator John Edwards (NC), Senator Joseph Lieberman (CT), and Representative Richard Gephardt (MO) – had all voted for a resolution granting Bush the authority to prosecute the war. Dean's personal charisma and energy also seemed to attract interest, particularly from young voters.

Dean's campaign organization was notable in its use of the Internet. First, the Dean campaign was able to raise a large amount of money via the Internet. Using the Internet in this fashion was not new, but Dean's campaign proved its effectiveness. Dean raised more money than his opponents ($53 million in the end) and a substantial fraction – e.g., half in the third quarter of 2003 – came from Internet contributions, many of which were in small amounts like $25. Second, the Dean campaign used the Internet as a tool for supporters to organize and interact. Whereas campaign events are often organized by the campaign staff, Dean's campaign encouraged supporters to plan their own meetings, fundraisers, rallies, and the like. One website in particular – meetup.com – became a forum where Dean supporters would coordinate their efforts.

The Dean campaign had the ingredients of a successful campaign for the presidential nomination: media attention, fundraising, and sizable support in pre-election polls. In presidential primaries all of these come together to create expectations about each candidate. The candidate's performance in the primaries is evaluated in light of those expectations, and expectations for the Dean campaign were high. Meanwhile, his opponents struggled to attain comparable recognition and support. In a January 2004 poll of likely Democratic voters conducted just before the first primary, 26 percent supported Dean. His nearest rival, General Wesley Clark, garnered 14 percent. John Kerry garnered only 8 percent. Dean seemed poised for victory as the first caucus was held in Iowa on January 19, 2004.

When the votes were counted, the outcome was somewhat stunning. Dean finished a distant third, with 18 percent of the vote. The victor was John Kerry (38%), who not two months before had mortgaged his house in order to loan his flagging campaign $6 million. John Edwards finished second, with 32% of the vote. That night, Dean gave a speech to supporters, punctuating his remarks with a yawp that became known as "the scream." This speech was widely lampooned, adding to his campaign's difficulties. Explanations for Dean's unexpectedly poor showing were various, and ultimately there is not yet hard evidence for any of them. In the weeks leading up to the caucus, Dean and Gephardt had engaged in an increasingly negative exchange of advertising that some observers thought had alienated Iowa voters. (Gephardt received only 11 percent of the vote, even though he is from a neighboring state. He dropped out of the race soon thereafter.) It may also have been that Dean's support base was simply not as well developed in Iowa as in other parts of the country. Finally, voters may have been thinking ahead to November and questioning whether Dean's background and message would serve him well in the race against Bush. Kerry, with his record of military service, may have seemed more likely to win an election so centered on national security. And, ultimately, perceptions of viability or electability are the driving force in presidential primaries (Bartels, 1988).

Two key aspects of presidential primaries are "front-loading" and "momentum." Front-loading refers to the tendency of states to schedule their primaries earlier and earlier in the year so that their outcomes are more influential in the process. Because of continued front-loading, in 2004, 18 states held their primary or caucus in January or February. Thus, the outcome was known very early, well in advance of the party conventions in July and August. Momentum refers to the fact that the candidate who does best in initial contests tends to win later contests, as other candidates drop out and as voters jump on the winning candidate's bandwagon. The Kerry candidacy was no exception. His strong showing in Iowa helped propel him to victory in the next primary, in New

Hampshire – a state where he had something of a geographical advantage because of his ties to neighboring Massachusetts. He won every other later primary, with the exception of the South Carolina primary (won by Edwards, who was born in that state). Thus, Kerry's improbable victory in Iowa was sufficient to propel him to the Democratic nomination for President. In July, Kerry selected as his running mate John Edwards, whose origins in the South complemented Kerry's in the Northeast and whose strong performance in the primaries after only six years in elected office had burnished his reputation significantly. The stage was now set for the fall campaign.

The general election

Figure 2.2 plots the fortunes of the two candidates from June 1 until November 1, with the party conventions and debates demarcated. It is important to note that the vertical axis ranges only between 42 percent and 52 percent, meaning that what appear substantial trends actually only reflect changes of a few percentage points. This figure reveals several notable things about the general election campaign. First, the race was quite closely contested, as predicted by the "fundamentals" discussed above. Second, as is common in competitive races, the lead changed hands

Figure 2.2 *Bush and Kerry poll standing (June 1–November 1, 2004)*

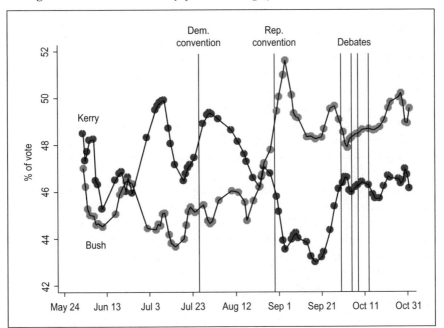

during the campaign (see Stimson, 2004). Had the election occurred in late June or July, Kerry apparently would have won.

These trends also illustrate the influence of campaign events. The Democratic Party convention, which occurred in late July, gave Kerry a "bounce" of about 2–3 percentage points. This is the typical effect of conventions, whose hoopla tends to rally partisans to the cause. However, Kerry's bounce proved temporary. Some attributed this short-lived bounce to the convention itself, which was accused of focusing on Kerry's biography while treating George Bush with kid gloves. The decline in Kerry's support during August also coincided with the first advertisements from the aforementioned Swift Boat Veterans for Truth, who criticized Kerry's service in Vietnam and claimed, among other things, that he did not actually deserve the medals he had won. These ads initially aired only a few times in a handful of states, and the Kerry campaign chose not to respond, believing that their impact would prove minimal. This decision may also have depended on financial considerations. After accepting the nomination, the presidential candidates can spend only a fixed amount of money that is given to them by the federal government. Because the Republican campaign occurred a month later (to avoid conflicting with the Summer Olympics), Kerry had to stretch this money over a longer period than did Bush. Kerry may have wanted to conserve his resources rather than counter these attacks on his record. However, the Swift Boat ads generated enough controversy to stay in the news for weeks. Even though the claims of this group were rebutted by military documents, the apparent damage was done. For the Kerry campaign, hoping to capitalize on Kerry's military service during a war that Bush had avoided, this was a low point. After the race was over and with the benefit of hindsight, various commentators would suggest that the Kerry campaign should have responded sooner and more forcefully.

The Republican convention began in late August and its effects were greater, as Figure 2.2 suggests. It gave Bush a substantial lead, one that would narrow but never vanish. Bush's performance in the first debate on September 30 did cost him a few percentage points. Commentators described his performance as "peeved" (*Newsweek*'s Jonathan Alter) and "repetitious" (the *Washington Post*'s Tom Shales). In a *Los Angeles Times* poll conducted just after the debate, 54 percent thought Kerry had won, 15 percent though Bush had won, and 30 percent though the outcome was "even." Even the First Lady, Laura Bush, chided her husband, "I don't know what happened. You've got to be yourself, and you weren't" (*Newsweek*, "Face to Face," 110).

The debate gave the Kerry campaign a much-needed shot in the arm, but little changed after that moment. The vice-presidential debate and the two subsequent presidential debates did not produce much change in the polls.

At the campaign's end, Bush had about a 2 percentage point lead. On Election Day, this same margin held: Bush won approximately 51 percent of the major-party vote to Kerry's 49 percent. Though Kerry won about 8 million more votes than did Al Gore, Bush won nearly 12 million more than he had in 2000. Exit polls on Election Day showed that, relative to 2000, Bush made gains among all types of voters – men and women, whites, blacks, Latinos, the young and the old, the rich and the poor. His vote share increased in "red" and "blue" states alike.

Table 2.1 (overleaf) shows the breakdown of the presidential vote by various demographic categories. By and large, these do not reveal any new patterns of behavior. There is a small gender gap, with women more supportive of Kerry than men. This gap, which has opened up because of the growing conservatism of men (Kaufman and Petrocik, 1999), was smaller in 2004 than in 2000. Differences across age, education, and income categories reveal that the young, the college-educated, and the less well-off were more supportive of Kerry than other groups – though as with gender none of these differences are very large. More potent cleavages in the American voting public have to do with ethnicity and religiosity. White voters are more Republican than black, Latino, and Asian voters by a considerable margin. Bush's support among Latinos (45%) was larger in 2004 than in 2000, where he won 37% of the Latino vote.* The influence of religiosity depends less on religious preference – though Jewish voters continue to be much more Democratic than Protestants or Catholics – than on religious practice. Those who attend church services at least one a week are much more likely than less frequent attenders to support Bush. Finally, these data also demonstrate the polarization of the parties: 88 percent of Democrats voted for Kerry, and 94 percent voted for Bush. Party identification continues to be a robust influence on the presidential vote (see Bartels, 2000).

Campaign messages

What was this election "about"? What agendas did the candidates pursue and what factors appear relevant in explaining the election's outcome? First, it is important to note that, by and large, presidential campaigns do not differ in their agendas (Sigelman and Buell, 2004). Both candidates tend to discuss the same issues. In 2004, Bush and Kerry focused on the war in Iraq, homeland security, the economy, Social Security, and health care. The differences came in how they framed or discussed these issues. Kerry's message was illustrative of what candidates challenging an incumbent frequently do: targeting the performance of the incumbent administration. Kerry focused on the economic downturn and in particular job losses. He

Table 2.1   *Demographic attributes and the presidential vote*

	% voting for Bush	% voting for Kerry
Gender		
Men	53	46
Women	49	50
Age		
18–29	43	55
30–44	52	47
45–64	54	45
65 and older	55	45
Ethnicity		
White	57	42
Black	14	86
Latino	45	54
Asian	34	64
Education		
Less than college	54	45
College degree or more	49	50
Income		
Less than $20,000	46	51
$20,000–$39,999	47	52
$40,000–$59,999	51	48
$60,000–$74,999	53	46
$75,000 or more	54	45
Religion		
Protestant	61	38
Catholic	55	44
Jewish	26	74
Church attendance		
Weekly or more	65	34
Less than that	43	57
Party identification		
Republican	94	6
Democrat	12	88

Note: Numbers may not add to 100 because of voters for other candidates or non-response.
Source: 2004 *Los Angeles Times* Exit Poll.

accused the Bush administration of having mismanaged the war in Iraq as well as the war on terror, especially given that bin Laden remained at large. He also accused the Bush administration of having devoted insufficient attention to homeland security. Kerry trumpeted his own plan to create job growth, reduce health-care costs, protect the country from terrorists, and win the war in Iraq.

Bush quite naturally defended his administration's record, pointing to recent economic gains. He tended to frame the war in Iraq as part of a broader effort to cultivate democracy, which he posited as crucial to winning the war against terror. Another prominent theme was an attack on Kerry's capacity for leadership in this war. Though it is typically the challenger rather than the incumbent who runs the more "negative" campaign, in 2004 Bush's strategy was to criticize Kerry early and often in an attempt to "define" him for voters. The crux of these criticisms was that Kerry was indecisive and vacillating, particularly with regard to the war in Iraq. The Bush campaign referred to Kerry repeatedly as a "flip-flopper." Kerry's own statements seemed to play into this characterization. Most famous was a statement regarding his votes on a September 2003 bill to appropriate $87 billion more for the war effort. Kerry initially voted for a version of the bill that included provisions repealing previously enacted tax cuts for the wealthy in an attempt to generate revenue for the war effort. When that version failed to win a majority, he voted against a subsequent version that did not contain those provisions. On the campaign trail, his attempt to describe his decision came out thus: "I actually did vote for the 87 billion dollars before I voted against it." The Bush campaign was ebullient. Bush strategist Mark McKinnon said later, "The greatest gifts in politics are the gifts the other side gives you" (*Newsweek*, 2004, 70).

In some sense, these messages worked. Though voters perceived Kerry as more knowledgeable and empathetic than Bush, they saw Bush as a stronger leader. Moreover, they tended to see Kerry as indecisive. In the 2004 National Election Study, 65 percent of respondents said that the phrase "strong leader" described Bush "very well" or "quite well." A smaller number, 52 percent, had this opinion of Kerry. At the same time, 47 percent of respondents described Kerry as someone who "can't make up his mind." Only 27 percent said that of Bush. These perceptions dovetail with voters' opinions about whom they trusted to handle issues like Iraq and terrorism. In pre-election polls, respondents preferred Bush over Kerry by a 2–1 margin. Kerry's inability to make headway on these issues may help account for his defeat.

Another explanation commonly offered for Bush's victory concerned the role of conservative Christian voters and the issue of "moral values." In the 2004 national exit poll, voters were presented with a list of seven issues from which they could choose their "most important problem": taxes, education, Iraq, terrorism, the economy and jobs, health care, and moral values. Commentators were caught off-guard when the plurality of respondents, 22 percent, chose "moral values," with 80 percent of these voters reporting support for Bush. Initially this poll result was interpreted as suggesting that it was conservative religious voters angry about issues like gay marriage who won the election for Bush. However, this interpretation has been largely discounted. Several prominent pollsters argued that the category "moral values" is amorphous and not strictly comparable to the other, more policy-oriented options in that poll question. Other scholars noted that there was no evidence that a larger number of conservative religious voters had turned out to vote, and that Bush's gains among churchgoers were actually smaller than his gains among non-churchgoers. Other polls that referenced specific social issues rather than the catch-all category "moral values" found that respondents prioritized terrorism and the economy more than gay marriage and abortion. Moreover, Bush did not get more votes in states with ballot initiatives related to gay marriage. In sum, it is fair to say that voters were truly focused on questions of economic and homeland security, and Bush's advantage on these issues was more consequential than religious conservatives' opposition to same-sex marriage (see Hillygus and Shields, 2005).

The "ground game"

The discussion above mirrors much post-election commentary in that it focuses on the messages of the candidates that were broadcast in advertising, debates, and elsewhere. This is the so-called "air war" of a campaign – one that became increasingly important in the 1970s as campaigns became centered more on the candidates and less on the party organizations that used to control the selection of candidates and various campaign tactics and strategies. When party organizations were more influential, television advertising was not yet a major part of campaigns. Thus, campaign strategy was not about persuading voters via carefully crafted messages but instead about mobilizing the party faithful on Election Day. Mobilization entailed a "ground game," which is to say a large number of volunteers and party workers who knocked on doors and made phone calls to remind voters to vote and to encourage them to vote for that party. The weakening of the party organizations and the advent of television shifted attention away from the ground game. Scholars noted that in the 1970s and 1980s, fewer voters reported being contacted by the parties, which may have helped produce an overall decline in turnout during this period (Rosenstone and Hansen, 1993).

A striking trend in the most recent elections, notably in 2004, is the renewed interest in voter mobilization. Television advertising continues to be important, and campaigns spend more money on that than anything else. However, advertising is not only expensive but it can be ineffective. Voters profess to dislike most campaign advertising, and typically ads do little to change voters' minds. Most voters have established partisan preferences and these do not change much over the course of the campaign (Lazarsfeld *et al.*, 1948; Finkel, 1993). The advantage of mobilization is that it targets voters who are already sympathetic to their cause and merely attempts to ensure that these voters are registered to vote and then turn out on Election Day.

New technologies have enabled the parties to target voters with greater detail. Both the Democratic and Republican Parties have assembled large databases that merge information about not just individual voters' political behavior but with other data about their consumer choices, such as whether they own a home and what kind of car they drive (see Gernter, 2004). If a party wants to target 40–year-old married women who have children and who drive minivans, they probably can do so. Having identified voters in this way, the next part of any mobilization strategy is contacting them. Here the parties have re-discovered the benefits of old-fashioned shoe-leather politics. In 2004, the parties and also various interest groups sent small armies of volunteers and paid workers to canvass neighborhoods and talk to potential supporters (Bai, 2004). Armed with handheld computers, these volunteers could record whom they had spoken with and the outcome of that interaction. These data were then collated by the parties so they could follow up as needed, especially on Election Day itself. Do these mobilization strategies work? Political science suggests that they do, particularly when voters are contacted face-to-face (Green and Gerber, 2004). In 2004, the evidence also suggests that mobilization mattered: turnout among the voting-eligible population was 60 percent, nearly 5 points higher than in 2000. In the future, the parties will likely continue to emphasize mobilization and to refine their strategies for targeting and contacting voters.

Races in the 50 states

The 2004 election saw comparatively little change in the party's delegations to the House and Senate. In part, this reflects the historic advantages of House and Senate incumbents. Incumbents have greater name recognition among constituents and typically raise enough money to discourage many potential challengers and outspend actual challengers. In 2004, approximately 98 percent of House incumbents (395 of 402) and 96 percent of Senate incumbents won re-election. The powerful advantages that incumbents possess create substantial stability in the composition of the House; large swings in the partisan balance are rare and have become increasingly so (Jacobson, 2004).

The conditions for dramatic changes in House and Senate delegations entail a political climate that overwhelmingly favors one of the parties, which then creates a "partisan tide." In 2004, the climate did not did not favor any tide. Bush's popularity, while increasing somewhat during the campaign, was not sufficiently high to provide "coattails" for Republican candidates to ride on, nor sufficiently low to help Democratic candidates. As a result, very few seats changed hands, and those that did occurred mostly in newly created House districts that were drawn to favor one party, or at the Senate level, in states where the partisanship of the population leans notably in one direction. In 2004, Republicans benefited from these factors more than Democrats.

In the House, the Democrats picked up two seats, one in Colorado and another in Georgia. The Republican Party picked up six seats, four in Texas, one in Indiana, and one in Kentucky. The four-seat gain in Texas was the result of an unusual and controversial redrawing of district lines in 2003–2004. After the Republican Party gained control of both houses of the legislature in 2002, they decided to redraw the lines to ensure a larger Republican share of the House delegation. The district lines had already been redrawn once after the 2000 Census, as is customary. It was a break with historical precedent to redraw them again. Despite protests by Texas Democrats, these new districts eventually went into effect and worked as intended. Three Democratic incumbents were defeated in newly redrawn districts.

The Republican Party also made gains in the Senate. It won six new seats, while Democrats won two. This altered the party balance in the Senate from 51–49 in favor of the Republicans, to 55–45. Most of the Republican gains came about because of retirements of Southern Democrats – including Edwards, as well as others in Louisiana, Florida, South Carolina, and Georgia. These Southern states have become more reliably Republican over the past 40 years, and thus these gains are perhaps not surprising. More surprising was the defeat of Senate Minority Leader Tom Daschle of South Dakota. He was a particular target in 2004 and faced a quality opponent in former Representative John Thune, who had very narrowly lost in the 2002 Senate race to incumbent Democrat Tim Johnson. Thune beat Daschle by only 4,500 votes out of almost 400,000 cast.

Only eleven governors were up for re-election in 2004, and the outcomes of these elections did not alter overall the partisan balance among governors. Republicans were able to defeat one incumbent Democrat, Governor Joe Kernan of Indiana. Democrats did likewise in New Hampshire. Perhaps the most dramatic race in the entire 2004 election was the Washington gubernatorial contest, featuring Republican Dino Rossi and Democrat Christine Gregoire. In a series of events eerily reminiscent of the 2000 dispute in Florida, Rossi was initially in the lead by less than 200 votes, a margin so close that Washington state law mandated a recount. The ballots were counted again by machine, and Rossi's lead narrowed to only 42 votes. The Secretary of State then allowed a manual recount. Gregoire gained enough votes, particularly in Democratic strongholds such as the area around Seattle, to win the election by only 129 votes out of over 2.6 million cast.

Also on the ballots in the states were a number of ballot initiatives, perhaps none more prominent than 11 initiatives that would ban gay marriage. All of these initiatives were passed, many by wide margins. The closest vote was in Oregon, and even there 57 percent of voters supported the ban while 43 percent opposed it. None of these outcomes was particularly surprising. Americans have grown more tolerant of homosexuality over the past 15 years, but when given an up-or-down vote on gay marriage, roughly a two-thirds majority is in opposition. More palatable are "civil unions," which provide gay couples with the legal rights that married couples have but are not "marriages" under the law. When survey respondents are asked whether they favor marriage, civil unions, or no legal recognition, a majority favors either marriage or civil unions. However, this was not the choice presented to voters in 2004. The passage of these initiatives emboldened opponents of gay marriage, who vowed to press ahead to amend the US Constitution. This issue will likely produce further controversy, though if long-term trends continue, the American public will continue to grow more accepting of homosexuality and of gay marriage as well.

Conclusion

The 2004 election stands in stark contrast to 2000 in that there was no prolonged controversy about the outcome. Kerry, after briefly considering a push for re-examining the Ohio ballots, realized that this would likely leave the outcome unchanged, and conceded the morning after Election Day. Though there were reports of difficulties with voting machines, there was less post-election discussion of issues related to election law and technology, in part because they had no apparent consequences for Bush's victory.

That said, reform of ballot design and voting systems remains a salient issue in American elections. In the last few years, political scientists have devoted increased attention to these issues and have discovered disparities in how ballots look (Wand *et al.*, 2001; Niemi and Hernson, 2003) and how different voting systems perform (Brady *et al.*, 2001; Alvarez, Sinclair, and Wilson, 2004). These disparities have very real consequences for whether voters can accurately cast a ballot for the candidate they prefer and have that voted counted. For example, scholars have demonstrated that punchcard ballots have a much higher rate of errors than other methods of voting, such as an "optical scan" system, where voters fill in an oval next to their choice.

In the wake of the 2000 election, Congress also acted, passing the Help America Vote Act of 2002 (HAVA). This legislation called for a new program that would provide states funding so they could replace punchcard systems like that used in Florida in 2000. This Act also established a new federal agency, the Elections Assistance Commission (EAC), to oversee this process. The overarching goal was "to establish minimum election administration standards for States," thereby reducing the considerable inter-state variation in how elections were conducted. A potential further goal for future elections is actually to achieve some national standardization so that voters in any one state or county are not disadvantaged relative to voters in other areas because they must rely on a different voting system.

One important consequence of the 2000 controversy in Florida and HAVA was to increase substantially the number of states that used electronic voting systems, which typically involve computerized screens that voters touch directly to indicate their preferences. These electronic systems mostly replaced older punchcard systems. In 2000, approximately 34 percent of the population used a punchcard system; in 2004, that had declined to 19 percent. By contrast, the percentage using an electronic system increased from 8 percent to 29 percent. Electronic systems, to be sure, are no panacea. Relative to punchcard systems, they improve only slightly on the number of "residual votes" – votes that are not counted because voters fail to enter a preference or make some other mistake – presumably because the technology of "touch-screens" is not intuitive to every voter (see Cal-Tech/MIT Voting Project, 2001). Thus, there is still much that can be done to improve the quality of voting technology and to ensure that every person's vote is counted.

A second goal, standardization of voting technology and ballot design across counties and states, will likely prove difficult because election oversight is the traditional responsibility of state and local governments, not the federal government. It thus takes significant effort to achieve standardization when the individual action of 50 state governments and even more numerous local governments is required. The recent resignation of the EAC's director in April 2005, who cited lack of commitment to reform within the federal government, suggests the challenges that lie ahead.

Despite these ongoing challenges, the 2004 election had positive implications, perhaps the most important of which was the high level of voter participation. The turnout rate, 60 percent of eligible voters, was the highest since 1992, when the candidacy of Ross Perot drew many to the polls. Before that, turnout of the eligible population had not broken 60 percent since 1968 (see McDonald and Popkin, 2001). If the participation of the citizens is a, and perhaps the, fundamental quality of a democracy, than the 2004 election is cause for some cheer. The irony, however, is that achieving such a high rate of turnout is likely predicated on other characteristics of elections that observers typically find less commendable – namely, an extremely competitive campaign featuring a lot of "attack" or "negative" advertising. On its face, the 2004 election seems to support the contention of some scholars that negative advertising – i.e., advertising in which the candidates criticize each other on various grounds – actually increases turnout (see Goldstein and Freedman, 2002). Negative information is likely more memorable to voters and may help clarify differences between the candidates and thus the stakes of the election. Thus, a "good fight" could actually help stimulate voters more than it disgusts them.

On the whole, the 2004 election was in some sense a return to normalcy after the uncertainty and controversy surrounding the 2000 election. The incumbent President won re-election, as typically happens (see Campbell, 2000). And so did most Congressional incumbents. Fundamental factors such as the state of the economy predicted a narrow victory for Bush, which is exactly what resulted. Party identification continued to influence strongly voters' choices. There were no fundamental shifts in the partisan preferences of important demographic groups. Given the race's competitiveness, campaign events such as conventions and debates were at least somewhat consequential. All of these suggest that campaigns and elections, though they may appear chaotic in the weeks and months before Election Day, also possess a considerable degree of predictability. The 2004 election, while solidifying the Republican Party's control of the Presidency and the Congress, continued to illustrate that politics in the United States is quite closely divided.

Though the 2004 elections brought victory for Bush and more seats for Republicans in Congress, subsequent events make it less clear that the upcoming 2006 elections will be similarly favorable. The war in Iraq has become increasingly unpopular, the price of gasoline has increased, and the tragedy of Hurricane Katrina has cast doubt on the federal government's ability to protect citizens in the event of an emergency. Bush's approval ratings have slipped to approximately 40 percent – about 10 points lower than when he was re-elected – although there continues to be substantial partisan polarization among the public in its views of Bush's handling of Katrina and his job generally. Moreover, the need to respond to Katrina, as well as the budgetary expense this response will entail, has reduced the ability of the Bush administration to pursue its other policy goals, such as reform of Social Security and the tax system. But this bad news may not necessarily bode ill for Republicans in 2006: because so many House and Senate seats are relatively safe, it is unlikely that Democrats will make big gains. A recent estimate located less than eight House races and five Senate races that could be considered "toss-ups" (*Cook Political Report*, 2005a, 2005b).

At this early stage, there are no safe predictions about the 2008 election. Interestingly, the 2008 election will be the first election since 1952 when there will be no incumbent president or heir-apparent (such as a vice-president) running in either party. Thus there is the potential for future shifts in party control depending on circumstances in the country and the candidates who step forward.

Note

* Some scholars, however, have contended that the exit poll data do not contain a representative sample of Latino voters and overestimate the Bush vote (Leal *et al.*, 2005).

Chapter 3

Parties in an Era of Renewed Partisanship

Bruce Cain and Darshan J. Goux

The conventional wisdom about American political parties is that they are comparatively weak, not only in contrast to European political parties, but also as compared to earlier periods in American history. Party discipline in the US Congress and state legislatures has traditionally been less than in European parliaments while incumbency factors and the personal vote have been stronger. Moreover, party identification has not typically predicted the vote as closely as in Europe, and political campaigns have centered to a greater degree on individual candidates, not on party platforms (Ranney, 1951). America, home to Downsian theory, had the best examples of Downsian parties: "teams" devoted primarily to winning by tracking the middle of the ideological spectrum as closely as possible. The result was often "echoes, not choices," candidates so indistinguishable as to nearly erase the rationality of voting.

But that conventional wisdom may be changing. Party-line voting and ideological division in the Congress and state legislatures has increased (Jewell and Morehouse, 2001; Polsby, 2004). Voter partisanship has also been on the rise, although to a lesser degree and somewhat later than in Congress and the state legislatures (Miller and Shanks, 1996; Jacobson, 2001). Where the reform focus in the 1970s and early 1980s was on the incumbency advantage, it is now on the over-heated and bitter resurgence of partisanship. Party bickering inside the beltway presently threatens longstanding traditions of legislative cooperation such as unanimous consent rules and respect for the right to filibuster on matters of deep conviction. The recent debate over the so-called nuclear or constitutional option in the US Senate is symbolic of a deeper breakdown in trust and cooperation between the two parties and the desire of the Republican majority to lessen the Democratic minority's influence. In the House of Representatives, always a less consensual body, Democrats claim that the Republicans have taken traditional majority prerogatives to the extreme, routinely moving forward with legislation at all stages without consulting the opposition members.

How did this come to be? Why did American political parties move from the periphery to the center of the political stage? Is it related to the increasing partisanship of the electorate? What role did institutional and legal changes, particularly in the area of campaign finance reform, play in these developments? How will the traditional party organizations fare in a new world of competing nonprofit partisan organizations?

There are no simple and definitive answers to these questions, but we will explore some of the more plausible explanations. First, loopholes in the federal campaign finance laws created a temporary demand and a short-lived opportunity in the mid-1990s for political parties to play a more central role in American politics than they had in the previous two decades as a channel for so-called "soft money." Secondly, a new campaign finance law, McCain–Feingold, intended as a plug for the regulatory and legal loopholes that soft money poured through, has created a more complex array of partisan group organizations. This raises important questions about the role that the traditional Democratic and Republican party structures will play in future elections. And lastly, there is a growing sense in America that organizational and activist partisanship is out of synch with public opinion: i.e. that elite polarization seems to exceed polarization in the general electorate, and that structural factors such as party resources and rule incentives will likely perpetuate this gap for the foreseeable future.

Legal loopholes and partisan opportunity

The universal function of political parties in Western democracies is to provide coordination and resources for groups and individuals with shared political beliefs. At the same time, the strength of party organization and ideology varies enormously across and within countries. Structural features such as federalism, the division of power between the branches and the presidential system have contributed to making US political parties seem like organizational outliers compared to those in other advanced democracies, particularly in Europe.

American parties have traditionally been considered "weak" in the sense that party platforms are largely irrelevant to how elected officials govern, campaigns are more candidate-centric, party-line voting in Congress is typically lower than in European parliamentary systems, and candidates are nominated by direct primaries in many states. Even the courts have contributed to this state of affairs: the Supreme Court decisions in several critical cases in the first half of the twentieth century defined the two major political parties as regulated utilities – i.e. mechanisms for conducting the state's elections rather than independent political entities with the right to control their own membership or nomination processes. In short, political parties had become relatively marginal players in American politics at the end of the last century, and there was no indication that that trend would be reversed. Some Democratic Party reforms in the presidential nomination process post-1972 tried to recapture the influence of elected officials in the presidential nomination process and to offset the democratizing effects of the McGovern reforms (Polsby, 1983), but the basic picture did not change. American parties remained basically weakened entities.

But the situation changed in the 1990s as an unintended consequence of efforts to cope with the constraints of existing campaign finance laws. Beginning in 1971, federal elections were covered by the Federal Election Campaign Act (FECA) as modified by the Supreme Court in a 1976 decision, *Buckley* v. *Valeo*. Striking down some parts of the law, the Court left in place a regulatory structure substantially different from the one designed by the law's proponents. Of critical importance to subsequent developments, it left total campaign expenditures uncapped, but limited individual and group (including party) contributions to candidates. Moreover, these contribution limits were not indexed to inflation or changes in the real costs of elections so in effect the limitations became more constraining over time. Parties were treated like just another interest group in the electorate that had to be regulated in order to prevent corruption, with comparable limitations on what the parties could receive and give directly to individual candidates in federal elections.

As the un-indexed contribution limits (termed "hard money" or money generated through the regulated and disclosed FECA system) became more onerous over time (i.e. due to the rising real costs of elections), candidates had to work harder to raise the large amounts of money they needed to run for election and re-election. Given the pressing need for more money, candidates, the parties and their interest group allies began searching for creative ways to bypass the stringent Buckley limitations. They got unexpected assistance from the Federal Election Commission, the regulatory agency charged with implementing and monitoring compliance with the federal campaign finance laws. In a series of administrative rulings, the FEC expanded the definition of "party-building" activities to include so-called issue ads (i.e. electoral ads that avoided key terms such as elect, defeat, etc. but indirectly conveyed the same message) and allowed the parties to raise money in unlimited amounts for such efforts. In effect, the political parties could underwrite many electoral activities without violating contribution ceilings or coordinated spending limits. "Soft money" used for party-building activities and solicited in unlimited amounts from individuals and groups effectively circumvented the "hard money" limitations of the Buckley regime.

Figure 3.1 *Party soft money 1992–1996*

	1992	1994	1996
Total* Democratic receipts	$36,256,667	$49,143,460	$123,877,924
Disbursements	$32,878,310	$50,383,546	$121,826,562
Total* Republican receipts	$49,787,433	$52,522,763	$138,199,706
Disbursements	$46,176,476	$48,387,091	$149,658,099

Source: Compiled by the FEC.

Note: *Includes each party's national, senatorial, and congressional committees.

Bolstered by aggressive soft money fundraising and the use of soft money dollars to finance issue advocacy ads, the role of soft money exploded in the 1996 election (Figure 3.1). Party building was expanded beyond registration and GOTV (i.e. get out the vote, or voter mobilization efforts on Election Day) to include issue advertising. Soft money disbursements increased by more than 200 percent for the Democratic and Republican Parties between 1992 and 1996 (Corrado, 1997). Parties were free to collect unrestricted amounts of money and spend them on attack ads that differed from normal attack ads only by omitting the magic words. In essence, the parties could direct these "soft money" resources to key races without the normal restrictions of contribution limits. And they did. Given that the limitations had not changed in over 20 years and the real cost of elections, particularly ones that involved TV advertising, were soaring, money gushed through the soft money loophole in larger and larger amounts. From 1992 to 2002, annual soft money contributions rose from $86 million to $496 million (Apollonio and La Raja, 2004). The prevailing pattern was not so much new groups coming into the political system and introducing new methods of campaign financing, but rather experienced donors, running the sectoral gamut from labor unions to corporations, supplementing hard money donations with soft.

By the mid-1990s the parties had a newly invigorated role as a conduit for large soft money. There was a contentious debate around McCain–Feingold (formally the Bipartisan Campaign Reform Act of 2002), the campaign finance law intended to fix this loophole, and whether passage would be a good or bad thing for the parties. On the one hand, putting political parties more in the mix of the electoral action seemed a good thing given the longstanding concern about the weakness of political parties in America. But critics questioned whether the parties were anything more than conduits for money. Paid professional consultants controlled the messages and strategy, and even dictated where the competitive races would be. Control over strategy did not flow to the parties. Rather, they were left with the more tactical tasks of raising soft funds and enrolling new voters (Plasser, 2001). On the other hand, some of this money built up state and national party electoral capacities, allowing for more professionalized staff, more sophisticated data processing and more expertise in fundraising, redistricting, media and campaign management (Jewell and Morehouse, 2001; La Raja, 2004).

It is important to distinguish between party goals and ideological goals. Party money, soft and hard, tends to flow in larger numbers to marginal and competitive seats. Money wasted on safe seats does not further the party's goal of winning elections. Other actors with different motives give in different patterns. Ideological donors give to the most loyal ideologues. Groups with business before Congress give money to incumbents to gain access and a hearing for their problems. But parties aim for maximizing seats, which means that they do not necessarily give to the most loyal candidates. The underlying logic is that it is better to have a party member in the seat than a nonmember, because in all but a few rare cases, the party member will vote with the party caucus at a higher rate than nonmembers. Moreover, party leaders who want to maintain or increase their majorities will let members in competitive seats dissent from the caucus if to do otherwise would create a serious electoral liability. After all, one cannot be a majority leader without controlling enough seats, so that given a choice between an unnecessary vote (i.e. the party caucus can win passage or defeat of a bill without the member's vote) with high electoral costs and a dissenting vote with no costs, the rational legislative leader will often allow some dissent in the ranks.

We will return to this point later on when we consider whether the enhanced role of the political parties in elections, especially competitive ones, has caused greater polarization at the state and federal levels. But to summarize, the important trend is that political parties became conduits for unrestricted soft money contributions in the 1990s and this put them in a more pivotal role than before. Indeed the revival of party organizations was one of the main arguments that opponents of McCain–Feingold used against the law, arguing that soft money bans would weaken the parties and empower interest groups.

There were other developments in the 1990s that contributed to the strengthening of party organizations. First, there was a remarkable Supreme Court decision, *Colorado Republican Federal Campaign Committee* v. *Federal Election Commission* (1996) that gave the parties the right to make independent expenditures in addition to the hard money contribution and the soft money expenditures. Under federal law, the political parties like the Democratic National Committee and the

Republican National Committee were restricted to making a $5,000 direct contribution to a US Senatorial candidate and an additional amount determined by a formula based on state voting age population for coordinated expenditures in connection with the general election campaign of candidates for federal office. In 1996, the Colorado branch of the Republican Party had spent above its allocated coordinated expenditure limit to run radio ads attacking the Democratic candidate, Tim Wirth, before the party had even nominated a Republican candidate. In a decision that surprised many election law specialists, the Court ruled that if these expenditures were done independently (i.e. without consultation and coordination with the candidate), they were classified as independent expenditures, and therefore could not be capped. Whatever the logic of assuming that political parties could be independent of their candidates, the decision gave the parties yet another mechanism for raising and spending money, and further incentives for donors to direct money their way. And, the two parties took advantage of this new ruling, spending $11.5 million in the remaining weeks of the 1996 general election campaign (Corrado, 1997).

The ability of state parties to assist federal candidates with resources and expertise increased during the late 1990s (Brox, 2004). State parties provided a conduit for hard and soft money and developed increasing campaign expertise. This pattern applied for both parties, although there are some temporal differences in the rates at which the Democratic and Republican party organizations have developed (Glasgow, 2002).

Aside from the increasingly favorable campaign finance laws and rulings in this pre-McCain–Feingold period, party organizations also received a boost from the more competitive situation in which states found themselves, particularly in the South. During the period of one-party domination, party organizations in southern states had no incentive to develop. Indeed, there were many anti-democratic practices, such as suffrage exclusions and party membership restrictions made possible because there was no competitive party to offer an alternative (Aldrich, 2000). But as the Republicans gained in the South, southern state party organizations gained strength and became the equal organizationally of parties in other states (Cotter *et al.*, 1984; Aldrich, 2000). This was especially true of the Republican Party and in the state parties' expertise in the area of fundraising (Aldrich, 2000). More generally, as the gap between Democratic and Republican party identifiers lessened, and the majorities in Congress became narrower, the parties benefited from the need for better coordination and wider avenues of fundraising (Jewell and Morehouse, 2001).

Finally, there is the question of the relationship between ideology and party strength. At first glance one might think that, since the parties became more polarized, ideology must have been on the rise. In fact, the work of Morris Fiorina and others indicates that there has not been much change in the underlying ideology of the electorate at the same time that the political parties became more polarized (a point we will return to in some detail later). But the realignment of the South, the persistent salience of so-called social issues such as race, abortion and the war in Iraq, has increased the distance between activists in the two major parties. Nothing unites political organizations as much as opposition to the other side. The parties, and the affiliated political nonprofits, like MoveOn and Focus on the Family, have benefited from a more highly charged and ideological debate among their activists and the politically motivated segments of American society. An invigorated base makes it easier to organize and mobilize. So, while changes in campaign finance rulings provided an opportunity for party organizations to be more relevant to political campaigns, the mobilization of the party bases on the issues of the day has also played an important role in strengthening partisanship among voters.

The new era

What the FEC gave in the 1990s, the Congress and the Supreme Court took away by 2004. The increasing sums of money flowing through the soft money loophole and the increasingly untenable distinction between attack ads that mentioned the "magic words" and those that did not created the conditions for a backlash from the reform community. A coalition of forces drawn from the media, key foundations such as Pew, and nonprofit advocacy groups like Common Cause and the Brennan Center pushed vigorously for legislation to plug the soft money hole. After several years, the McCain–Feingold bill emerged in 2002, ending unlimited party-building donations to the parties, broadening the definition of electoral ads, limiting local party funding activities that impacted a federal election and prohibiting attack ads within 90 days of an election funded by unregulated money. Defying the expectations of many legal experts, the Supreme Court upheld most of the new law's provisions in *McConnell v. FEC* (2003).

It was by no means certain that the hole would be plugged and the Court would sanction these fixes. To begin with, the Congress and the presidency was controlled by the Republican Party, and Republicans have historically been more skeptical of campaign finance reform efforts. Had the final bill only addressed campaign finance reform, it would likely have failed. But instead, it increased the contribution limits and provided for inflation indexing in the future, which in effect put more money in the hands of the candidates and their consultants. Moreover, while both parties made use of the soft money loophole, the Democrats were more dependent on it than the Republicans, a fact that some Democratic operatives used to argue against the reform. Also, the Republican Party has historically been better at building an individual contributor base so that raising the hard money amounts individual donors could contribute played to a Republican strength. Even though Republican control of the government would normally mean a harder, if not impossible, path for campaign finance reform, elements of the McCain–Feingold bill, especially its increased contribution limits, helped to facilitate Republican acceptance and ultimately support for its passage.

Similarly, Court approval of the bill was uncertain. In *Buckley*, the Supreme Court made it clear that preventing *quid pro quo* corruption was the primary rationale for campaign finance restrictions. But with parties acting as funding conduits for new and large unrestricted dollars, the old corruption model – money given to a legislator in exchange for official action – was not quite applicable to the new reality. Hence, the Court in its decision upholding most of McCain–Feingold developed a new concept, conduit corruption. In other words, big donors bought favors and access to Congress by giving unrestricted soft money to the party for issue ads. In essence, the Court saw the parties as a tool of circumvention, introducing new means of corruption outside the regulated direct contributions to candidates. There was no real solid evidence of conduit corruption offered in the case. The Court relied heavily on the testimony of members of Congress who said they knew of other members who acted in this corrupt way. And, it was never clear why if groups and individuals were restricted from giving unlimited amounts of money, it was also necessary to restrict how much the party gave to the candidates. Can a party corrupt a candidate if it is not the conduit of large interest group donations? These questions were never really addressed or answered in the Court's decision.

At the time the bill passed, there was considerable debate over whether the new law would weaken the parties. Some pointed out that the BCRA's provisions would hinder legitimate party-building activities, such as registration drives and GOTV, in the name of curbing issue ads. Moreover, the trend toward better cooperation between local, state and national party organizations would be weakened (Alexander, 2003; Pomper, 2003). And, most importantly, with the party soft money loophole plugged, the unrestricted money would flow into the hands of interest groups, which might have even more deleterious effects on policy-making.

To some extent, the latter concern was mitigated by increasing the limits on how much individuals and groups could give directly to candidates, PACs and the political parties. For the Democratic Party in particular, the new law would mean building up its network of hard money donors to match the Republican base, and that would not happen immediately. Consequently, it was clear to many critics that the parties would respond by increasing their use of independent expenditures and nonprofit pseudo-party organizations (Malbin, 2004). That is precisely what happened. Known by their IRS designations – 527 and 501(c)(4) – a number of new nonprofit political organizations leaped into the void left by the political parties as a result of the BCRA. As all who followed the 2004 presidential election will remember, organizations like MoveOn.org and ACT helped the Democratic Party erase Republicans' natural advantage with individual hard money donors. These organizations, in essence, performed party-like functions – recruiting volunteers, producing TV ads, fundraising, etc. – but since they were independently operated, they could not be regulated, except by the provisions of their IRS exempt status. A number of these organizations have the capacity to act as nonprofits (limited in the amount and type of electoral work they can do) and as PACs (devoted full time to electing candidates and able to give money directly to candidates).

It is fair to say that party influence has not lessened in the post-BCRA era. Parties are taking advantage of new hard money opportunities so they have not been left out of the game (Corrado and Mann, 2004). But, at the same time, there has been an increase in giving to the 527s by those who had given soft money in the past and by individuals and unions in particular (as opposed to corporations). It is also clear that the parties and their consultants were involved in funding, operating and creating the 527 organizations. It is, of course, ironic that the Democratic Party pushed so hard for the BCRA, but beat the Republicans to the punch in exploiting the nonprofit loophole, which in essence brought unrestricted money back into play.

The unintended consequence is that the partisan environment has not lessened, but has become more complex and less efficiently coordinated. To some degree the independence of the nonprofits has opened up harsher and more personal lines of attack. In 2004, the Swift Boat Veterans' personal and devastating attack on John Kerry's war record was allegedly done without the consent and approval of the Bush campaign. This allowed candidate Bush to disavow any role in mud-slinging and to benefit from the effects of the attacks at the same time. Similarly, the Kerry campaign could benefit from the sometimes over-the-top ads of MoveOn.org (e.g. comparisons between Bush and Hitler) without taking the blame for them. When a candidate makes unfair and tasteless attacks on his or her opponent, there is a danger the attack will backfire and cause a loss of support. But, if another ostensibly independent group makes the same attack, the candidate is more immune to the consequences. If candidates believe this logic, the prognosis is that campaigns may get more bitter and personal in the future.

The independence of nonprofit organizations also undercuts efficiency. Soft money drove more cooperation between local, state and national party organizations. But, for the party to exercise its independent spending option, it must avoid direct communications with candidates and their staff. Having separate nonprofit organizations doing grassroots activity can lead to duplication and wasted effort. In 2004, volunteers for the Kerry campaign in battleground states like Ohio, Pennsylvania and Florida reported horror stories of independent groups canvassing the same neighborhoods, inexperienced volunteers using the wrong voter lists, and the like. The splintering of party effort and the need to avoid actions that would violate the BCRA and the tax code will make for less coordinated and efficient campaigns in the near future. With the increased financial resources of independent organizations, some worry that candidates will become more loyal to these organizations than to the parties (Alexander, 2003). And, the addition of these new players to electoral politics has only decreased the ability of ordinary citizens to get involved in the campaign process. Without the simple party heuristic as a guide, it is harder than ever for citizens to keep track of the funding sources in a campaign, and the new stricter rules may make it harder for amateurs to get involved in the political process (La Raja, 2004).

In sum, an unintended aspect of campaign finance reform has been a complication of the meaning of party in American politics. V.O. Key's much venerated and often cited tripartite distinction between the party as legislative caucus, the party as organization and the party in the electorate must now be expanded. Today, the parties comprise at least six national committees: the Democratic National Committee (DNC); Republican National Committee (RNC); Democratic Congressional Campaign Committee (DCCC); National Republican Congressional Committee (NRCC); Democratic Senatorial Campaign Committee (DSCC); and National Republican Senatorial Committee (NRSC). Each party has its own state branch in the each of the 50 states and numerous local party organizations. Making matters more complicated, the party as official party organization co-exists with a parallel constellation of parties as nonprofit organizations which provide "independent" party support functions that include voter mobilization and persuasion. Even the party as legislative caucus includes a bewildering array of organizations controlled by elected officials, including so-called leadership PACs. These are organizations formed by elected officials, candidates and other political leaders outside of their own campaigns as a way to raise money for other candidates at the national, state and local levels. Leadership PACs have become a popular way of raising an individual's political profile and gaining political clout. In the 2004 election cycle, there were 222 such PACs which contributed $27,520,592 to federal candidates (Center for Responsive Politics, 2005).

Partisanship in the electorate and party resurgence

Campaign finance reform has shaped the role that American political parties can play in campaigns. Regulatory loopholes and now increased hard money contribution limits have made the party organizations more complex and important at the same time. But can we say more?

Is there any connection between the resurgence of party as organization and polarization in the electorate and in US legislatures?

The answer is possibly.

The trend toward greater voter partisanship has been more gradual and does not detract too much from the general picture of a predominantly moderate electorate. Since the 1970s, voter partisanship has been on the increase. Partisan voting has increased over the last six presidential elections, rising to levels 80 percent higher in 1996 than in 1972 (Bartels, 2000). Attitudes toward the parties have hardened as citizens today are more likely to have positive feelings about one party and negative feelings about the other, are less likely to feel neutrally about either party, and are better able to list reasons why they like and dislike the parties (Hetherington, 2001). Citizens are likely responding to more consistently partisan behaviors by political elites, but the extent and nature of this influence is unclear (Hetherington, 2001; Layman and Carsey, 2002).

Until recently, charges that increases in the proportion of independents and in split-ticket voting were evidence that the parties had lost their bases of electoral support predominated (Niemi and Weisberg, 1976). More recently, these claims have diminished as the proportion of strong party identifiers has grown and the proportion of pure independents, that is independents who do not lean toward one party or the other, has grown since the mid-1970s. Partisan loyalty is even stronger among voters (Bartels, 2000).

Some scholars attribute the growth in partisanship to an ideological realignment among segments of the American electorate, like white Southern males, that has been driven by the parties' policy positions (Meffert *et al.*, 2001; Schreckhise and Shields, 2003). Realignment is disputed, however, as only those party identifiers who are aware of elite polarization on multiple issue dimensions have brought their own attitudes in line with party elites on those issues (Layman and Carsey, 2002).

At the same time there has been an increase in polarization in the US Congress (Figure 3.3). The parties in Congress have become more internally homogenous and more distinct from each other. Using both sophisticated scaling measures and simple interest group scores, there has been an increase in polarization along the left–right continuum. There is some question as to the degree to which the polarization is caused by party as opposed to other factors such as the increasing income inequality in

Figure 3.2 *Distribution of party identification (1952–2004)*

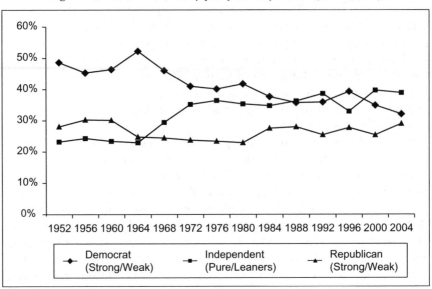

Source: Data from the American National Election Studies.
See < www.umich.edu/~nes/nesguide/toptable/tab2a_1.htm > .

Figure 3.3 *Ideology of House party coalitions, 1947–2003 (party mean)*

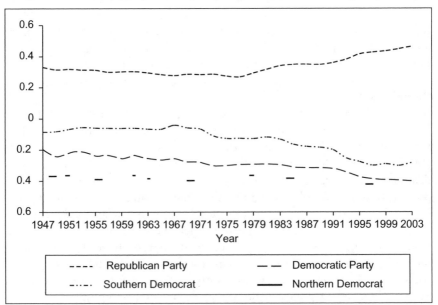

Source: Data from Poole and Rosenthal's DW-NOMINATE scores.
See < www.voteview.com >

America, incumbent-oriented redistricting that leads to safe seats and demographic shifts, but party influences are likely an additional cause. There are several types of party influence to consider. The first is the impact of party leadership in government. One way to measure this is the impact that party seems to play on close votes, and so measured, there seems to be an effect in this sense. Party leaders may be more effective at compelling members to vote the party line or party discipline may be manifest in an individual member's preferred policy outcome. The growing cohesiveness and polarization of the parties in Congress may reflect stronger party leadership or the increasing polarization of individual members' preferences or both (McCarty *et al.*, 2001; Snyder and Groseclose, 2001).

Parties' ability to raise needed funds also influences the selection and support of candidates and thus office holders. As the party in its many guises has become more important in the financing of candidates, it gains more leverage over those who get elected to office with their assistance. Since the parties tend to focus on the most marginal seats, this is a delicate calculation. The party leadership does not want to put its marginal members in a no-win position by forcing them to adopt unpopular positions, but, at the same time, there will be times when loyalty is needed for crucial votes. If party activists control the purse strings and take more extreme ideological positions than the general electorate, then candidates will be torn between adapting those issue positions that generate campaign revenues and moderate positions that could win them a majority of votes (Moon, 2004). Signaling the changing composition of party elites, surveys of delegates to the national conventions in the 1990s found their preferred issue positions were more polarized than in previous decades (Jackson *et al.*, 2003).

Party activists, of course, control more than the purse strings. Networks of donors, volunteers, political consultants, the staffs of elected officials and campaign professionals form informal party organizations for candidates that may influence the nomination process and the general election campaign. For example, far from being personal factionalized campaign staff in 2000, the leading candidates' campaigns were mostly run by long-time party loyalists and not by staff particularly loyal to the candidate (Bernstein and Dominguez, 2003).

Now that interest groups have adopted party-like functions and directly finance campaign operations, they too are in a better position to extract promises from candidates on issues that the groups care about most intensely. Knowing that these groups are monitoring what elected officials say and do, no doubt puts pressure on members to toe a more orthodox line on critical issues. Some of this will be reflected in the higher polarization and evidence of party-line influence.

The implicit assumption of the V.O. Key party analysis is that the three components of party are at some equilibrium level of consistency. If the party in the legislature is highly polarized then we would expect the same of the party as organization and the party in the electorate. But, they might not be completely in synch, particularly the party in the electorate. Morris Fiorina's work suggests that the polarization of party activists, political insiders and elected officials far exceeds that of the general public (Fiorina *et al.*, 2004). Analyzing public opinion data he argues that Americans' ideological and policy positions are no more polarized today than they were 20 or 30 years ago. In his view, the mass public holds moderate or ambivalent policy positions and prefers centrist candidates. The popular image of a polarized America reflects increased polarization among elites and a series of misrepresentations by the parties and the media.

The possibility that the parties may not be in tune with the electorate mirrors a debate in both parties about the best strategy to pursue to win seats in the national and state governments. Bill Clinton won the presidency with an explicit tack to the right, so-called triangulation or downplaying the more extreme positions of party caucuses and adopting moderate versions of conservative policies such as welfare reform and curbing aggressive affirmative action. Similarly, George W. Bush won in 2000 with his compassionate conservative theme, explicitly trying to lure independents and moderate Democrats. But, beginning in 2001, Bush strategist Karl Rove turned away from such "median voter" tactics and focused on mobilizing higher turnout from the party base by promising and delivering conservative policies like lower taxes, less regulation, strong responses to terrorism, etc. This has left party tactics and debate among party strategists in a state of confusion. Should parties cater to their bases, or move to the middle? Should campaigns continue the tradition of expending most of their resources reaching swing and independent voters, or should they allocate more resources getting their core supporters to the polls?

The controversy over Howard Dean's election to the Democratic National Committee's chairmanship after the 2004 election illustrates this quandary quite well. Party activists, fed up with weak responses to Republican policies (especially the Iraq war) by their elected representatives, wanted a strong forceful spokesperson to articulate their anger and opposition. Others from the party establishment and Clinton wing in the party wanted the party to return to what worked in 1992. Similarly, while the Bush administration continues to push strongly conservative policies approved by their base, they have encountered nervous resistance from moderate representatives, especially those from so-called blue states (i.e. that supported Kerry). The outcome of the 2006 election may determine the long-term fortunes of Karl Rove's base strategy: if moderate candidates and tactics prevail, we may see a return to median politics.

Parties and the Internet

Finally the role of political parties will be shaped by the rapidly evolving information age. In particular, the Internet is changing the way information is disseminated and lowering the cost of mass organization. The peculiar attributes of the Internet are likely to continue to encourage ideological polarization among activist segments of the electorate, but the parties may not lead this drive. While political reformers carry high hopes for the transformative powers of the Internet for American democracy, evidence of its effect has been slow in coming. The Internet is widely seen as an opportunity to strengthen democracy by leveling the playing field and redistributing power. The evidence is mixed. In politics, the greatest on-line success has come not from the parties but from interest groups and outsider candidates. Aided by the Internet, activists play an increasing role in the distribution of campaign resources and candidate selection, and large resource-rich groups have had the most success. Rather than diversifying democratic debate or forcing coalitions to communicate as a traditional party meeting might do, many critics counter that the on-line environment encourages specific homogenous on-line forums that do not force accountability or compromise (Winner, 2003).

The parties have been slow to take advantage of on-line opportunities. As late as 2000, state party websites lacked technical sophistication and did little beyond providing services for specific campaigns (Farmer and Fender, 2003). In 2004, the Kerry and Bush on-line strategies received flattering press, but in practice the sophistication of these strategies and utilization of on-line resources was limited (Fowler and Levey, 2005). In contrast, interest groups like MoveOn.org recognized the strengths of the Internet early on and have used it to build highly successful networks for volunteers and fundraising (Cornfield, 2004). Beginning with frustration over the impeachment of President Bill Clinton and the media handling of the impeachment, MoveOn.org began raising money and letting its members decide how and for whom to spend it. MoveOn became a powerful player in the 2004 election financing candidates and running independent expenditure campaigns.

The Internet also played a prominent role in the unexpectedly prominent campaign of Democrat Howard Dean for the party's presidential nomination. Like MoveOn.org, the Dean campaign used the Internet to raise money and organize its supporters, and like MoveOn.org the Dean campaign was perceived as operating outside the party mainstream until its on-line success propelled it into public view. Unlike other campaign websites that focused on providing informational content, the Dean site gave visitors the opportunity to interact with each other and the campaign, to chat with other Dean supporters on-line and to meet up with them in person. The site created a social network and encouraged visitors to spread the word (Cornfield, 2004).

Political web sites have had more luck when they adopt decentralized approaches that give individuals the opportunity to employ the Internet as a tool for establishing relationships and sharing information with like-minded individuals. It remains to be seen whether parties can adapt to this approach or find some new approach to the on-line world. In politics, the greatest on-line success has come not from the parties but from interest groups and a few candidates, who have made great strides in the areas of fundraising and network development and have shown a greater willingness to abandon hierarchical organizational structures. In contrast to other areas of party activity, the party on-line remains relatively weak today. Still, despite concerns that the Internet makes it easier for individuals to get information on their own and to communicate directly with elected officials and each other, thus limiting the role of organizations like parties, early empirical research suggests resource-rich organizations could still have the edge (Davis, 1999).

Conclusion

The recent changes in the role of American political parties reminds us that weak parties and ideology in the US is not necessarily a given. While the days of ward bosses and genuine grassroots machines are long gone, political parties can be useful tools for mobilizing money and channeling resources in strategic ways. The forms that political parties take in the US are becoming more complex: to focus only on the official party apparatus (e.g. the DNC, RNC, state central committees, etc.) is to ignore the vast partisan network of political consultants, PACs controlled by elected officials and caucuses, and the new array of partisan nonprofit organizations. There are a lot of party organizations in the US and they do not always coordinate very well, but they are still formidable in their impact on American elections. For a country steeped in Madisonian and populist prejudices against partisan factionalism, the US is surprisingly divided along party lines. US parties may not be organized in a simple and united structure, but they define politics in increasingly important ways, especially at the representative and activist level. This trend is likely to continue for the foreseeable future.

Chapter 4

Interest Groups

Graham K. Wilson

Interest groups have long been recognized as a fundamental feature of American politics. Tocqueville celebrated their importance in his famous *Democracy in America* (Tocqueville, 2002) based on his travels in Jacksonian America in the 1830s. Over a century later, the pluralist tradition that dominated American political science for several decades after the Second World War argued that an understanding of interest group politics was central to understanding politics in the USA, and probably in other nations as well (Truman, 1971; Dahl, 1956; Polsby, 1963). Yet interest groups come in many different types, are only one of the means by which people can try to influence politics or policy and vary their tactics as changes in factors such as the law and technology create new strategic opportunities. This chapter focuses on the changing roles of interest groups, the changing balance of power between interest groups and the changes in interest groups tactics that have occurred in recent decades. As we examine these changes, we shall keep in mind the normative questions that have long been raised about interest groups in the United States.

The dominant pattern in writing on interest groups has been to celebrate their contribution to democracy. Tocqueville argued that interest groups played a crucial role in providing citizens not only with a means of expression but with education in the practices of democratic deliberation. The pluralists of the 1950s and 1960s also argued that interest groups played a crucial role in democratic politics. The right to "petition government" exercised by interest groups is both a right recognized by all democracies and one enshrined in the US Constitution. Moreover, interest groups ensured that public policies damaging to minority interests or groups in the population were not ridden over roughshod by the majority. Interest groups therefore made it likely that that new public policies were reflective of more than a bare 51% majority of the population. Interest groups also improved the quality of public policy by providing information and technical insight into policies.

The critics of pluralism argued that interest groups played a deleterious role in politics. The critics made three major criticisms. First, because it takes resources to operate and maintain organizations, the interest group system reflected and reinforced inequalities in American life; as Schattschneider (1960) commented, the choir in the pluralist heaven sang with an upper-class accent. Second, interest groups necessarily advantaged particular groups or sections of society at the expense of the public interest. Those who received a benefit from public policy such as a subsidy or trade protection (a "rent" in the contemporary language of rational choice political science) would rally to defend it; those who paid the cost for perfectly rational reasons would probably not do so (Stigler, 1975). Third, American interest groups tended to be highly fragmented, competitive organizations in contrast to their counterparts in other countries and thus in practice could contribute little to solving the problems of governance. Whereas in "neocorporatist" countries such as the Netherlands, highly organized, cohesive interest groups could work with government to solve problems, in the United States interest groups vied with each other in competition for members by taking inflexible and extreme positions on the issues. When the Chamber of Commerce showed signs of being willing to compromise with the Clinton administration on finding a solution to the problems of America's health care system, it immediately lost members to the National Federation of Independent Business (NFIB), which simply opposed any change in the current system and accused the Chamber of betraying its members. It has been easier for environmental groups in the less competitive British interest group system to explore cooperation with industry and alliances with financial institutions interested in improving the environment; in the United States any group that shows similar interests in cooperation and fresh approaches is again attacked by its rivals as having "gone soft" and of betraying the environmental cause.

The structure of interest group politics at the accession of George W. Bush

It has been common to distinguish several types of interest groups in American politics and, with just a little bending of the facts, to associate the founding of each type of interest group with a particular era.

Prior to the 1960s, the best-known mass membership groups were related to economic interest. Farmers' organizations had led the way; the American Farm Bureau Federation (AFBF) was a major force by the late 1920s. (Wilson, 1977; Hansen, 1991). Labor unions have played a crucial role in American politics since the New Deal, supporting liberal policies for the most part including both welfare state type policies such as

Medicare and civil rights legislation (Greenstone, 1969; Wilson, 1979). The unions have also been a crucial source of support for Democrats in Congress, nearly always, in practice, the more liberal members of the party. Extensive political involvement in politics by unions can be traced back to the New Deal era; many of the unions that emerged at that time, such as the International Union, United Automobile, Aerospace and Agricultural Implement Workers (UAW), did so under the protection of the federal government. In consequence, these unions had a powerful memory that politics matters in contrast to the apolitical approach that had previously dominated American craft unionism. For many years, the AFL-CIO's Washington lobbyists were regarded as among the best in the business and its political action arm, the Committee on Political Education (COPE) was effective in organizing financial and help for liberal Democrats. In more recent times the unions have struggled to remain at the forefront of interest group technology. Much more important than doubts about the technical capacity of unions as interest groups, however, is the fact that their memberships have declined precipitously. In the early 1950s, about one third of American workers belonged to a union; today the proportion is about one in twelve. The proportion of workers unionized in the private sector is even lower. The UAW saw its membership decline from 1.6 million to 700,000 between 1980 and 2005. As the UAW has been one of the most liberal and most politically active of American unions, this decline has serious implications for American politics in general and the Democrats in particular.

In 2005, a group of unions grouped around the Teamsters and Service Workers International resigned from the AFL-CIO accusing it of devoting too few resources to recruiting new members. The most likely consequence of this defection was to accentuate further the widespread belief that strong unions were children of the New Deal and that they had declined inexorably and irreversibly in the latter decades of the twentieth century.

In contrast, business has gained strength considerably since the late 1960s. The proportions of corporations employing a lobbying staff based permanently in Washington DC, making campaign contributions and seeking actively in other ways to influence public policy, has increased dramatically in the last three decades. Trade associations such as the American Chemistry Council (formerly Chemical Manufacturers' Association) have increased the number and quality of their staff considerably over the same period. The Business Roundtable was created in the early 1970s to represent the interests of the largest businesses while the Chamber of Commerce, once written off as shrill voice for predictable right-wing views, has emerged under the leadership of Thomas Donoghue as one of the best interest groups in terms of its ability to lobby effectively (Wilson, 1981; Mucciaroni, 1995; Smith, 2000). In the 1970s, business executives feared that they were bound to lose in Washington. In the early twenty-first century, the voice of business in Washington seemed dominant and privileged as the Bush administration gave business exclusive and early access in writing its energy policy.

Business is far from being the only interest to bolster its representation in Washington in recent decades. Most large American universities now maintain Washington lobbying offices in part to deal with the raft of intrusive regulations (for example on research on "human subjects") that bedevil American academics and in part to try to have Congress "earmark" funds or research for grants for their university rather than have the money awarded through a competitive "peer review" process.

The most surprising development of the last third of the twentieth century was the rise of the public interest groups (McFarland, 1984; Berry, 1999). As we noted earlier, a common criticism of pluralism was that whereas vested interests with a stake in public policy were well represented by interest groups, general or public interests were not. Consumers, breathers of the air and drinkers of water (which is to say everyone) did not have an interest group to represent them; businesses that provide shoddy products to consumers or were polluting industries did. In the late 1960s and 1970s, defying political scientists' prognostications that interest groups to defend public interests could not be successful unless they also provided individualized benefits because it was not rational for individuals to mobilize to promote public goods (Olson, 1968), "public interest groups" mushroomed. Groups targeted on causes such as more honest politics (Common Cause), defending consumers (Public Citizen) and the environment (Greenpeace) were created or rejuvenated (the Sierra Club). There is still much debate about why this surge in public interest groups occurred. However, the change in the interest group system that occurred then seems to be permanent; public interest groups have withstood a sequence of unsympathetic administrations; indeed, radical right-wing administrations such as those of Ronald Reagan or George W. Bush have been good recruiting sergeants for liberal public interest groups as generally sympathetic but inactive citizens have felt compelled to join. A similar story can be told of the Women's Movement. Modern feminism took off in the early 1970s but today the National Organization for Women (NOW) is an established feature of the Washington landscape and is particularly prominent during Democratic administrations and in debates over Supreme Court nominations.

The third type of interest group that is active is hard to associate with any particular historical period. It consists of membership organizations which people join to receive some individualized benefit but which then also play a role in politics. In his influential work, Mancur Olson argued that the National Farmers' Union overcame the problems of the logic of collective action by providing the individualized benefit of access to its grain elevators. Its rival, the American Farm Bureau Federation (AFBF), attracted members by offering discounts on insurance (Olson, 1968). Perhaps the best example today is the largest membership group in the United States today, the American Association of Retired People (AARP), which attracts members through discounts on hotels and other services. However, the AARP does also play a major role in debates on public policy such as the proposed partial privatization of retirement pensions (Social Security). While it is difficult to identify a short-term trend in the degree to which such organizations practice interest group politics, it is clear that over the longer term there has been a substantial increase. In nineteenth-century America, there were numerous mutual help organizations that provided insurance and other individualized benefits without being at all active politically. Today, because the reach of government in American society is so much greater, there are very few membership organizations that are not drawn into lobbying on issues of concern to them.

The final type of interest group we shall consider is a campaigning interest group mobilizing people with passionate concerns about a particular issue or group of issues. Although organizations of this type (such as the Committee of One Million in the 1950s opposed to recognizing communist China) have existed for years, it is seems that they are more common today. In recent years, organizations such as Swift Boat Veterans for Truth, MoveOn.org and ACT (America Coming Together) have been highly conspicuous. Indeed, as Table 4.1 shows, in recent campaigns organizations of this type have spent more money than the parties and a significant proportion of the amount spent by the candidates themselves. This seems to be a distinctly modern phenomenon.

Table 4.1 *Expenditures by groups, parties and candidates, 2004 presidential election*

- Total candidate expenditures: $858,288,053
- Kerry and Bush expenditures: $665,917,403
- Total expenditures by 527s: $542,765,635
- Total expenditures by DNC: $394.41 million
- Total expenditures by RNC: $392.41 million
- Total expenditures by all federal committees of both major parties: $1.41 billion

Source: candidate data and national committee data were taken from the FEC website and the 527 data was displayed on the < www.opensecrets.org > website using IRS figures.

Tactics: an era of mobilization

It is difficult to generalize about interest group tactics. The determinants of interest tactics are numerous but include the following. The first is the expectations of stakeholders. Shareholders in BP or Shell probably hope not to see their company's name on the political pages of the newspapers very often; members of Greenpeace are disappointed if they do not. In consequence Greenpeace will pursue tactics that catch the headlines and BP will not. Second, interest groups can use only those tactics that they can afford. Every interest group would probably like to place issue ads on television, hold focus groups and conduct opinion polls to discover how to tailor its message most effectively. Many groups cannot afford to do so. Finally, all interest groups respond more or less rationally to the incentives that the law provides in terms of what activity is possible and effective. For example, interest groups gave larger and larger quantities of "soft money" in the 1990s when the law permitted the practice. Soft money, which could come from the general coffers of an interest group rather than from money raised in special contributions, was easy to raise and spend even though it had to be funneled through the parties to candidates rather than given directly. By 2000, interest groups were donating as much in "soft money" as they were through PACs in "hard money." After the practice was outlawed by the McCain–Feingold Act of 2002, interest groups had to redirect their resources into other activities.

Before we attempt to generalize about changes in interest group tactics, it is useful to set out the range of possible tactics.

Lobbying

Nearly all interest groups seek to persuade legislators and executive branch officials to adopt policies that the group favors. There is a constitutional right to lobby, although laws have increasingly placed requirement and restrictions on this right. In particular, recent laws have required more extensive and accurate reporting by interest groups on the amounts they spend on lobbying, and techniques once common, such as employing recently retired legislators to lobby their former colleagues have been limited.

Campaign contributions

Probably the best-known interest group activity is making contributions to the campaigns of candidates for office. Numerous studies have been conducted in attempts to identify the impact of campaign contributions (Wright, 1996; Baumgartner and Leech, 1998). While it might seem obvious that if an interest group gives a campaign contribution it will be treated better, the results of these studies have been contradictory and inconclusive. There are several reasons for this. First, so many interest groups offer contributions that politicians denied contributions by one group (business) are likely to be supported by others (unions, environmentalists). Second, if interest groups give to ideological friends, it is hard to disentangle the impact of the contribution from that of the politician's beliefs or constituency interests. If – as is commonly the case with corporations – the interest group gives to the powerful rather than the friendly (e.g. to a committee chair), that politician is likely to be able to command donations from such a wide array of groups that no one contribution is likely to have a determining influence. Finally, interest group influence may manifest itself in behind-the-scenes activity rather than in the roll call votes observed by the political scientist.

Campaigning for candidates or for public support

As the controversy over McCain–Feingold suggested, interest groups had increasingly come to enter political campaigns themselves, often maintaining a degree of separation from the candidate's own campaign so as to evade limits on campaign contributions. In theory, supporting a candidate's policy positions and criticizing the opponent's was not subject to campaign contribution limits, particularly if "magic words" explicitly urging people to vote for or against a named individual were avoided. Unions – particularly the AFL-CIO – have mounted hugely expensive campaigns in support of candidates but parallel to the candidates' own efforts. Indeed, in some state legislative races, the campaign has seemed to be fought between contending interest groups (such as the Wisconsin Education Association – a teachers' union – and the employers' organization, the Wisconsin Manufacturers and Commerce) rather than between candidates. These interest group campaigns have used all the tactics of modern campaigning – focus groups, polling, television advertising, phone banks, mailings and computerized efforts to identify and mobilize voters in support of the candidate or party favored by the interest group.

Establishing friendly relations with an executive branch agency

A great deal of public policy either originates in executive agencies or is shaped by them as policy is implemented. Executive branch agencies such as the EPA have significant latitude in writing regulations that give effect to the broad mandates of legislation such as the Clean Air Act or the Clean

Water Act. It was common between the New Deal and the 1970s to suggest that interest groups could establish exclusive "iron triangle" relationships between themselves, the executive branch agency most relevant to them and the congressional committees that oversaw the agency. Iron triangles persisted over time, transcended political party and carried over from one administration to the next. Influential political scientists such as Theodore Lowi expressed great concern that the iron triangles produced a federal government that was a congerie of special interests each serving its own purposes at the expense of the public's (Lowi, 1969). Iron triangles held enormous potential for interest groups, however. A strong relationship with a sympathetic executive branch agency would mean that the agency would make only those policy proposals acceptable to the interest group and would implement the resulting legislation as the group wished.

Going to court

Interest groups of all types pursue their goals in court arguing that executive agencies have exceeded their legal power as set out in an Act of Congress, failed to implement legislative mandates, have adopted regulations without complying with onerous procedural requirements of the Administrative Procedures Act and similar laws or that the law itself violates the Constitution. Although the greatest publicity is given to interest group involvement in cases involving issues such as affirmative action or abortion rights, business organizations bring many more cases each year challenging regulations adopted by agencies or their enforcement of them.

Changing the climate of opinion

Interest groups do best when public opinion is on their side. As Smith has argued (Smith, 2000), when a unified business community fights against public opinion, it usually loses. Business has also adopted longer-term strategies to protect its interests including supporting pro-business think-tanks to generate favorable policy proposals and programs involving charitable giving or community service to burnish its image and diffuse criticism. The controversial retailer, Walmart, for example, promotes itself as helping communities and individuals in part to diffuse criticism of its low pay and lack of health insurance for its employees.

Interest groups choose between a variety of tactics in pursuing their goals. For example, a large business corporation probably has its own lobbyists in Washington, a PAC, contract lobbyists on hire and a

Washington law firm on a retainer to engage in lobbying as well as legal work. It would also belong to at least one trade association representing the industry or industries in which it operates and at least a couple of the organizations that claim to speak for business as a whole – the Chamber of Commerce, the National Association of Manufacturers and the Business Roundtable. Deciding on a political strategy that uses the right mixture of these resources is obviously a complex decision that can be influenced by commercial as well as political calculations. Corporations often prefer trade associations rather than themselves to bring court cases challenging regulations in case in the process the corporation generates bad publicity for itself by seeming to show indifference to the environment, workers' health or the interests of consumers.

Are any of these tactics compatible with each other? Some clearly are. An industry could easily lobby Congress on a law, try to influence an executive branch agency's implementation of the law and bring court cases challenging regulations adopted under the law without any concern that these tactics might get in the way of each other. It is trickier to combine strategies that seek to mobilize the public or influence elections with strategies that take the composition of Congress as a given and simply try to maximize influence within that constraint. At an extreme, it is difficult to lobby a legislator effectively if you have just campaigned against him or her in the last election.

Changes in tactics

Changes have occurred within each of the types of strategy we identified above.

First, *lobbying* has changed in interesting ways since the ground-breaking study by Bauer, Pool and Dexter (1963). While changes in the law and reporting requirements make it hazardous to estimate changes over time in the number of lobbyists, it is striking that the number of lobbyists in Washington has increased from 16,342 in 2000 to 34,785 in 2005. Much of this apparent increase is no doubt due to people who have not changed their day-to-day activities deciding that it is legally safer to declare themselves lobbyists. However, both the number of lobbyists today – 65 lobbyists for every Senator and Representative – is evidence that lobbying as a career has never been more promising. Lobbying has become more professional and, in a sense, it has become a profession. This is partly a matter of a general increase in the education, training and skill of lobbyists. It is also a matter of the rise of lobbying as a career path distinct from both the law and a career in government. While a career in government is often a precursor to a career as a lobbyist, lobbyists are expected to have knowledge as well as connections. While most lobbyists continue to work for individual interest groups, an important change has been the development in the last 30 years of contract lobbying firms. Why do these firms flourish even as individual interest groups employ more and better lobbyists themselves? There are two probable explanations. The first is that many modern lobbying campaigns take the form of temporary coalitions of interest groups that come together to fight a specific campaign and then disband. The contract lobbyists brings the coalition together and manages it for the duration of the campaign. The second explanation is that contract lobbyists provide services to take the campaign beyond Washington through developing and placing advertisements, conducting opinion polls and stimulating grassroots campaigns.

What has driven the expansion in lobbying? The brief explanation is that government today matters more to more interests than ever before. Tax, trade, affirmative action, safety and environmental policies affect almost every business. Government is also a major customer for many firms. The considerable increase in federal expenditures under George W. Bush – not only or even primarily – on Homeland Security and, of course, oddly accompanied by tax reduction – has resulted in increased opportunities for businesses to obtain government contracts. Government contracts however make businesses subject to vast numbers of rules and regulations (such as affirmative action) unrelated to the nature of the contract itself. These firms therefore come to have a huge stake in what those rules and regulations attached to all government contracts specify. Public policy has also in effect encouraged lobbying. Provisions of the tax code – particularly Section 501c(iii) of the tax code – have been interpreted in a very permissive way so as to give interest groups freedom to lobby while still receiving tax benefits as charities.

Lobbying has also been affected by the marked increase in partisanship that has occurred in American politics. Republican leaders have exerted tremendous pressure on interest groups to hire Republicans as lobbyists. When Tom DeLay became majority whip after the Republicans gained control of the House in the 1994 midterm elections, he started a program known as the K Street Project which was intended to force lobbyists to hire only Republicans and donate money only to Republicans. Early targets of the campaign were the Electronic Industries Association and Microsoft, both of which surrendered to pressure to hire Republicans. In recent years 29 DeLay former staffers have secured major lobbying positions representing 350 key corporations and institutions. Interest groups not only contributed $14.3 million to between 1908 and 2004 to DeLay's political action committee, ARMPAC (Americans for a Republican Majority Political Action Committee), but gave large sums to other, less legally secure organizations created by DeLay (Judis, 2005). In 2005,

DeLay was indicted for breaking Texas campaign finance laws with one of these organizations, TRMPAC (Texans for a Republican Majority Political Action Committee), leading to his resignation in Spring 2006.

Campaign contributions have in fact been subject to numerous attempts at control over the years. The making of campaign contributions has been subjected to (often ineffective) legal limits since the 1920s (Malbin, 1980). In the post-Watergate era, interest groups were required to funnel campaign contributions through Political Action Committees that were subject to oversight by the Federal Election Commission (FEC) and were required to report fully the sources of their income and destination of their contributions. Initially, PACs were limited to $5,000 contributions per election (primary or general), an amount that rapidly seemed puny as campaign costs escalated. In the 1980s, interest groups increasingly evaded these limits making "soft money" contributions that were given initially to parties (supposedly for party-building activities) but in practice were redirected to individual political campaigns. Soft money contributions had the advantage for interest groups of being both unlimited in total and of being legally fundable from general accounts and not, as with PACs, from the specially earmarked donations of individual members, workers, executives or stockholders. By 2000, soft money contributions exceed PAC donations. Thereafter, new legislation (McCain–Feingold, or the Bipartisan Campaign Reform Act of 2002) prohibited soft money contributions and placed limitations on campaigning for candidates by supposedly independent interest groups. Somewhat surprisingly, these limitations survived constitutional challenges in the Supreme Court. McCain–Feingold also increased the limits on contributions by individuals and PACs so that individuals could contribute $2,000 a year rather than $1,000 per election and PACs could contribute $5,000 a year rather than $5,00 per election to candidates. Clearly the intent of McCain–Feingold was to weaken the impact of interest groups on candidates by prohibiting soft money donations which provided a particularly easy way for corporations to funnel large quantities of cash into campaigns. Yet the history of campaign finance reform in the United States is that, like water flowing down hill, money always finds a way into politics. The increased limits on donations by individuals provide a relatively easy way for corporations to evade limits by having large numbers of their executives make coordinated contributions to candidates. Unions may have a harder time adapting to the new law.

Other interesting changes concern the degree to which donations are given for strategic reasons rather than because the interest group genuinely supports the candidate. Business used to be heavily criticized by conservatives for giving money to liberal Democrats who happened to hold strategic positions in Congress; sometimes corporations gave to both candidates in the same election. This strategic giving was practiced mainly by business and has declined because the power of the Democrats has declined. As the Democrats have held neither chamber of Congress since 1994 with the exception of a brief Democratic control of the Senate in 2001–02, there has been less need for business to make strategic contributions; corporations have been freer to follow their heart and give to Republicans.

Campaigning for candidates or public support

As we have noted, there has been an explosion in electoral activity by interest groups. The most obvious aspect of this explosion was the growth of "527s" named after the section of the federal tax code providing tax-exempt status to organizations that exist primarily to influence elections. These 527s provided an easy and tax-exempt way to circumvent limits on contributions to candidates. Individuals could give only $2,000 to John Kerry's campaign directly but, as George Soros realized, they could give millions to American Coming Together or MoveOn.org to promote the positions that he took or to criticize the Bush administration so long as there was no formal coordination between the 527 and the candidate it favored. Informal coordination almost certainly occurred in 2004 as 527s often had the same lawyers as party organizations and had prominent members of the parties or candidates' organizations on their boards of directors. A large body of case law established that 527s were obliged to avoid using the "magic words" that called explicitly for citizens to support a particular candidate. Otherwise the 527s faced no serious limits on their activities until McCain–Feingold. McCain–Feingold required that they cease advertising related to a campaign 30 days before a primary and 60 days before a general election. On the face of it, this was an extraordinary limitation on the First Amendment's promise of freedom of speech. Supreme Court doctrine since *Buckley* v. *Valeo* in 1974 has held that as in modern societies effective political speech (advertisements) cost money, any attempt to limit advertisements or spending on them is a breach of the First Amendment. However, in December 2003, the Supreme Court upheld the provisions of McCain–Feingold that prohibited 527s running election-related advertisements towards the end of a campaign on a 5–4 vote. Justices Stevens and O'Connor for the majority argued that the prevention of corruption or even the *appearance* of corruption was such an important goal that it justified curtailing free speech.

A second factor driving increased public campaigning by interest groups is the growing doubts about efficacy of advertising. Although television advertising is the largest item of expenditure for political campaigns, it is often highly inefficient. Many races take place in states or, more commonly, districts, served by television stations that cover more than one state (New York, New Jersey, Connecticut) and multiple House districts. In consequence, many of the viewers who see an advert cannot vote for the candidate who paid for it. Moreover, with new technologies such as TiVo® or even the humble remote, viewers can tune out of advertisements. Interest groups have therefore tended to move resources toward trying to contact voters directly. This process has been aided by technology too. Software programs help identify likely supporters; e-mail and ever cheaper phone charges facilitate contacting these voters individually. The National Abortion Rights Action League (NARAL) and the National Rifle Association (NRA) both shifted resources at the turn of the century away from advertising and into attempts to reach individual voters directly. So, more surprisingly, did business. The Business Industry Political Action Committee (BIPAC) developed programs to help corporations contact their employees directly in order to try to persuade them how to vote. Whether these attempts to reach individual voters succeeded or not is unclear. However, surprising interest groups proved to be important elements in some campaigns; Planned Parenthood, for example, sent out 90,000 "voter guides" in the 2000 Missouri Senate race and operated a phone bank that was able to make 15,000 calls in the last stages of the race (Wilcox, 2002).

It is also striking in between elections, the distinction between lobbying and campaigning has more or less disappeared. (Goldstein, 1999). Interest groups, like presidents, increasingly "go public" by taking their message to the country and not just to decision-makers in Washington. Liberal and conservative interest groups were planning to spend up to $100 million on campaigns for and against George W. Bush's nominations for the Supreme Court in 2005. The very topic that had been the policy – trade – whose politics underpinned Bauer, Pool and Dexter's portrait of the subservient lobbyists was now a topic that occasioned considerable mobilization in the country and not merely discrete lobbying in Washington. The major trade legislation of the 1990s (the Uruguay Round, NAFTA) prompted considerable mobilization. The prospect of further trade liberalization in the Doha Round was the excuse for violent protest in Seattle in 1999 and Washington DC the following year. Within the boundaries of democratic politics, both unions and environmentalists opposed to trade liberalization and businesses that were in favor launched major campaigns across the country.

Relations with executive branch agencies

The vast majority of political scientists agree that iron triangles are a thing of the past (Heclo, 1975). The explosion in the number and variety of interest groups from the late 1960s onwards made it unlikely that there would be a single interest group that controlled any important policy area. A classic example of the iron triangle used to be the control of federal lands by the Bureau of Land Management (BLM) within the Interior Department; the BLM was long responsive to the National Cattlemen's Association and its allies on the House and Senate Interior Committees. Today the National Beef Cattlemen's Association must contend with environmental groups as it seeks to dominate the Bureau of Land Management in the Interior Department that controls grazing rights. However, if circumstances are propitious (such as there being a conservative administration in power), the Cattlemen can still achieve a close relationship if only on a temporary basis until the Democrats return to the White House.

The example of the BLM also serves to remind us of the increased importance of partisan politics in relations between interest groups and the executive branch. Executive branch agencies have become markedly more linked to partisan politics in recent decades. As Paul Light has shown (1995), an ever thicker layer of political appointees stretches down from the top of agencies so that the career civil servants are ever more removed from policy-making. Moreover, an extraordinary range of decisions that might once have been thought to be technical are now in the United States political; Democrats and Republicans differ on what is good policy in a wide array of policy areas as distinct as monetary policy, climate change, counter-terrorism and education (including teaching whether Darwin or Genesis provides the more accurate description of the creation of human life). In this era of polarization in American politics (at least at the elite level), the effectiveness of interest groups in relations with the executive branch depends very much on their relations with the President's party. The election of George W. Bush increased considerably the access and influence enjoyed by groups such as corporations (particularly the energy industry), ranchers and the Christian Right. The access and influence of groups such as unions, feminist organizations and environmentalists was reduced correspondingly from the days of the Clinton administration. If the Republicans were to lose the White House in 2008, the balance would shift back.

Going to court

There have been no significant recent changes, though conservatives hope that they are on the verge of some. For many decades, largely because of the impact of the Warren Court on areas such as race relations, the belief held sway that the courts were a particularly useful forum for liberal groups such as the National Association for the Advancement of Colored People (NAACP). The courts' continued defense of the right of pregnant women to decide to have an abortion during the first two trimesters of pregnancy strengthened this image of the courts as promoters of liberal causes. Conservative attacks on "judges who make laws from the bench rather than enforcing them" have continued since the Warren era to the present day even though the court today is heavily dominated by judges appointed by Republican presidents. Whether the courts as a whole have been more useful to liberal interest groups than to others is, however, an interesting question. The high-profile civil rights and abortion cases are not necessarily typical of the work of the courts as a whole. The role of the appeals courts in constraining regulatory agencies such as the EPA was very useful to business during periods when regulatory agencies were asserting their powers very vigorously.

The future role of the courts in interest group politics rests on how a number of trends, evident in the courts but not yet clearly defined, play out. First, there has been some possibility that the courts will revert to a narrower interpretation of the role of the federal government in economic and social issues. There seemed to be a clear trend in this direction starting with the *Lopez* case that marked the first time that the Supreme Court had asserted that Congress had gone too far in using its power to regulate inter-state commerce since the New Deal. However, the Supreme Court's decision in 2005 asserting the power of the federal government to ban the medical use of marijuana as permitted by several states seemed to mark the end of this trend. If, however, George W. Bush succeeds in appointing radical conservatives to the Supreme Court, lawyers from the conservative movement that believes in a "Constitution in exile" usurped by New Deal jurisprudence, this trend might be revived. His successful nomination of Chief Justice Roberts in 2005 and the confirmation of Justice Alito in 2006 are certain to strengthen the conservative wing of the court. Whether or not either Roberts or Alito have the radical instincts of Justice Scalia or are prepared to overturn longstanding precedents remains to be seen. If they do, they would provide enormous opportunities for business and conservative groups to constrain the regulatory role of government in areas such as environmental protection. Second, it is unclear how activist or deferential the courts will be to this and future administrations. Courts can constrain the ability of conservative administrations to repeal regulations adopted by more liberal administrations just as they can constrain the ability of liberal administrations to adopt new ones. It seems so far that the current Supreme Court has been deferential toward this administration, refusing, for example, to question the way in which the administration has developed its energy policy in closed-door meetings with energy companies.

Conclusion

American interest groups are so varied that generalizations about changes in tactics are hazardous. A number of generalizations do seem safe, however.

First, as has been true for the presidency and Congress, the division between "inside the Beltway" and "outside the Beltway" politics has disappeared. Successful lobbying strategies rest on combining close relationships between lobbyists and legislators with activity back in the district that persuades legislators to listen to the lobbyists. That activity can encompass both raising money and mobilizing voters. It almost certainly includes producing television commercials. The discrete gentlemanly world of lobbyists and legislators in the past has been replaced by a more campaigning style of politics. Similarly, interest groups no longer merely work with whatever Supreme Court (or federal appeals courts) they have been given but campaign hard to secure or oppose the nominations of justices.

Second, and following from this, interest groups have been driven to develop techniques of mass mobilization and campaigning in addition to honing skills in lobbying (Wilcox 2002). The extreme example in 2005 was Walmart, which developed a "war room" to respond to criticism of the company anywhere in the United States. The Walmart war room was not merely modeled on those of presidential campaigns but was staffed by people Walmart recruited who had worked in presidential campaigns for both Democrats and Republicans.

Has the trend toward the politics of mobilization made interest group politics more democratic? Tocqueville argued that Americans were unusually likely to join interest groups and that interest groups in turn helped train American citizens for democracy. On first glance, Tocqueville should be delighted by the situation today. A larger number of interest groups than ever before, representing a wider array of interests than ever, play a more conspicuous role in American politics. Interest groups create and channel an enormous amount of political energy from citizens and do so for a wide range of interests and causes. Many of the old criticisms of pluralism, such as the claims that interest groups represent only privileged self-interested sectors of society, are manifestly false. Environmentalists, consumers, feminists, liberal religious groups, conservative groups and advocates of increased aid to the third world have a visible presence as well as oil companies, pharmaceutical companies, farmers and other familiar examples of special interests.

Yet the Tocquevillian dream differs in important respects from the reality of contemporary American politics. The most obvious concern is that much of the interest group activity that takes place is carried on by organizations that are not intended to promote deliberation or even meaningful participation by citizens. A simple example of this is business which, as we have noted, is very heavily involved in interest group politics. American corporations no doubt have many virtues and should certainly express their concerns within the political process. Yet they are very hierarchical organizations and as such do nothing to promote the deliberation and civic training of citizens that Tocqueville expected from associations. It is more disturbing to find that much the same criticism can be made of the mass membership organizations, including both the "public interest" environmental and consumer groups and the 527s that have been so prominent in recent election campaigns. Most interest groups that claim to be speaking for the public are in reality organizations that encourage contributions on the basis of visceral reactions to people (such as Hillary Clinton, Ted Kennedy, Dick Cheney) or policies (abortion, equal rights for gays, Iraq) rather than deliberation on the issues. The modal relationship between a "member" of these groups and the organization is limited to writing a check or giving a credit card number. Tocqueville's fundamental argument about interest groups was that they raised the quality of democracy. It can be argued that today many of these interest groups lower the quality of democracy by accentuating disagreements in the quest for subscriptions; all the interest groups involved in the abortion debate, for example, adopt more polarized positions than do the American people. Relying on anger to attract members, these interest groups do little to promote deliberation or compromise on the political system as a whole.

One of the traditional criticisms of pluralism remains true and is probably truer than ever. The interest group system is very unequal. Lots of interests are represented within it but they are not represented equally. The interest group system is tilted heavily in favor of business, which is by far the best represented interest. Most of the lobbyists in Washington work for business, business supplies more campaign contributions than any other interest and most of the cases brought before the courts by interest groups are brought by business groups. Little can be done about this. Interest group politics requires resources to employ lobbyists, place advertisements and make campaign contributions. Business has more of these resources than any other interest, and the gap has been growing. This is not necessarily to say that the entire political system is similarly unequal; other parts of the political system may compensate for the inequality that characterizes the interest group system. Its inequality is, however, a troubling aspect of the interest group system.

Chapter 5

The Presidency

Gillian Peele

The two-term presidency of George W. Bush, the 43rd President of the United States, is one which combines elements of continuity and distinctiveness in a manner which is both intriguing and politically controversial. The continuities to be found in the Bush administration reflect both the incremental development of strategies for coping with the problems of exercising leadership in a highly fragmented political system and the experience of successive presidents in managing the executive branch. But they also reflect a continuity of political vision which has produced intriguing echoes of the Reagan presidency (Keller, 2003). The distinctiveness stems from the unusual character, ambitious agenda and convictions of George W. Bush himself and of his style of government as well as from the dramatic events of his time in office.

The Bush presidency as it stands in the second year of the second term is in many ways a very different entity from the administration which took office in 2001. All presidencies evolve as they respond to external pressures and develop new priorities but the Bush presidency has been subjected to external shocks of an unusually dramatic kind. The terrorist attacks of 9/11 transformed America's political situation and catapulted Bush into a very different kind of presidency from the one he had envisaged on taking office in January 2001. But, if the war on terror in many ways strengthened Bush's short-term position, it also presented challenges which it was not clear his administration could meet. Thus, although Bush's initial response to the attacks of 9/11 was the adoption of an assertive and ambitious foreign policy built upon an optimistic understanding of America's global influence, by the end of his first term of office Bush had been given plenty of evidence of the limits on American power on the international stage. Equally importantly, the Bush administration's foreign policy activism in the wake of 9/11 had the effect of alienating much international sympathy and provoking widespread hostility to the United States abroad, including in Europe where it might have expected more support.

The attacks of 9/11 had given Bush an opportunity to transcend the bitterness and division that had occurred in the wake of the disputed election of 2000. Yet the unity and record levels of support which Bush enjoyed in the immediate aftermath of 9/11 did not endure. Indeed Bush's opinion poll ratings resemble a roller-coaster in their highs and lows, making leverage over the other parts of the political system uncertain. Although Bush achieved a second term in 2004 and claimed a mandate of his own, he entered his second term with an approval rating hovering around 50% – a low figure compared with other presidents who have secured re-election in the recent past. When Bush's second term was confronted by a massive natural disaster in the form of Hurricane Katrina in the summer of 2005 there was extensive criticism of the President's policies, especially the impact of his approach to environmental policy and early spending priorities as well as his choice of administrative appointees. (The agency allegedly responsible for such emergencies – Federal Emergency Management Administration (FEMA) – was commanded by Michael Brown, a personal Bush appointee with no expertise in the field who was forced to resign in 2005, shortly after Bush had praised him publicly.) And there was much bitterness about the extent to which the victims of Katrina in New Orleans were overwhelmingly poor and black.

It remains to be seen how far Katrina, in addition to its physical destruction, will impose long-term damage on George W. Bush's presidency. What the hurricane has highlighted, as 9/11 did in 2001, is the extent to which presidents are only partly in control of their political fate. Although public approval ratings seemed to pick up slightly in the early days of 2006, the poll ratings for most of 2005 made grim reading for the president (see Table 2.1). The significance of the ratings which absorb so much presidential attention is that they can limit or constrain an incumbent's room for maneuver in relation to other actors and his ability to set the political agenda. While it is true that Bush's personal characteristics were perceived more positively than his policy achievements, he was increasingly seen as a divisive figure in an increasingly polarized political system. And when in November 2005 the Democratic Party scored important victories in the off-term elections, there was much discussion of a revival of that party's fortunes and a rejection of the Republican Party's policies.

Yet even if – and it is a big if given the fluid character of politics in the United States and the confident grip on power of the Bush administration – the public continues to view George W. Bush's presidency unfavourably, Bush's period in power raises important issues both about the capacity of the executive within the United States system of governance and about the character of policy and politics in twenty-first century America.

The problem of the twenty-first century presidency

Any analysis of the modern presidency has to begin also by noting the daunting difficulties associated with the office. Scholars of the American presidency are generally agreed that the institution is a difficult one to work effectively (Hodgson, 1980; Franck, 1981). By comparison with many other executives the American presidency appears a "weak reed", in Neustadt's phrase, reflecting an imbalance between the expectations of a president and his political resources (Neustadt, 2001). The American polity was constructed against the background of suspicion of strong government but fortunately for its survival the Constitution defined the scope of executive power in an open-ended way. Although the Constitution provides a range of specific powers, the executive was also granted a substantial amount of discretion which successive incumbents have used to expand their authority. Nevertheless the executive power in the United States is one which scholars and politicians have generally acknowledged to be constrained by constitutional design. The logic of the constitutional order requires a president to negotiate in a system of shared powers.

Not surprisingly many presidents have found the constraints imposed by the constitution frustrating and sought to circumvent them. In the twentieth century also there has been an increasing demand for strong political direction and a growing assumption that only the presidency has the capacity to provide the leadership which a modern state requires. It is a short step from that argument to the theory that the executive, backed by a national mandate, has an obligation to provide strong executive leadership and the right to pursue policies he perceives as in the national interest. Thus some scholars have identified two theories of the executive's role in the constitutional system. On the one hand there is the approach which sees the president operating within a system of checks and balances and shared powers and which relies on persuasion to promote presidential goals (Neustadt, 1960; Jones, 1999; Jones, 2005). On the other hand there are approaches which see the presidency as the dominant institution in the American system, and one which will seek to strengthen its strategic position by exploiting ambiguities in the constitution and by following policies which increasingly centralize and politicize the governing process (Moe, 1985; Aberbach, 2005a).

Part of the problem of the modern presidency is the sheer magnitude of the task which a president has to confront. On the domestic side the role of the federal government has expanded massively in the period since the New Deal of the 1930s, creating an administrative state of enormous proportions and complexity and one which presidents find it difficult to control. On the foreign policy side, the expanded role of the United States after 1945 meant that the American president became the *de facto* leader of the free world and guarantor of the international order. The transformation which has occurred as a result of the collapse of communism since the late 1980s has not reduced America's world role, although it has provided more room for debate about how and when its power should be used. In addition the president has to perform a number of domestic functions including the often conflicting ones of national leader and chief standard bearer of his party.

Many scholars of the American presidency have addressed the weaknesses and difficulties inherent in the contemporary executive and many have seen the presidency as an institution whose problems have been exacerbated in recent years (Neustadt, 2001). This weakening can be traced partly to the disillusion with the "imperial" presidency after Watergate (Schlesinger, 1973). The subsequent strengthening of Congress circumscribed the executive's freedom of maneuver especially in a period when divided government has become a frequent but not inevitable feature of American politics. In addition to the formal constitutional checks on the executive, American presidents also found it harder to mobilize consensus in a country marked by deep divisions of opinion and increasingly well-organized interest and advocacy groups.

Presidents have necessarily had to devise ways of governing within these new limits. Two such strategies – that of "going public" (Kernell, 1997) and an administrative strategy involving the exploitation of the resources available within the executive branch so that dependence on the legislature is minimized (Nathan, 1975; 1983) – have become part of the repertoire of all modern presidents. The "going public " strategy reflects the insight that if modern presidents are to get what they want, they must appeal directly to the public (and use their popularity to pressure institutional rivals such as Congress) rather than engage in intra-institutional bargaining. Although the ever-increasing emphasis placed on communications within the White House underlines how crucial the role of public opinion is, the strategy has to some extent been rendered more difficult by structural developments in the media, especially the proliferation of news media and the 24-hour media time frame. The executive strategy reflects the perception that executives must squeeze every ounce of advantage from their position to overcome the constraints of the constitutional order. First Richard Nixon and then Ronald Reagan developed an approach to the presidency which relied heavily on the inherent powers and prerogatives of the office (including the appointments powers and the use of devices such as executive orders and signing statements) to side-step Congress, especially when it was in the hands of the opposing party. Although the strategy was discredited as a result of Nixon's period in the White House, the Reagan variant provided highly successful when combined with the skillful exploitation of the media and a popular incumbent. For some observers

George W. Bush has built on this executive strategy to produce a plebiscitary theory of the presidency which is more in tune with populism than constitutionalism (Aberbach, 2005b).

Certainly, whatever the difficulties, the president is the one nationally elected office in the American system and as such he has to try to provide leadership in a system which is almost deliberately calculated to frustrate it. How to provide the leadership which this office alone can deliver within the American system is a problem which confronts presidents from the moment they enter the Oval Office to the moment they leave. Of course different presidents bring different conceptions of the presidency and different policy priorities with them to the White House just as they bring to it different personal skills and attributes.

Newly inaugurated presidents will frequently emphasize fresh beginnings and a break with the past, especially if – as was the case with Bush in 2000 – they take over from a president of a different party. But presidents cannot completely begin afresh and they have to manage their responsibilities against the background of the legacy of expectations and assumptions left by their immediate predecessor and in the knowledge that their actions will have implications for their successors.

The Bush presidential style

The American presidency is a peculiarly personal office. Of course there is a massive bureaucracy supporting the president and scholars rightly pay attention to the institutional presidency as well as emphasizing the importance of relationships with other constitutional and political actors. But the quality of an administration is set by the individual who occupies the White House. An individual president leaves his mark on the presidency in a range of different ways, not least the people he appoints, the policies he prioritizes and the way he communicates with the public. Hence it is understandable that analysts will seek not merely to probe a president's policy preferences and political philosophy but also his character and style. Although this may sometimes seem unscientific, the disposition, skills and working habits as well as the formative experiences of an incumbent have an impact on the presidency (Minutaglio, 1999; Greenstein, 2003; 2004; Renshon, 2004).

George W. Bush, despite the strong family political tradition, was in many ways a highly unlikely candidate for the presidency even in a system where the selection process is regularly criticized for producing weak candidates. The general perception of George W. Bush, the eldest son of the 41st President, was that he was a lightweight by comparison with his father and by comparison also with his brother Jeb, Governor of Florida

(Ivins and Dubose, 2000). Certainly there was little in Bush's early career to suggest presidential ambition or calibre. After undergraduate study at Yale, Bush attended Harvard Business School and then went into business in Texas with, at best, moderate success. Much of Bush's early life had been directionless, but marriage in 1977 and a family to some extent changed his playboy behaviour though he remained a heavy drinker. A new commitment to religion in the mid-1980s had a profound effect on his politics, making his presidency, in the words of one commentator, "the most resolutely 'faith-based' in modern times, an enterprise founded, supported and guided by trust in the temporal and spiritual power of God" (Fineman, 2003). He gave up drinking and developed political ambitions, building up contacts with the increasingly important religious right. Religion has brought Bush significant political support; but it melds with his own instinctive style and persona, which distrusts complexity and doubt, and is suspicious of intellectualism.

Bush successfully campaigned for Governor of Texas in 1994, over-whelmingly securing re-election in 1998 (Ivins and Dubose, 2000; Lind, 2003). The timing of that re-election victory was important because it occurred at a moment when the Republicans in Congress were losing support as a result of backlash against Newt Gingrich. Bush's position as Governor of Texas made him strategically well-placed to secure the nomination for 2000 since it was thought that Bush could attract the center ground and neutralize the harsh image that Republicans had acquired during the Clinton presidency. Moreover, as the son of a former president (albeit one not greatly popular with either the GOP activists or the electorate) George W. Bush offered a link to the Reagan era and excellent fundraising potential. Indeed one of the themes which frequently recurs in discussion of the George W. Bush presidency is the extent to which there is a parallel between the Reagan and George W. Bush presidencies, both in terms of its strategy and its ideological ambition (Aberbach, 2005a; Edwards, 2006).

Texas provided George W. Bush substantive governmental experience and it is worth noting the extent to which many of the people who had served Bush in Texas went on to work in the White House as key advisers and members of Bush's cabinet. Texas was also a source of some policy initiatives, although because Texas is not a strong gubernatorial state Bush's control of the state executive was limited. Thus when he ran for the presidency, Bush had atypical executive experience and his knowledge of Washington had mostly been learned indirectly through his father. Yet he quickly became the Republican front-runner – the inevitable candidate and the one who galvanized financial support (Bush's ability to raise money was prodigious and his 2004 campaign expenditure of $300 million made it the most expensive on record). Of course Bush had many advantages for a

Republican Party anxious to regain the White House. He projected a personality that had electoral appeal: despite the patrician background he looked populist, and had a manner of speaking that appeared warm and direct (Rockman, 2003; Campbell and Rockman, 2003). Unlike Clinton, George W.Bush had little interest in policy detail and in the field of foreign policy he was not merely uninformed but ignorant. However, this apparent defect in a presidential candidate was overcome by careful reliance on experienced advisers, many of whom had worked in the previous Bush administration. But there was also an explicit elevation of morality, character and organization over intellectualism in the Bush campaign and an implicit symbolic appeal to a vision of America which stood in marked contrast to that offered by the Democrats. And if Bush did not seem keen to become absorbed in policy detail he was able to concentrate on important themes and to bring out the big picture in a way which arguably made him more appealing to voters than either Gore in 2000 or Kerry in 2004.

George W. Bush was in many ways a natural standard bearer for the Republican Party at the turn of the twentieth century. Unlike his father, he enjoyed electoral politics and he was thoroughly at home in the cultural environment of Texas and the South which had become such an important base for the Republicans. His own increasingly Bible-based religious faith enabled him to identify with important constituencies on the right which had developed around key social issues such as opposition to abortion and homosexuality. His approach to politics was practical rather than ideological, although on economic and environmental issues his Texas background and strong links with the oil industry would have made him instinctively hostile to government regulation and sympathetic to business. His speaking style was friendly and homely and, although his use of words might provide endless humour for opponents, it did not necessarily alienate voters. Bush's public image has, of course, been carefully crafted to project a man who is at home with ordinary Americans but there is a sense in which his preferences and tastes really do coincide with those of middle America.

In two important respects at least the image and the reality may be at odds. Some observers suggest the real Bush is both less sociable and more status-conscious than the public image would suggest (Dean, 2004). But George W. Bush is also much more ruthless and determined a figure than the amiable image might imply. That ruthlessness has come in election campaigns where Bush has sanctioned negative tactics against opponents, for example the Swift Boat Veterans' attack on Kerry in 2004. And it is implicit in the close relationship with Karl Rove, a political tactician who learned his skills with Lee Atwater who was the campaign strategist for Bush's father in the 1988 presidential race (Moore and Slater, 2003). Rove has long been a key player in Bush's inner circle and his "laser-like vision" is seen as a crucial component of Bush's political strategy (Kettl, 2003).

Part of George W.Bush's appeal as a Republican candidate was that he appeared to offer a moderate and centrist style of Republican politics that could give Republicans a majority again. As a candidate Bush emphasized the theme of "compassionate conservatism", which, though vague, evoked a softer image than that associated with the Contract with America and Newt Gingrich's strongly anti-government message. But the content of Bush's brand of conservatism was not well defined as he successfully balanced his appeal to different electoral and party constituencies. The highly contested nature of the 2000 election result, apart from shortening the transition period, initially had a debilitating effect on Bush's first term, because the election was widely seen to have been stolen. Although some assumed that the circumstances of the 2000 election would produce a president who would seek compromise and govern in a relatively nonpartisan manner, Bush's strategy even in the first term before 9/11 was to pursue a right-of center-agenda that would please the Republican Party, hence the emphasis on cutting taxes. He spoke the language of bipartisan consensus but pursued an agenda that was highly conservative, especially in relation to moral issues, the environment and tax cuts. Not surprisingly, therefore, early efforts to reach out to congressional Democrats largely failed and the President found himself facing an increasingly united Democratic opposition in Congress.

It is not clear how well-formed a conception of his presidency Bush had on entering the office in 2001. An important part of his campaigning strategy was to attack Clinton for demeaning the office and certainly one of Bush's imperatives has been to restore respect for it. (The ethical problems and scandals which beset Bush and some senior Republicans such as DeLay in the second term occasioned an unusual lecture on standards for all presidential aides.) Alongside an emphasis on personal integrity in the presidency, however, has gone a determination to strengthen its powers and prerogatives, including the notion of executive privilege where Bush has attempted to broaden his power to withhold executive doucuments from congressional and judicial investigations and, equally controversially, to protect their own and previous presidents' papers and records (Rozell, 2002). Some commentators have seen this approach as reflecting an administrative strategy akin to that pioneered by Richard Nixon and developed by Reagan (Aberbach, 2005b). Others have seen it as part of a sinister movement to avoid democratic accountability (Dean, 2004).

Certainly Bush's approach to the job of being president has been noticeably different from that of Clinton. While Clinton was fascinated by policy issues and liked to engage in open-ended policy debates, Bush made it clear that his would be a presidency which operated in a more tidy, disciplined and structured manner. As a result it has relied much more heavily on delegation, and direct presidential involvement in the evolution of policy detail is limited. In particular George W. Bush has relied extremely heavily on his vice-president, the seasoned Washington insider Dick Cheney. The extent of Cheney's power and influence has caused commentators to talk of a co-presidency, although others have emphasized the extent to which it is a mark of Bush's decision-making capacity that he is able to delegate effectively without feeling threatened (Edwards, 2006). Certainly the strengthened role of the vice-president is one of the distinguishing features of the Bush administration and its implications will be further discussed later in the chapter. At this point it is worth noting that the selection of Cheney as Vice-President was in large part the result of Bush's father's influence and concern that his son's inexperience should be balanced by those familiar with Washington. Cheney's ubiquitous influence has brought to the White House more than efficiency and experience, however. For Cheney is a hard-line conservative who shared the values of a new generation of neo-conservatives; and as he helped construct the first Bush administration he inevitably brought many of the neo-conservative network into government, making it a job centre for the Project for the New American Century, as one critic put it (Nichols, 2004).

It is difficult to tell how the George W. Bush presidency might have developed in the absence of 9/11. The terrorist attacks on the United States and the subsequent engagement of the US in Afghanistan and Iraq have meant that Bush's administration has been on a continuous war footing. This has had advantages and disadvantages; 9/11 galvanized the Bush presidency and enhanced George W. Bush's role as national leader, creating legitimacy and making him appear presidential. The crisis also created a situation which allowed the executive to take the initiative and, for a time at least, reduced the willingness of Congress to challenge the president's authority. But it has subjected Bush's presidency to more than usual strain, exposed its decision-making flaws to relentless criticism and deflected him from his domestic agenda. Ironically the inept response to Hurricane Katrina just nine months into his second administration has set off another round of inquiries and investigations, while redefining the political agenda and seriously altering the mood in Washington.

Managing the executive branch

Although the federal government was tiny at the inception of the republic, its growth since 1789 has been prolific and messy. New functions have been added, the scope of government has expanded and the numbers employed by the federal government have rocketed upwards, despite efforts of many recent presidents to cut back the size of federal government. (Figures for 2003 show 2,743,000 working for the federal government of whom 2,677,000 worked for the executive branch with a payroll of $143,380,000,000 p.a. for the federal government as a whole; *Statistical Abstract of the United States.*) In addition to the 15 executive departments (Bush inherited 14 but the number expanded to 15 in 2002 with the creation of the cabinet-level Department of Homeland Security) there are a range of diverse agencies and bureaus. The Constitution places executive power in the hands of the president which makes him in theory the manager of this extensive web of federal departments and agencies. In practice one of the principal challenges for any president is how to make the executive responsive to the president both with respect to policy-making and to the implementation of policy (Aberbach and Rockman, 2000).

Presidents use a variety of techniques for trying to secure an executive branch which is responsive to their wishes. One of the most important techniques is the use of appointments. These exist at a number of different levels and, while some (such as cabinet secretaries and ambassadors) need senatorial confirmation, others do not. While some posts such as ambassadorships may be given as a reward for political favors and fundraising help or even on the basis on friendship, many are used to strengthen the president's political control of the bureaucracy. Within the executive branch appointees may be career civil servants whose career is dependent on merit. But in addition there are a range of appointments which the president can make on his own authority. These political appointments can be used to try to inject new policy direction into an agency. The percentage of political (as opposed to merit) appointments at any one time varies depending on the sensitivity of the subject matter and a range of other factors. Generally, political appointees have been seen as increasing in recent years as presidents try to gain leverage over policy (Light, 1995). The Bush administration has used the appointments power not merely to secure greater political control over policy within departments but also to ensure that, even in areas which have traditionally been seen as apolitical, appointees are sympathetic to the Bush administration's ideological preferences. This strategy has been used most controversially not merely in judicial appointments but also in relation to appointments to scientific and medical advisory boards such as those within the jurisdiction of the National Institute of Health (Silberstein, 2002).

Managing the executive branch is a challenge which few presidents meet successfully: not only do those nominally in charge of the executive agencies develop conflicting loyalties but many presidents soon lose interest in much of the detail of what goes on inside the departments. Moreover, as an administration ages, it loses some of its key players and, if a president gains a second term, he may find that he has to refill a large number of executive vacancies.

The shape of an elected president's government, and many other matters to do with the process of governing – such as making appointments and identifying legislative priorities – will be worked out in the transition period. For George W. Bush the extraordinary events of his first election victory meant a foreshortened transition period (Kumar and Sullivan, 2003). Yet even with that shortened period the Bush transition appeared highly successful. The detailed work of the 2000 transition was closely supervised by the vice-president-elect Dick Cheney who, together with Andrew Card, the Chief of Staff, and Clay Johnson, an old Texas ally, put together the cabinet, the personal staff and the policy agenda for the new president. Although George W. Bush on entering office had an unusual personal familiarity with the White House, it was Cheney and Card who brought their inside knowledge of administration to the new president's aid. Card was replaced by Joshua Bolten in 2006.

While the process of planning the Bush presidency was handled efficiently, the actual filling of appointments was slow. Delay in filling of administration vacancies has been attributed to a number of causes over the years : divided government, the amount of paperwork required and the sheer increase in the number of appointments so that Bush had about 3,300 to fill in 2001 (Mackenzie, 2002). Whatever the reason, the Bush White House had a number of vacancies in the administration through the first year.

The cabinet: reshuffling team Bush

The role of an American cabinet is, of course, very different to that of a cabinet in the Westminster system. It is not mentioned in the Constitution. While it is a body which can provide administrative linkage, it rarely provides collective political advice. Indeed the Constitution specifies that the president may request advice in writing from the individual secretaries about their departments, though it may have some residual political use as a sounding board if the president wants so to use it (Fenno, 1959; Bennett, 1996; Warshaw, 1996).

Increasingly also it has been seen as having symbolic significance so that presidents will strive to include an ethnic and gender balance in their top appointments. Here there has been substantial disagreement about the character of Bush's appointees with some pointing to the diversity of cabinet-level appointments, especially the inclusion of women (including Gale Norton, Ann Veneman and Elaine Chao as well as Christine Todd Whitman and Condoleeza Rice), blacks (Powell and Rice) and Hispanics in the first Bush administration. Others, however, have pointed to the paucity of women (who constituted just 26.1% of the 264 nominations requiring Senate confirmation in January 2001) and black Americans lower down the government (Brookings Presidential appointee initiative; Tessier, 2001). And many have made the point that, whatever the symbolic significance of appointing minorities to important government positions, what really matters is policy and that here Bush is in many ways out of step with the key interest groups representing minorities.

Who is in the cabinet is indicative of presidential purpose; and cabinet officers may enjoy a degree of public status and exposure which makes them dangerous critics if they fall out with the President. The first Bush administration compensated for the new president's lack of direct experience in Washington by bringing into key posts an unusually large number of experienced Washington players, largely people who had served in his father's 1989–1992 administration or that of Reagan. Dick Cheney and Donald Rumsfeld were government "retreads" (though personal antagonism meant that Rumsfeld had not served in the George H.W. Bush administration) as was Colin Powell, who moved from being Chairman of the Joint Chiefs of Staff to being Secretary of State. Dick Cheney as Vice-President was a key link and indeed the role of the vice-president under Bush became so powerful as to be widely described as a co-presidency or the real president. (Similarly strong language is frequently used also about Bush's relationship with Karl Rove.) Initially it was expected that Cheney's influence would be most marked on the international and defense fronts where Bush's own input was limited. In fact Cheney's influence has been much more extensive and touches all aspects of the administration. Certainly at the beginning of the second term Cheney's domestic policy influence was publicly acknowledged and he was regarded as having a pivotal role in shaping the Bush agenda, especially on Social Security reform and on legislative strategy. He was also said to be a key player in the politics of the President's agenda and "holding the increasing fractious Republican party" together (Stevenson and Bumiller, 2005).

Though loyalty and tight control have generally been seen as hallmarks of the George W. Bush administrations, Bush's first cabinet still exhibited some internal dissent. Colin Powell frequently found himself at odds with Donald Rumsfeld and others because of his preference for multilateral policies rather than unilateral ones. Christine Whitman at EPA found herself undercut on the controversial environmental issues where the Bush administration took a stance which increasingly undermined, to put it mildly, established environmental policy goals. Paul O'Neill at Treasury found himself at odds with the President over economic policy and policy presentation and was fired in December 2002 along with his deputy Lawrence Lindsay. Such internal conflicts are common in any administration but the Bush administration, which always placed a strong emphasis on unity and indeed on secrecy, became increasingly keen to eliminate such friction as time went on. The careful vetting of appointees and the assertion of a strong team spirit created pressures which marginalized dissenters.

At the beginning of his second administration it was made clear that there would be some key changes in the personnel at the top of Bush's administration. While it was noted that these shifts would be handled in an orderly manner, it was evident that Bush's second term would see an executive molded much more to his personal liking than the first and more committed to Bush by personal loyalty. The changes for the second term were made fast and indeed only a few cabinet secretaries have served from the beginning, although many departures were at their own request. The survivors from the first administration (at the time of writing) include John Snow at Treasury who had been appointed in the middle of Bush's first term to replace Paul O'Neill, Alphonso Jackson at Housing and Urban Development, Gail Norton at Interior, Elaine Chao at Labor and Norman Mineta, Bush's gesture to bipartisanship, at Transportation. Donald Rumsfeld, despite early run-ins with the military and its Congressional supporters and suspicion of empire-building, survived at Defense, as did Bush's drugs czar, John Walters. Margaret Spellings (who had served with Bush in Texas and had acted as domestic policy counsellor in his first administration) replaced Roderick Paige at Education, bringing more detailed expertise to the job (Light, 2004). Michael Leavitt at Health and Human Services replaced Tommy Thompson; Samuel Bodman at Energy replaced Spencer Abraham. Carlos Guttierrez replaced Donald Evans at Commerce; former Nebraska Governor Mike Johanns, who replaced Ann Veneman at Agriculture, was seen not merely as a committed Christian but a supporter of the farm industry.

Thus Bush's new cabinet appointments reflected his preference for people who would not be divisive and he promoted people unlikely to rock the boat on policy grounds. As a result Bush, like many before him, compounded the isolation of the presidential office by preferring compliant members to critics, eliminating dialogue. Bush also wanted to exert more control over the departments and one way of doing that was to strengthen the role of his personal advisers, sometimes by moving them into key cabinet positions. Condoleeza Rice, a long-time and loyal adviser to Bush and a member of the group of neo-conservatives nicknamed "Vulcans", replaced Powell as Secretary of State. Yet Rice's appointment, while acceptable to the neo-conservatives, is in many ways more the product of her personal loyalty to Bush than to ideology (Mann, 2004; Mashall, 2005). And one of Bush's most controversial first-term appointments, Attorney General John Ashcroft, was replaced when Ashcroft resigned on health grounds. The replacement Alberto Gonzales, a long-serving legal adviser to Bush, though widely criticized for narrowing the definition of torture used by government was a much more measured and moderate figure than Ashcroft.

In response to 9/11 a new Department of Homeland Security was set up in 2002. Initially Bush responded to 9/11 by the creation of an Office of Homeland Security rather than a fully fledged department but the need for greater muscle in coordinating various security-related agencies prompted the expansion in 2002. It has not functioned entirely satisfactorily and has been severely criticized as bureaucratic and inflexible. After losing one nominee to head this new department in the second term, Bush finally secured the appointment of Michael Chertoff, a former appeals court judge and former Assistant Attorney General at the Department of Justice.

The Executive Office of the President

The rapid expansion of the scope of the federal government under Franklin Delano Roosevelt prompted an expansion of the staff available to support the presidency in his constitutional tasks. The Executive Office of the President (EOP) was created with the mandate of reporting directly to the president. EOP is, as has been noted, the structural basis of the institutionalized presidency and its different agencies have different institutional histories and degrees of politicization (Lewis, 2005).

Organizationally EOP is itself complex and is not so much a single office as an umbrella organization that "shelters more than a dozen staff agencies of varying significance" (Dickinson, 2005). Since Roosevelt's time the EOP has itself grown exponentially, creating new problems of managements and control. The expansion of the EOP has reflected the changing nature of the presidential office and the priorities of particular presidents. Thus in 1946 a Council of Economic Advisers was added to the structure of the EOP. Eisenhower added a congressional relations unit. Specialist units have been added to deal with the media. Under George W. Bush some of Clinton's units were dismantled including the Office for Women's Initiatives and the staff supporting his Initiative for One America. Instead a new unit to deal with Faith-Based and Community Initiatives was added by executive order at the very beginning of the new Bush administration.

Despite its ostensible role as a support for the president's agenda, the task of managing the Executive Office has itself become a problem in its own right. Presidents must find a style of control which suits them and which reflects their own agendas and priorities.

Given that, presidents will frequently prefer to put their closest advisers in the White House Office rather than in key executive positions, although there may be as in the Bush administration movement between the two sides of the administration.

Within EOP is the White House Office (WHO) – the politically sensitive nerve center of the presidency, the site of the key staff and advisers who are closest to the President. The composition and structure of the White House Office will be the most important clues to the president's way of thinking The overall size of the White House staff has varied. The size of staff grew under Nixon but was cut back under the Carter presidency. However, despite these cuts the number of staff has again grown. Currently the White House Office employs perhaps 450 policy analysts and political advisers.

Although there may be variations in detail, the organization and staffing of the administration tends to fit within the parameters of a broad model which many commentators now see as standard (Walcott and Hult, 2005). Broadly two models of organization have appealed to presidents in the approach to managing their closest staff (Campbell, 1986). In one the staff have been organized hierarchically so that there are strict controls on access to the president as information is filtered upwards. In the other model, the so-called "spokes of a wheel" model, the president remains open to a number of advisers. The hierarchy model gains order and control at the expense of building up powerful staff and excluding the president from formative stages of discussion. The spokes-of-a-wheel model encourages creative discussion at the expense of efficiency. The spokes-of-a-wheel model has generally appealed more to Democratic than to Republican presidents, who have placed more emphasis on organizational clarity.

Both Democrats and Republicans have used a chief of staff in their organization of the EOP, although, as Clinton's White House showed, much depends on the amount of power granted to the chief of staff (Kernell and Popkin, 1986). The role of chief of staff is one which Eisenhower introduced in an effort to bring more streamlined processes to White House operations. For some time this development was regarded with suspicion by those who saw it as an undermining of the flexibility and creativity which should suffuse White House operations. Although a president must select people with administrative experience to fill the major departmental positions, the choice of personal staff is much more likely to reflect his own preferences and friendships. Initially George W. Bush appointed Andrew Card as Chief of Staff but Card shared power with two other key figures, Karen Hughes and Karl Rove, his Deputy Chief of Staff. After Hughes's departure from her key communications role early in Bush's first term, Rove increased in influence and in the second term he was given an enhanced coordinating role across the spread of domestic and foreign policy (Fletcher, 2005). But in Bush's second term Dan Bartlett, Bush's Communications Director, also increased his influence taking a bigger role in policy advice on the domestic front as well as communicating the President's message (Walsh, 2006).

Coordination

Meetings of the American cabinet are not the place in which policy conflicts are resolved. Under Bush cabinet meetings take place perhaps once every 45 days and are not substantive. Given that, the cabinet in the American system cannot provide much linkage or coordination within the administration. Those functions are performed by cabinet councils which contain groups of cabinet officials, sub-cabinet officials and White House staff across related policy areas. One of the imperatives of the Bush White House has been to exert more control over departments and to ensure better coordination. A variety of tactics have been used to this end including a directive which was issued by Card at the beginning of Bush's second term to force all cabinet secretaries to spend time in the White House (as opposed to their departments) to coordinate policy and tactics. The White House is also increasingly the source of policy initiatives (Fletcher, 2005). Although some scholars see this innovation as eroding the autonomy of cabinet secretaries, others recognize that the trend toward greater White House control has been gathering momentum since before the Bush administration. And for some cabinet secretaries the change makes it easier to get the attention of the White House for their departments.

Enhancing presidential power

From the beginning Bush wanted to reassert the powers of the presidency which he saw as having eroded since Watergate and having been further eroded under Clinton (Rozell, 2002). George W. Bush sought to do this a number of ways. On a personal level he hoped that protecting the presidency from the kind of scandal that engulfed Clinton would allow it to regain respect and authority. But Bush was also determined to assert the prerogatives of the presidency more strongly than before. In particular Bush has been keen to assert executive privilege over information and records related to White House policy-making.

In addition Bush, like Clinton, has used executive orders and other devices such as proclamations, signing statements and memoranda, and national security directives extensively. Executive orders can be used to bypass Congress especially if a president has difficulties with the legislature. Executive orders, along with these other devices, allow a president to act unilaterally and to seize the policy initiative. Although they can be challenged in the courts and by Congress, the ability to do things on his own authority is a powerful resource for a president in a system where legislative action is often slow. Not surprisingly presidents have made regular use of executive orders and used them for increasingly substantial and significant matters (Howell, 2005). In Bush's case executive orders and national security directives have been used controversially to create military tribunals, to freeze the assets of suspected terrorist organizations and to reduce the effectiveness of environmental and industrial regulation. Executive orders are not the only techniques at the President's disposal for effecting policy without recourse to Congress. Also of importance are proclamations, which can be used, for example, to designate special days. Bush used this technique to designate a Life Day, thereby signaling his commitment to the values of the Right to Life movement. And signing statements (presidential statements on signing a bill into law) can be used to achieve a number of presidential objectives including highlighting constitutional objections to a bill or inviting the courts to interpret the law in a particular way. As has been noted, a president's appointment power is central to his ability to influence policy. Even in those areas where the Constitution specifies confirmation by the Senate the executive may get round this by making a recess appointment. Bush used this strategy to secure the appointment of John Bolton, as the Ambassador to the UN which the Senate had blocked. The President's power to appoint to the federal judiciary is also crucial and has been seen as a crucial part of the conservative movement's strategy since the Reagan years.

Managing the agenda: Congress

The President's relationship with Congress is one of the keys to the success of his presidency. The Constitution sets up a system of separated powers which means that the executive and the legislature respond to different constituencies. Although the electoral cycles of the president and the two houses of Congress are different, the president's relationship with Congress is deeply affected by the rhythms of congressional elections. Each Congress is different not just in terms of the obvious factors of party composition but also in terms of each chamber's internal politics. (The House is generally more disciplined and majoritarian in outlook than the

Senate which, with its powerful weapon of the filibuster, can frustrate a president's legislative agenda as well as his ability to secure important nominations.)

Bush's relationship with the 107th Congress (2001–2002) was in some ways the most strained. The contested election of 2000 meant that Bush came into office with none of the customary legitimacy which helps a newly elected president promote his agenda. In his first two years he faced a Senate where Republicans had the advantage briefly only because of the Vice-President's role as tie-breaker and was then narrowly Democratic because of the switch by Senator Jeffords away from the Republican Party. This tight situation encouraged Bush to intervene in the midterms of 2002 in support of Republican candidates and the 108th Congress saw Republicans in control of both the House and Senate, a position which was strengthened in the 109th Congress.

Bush's legislative strategy in his first administration was to set out a few priorities and go public with them (Edwards, 2006). In particular the tax cut which was signaled early in the administration was seen as crucial both for rallying Republican sentiment and for steering the direction of domestic policy. Bush was also strongly committed to educational reform and made his "No Child Left Behind" initiative a major issue. Educational reform was seen as a shrewd issue for Bush to prioritize because it could be pursued across party lines; and even though there were elements (such as vouchers) which Congress could not swallow, Bush was willing to compromise. Compromise has in fact been a major feature of Bush's relationship with Congress, on the theory that some success is better than none. But he has been careful to claim credit for legislative achievements and to turn apparent concessions into victories (Edwards, 2006).

Bush unusually among recent presidents has not exercised the veto on any legislation coming from Congress. Perhaps this is not surprising since he has enjoyed a Congress which has been in Republican hands at least since 2002 and where Bush has taken care to strengthen GOP support for his policies through the strategic use of federal money. It should also be noted that Bush's use of signing statements to put his gloss on law has been marked. These signing statements represent an important expansion of presidential power since they allow the executive the opportunity to put its selective interpretation on Congressional measures.

Given the lack of legitimacy Bush had when he took office for the first time, the 2004 election victory was hailed as a decisive endorsement of the President and his policies. Although the margin of victory was in fact quite narrow (51% of the vote to Kerry's 48% and a margin of 286 to 252 in the Electoral College) it was enough for Bush to claim that he had acquired political capital and that he was going to use it. The elections of 2004 also saw Republicans increase their control of both chambers of Congress, although Republicans still had insufficient support in the Senate to defeat a filibuster. This had an impact on the legislative agenda and on nominations. Judicial nominations in particular had been blocked by Democrats keen to prevent ideologically conservative judges reaching the federal courts.

Republicans began the 109th Congress in a mood to achieve radical change and to work with the President on social security reform and reform of the legal system. But Democrats have become more united in their opposition to Republican policies and there had been little legislative progress with the Bush agenda by the end of the first year of his second term.

As in the first administration Bush had talked about rising above partisan politics but had pursued a distinctly partisan strategy. In his first term Bush had placed emphasis on educational reform and the tax cuts. After the election Bush made clear his wish to push forward a radical agenda centered on the reform of social security. While supporters lauded Bush's courage in taking up one of the most controversial and difficult issues in American politics, critics saw this as another stage in the dismantling of the welfare state. However, such was the sensitivity of the issue in Congress that by the end of December 2005 extensive radical reform looked doomed.

Foreign policy

Foreign and security policy were initially seen as the areas where Bush would need to rely on the experience of others, especially his Vice-President Dick Cheney. Yet ironically national security issues have dominated the Bush presidency, submerging to a large extent the domestic agenda. Although the detailed discussion of Bush's foreign policy occurs in another chapter (see Chapter 14), here we should note the way Bush's ambitions in this field have unfolded and developed. When Bush appointed Colin Powell as his Secretary of State in his first administration he was building in expertise but also generating conflict into his administration. Powell, as noted earlier, was skeptical about the unilateral exercises of force and keen to explore multilateral options. His outlook was very different from that of the more conservative players in the cabinet – Dick Cheney and Donald Rumsfeld – and also from the ideologically assertive lieutenants such as Paul Wolfowitz and Richard Armitage. Increasingly Bush seems to have sided with them and, when Powell left the administration in 2004, he appointed Condoleeza Rice as his National Security Adviser. Although young by comparison with Rumsfeld, Cheney and Powell, she was close to Bush personally and had strong academic credentials. Intellectually and ideologically she was close to the neo-conservative activists who wanted the United States to assert its power in the world on behalf of democratic values. In the first term she expanded her influence while acting as a broker rather than a policy-maker. In the second term Bush elevated her to the position of Secretary of State.

Despite his initial weaknesses in foreign policy, Bush developed confidence in the aftermath of 9/11. The National Security Council machinery was supplemented by a war cabinet in which Bush was keen to secure agreement and clarify policy. He was also determined to chair key meetings himself rather than delegate them (Woodward, 2002). After 9/11 the Bush administration developed a foreign policy approach which was a radical departure from that of previous administrations, especially in the extent to which it urged unilateral rather than multilateral action and propounded a vision of a world based on values which the United States could endorse. The Bush doctrine, as it came to be known, expressed the idea that the United States would be justified in taking pre-emptive action to remove regimes which threatened its security.

Conclusion

George W. Bush's presidency exhibits a number of features which, although not entirely novel, together constitute a distinctive approach to the problems of the office. The determined use of unilateral powers including executive orders and signing statements underline a conception of the presidency in which the executive should be able to mobilize a variety of weapons on behalf of its agenda. The centralization and tight management of Bush's team reflects a belief in the importance of discipline and focus in getting things done in Washington and a personal preference for clear and decisive management over policy debate. The preference for ideologically sympathetic appointees – for politicization over neutral competence – is in keeping with an approach pioneered by earlier Republican Presidents Nixon, Reagan and, to a lesser extent, George H.W. Bush who sought to reverse the values of the governmental structures they inherited. These features of the George W. Bush presidency inevitably have their weakness. The assertive approach to presidential powers, however much it may be tolerated in a period of crisis, sits uncomfortably with the notion of shared powers and constitutional balance. Centralization and tight management exclude the input of voices which may contribute to the policy debate and may create a siege mentality in the executive. By reducing the expertise of policy-makers in the quest for control, politicization may damage policy-making effectiveness and thus frustrate the very end it is designed to promote. Moreover, as observers of Bush's managerial style of leadership have noted, Bush's fundamental values and his tendency to see the world in stark black-and-white terms make it uncertain that he can solve the problems of a country where policy dilemmas are more frequently coming in shades of grey (Kettl, 2003). To that extent Bush's personal recipe for good government in Washington is ill-suited to the policy needs of the wider American society in the twenty-first century. Moreover, although the Bush presidency has moved into an increasingly confident and assertive stance across the range of foreign and domestic policy, that assertiveness seems likely to provoke a constitutional and political reaction. For however much George W. Bush asserts the idea of presidential supremacy and however much that assertion is supported by the unusual circumstances of his presidency, it remains the case that the President must operate within a constitutional context in which other actors have the capacity to check executive action. That said, George W. Bush's presidency is suggestive of how successor presidents may harness executive resources within the American polity and provides a template for a style of presidency far removed from that envisioned by the Founding Fathers.

Chapter 6

Congress

Ross English

Following September 2001, it appeared that the terrorist attacks on New York City and Washington DC had brought about a change in Congressional politics. The two parties came together to pass a series of measures from those specifically directed at tackling terrorism at home and abroad to more domestic issues such as corporate accountability following the Enron scandal. Even the party leaders, previously whose relationships had ranged from strained to the outright hostile, came together in a show of unity.

Such demonstrations of bipartisanship proved to be short-lived. By the end of the 108th Congress (2003–4) the legislative process had become characterized by partisanship, rancour and stalemate. Frustrations became such that at one point Senator John McCain (R-AZ) angrily complained, "why don't we just go home ... rather than go through this charade of telling Americans that we are legislating" (Congressional Record, April 27, 2004: S4411). The apparently rapid breakdown of any post-9/11 consensus was a combination of several factors: the relatively even balance between the two parties in both chambers of Congress, an increasing ideological homogeneity within both parties that are also moving further apart from one another, the attempts by the Republican leadership to pursue a party agenda despite the small size of their majority and the Democrat tactics used to try and stop them.

It is these factors that this chapter considers, while also considering whether the Republican majority has been able to overcome those difficulties to pass important legislation.

An age of parity

According to Norman Ornstein, the American political system has entered an "age of parity" (Ornstein, 2002). Indeed whichever way one looks at the parties, there is little to separate the Democrats and Republicans in terms of public support. Whether it is in terms of representation in Congress, state legislatures and governorships or party identification, the era of one-party national dominance at any level of government is, at least temporarily, over.

Since the Republican victories in the 1994 midterm elections, which gave them control of Congress for the first time in 40 years, the size of majorities in both the House of Representatives and Senate have remained relatively slim (see Figures 6.1 and 6.2). While the Republicans have been mostly successful in maintaining their control of Congress – only losing the Senate between 2001 and 2003 when the defection of Senator Jim Jeffords of Vermont from Republican to Independent gave the Democrats a one-vote majority – their numeric advantage has been a far cry from the dominance the Democrats enjoyed in the 1960s and 1970s.

The prospects for any immediate return to overwhelming majorities for either party in Congress appear remote. This is because the dynamics of Congressional elections make a party landslide in any one election most unlikely. In some ways there is a paradox here – if there has been genuine competition between the two main parties for control of Congress as a whole, the same cannot be said for the vast majority of individual House and Senate seats. Looking at races district-by-district or state-by-state, it is clear that party competition has been in decline. Indeed, at present, one would estimate that only around 10 percent of seats in Congress can be said to be winnable by either party at election time (Campbell and Jurek, 2003).

This trend can be attributed to three factors. First, the electorate is seemingly becoming increasingly partisan. The rise in split-ticket voting (casting a vote for candidates of different parties for various posts on one election day) witnessed in the 1970s has declined and, accordingly, some areas of the country are becoming dominated by one party – most noticeably the Republican South.

Secondly, in most states the drawing of district boundaries for seats in the House of Representatives is in the hands of the party which controls the state legislature and as such is often a partisan exercise. Every ten years, following the nation-wide census, the states are required to undergo a process of "redistricting" – to consider the shape of their House districts to ensure that population shifts have not caused some to become significantly over-populated. In many cases the party in control of the state government has used this exercise to manufacture an electoral map that will favor their own candidates, creating numerous districts whose demographics ensure that they will be steadfast in their support for one party. In 2003, the Republican-controlled Texas state legislature passed a controversial redistricting plan that explicitly set out to target the seats of a number of Democrat members of the House of Representatives with an electoral map that was likely to return more Republican members. There was nothing unique to Texas or Republicans about such partisan scheming, but it was particularly contentious as the changes were not a response to population movement – Texas had already redistricted

Figure 6.1   *Party majorities in the House of Representatives, 1945–2005*

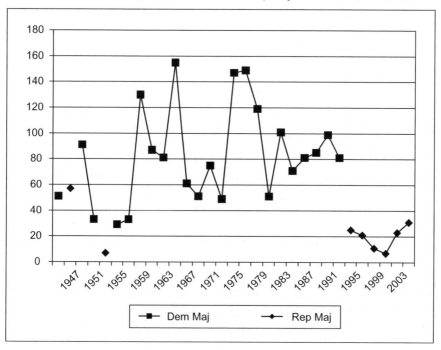

Figure 6.2   *Party majorities in the Senate, 1945–2005*

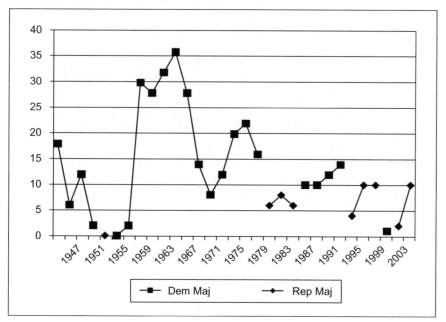

following the 2000 census – but was simply a matter of political maneuvering that followed the Republican takeover of the Texan legislature. The dispute came to national attention when it began to take on the appearance of farce as, in a vain attempt to prevent the approval of the new map, Texas Democrats fled the state and hid out in a hotel in Oklahoma.

Thirdly, the advantages of incumbency still make it difficult for challengers to unseat members of Congress seeking re-election. Members of the House and Senate have access to the resources of the federal government that subsidize the costs of mailing their constituents ("the franking privilege"), travel costs between Washington DC and their home state and the expense of maintaining staffed offices in their constituency. Two or six years (House and Senate respectively) of public appearances and media interviews gives incumbents the sort of name-recognition that it would take most other candidates millions of dollars to buy. For several reasons, interest groups and private donors are more likely to donate money to incumbents and consequently they are usually able to raise more campaign funds than their challengers. Finally, incumbents simply by virtue of being members of Congress are in a position to work to satisfy their core constituencies by introducing legislation, engaging in "position-taking" and ensuring they receive their share of federally funded projects (Fenno, 1973).

The effect of the continuing fine balance between the two parties in Congress has often been to increase the partisan tensions that exist. Because of the genuine party competition within Congress the minority have expectations that they can prevail on certain issues and even have a realistic opportunity to retake one or both of the chambers at a not-too-distant future election. As such, every action in Congress – votes, speeches, committee hearings – becomes imbued with political significance would not be there if one party was numerically dominant. The defection of five or ten members of the majority in a vote on legislation that divides the party leaderships would have meant very little in the 1970s, but in the current climate such movement can mean the difference between success and failure. There is also a wider game being played as actions in Congress are aimed at the public in general as part of a partisan battle in advance of the next election. Such an atmosphere does not make bipartisan cooperation easy to achieve.

Ideological balance

A Congress finely balanced between the two parties does not automatically mean that measures will pass or fail with narrow majorities or that every issue will be the subject in contention. This is because, unlike many of their European counterparts, American political parties within Congress have traditionally been "broad churches" containing legislators with a wide range of views even on important issues. This is due to the diversity of the nation itself and to the fact that to sustain a two-party system the Democrats and Republicans must allow their members to reflect the views and interests of their own constituents if they are to continue to win election. During the 1950s Congress featured a dominant conservative coalition opposed to federal intervention in matters of civil rights. This coalition was largely successful regardless of which party held the majority as it was composed of both Republicans and many conservative, often southern, Democrats.

It would be a mistake to conclude that parties do not still contain a range of views on any one issue, however it can be said that the Congressional Democrats and Republicans are, in the first decade of the twenty-first century, more ideologically united than at any time since the Second World War. Indeed, not only have the parties seemingly become more homogeneous but in the process they have moved apart from each other on the ideological spectrum. This is largely due to shifts in the electoral map.

Because so few incumbent members of Congress are defeated on election day, changes in voting trends in different areas of the country can take a long time to be truly reflected in terms of Congressional representation. For instance, most southern states have consistently voted for Republican candidates for the White House since the mid-1960s, yet continued to return Democrats to the House and Senate for decades after. In the South though, the pattern of Congressional representation is slowly catching up as southern Democrats retire, opening an opportunity for the Republican Party to capture those seats.

The effect this has had on the ideological make-up of both parties is attributed to the fact that those members who represented constituencies in areas considered to be their opponents' natural territory – particularly southern Democrats and Northeastern Republicans – were frequently either ideologically centrists or, in some cases, closer to the ideals of many of their opponents than they were their own mainstream party colleagues. As those seats switch parties so do many conservative Democrats and liberal Republicans begin to disappear, causing the parties to drift apart ideologically while becoming increasingly homogeneous in themselves. In the 2004 election alone, the retirement of Democrat Senators in South Dakota, Florida, Louisiana, Georgia, and South and North Carolina saw the Republicans capture those seats, consolidating its grip on the South.

The reduction in the number of moderates or centrists in both parties has added to the tensions between the two parties. Not only were centrist legislators the key to fostering bipartisan negotiation over legislation, but also, as their numbers dwindle, the need for the party leadership to compromise or soften legislation to ensure their support diminishes. As we shall see, though, the effect of this trend is more stark in the House than in the Senate.

The rise of party government?

Even though the parties have become tighter ideological groupings it would still be reasonable to assume that, with the Republicans holding only relatively narrow majorities in either chamber, the ability of the party leadership to pursue any sort of policy agenda would be seriously undermined. Indeed, it could be expected that slim majorities would mean that in order to obtain the passage of a legislative programme many minority concerns would have to be accommodated, especially as, traditionally, parties within the United States Congress have been viewed as weak: unable to exert control over its legislators. They lack many of the sanctions that enable most of European parties to enforce party discipline, including the ultimate power to control who can stand for election under the party label. At election time members are judged more on their own performance and how they served their district or state than by any perception of their party as a whole and as such their first priority will be their own electoral comfort rather than the wishes of their leaders.

Despite such assumptions, over the last two decades, some commentators have identified the growth in what is termed *conditional party government* (Rhode, 1991). With parties becoming increasingly ideologically homogeneous, there are circumstances where legislators look to their leaders to use the rules of the chamber to facilitate the passage of party-backed legislation. In this way, parties are able to impose discipline at the behest of rather than despite their members. Accordingly the Republican majority has looked to use the rules of Congress to impose control over their rank and file and push a policy agenda without the need for significant compromise. Some of the most significant developments in this direction have concerned the role of committees.

Committee control

In the House at least, changes in the relationship between the majority party leadership and Congressional committees date back to the Speakership of Newt Gingrich (R-GA, Speaker 1995–1998). Gingrich had ensured, in the successful attempt to wrest control of the House from the long-time Democrat majority, that during the 1994 election campaign Republican candidates would base their campaigns around a centrally agreed plank of ten policies known as the "Contract with America". Part of the idea was to provide a contrast to the previous Congress that, probably unfairly, was being portrayed as controlled by "do nothing" Democrats – a perception largely based around the failure to pass health care reform, a central policy commitment of the Clinton administration. Consequently, once in the majority, Gingrich needed to make good to the promises contained within the Contract (McSweeney and Owens, 1998).

The difficulty for any leader within Congress is that the fate and shape of legislation is largely in the hands of the committees and subcommittees and particularly the committee chairs. In many ways the committees are the gate-keepers of Congress, deciding which bills will be reported for consideration by the whole chamber and which will quietly die. Throughout recent Congressional history the plans of party leaders have been frustrated by uncooperative committee chairs who have established "little fiefdoms" over the policies under their jurisdiction (Fenno, 1997).

Gingrich succeeded in gaining the support of his party to institute changes that attempted to limit the autonomy of committees. He oversaw a cut in the number of committees as a whole and in the number of subcommittees each was allowed to establish. The staff available for all committees was also cut, virtually all committee meetings were to be held in public, vote tallies were to be published and the practice of allowing the chair to cast proxy votes on behalf of absent members was abolished. Each member was restricted to serving on only two committees and each chair, after serving three terms, would have to step down. Gingrich also used the ability of the party caucus to vote on who receives a chair to appoint members considered party loyalists over the heads of members who, through the custom of seniority, were thought to be in line for the post.

The grip that Gingrich sort to impose over House committees proved to be short-lived and by the end of his tenure as Speaker they were again functioning with a significant degree of autonomy from the party. However, attempts to impose discipline have not disappeared, especially under the direction of House Majority Leader Tom Delay (R-TX) and, on occasions, his actions have caused some controversy. During the 108th Delay was admonished by the House Standards of Official Conduct (or more commonly known as "Ethics") Committee for three separate violations of the ethics rules. Seemingly in response to this action the Republican leadership ensured that the chair of the committee Joel Hefley (R-CO) was replaced by the party loyalist Representative Doc Hastings (R-WA), Delay's most outspoken Republican critics found themselves removed from the panel and two senior aides were fired. In addition the rules of the committee were changed so that the agreement of an overall majority of the committee would be needed to allow any investigation to proceed – meaning in reality that at the support of at least one Republican would be needed to consider the charges against DeLay.

The attempts to bring the committees in line behind a party-led policy agenda has seemingly had some success. Within the House of Representatives, Democrats have complained that many committee chairman have almost entirely ignored minority representatives during the writing of legislation to be presented to the floor. They argue that deals have been cut between the Republican members before the committee convenes and with a majority ensured on each vote, the chairman gavels through the legislation without allowing meaningful Democrat input. As a result of such accusations, relations on the House Judiciary Committee plunged to such a depth in 2003 that one session led to physical threats being made and the chairman calling the Capitol Hill police to remove Democrat members from an adjoining room. The level of cooperation between the two parties, however, has always varied between committees depending on the personalities and issues involved and will continue to do so.

The tactic of attempting to increase the influence of party over the committees by using rules changes is easier to achieve in the House of Representative than it is in the Senate. The Senate has always been a more informal body willing to accommodate the wishes of Senators from both parties. As such, the day-to-day running of the Senate is conducted with the unanimous consent of all present, rather than determined by a powerful majority-dominated Rules Committee, as is the case in the House. Despite this, the Republican Senate leadership has also attempted to use what powers they do have to rein in potentially troublesome committees. At the start of the 109th Congress (2005–6), the moderate Republican Senator Arlen Specter (R-PA) was in line to become the chairman of the Senate Judiciary Committee. The Judiciary Committee plays an important role in the consideration of the president's nominations to fill vacancies on federal courts; an issue that had caused controversy in the previous Congress. Specter, as chair, would potentially have a great deal of influence over the success or failure of future nominations, including those to the Supreme Court, should a vacancy arise. Consequently, the conservative wing of the Republican Party were alarmed when Specter announced that he thought it "unlikely" that the Senate would confirm any judicial nominee who was hostile to *Roe* vs. *Wade*, the court case that established the principle that state laws banning abortion are unconstitutional. A campaign was launched to prevent Specter from gaining his promotion to committee chair. While this was happening, majority leader Bill Frist (R-TN) publicly cautioned Specter, describing his comments as "disheartening" and saying that the Senator had "not yet" made a persuasive case for the awarding of the chairmanship. Specter was eventually allowed to take up his position after pledging that his committee would promise "prompt action" on any nominee that President Bush proposed. In addition to placing pressure on Specter, Frist was handed by his party the power to handpick the Senators to fill half of all vacancies on the 12 most prestigious committees including Agriculture, Armed Service, Appropriation and Judiciary.

Conference committees

Even if the party leaderships have been able to impose greater control, there has still been a significant barrier to the rise of any form of true party government because of the simple fact that in a bicameral system, the approval of both chambers is necessary to turn a bill into a law. Indeed, the failure of the Republican House leadership to pass many elements of the Contract with America in the 104th Congress was due to the reluctance of the Senate. Even if the Senate leadership is able to obtain the passage of party-backed legislation, the more conciliatory nature of Senate delibera-tions will mean that the input of minority views may well move the content of legislation away from the majority party's ideal. Throughout the 108th Congress House Majority Leader Tom DeLay and the Republican leadership looked to use the rules of Congress to overcome this problem.

On party-backed legislation, the Republican leadership has pushed many votes on the floor of the House to the brink rather than compromise the policies to guarantee passage. This was notable as usually party leaders will ensure that they have the support of enough of their colleagues before a bill is called up for a vote. However, during the 108th Congress, legislation on prescription drug coverage (The Medicare Prescription Drug and Modernization Act), Head Start funding (School Readiness Act) and school vouchers in DC (within the District of Columbia Appropriations Act) all passed the House by a margin of a single vote. By using this tactic of House floor brinkmanship, pressure could be placed on one or two reluctant Republican members and minor compromises worked out with them that did not fundamentally affect the policy. In order to achieve success by the application of last-minute pressure on reluctant Republicans the leadership adopted the tactic of keeping floor votes on legislation open for as long as necessary to twist enough arms to gain a majority. In 2003 during a vote on President Bush's Medicare package, voting continued for an unprecedented 2 hours and 51 minutes, until a one-vote victory was ensured. Such brinkmanship continued to be used in the 109th Congress, with the vote on the controversial "Gasoline for America's Security Act of 2005" being held open by the Republican leadership until a 210–212 "No" vote was turned into a 212–210 victory. At the heart of this approach was a knowledge that the legislation that emerged from the Senate, if in fact it ever did, would likely to have been watered down to an extent that would be unacceptable to the House leaders.

For legislation to become law, a single piece of legislation must be sent to the president for his signature. If the bills emerging from the House and Senate contain significant differences, a conference is held where the key members of each chamber (usually from the reporting committees) meet to hammer out a compromise bill. This arrangement was used by Republican leaders to achieve their policy goals. By assuring the House bill was as close to their ideal as possible, the conference procedures could then be used to engineer a victory for the House viewpoint. Frequently that required working out an agreement between the House and Senate Republican conferees before the committee convened, effectively removing any Democrats from the conference deliberations. Such tactics led Congressional scholar Thomas Mann to comment that "We've been moving away from genuine deliberation on conferences for some time, but it's now gotten to the point of embarrassment."

Obstruction in the Senate

Whatever efforts are made by the majority in the Senate to unite behind party-backed initiatives, they still face the prospect that the rules of the body can be used by opponents to frustrate. The fact that the Senate is run on the basis of unanimous consent leaves open the opportunity for any member or group of members for obstruction or *filibuster*. Filibuster is a term that can be used to describe any attempts at delay or obstruction by Senators designed to deny the passage of a measure they oppose, although in the popular imagination it is closely associated with very public displays of obstruction on the floor of the Senate.

An increase in the use of obstructionist tactics by the minority in the Senate is perhaps inevitable when the majority are able to unite on issues and use the legislative process to achieve some degree of party government. Under such circumstances the need to accommodate the wishes of minority party senators to guarantee passage of a measure is diminished and as such the minority will turn to other methods to make their voice heard.

During the Bush administration, the filibuster has become the center of controversy in the Senate. Much of the coverage has focused on the use of the filibuster to prevent the approval of some of President Bush's judicial nominations. Democrats, claiming that the nominees were out of step with mainstream America's attitudes on issues including abortion, and protesting that their concerns had been ignored by the Republican majority, set about blocking votes on 10 of the appointments. The deadlock that ensued was enough to prompt one of the controversial nominees, Miguel Estrada, to withdraw his name from consideration. Republicans have argued that the use of the filibuster on the consideration of judicial nominees is a breach of Senate traditions (although Democrats noted that some of President Clinton's judicial picks were also blocked when the Republicans were in the minority). The Republican Senate leadership has gone so far as to suggest that the action may be unconstitutional as it prevents the Senate from exercising its constitutional duty to offer "advice and consent" on presidential nominations.

Under Senate rules, any filibuster can be stopped if 60 Senators agree ("cloture"). However, with only a relatively thin majority, Senate Republicans have consistently fallen short of achieving the required votes. As a result, the Republican leadership issued a threat that they might ask for a ruling by the president of the Senate (a role played by the vice-president) to outlaw those filibusters as unconstitutional – a ruling that would only need a simple majority to be upheld. Such action would alter the fundamental basis of Senate procedures, that of respect for the rights of the minority. The threat – and desire by some Republicans – of employing this "nuclear option" was averted when, in May 2005, a bipartisan group of 14 centrist Senators reached an agreement that they would oppose the use of filibusters on judicial nominations (except in "extraordinary circumstances") while also opposing any attempt to use the rules of the Senate to outlaw them.

The use of the filibuster in the Senate has not been limited to judicial matters. The period of bipartisan cooperation following 9/11 that saw the passage of the controversial Patriot Act, the creation of the Department of Homeland Security and funding of military action in Afghanistan and Iraq, gradually gave way to increasing levels of partisanship. By the end of the 108th Congress the Senate had become characterized by stalemate, obstruction and partisanship. Both John McCain (R-AZ) and Robert Byrd (D-WV) voiced their frustrations publicly, Byrd accused the Senate of having become "a factory that manufactures sound-bite votes that make great fodder for 30-second political ads" and warned that Congress was in danger of turning into "little more than an insignificant arm of the political parties" (Congressional Record April 28, 2004: S4474). Relations between the two parties had descended to such a state by the early summer of 2004 that Republicans were reduced to bringing up bills they knew would be filibustered – so as to accuse their opponents of obstruction – and Democrats were repeatedly proposing amendments they knew would be defeated but that they considered politically sensitive for Republicans.

Congressional Republicans attempted to use Democrat obstruction in the Senate as an electoral issue. A central target for this tactic was the Democrat Senate leader Tom Daschle (D-SD) who was repeatedly labeled by his opponent John Thune as the "chief obstructionist" to President Bush's agenda. The race was also a further indication of the declining state of relations between the two parties in Congress reflected in the fact that Republican Senate leader Bill Frist campaigned against Daschle in South Dakota, breaking an unspoken convention that leaders would not actively work for each other's defeat during the election period. That Daschle lost his seat to Thune in the November election was acclaimed by many Republicans as evidence of the public's disapproval of Democrat tactics in the previous Congresses, although the fact that he was the only sitting Democrat Senator to be defeated cast some doubt on those claims.

Relations between the two party leaderships looked little better in the 109th Congress. In an attempt to force the issue of pre-Iraq war intelligence onto the agenda the Senate Democrat leadership invoked a little-used rule to take the Senate into closed session – ordering that all visitors, journalists and staff leave the chamber, closing the doors and turning off the television cameras. This stunt infuriated the Republican leadership. An outraged Majority leader Bill Frist told reporters that he had been "slapped in the face" by the action and that he could no longer trust Minority leader Harry Reid (D-NV). The trick worked, however, as Frist agreed to a bipartisan task force to look into the issue.

Assessing Republican success

Despite their consistent majorities, Republican leaders have also found that since 2001 the traditional difficulties of pushing an agenda through two very different chambers – a conservative House and a more centrist Senate, both with a tight partisan balance – have proven a stumbling block. Many high-profile proposals supported by the House stalled in the Senate. Such legislation that failed to find its way into law during the 107th and 108th Congresses included bills concerning legal reform, energy policy, welfare and tax breaks for religious and other charities. On the other hand, Senate-backed proposals on hate crimes and tobacco regulation were killed by House Republicans.

Problems also arose when the priorities of the Bush administration differed from the needs of the Congressional Republican leadership or the rank and file. In the 108th Congress a mass-transit bill ran into difficulties as the White House and Congress disagreed over the amount and destination of federal funds. Even with increased Republican majorities following the 2004 elections, there still remained a question of reconciling difference between Republicans in either branch of government over the fundamental issue of the federal budget. The disagreements have tended to center on how to stem the growth of the budget deficit. Some House Republicans on the Budget Committee have demanded wholesale reform of the budgetary process to prevent deficit increase in the future.

Such disagreements over fiscal policy go to the heart of the politics of Congress where it is often easy to get agreement that spending needs to be reduced, but difficult to implement specific reductions as members weigh the effect of the reality of those cuts on their own districts and states. Indicatively, the spending reduction proposals (which were contained within President Bush's budget for 2006 and meant cuts in subsidies for cotton farmers) were given a very cool reception from leading Republican Senators, many of whom represent southern cotton-farming states. Congressional Republicans who, in their years in the minority, decried Democrat addiction to so-called "pork-barrel" spending aimed at easing re-election attempts have seemingly, now in the majority, become equally attached to the projects that advantage their constituencies, and their leaders have discovered the benefits of using the promise of federal funds to build coalitions in order to pass other policy goals (Evans, 2004).

The issue of the deficit began to grow in salience as the 109th Congress wore on. The passage in August 2005 of a $286 billion highway appropriations bill (The Safe, Accountable, Flexible and Efficient Transportation Equity Act of 2005) brought accusations of pork barrel spending. One project that was frequently singled out by critics was the so-called "bridge to nowhere" that linked the small Alaskan Island of Gravina to the mainland at the cost of $223 million.

Even on some issues that were seen as central to the Republican and Bush administration's agenda the Congressional leadership has been forced to compromise to keep other elements of the program on track. In November 2005 the House Republican leadership was forced to drop plans to allow drilling in the Alaskan wilderness in order to assure the passage of wider budgetary legislation. The Alaskan drilling plan had been a key part of the White House's energy proposals since 2001. Similarly, the Bush administration experienced defeat over a sensitive political issue for conservatives when in May 2005 the House voted 238–194 to repeal restrictions on federal funding for embryonic stem cell research.

Public confidence

The politicking and partisan bickering that has characterized recent Congresses has begun to have a detrimental effect on the perception of the institution by the voters. In opinion polls public satisfaction with Congress has fallen rapidly since 2001. According to a Gallup poll in November 2005 only 29% of those questioned indicated that they approved of the job Congress was doing, with 63% disapproving and 8% having no opinion (Gallup Poll, November 7–10, 2005). This figure was significantly lower than even those produced in 2004 and 2003. While satisfaction with the Republicans in Congress was lower than that of the Democrats, neither party could boast an approval rating higher than its figures for disapproval.

A contributory factor to this decline in public support has been a series of financial scandals that hit the 108th and 109th Congresses. Accusations ranging from improper use of campaign donations to outright bribery have rocked Congress and have involved some of the highest-ranked members. Many of the charges surrounded lobbyist Jack Abramoff who was alleged to have extracted $82 million from Native American tribes in order to court members of Congress on their behalf; handing out sweeteners, including fully paid golfing trips to St Andrews in Scotland, to members of Congress. A former partner of Abramoff, Michael Scanlon, admitted to a role in conspiracy to attempt to bribe a Congressman. In unrelated cases, House Majority Leader Tom DeLay stepped down from his leadership position to fight an indictment for money laundering connected to an election campaign in Texas and Representative Randy "Duke" Cunningham (R-CA) resigned his seat after pleading guilty to tax evasion and conspiracy. In the Senate, Majority Leader Bill Frist was subpoenaed in connection with an investigation surrounding his sale of stock in a family-founded company. Frist vehemently denied any wrongdoing.

Learning to govern?

Despite the problems experienced by the Republican leadership in pursuing a partisan policy agenda, there have been notable successes that indicate that they have begun to "learn how to govern" (Fenno, 1997). Central to the passage of reform of Medicare and prescription drug coverage, opposed by many Democrats, was the wooing of the leadership of the American Association of Retired Persons and their eventual support of those measures. Tax cuts wanted by the Bush administration were passed in three consecutive years. Controversial legislation banning late-term abortions (the Partial Birth Abortion Ban Act of 2003) and providing for a separate crime of killing an unborn child (the Unborn Victims of Violence Act of 2004) made their way into law. Even the "lame duck" session of Congress (that is held after the elections have taken place, but before the new Congress convenes) was made use of to assure the implementation of significant reforms to federal intelligence gathering in response to criticisms received in the recently published report on 9/11.

Figure 6.3 *Public bills becoming law, 1983–2003*

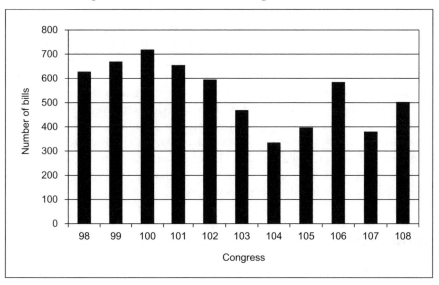

Source: Congressional Record.

In terms of sheer Congressional activity, there have also been signs of a revival. Following the Republican takeover in 1995, the number of bills passing into law fell dramatically (see Figure 6.3). During the 1980s Congress regularly placed over 600 separate items onto the statute book, in the 104th Congress that fell to nearer 300. Despite the partisan machinations of recent Congresses, that number has risen again. The 106th Congress saw the figure approach 600 once more and in the 108th Congress almost 500 laws were passed.

At the start of the 109th Congress the Republican leadership also demonstrated that it could use its majority to act quickly to legislate to meet the concerns of its conservative base. It did this by taking the unusual step of intervening in the case of Theresa Schiavo. Schiavo was a Florida woman who had been hospitalized since 1990 with brain damage caused by a cardiac arrest. Doctors at her hospital had concluded that she was in an unconscious "persistent vegetative state" and had no hope of recovery. Her husband indicated that he felt that Schiavo would not have wished to be kept alive under those circumstances and agreed that the feeding tube that sustained her should be removed. The decision was contested in Florida courts by her family who argued that Schiavo, rather than being effectively brain dead, showed signs of connection with her surroundings. The courts found in favour of her husband and with the feeding tube removed, the case hit the national headlines and became a cause adopted by the pro-life movement.

Congressional Republicans moved swiftly to intervene in the *Schiavo* case by passing an Act ("For the Relief of the Parents of Theresa Marie Schiavo") that explicitly gave her parents standing to appeal to the Middle District Court of Florida and directed that court to determine whether her rights had been violated. Following the passage of Act, a case was brought to that court, which eventually found against Schiavo's parents; the tube remained withdrawn, leading eventually to the patient's death.

The intervention of Congress and the president proved controversial, with a vast of majority of Americans in opinion polls expressing disapproval of government action in an individual ethical medical dilemma. However, what it did show was that, even with their thin majorities, the Republican leadership managed to act quickly and successfully over a highly controversial issue.

Conclusion

The unity that followed 9/11 notwithstanding, the contemporary Congress has been characterized by partisanship and, on occasions, obstruction. At the heart of this is that the parties in both chambers of Congress are not only relatively evenly balanced but have moved apart ideologically. Despite this, using the control over the rules and procedures of the legislative process afforded to the majority, the Republican leadership has attempted to marshal their majorities to pursue a partisan agenda. Feeling sidelined in this effort, the Democrats have frequently turned to obstruction to stymie Republican plans. While the Republican agenda has often stumbled due to the traditional difficulties of legislating in a decentralized and bicameral system, the successes that have occurred have shown that they have learnt how to govern within a finely balanced Congress.

Chapter 7

The United States Supreme Court: Continuity and Change

Chris W. Bonneau and Tara W. Stricko-Neubauer

The United States Supreme Court is a judicial institution unlike any other in the world. The Court sits at the pinnacle of the American judicial system and is a powerful court of last resort with extensive discretionary powers of judicial review. Additionally, Supreme Court justices are institutionally insulated from the political process and the Court itself enjoys high levels of public support and confidence despite its lack of electoral accountability (Caldeira and Gibson, 1992; Durr, Martin, and Wolbrecht, 2000). Generally speaking, when the Court makes a decision the majority of the American public and political leaders accept it as legally binding even if they disagree with the substance of the decision.

During the last few years there has been no shortage of important and politically relevant judicial decisions. The Court has made noteworthy rulings in areas of traditional importance including the death penalty, free speech, and voting rights. However, the Court has also shown a willingness to assert its legal authority in areas of contemporary political controversy. Court decisions on the rights of criminal detainees, the rights of homosexuals, and school vouchers are clear examples of this fact.

In this chapter, we examine some of the Supreme Court's most important decisions over the period of the George W. Bush presidency, focusing especially on the 2001 to 2005 terms. We also discuss the likely impact of membership changes on the Court in terms of the outcomes of cases. The Supreme Court enjoyed an unusually long period of uninterrupted membership from 1994 through early 2005, but the recent confirmations of John Roberts as Chief Justice and of Samuel Alito as Associate Justice seem likely to make a major change to the dynamics of the Court. Justice Alito is most likely to make an impact through his replacement of Justice O'Connor who was a crucial swing vote. In contrast, John Roberts is most likely to have an impact on the Court through his affable personality and his special role as Chief Justice. We begin, however, with a brief overview of the American judicial system and the role of the Supreme Court in that system.

The organizational structure of the American judicial system

In order to understand the significance of judicial decisions it is important to understand the institutional context within which the highest court in the US operates. Unlike many other countries, the United States government is a federal system with two levels of government: the national and the state. While the tripartite nature of government (with the executive branch, the legislative branch, and the judicial branch) is fundamentally the same across both levels, the specific structures and arrangements of the judicial systems vary a great deal between the federal government and the state governments, and between each of the 50 individual states.

Formally the United States utilizes a system of shared federalism. This means that the federal government has the final say in some areas of law (for example in such policy areas as coining money, providing for national defense, and regulating inter-state commerce) while the state governments have the final say in other areas (such as education, elections, and police powers). Nevertheless, in practice the division of responsibilities is not so clear and power is biased toward the federal government. When federal and state laws are in conflict, the federal law is enforced, due in part to the supremacy clause in Article VI of the US Constitution. Cases tried in the federal court system typically include cases of federal law or rights guaranteed in the US Constitution. Federal cases also include disputes between states, between citizens of different states, and some special situations such as maritime law and cases involving foreign ambassadors or other foreign nationals (see Article III, Section 2 of the US Constitution).

The structure of the judiciary is briefly discussed in Article III, Section 1 of the Constitution. Only the US Supreme Court is mentioned directly, but the writers of the Constitution left it up to Congress to create "such inferior Courts as the Congress may from time to time ordain and establish" as needed. Over time the federal judicial system has come to be composed of three levels of courts. As can been seen in Figure 7.1, the United States District Courts are the first level. The District Courts are the trial courts. They hear arguments, evaluate evidence, and make decisions about who wins the case (sometimes with the help of juries). The cases are heard by individual judges exercising original jurisdiction and these are the courts of first instance for the bulk of federal cases in the US The vast majority of these 94 courts are allotted geographically. Two of these courts are specialized District Courts: the Court of International Trade and the Court of Federal Claims.

The second level of federal courts is composed of the 13 United States Circuit Courts of Appeals. The Appeals Courts are also based on

Figure 7.1 *The judicial system in the United States*

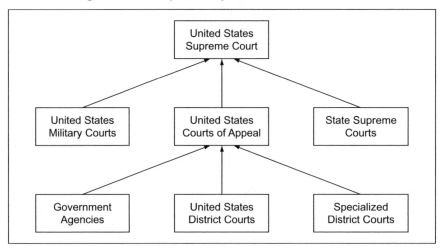

Source: Administrative Office of the US Courts, < www.uscourts.gov >.

geographical regions of the country. Each Appeals Court handles appeals from the District Courts of the states in their circuit, except for the D.C. Circuit Court which handles appeals for the nation's capital, the District of Columbia, and the Federal Circuit which hears appeals from the special District Courts. If a losing party is dissatisfied with the outcome from the District Court, she has the right to appeal the decision to the Circuit Court. Not surprisingly, many of these cases are criminal cases. If a defendant is convicted of a crime, she is likely to appeal. After all, she has little to lose by doing so. The circuit courts typically hear appeals in panels composed of three judges. Occasionally particularly important or contentious cases are heard *en banc*, with all the judges of the circuit sitting as a whole. These courts do not retry cases; rather, they simply rule on alleged errors of law that were committed by the lower court. Courts of Appeals must make a decision on every case that is appealed to them; in other words, they have mandatory jurisdiction.

At the apex of the judicial system is the United States Supreme Court. Most of the Court's workload consists of appeals from the US Courts of Appeals. The US Supreme Court also hears appeals from the state courts of last resort (generically referred to as state supreme courts) and military appeals courts when the cases involve federal issues (often constitutional rights). Article III, Section 2 gives the Court original jurisdiction in cases involving ambassadors and conflicts between states, but these cases make up a rather small portion of the Court's docket. Besides cases involving the Court's original jurisdiction, the Court has discretionary jurisdiction over its docket; that is, the Court can decide which cases it wants to hear. The

Court's nine justices generally make the most of their discretionary jurisdiction and heard oral arguments in only 87 of the 7,496 cases appealed in 2004. Of those 87 cases the justices resolved 85, of which 74 were decided with signed opinions The number of cases appealed to the Court's in 2005 was down by some 400 compared to 2004 (Rehnquist, 2005; Roberts, 2006).

All federal judges are nominated by the president and confirmed by a simple majority vote in the United States Senate. In contrast to many other judicial systems, the judges have lifetime appointments and are unusually insulated from political pressures. Once confirmed, federal judges can be removed only through the impeachment process (impeached by a majority of the House and convicted by two-thirds of the Senate). While lower federal judges (such as John Pickering) have been impeached and removed from office over the years, it is a relatively rare occurrence: no Supreme Court justice has ever been removed from office and indeed only one – Samuel Chase in 1805 – has ever been impeached.

Most states have court structures that generally mimic the federal court system. The most notable differences between the federal judicial system and the state systems are their appointment processes and insulation factors. The 50 US states appoint and retain their judges using various procedures, the most common of which include some kind of electoral retention procedures (either in a contested election or in a retention election). In contrast to the federal court system, few state judges are appointed for life and therefore state judges rarely have the same security of tenure and decisional freedom that US Supreme Court justices enjoy.

Typically US presidents are able to appoint a Supreme Court justice at least once per four-year term. While a Supreme Court appointment can be vital, especially with a closely divided court, the primary way that presidents are able to influence the development of federal law is with lower court appointments, which are much more frequent. Lower court judges make the majority of decisions in the federal judicial system and therefore by selecting these judges presidents have greater opportunities for influencing the course of law in the United States. As of early 2005 George W. Bush had appointed 168 District Court judges out of 680 District Court positions. This means that he had appointed 25 percent of all federal trial judges. At the same time (early in his second term) George W. Bush had appointed 34 out of 179 Circuit Court judges, a total of 19 percent, according to Alliance for Justice. While these figures may not seem to be particularly large, George Bush will have the majority of his second term to continue to leave his mark on the nation's federal judiciary. By way of comparison, during the same time frame Bill Clinton's appointees comprise only 41 percent of District judges and 33 percent of Circuit

Table 7.1 *Current Members of the United States Supreme Court*

Name	Year appointed	Appointing president	Previous position	Year of birth
John G. Roberts Jr	2005 (CJ)	G.W. Bush	DC Circuit	1955
John Paul Stevens	1975	Ford	Seventh Circuit	1920
Antonin Scalia	1986	Reagan	DC Circuit	1936
Anthony M. Kennedy	1988	Reagan	Ninth Circuit	1936
David H. Souter	1990	G.H.W. Bush	First Circuit	1939
Clarence Thomas	1991	G.H.W. Bush	DC Circuit	1948
Ruth Bader Ginsburg	1993	Clinton	DC Circuit	1933
Stephen G. Breyer	1994	Clinton	First Circuit	1938
Samuel Alito	2006	G.W. Bush	Third Circuit	1950

Source: United States Supreme Court < www.supremecourtus.gov/ > .

judges, appointments made after two full terms in office (Alliance for Justice, 2001).

Table 7.1 lists the nine current members of the US Supreme Court. The current court has one woman (Justice Ginsburg) and one African-American (Justice Thomas). While there are no formal qualifications specified in the Constitution (not even the requirement of formal legal training) traditionally the Court has been staffed with wealthy well-connected white males who graduated from Ivy League law schools and who had previously held high-ranking positions within government as well as having significant judicial experience before their elevation to the high court. Due to the Republican Party's recent dominance of presidential elections, seven of the current Court's nine members were nominated by Republican presidents.

While presidents typically pick Supreme Court justices who will reflect their particular political ideology (Segal and Spaeth, 2002), the current Court is a perfect example of how difficult it can be accurately to predict a judge's true ideology. The current court is closely divided and several recent decisions have been decided by a five to four margin. Five to four decisions are significant because an opinion must gain the support of five out of the nine justices to be considered a majority opinion. Majority opinions are preferable to a plurality opinion which is an opinion that has the greatest number of justices agreeing with it, but not a majority (usually three or four justice coalitions). In recent years the justices widely regarded as centrists and most likely to play a critical role in providing the final vote needed to form a majority opinion were Sandra Day O'Connor and Anthony Kennedy, both Ronald Reagan appointees. Often joining O'Connor and Kennedy in ruling liberally was David Souter, an appointee of George H. W. Bush. While Souter was regarded as something of a judicial enigma at the time of his appointment (Rabkin, 1996), and O'Connor was vilified by the religious right for taking pro-choice stances as an Arizona state legislator, it is clear that both appointing presidents expected their nominees to be much more reliably conservative in their judicial decision-making than they in fact turned out to be.

On the other hand, it is usually possible to have a good sense of a judge's general ideology. This is why the recent replacement of Chief Justice Rehnquist with John Roberts is likely to have a leadership impact on the future decisions of the Court. Toward the end of his tenure, court watchers noticed a decline in the influence of the conservative Rehnquist in shaping the decisions of the Supreme Court. During the 2003–2004 term there were 18 cases decided by 5 member majorities and Rehnquist was in the majority in only 8 of the 18 (Greenhouse, 2004). Court observers reasoned that Rehnquist's influence was replaced by more centrist members of the Court such as Justice Sandra Day O'Connor. During the same term O'Connor was in the majority in 13 of the 18 cases and dissented only 5 times during the 2003–2004 term (Greenhouse, 2004). While Roberts and Rehnquist are both ideologically conservative, the replacement of the old and infirm Rehnquist by the much younger and energetic Roberts should increase the potential for him to shape the decisions of the Court through the exercise of strong leadership as Chief Justice. The potential for a swing in the conservative direction can only be enhanced by the appointment of Alito (by most accounts, a reliable conservative) as a replacement for the moderate O'Connor whose vote was often pivotal in close decisions.

The Court's changing agenda

As noted by Alexis de Tocqueville (1840), most political issues eventually become legal issues. This means that the judicial system, especially the United States Supreme Court, often hears politically charged cases with widespread social implications. For example, recent decisions have limited the application of the death penalty (which enjoys high levels of public support), provided additional rights for criminal defendants (including those held in conjunction with the "war on terror"), and interjected the Court into electoral disputes that are fundamental to the political process. Additionally the Court has made important decisions regarding the president's power to conduct foreign policy, the rights of same-sex couples, and age discrimination.

The Bush Presidency has seen a number of important Supreme Court decisions in cases which either signal a noteworthy development in jurisprudence or seem likely to exert a major impact on the evolution of US constitutional law. Readers must be mindful that the Rehnquist Court was closely divided ideologically so many of the recent landmark decisions were resolved by small five-member majorities. Such narrow majorities increase speculation over the impact that Roberts and Alito will exert in the future.

Civil rights and liberties

Changes in the law are often prompted by technological advancements. The Internet is a relatively recent technological innovation that has revolutionized the way people research and access information. The Internet has made it easier and quicker to look up virtually any topic and has helped advance knowledge and learning in ways unimagined even 15 years ago. At the same time the Internet has become a center of commercial activity, some of which involves pornography and adult entertainment. In an attempt to eliminate child pornography on the Internet, Congress passed the Child Pornography Prevention Act of 1996 (CPPA) which forbade visual depictions of minors (or persons who appear to be minors) engaging in sexually explicit actions. In *Ashcroft* v. *Free Speech Coalition* (2002), the Court struck down portions of the CPPA for being overly broad and unconstitutional. The Court held portions of the law invalid because it banned depictions that were not actually children, which triggered free speech protections without invoking the need to protect actual minors (as held in *New York* v. *Ferber*). However, in *Ashcroft* v. *American Civil Liberties Union* (2002) the Court refused to hold other legislation, the Child Online Protection Act (COPA), as overly broad for relying on general notions of "community standards" in identifying material harmful to minors. COPA was more restrictive than CPAA and had three provisions: it applied only to material on the World Wide Web which was communicated for commercial purposes and restricted only material that was harmful to minors. This ruling is significant because the Court decided that reliance on vague notions of community standards did not inherently make legislation overly broad. Finally, in *United States* v. *American Library Association* (2003) the Court held that federally funded libraries could be required to install filtering software on their public computers in order to prevent minors from accessing pornographic websites. These decisions continue a line of precedent set by *Miller* v. *California* (1972), which established a rather flexible standard with which to identify obscenity. Generally, to be found obscene a work must be judged obscene by an average person applying community standards and the work as a whole must appeal to prurient interests. The Court's recent decisions have upheld the notion of community standards while also upholding reasonable limits designed to protect children.

In the past few terms the Court has also made a number of decisions protecting an individual's right to free speech. In *Virginia* v. *Black* (2003) the Court struck down Virginia's law against burning a cross with the intent to intimidate as a violation of free speech because the law treated all cross burnings as being inherently intimidating instead of making provisions for evaluating evidence of the respondent's intent to intimidate (the state can ban cross burning if it is done with the intent to intimidate). This decision is essentially a furtherance of its unanimous decision in *R.A.V.* v. *St Paul* (1992) that held that cross burning is constitutionally protected symbolic speech. In *Scheidler* v. *National Organization for Women* (2003) the Court declined to allow anti-abortion protestors to be charged with extortion under the Racketeer Influenced and Corrupt Organizations Act of 1970 (RICO). In an 8–1 decision the Court held that since the protestors did not gain anything of value that could later be sold they did not engage in extortion. This directly reverses a unanimous decision made in 1994 (*National Organization for Women* v. *Scheidler*) that held that RICO could be used to stop abortion protestors as protestors could interrupt commerce despite the lack of an economic motive. While this decision turned on an interpretation of the intricacies of RICO, the decision allowed anti-abortion protestors to continue disruptive activities outside of clinics. Finally, in a 5–4 decision the Court held that regulations prohibiting judicial candidates from publicly announcing their views on disputed political and legal issues violated the First Amendment right to free speech, *Republican Party of Minnesota* v. *White* (2002). The Minnesota Supreme Court's canon of judicial conduct, which prohibited candidates for judgeships from announcing their views, was premised on the need for the impartiality of judges in order to maintain the legitimacy of the judiciary. Despite these important concerns the Court held that the importance of free and open in discussion of issues – a central purpose of elections – outweighed the possible harm of the appearance of impartiality. However, in *McConnell* v. *Federal Election Commission* (2003) a 5–4 Court ruled that bans on soft money (money given to political parties not candidates) and regulations on advertising do not violate the First Amendment. The Court held that government interests in preventing corruption (or the appearance of corruption) justified minimal infringement of speech rights.

Recently the Court has continued to step away from the strict separation of church and state originally announced in *Lemon* v. *Kurtzman* (1971), and has continued to break down the barriers between church and state in the educational context. In *Zelman* v. *Simmons-Harris* (2002) the Court upheld the constitutionality of a state school voucher program that allowed lower-income parents to choose to send their children to religious schools. The Court held that the program was not a violation of the establishment clause because it provided parents with a school choice program that was religiously neutral in its intent and merely provided parents with school choice that allows them to choose from both religious and non-religious schools. However, in *Locke* v. *Davey* (2003) the Court held that a state may choose to prohibit scholarship funds from going to students who choose to major in theology. The Court held that Washington state's "historic and substantial" interest in excluding religious instruction from public funding did not violate the Free Exercise Clause. The differences between outcomes in these two cases neatly illustrate how a closely divided court can easily reach differing outcomes which appear to some to be inconsistent (though, here, the Court decided *Zelman* under the Establishment Clause and *Locke* under the Free Exercise Clause).

In *McCreary County* v. *ACLU* (2005) the Court ruled that a display of the Ten Commandments in a courthouse was unconstitutional because it lacked a primary secular purpose under the *Lemon* test. Interestingly, the Court reached an opposite ruling in *Van Orden* v. *Perry* (2005) and upheld the display of a Ten Commandments statue on the grounds of the Texas State Capitol. These decisions noted the difficulty judges face in reconciling the separation of church and state while also paying homage to the country's religious heritage. A further case dealing with religious freedom was decided and affirmed the duty of prison officials to accommodate prisoners' religious practices and held that such accommodations did not violate the First Amendment–*Cutter* v. *Wilkinson* (2005).

Two closely watched educational cases involved the University of Michigan's affirmative action policies. Affirmative action was originally designed to help disadvantaged minorities compete on an even playing field with other individuals; however, many now view affirmative action as reverse discrimination against non-minority individuals. In *Gratz* v. *Bollinger* (2003) the Court struck down the university's undergraduate admissions policy because it violated the Equal Protection Clause of the Constitution by automatically awarding minority students additional points in the scoring systems used to calculate admissions. However, in *Grutter* v. *Bollinger* (2003), the Court held in a 5–4 decision that Michigan's law school may use an admission system that simply takes race into account as one of the factors used in order to achieve the educational benefits of having a diverse student body. The decisions in these two cases were based upon Justice Powell's famous opinion in *Regents of the University of California* v. *Bakke* (1978) which argued that affirmative action programs are constitutional as long as they do not utilize a strict quota-based criteria for admitting minority students.

Criminal procedure and the death penalty

Over the last few terms the Court has made landmark decisions on the rights of criminal defendants (modifying to some extent the protections afforded by the 1966 *Miranda* ruling requiring suspects to be advised of their constitutional rights prior to interrogation and excluding illegally acquired confessions from court) and on the death penalty. Notable decisions on the rights of suspects include *Chavez* v. *Martinez* (2003), *Missouri* v. *Seibert* (2004), and *United States* v. *Patane* (2003). In *Chavez* the Court held that suspects who were not read their rights but made statements to police could not later claim violation of their Fifth Amendment rights as long as the statements were not used against the suspect in legal proceedings. This case is significant because it held that police cannot be sued for not following the dictates of *Miranda* if the plaintiff was not actually charged with a crime based on un-Mirandized statements made to police. However, in *Seibert* the Court ruled that police officers had violated the Fifth Amendment by inducing a suspect to confess before reading the suspect her rights and then compelling her to repeat her confession. In *Patane* a divided Court held that evidence produced as the result of un-Mirandized voluntary statements may be used in court without violating the Fifth Amendment. In *Hiibel* v. *Sixth Judicial Circuit of Nevada* (2004) the Court ruled in a 5–4 decision that state laws requiring individuals to identify themselves to police were not in violation of either the Fourth or Fifth Amendment. The majority decided that answering such a minor question was not self-incriminating. In an issue involving a trial judge decision of a different sort, *Sell* v. *United States* (2003), the Court ruled that a defendant may be involuntarily medicated with anti-psychotic drugs so that he was able to participate fully in a trial to determine his guilt or innocence. These decisions represent a rather narrow approach to the rights of the accused.

Search and seizure decisions have long been the center of controversy at the high court. Recently the justices took a restrictive view of the Fourth Amendment and ruled that police to do not need to advise citizens of their right to refuse random searches despite the coercive environment in which those searches might take place, *United States* v. *Drayton* (2002). The Court also held that a school district may engage in random drug testing among student athletes because of its interest in preventing drug use among students, *Board of Education* v. *Earls* (2002). The Court also affirmed the legality of a drug charge even though the defendant was stopped for a traffic violation and only later was a drug sniffing dog brought in to search the vehicle. In *Illinois* v. *Caballes* (2005) the Court upheld the arrest and probable cause search of the car trunk for drugs despite the argument that it was unrelated to cause for the initial stop which was speeding.

The Court has recently taken a generous view of the Sixth Amendment's right to confront witnesses and have the advice of counsel. In *Crawford* v. *Washington* (2004) a unanimous Court held that the introduction of out-of-court testimony violated a defendant's right to confront and cross-examine witnesses. In *Alabama* v. *Shelton* (2002) a 5–4 Court held that defendants facing suspended sentences must still be offered state-appointed counsel because of the potential for imprisonment. In *Blakely* v. *Washington* (2004) a divided Court held that judges could not impose a sentence increase on a defendant unless the facts had been submitted to a jury. Without the jury approval the majority ruled that such actions constituted violations of the right to trial by jury. This essentially invalidated the sentencing schemes in several states as well as the federal government, casting doubt on the constitutionality of thousands of sentences.

The Court has also been undergoing a reinterpretation of the Eighth Amendment's prohibition on "cruel and unusual punishment." Nowhere has the importance of the Court's decisions on the lives of criminal defendants been more obvious than in cases relating to the death penalty. In recent terms the Court has made a number of critical decisions in the area of capital punishment. Since the death penalty was declared constitutional in 1976 in *Gregg* v. *Georgia* (after earlier being declared unconstitutional due to inconsistent application in *Furman* v. *Georgia* in 1972), the Court has continued to define the contours of constitutionality in the execution of criminals. Recent noteworthy decisions include *Atkins* v. *Virginia* (2002) and *Roper* v. *Simmons* (2005). In *Atkins* a 6–3 court held that executions of the mentally retarded violated the Eighth Amendment's proscriptions of cruel and unusual punishment. The majority cited state decisions to disallow such sentences as evidence of evolving standards of decency as well as skepticism of the ability of the death penalty to provide a deterrent to crime in the case of the mentally disabled. This decision was reinforced by the Court's decision in *Tennard* v. *Dretke* (2004) where the Court held that jurors should have been presented with evidence of the defendant's mental capacity when they considered whether to impose the death penalty. Moreover, in *Roper* v. *Simmons* the Court reversed prior rulings in *Thompson* v. *Oklahoma* (1988) and *Stanford* v. *Kentucky* (1989) and ruled 5–4 that no minor under the age of 18 could be sentenced to death because of evolving standards of decency which held that such a punishment was in violation of the Eighth Amendment. Despite these Eighth Amendment rulings favorable to defendants, the Court upheld the popular "three strikes" laws and held in *Lockyer* v. *Andrade* (2003) that two consecutive prison terms of twenty-five years to life for a rather petty crime under California's three strikes sentencing guidelines did not offend the Constitution.

The Court has also further refined the procedures that must be followed in death penalty cases. In a ruling similar to that of *Blakely* v. *Washington*, in *Ring* v. *Arizona* (2002) a 7–2 majority held that findings of aggravating circumstances that lead to imposition of the death penalty must be decided by a jury to be acceptable under the Sixth Amendment. However, in *Schriro* v. *Summerlin* (2004) a 5–4 Court declined to retroactively apply the jury requirements announced in *Ring*. This limited the impact of the *Ring* decision to defendants convicted after 2002. The Court's decisions in capital cases represent a new approach by a divided court to a policy long supported by a majority of the American public even though the United States retention of the death penalty increasingly incurs international condemnation.

Presidential power

Traditionally the president has been granted a great deal of discretion by the courts in his conduct of foreign affairs. However, several recent cases have tested the degree of freedom the president (and military) has in detaining individuals in pursuit of the war on terror. In *Rasul* v. *Bush* (2004) the Court held that foreign citizens detained at the Guantanamo naval base in Cuba were in fact under the control of the United States (despite the fact that Cuba retained "ultimate sovereignty" according to a treaty it has with the US) and therefore could file habeas corpus petitions with the federal courts. In *Hamdi* v. *Rumsfeld* (2004) a highly divided court announced in a plurality opinion that despite the fact that Congress had authorized the president to detain enemy combatants by authorizing the use of force, Hamdi (an American citizen captured in Afghanistan) could challenge his designation in federal court and the courts were not prevented from hearing that claim by the separation of powers. Finally, in *Rumsfeld* v. *Padilla* (2004) an American citizen who was returning from Pakistan and arrested in Chicago challenged his detention as an enemy combatant. In a 5–4 decision the Court declined to decide his challenge and instead ruled on a technicality, holding that Padilla should have filed his habeas writ in a different jurisdiction. While these three decisions nominally challenge the president's right to designate individuals as enemy combatants, they do not resolve the issue of what constitutional protections and rights these defendants have and instead put that issue off for another day. However, the outcome of *Demore* v. *Kim* (2003) may be instructive as to what will happen in the future. In *Demore*, a 6–3 Court held that the federal courts could hear the habeas challenges raised by resident aliens detained by the Citizenship and Immigration Services (formerly the Immigration and Naturalization Services—INS) prior to deportation. That being said, the court ultimately ruled in favor of the United States government holding such individuals in custody prior to their deportation trials. Thus, while individuals challenging the federal government's power to detain them are able to challenge their detention in federal court (no small victory), they are not necessarily likely to win their case.

The Court has recently decided a number of other cases pertaining to the jurisdiction of US Courts in cases involving foreign entities and events. In *Sosa* v. *Alvarez-Machain* (2004) the Court held that a Mexican citizen who was wanted for crimes in the US and was kidnapped in Mexico by fellow citizens on behalf of the United States government could not sue his kidnappers in the US court system. In *Austria* v. *Altmann* (2004) the Court ruled that Altmann (a descendent of Holocaust victims) could sue Austria in federal court for the return of paintings owned by her uncle before World War II and now housed in the Austrian Gallery. Finally, in *F. Hoffmann-LaRoche Ltd* v. *Empagran SA* (2004) a unanimous Court ruled that the American courts have no jurisdiction in foreign price-fixing schemes if those schemes have no domestic effect. This case turned on a technical reading of a 1982 amendment to the Sherman Act but signaled the Court's recognition of the need for individual national legal systems to accommodate the complexities of international law in an increasingly complex and interconnected world.

Federalism

Federalism cases determine the proper relationship between the states and the federal government. Traditionally the federal government enjoys wide discretion in numerous areas and usually wins when federal and state laws come into conflict. For example, in *American Insurance Association* v. *Garamendi* (2003) the Court ruled that a California law designed to facilitate the processing of claims of families of Holocaust victims violated the president's right to conduct foreign policy. In *Gonzales* v. *Raich* (2005) the Court struck down state laws permitting the medicinal use of marijuana under the Commerce Clause because of the threats posed by such statutes to federal regulation of inter-state commerce. Finally, in

Granholm, Governor of Michigan v. *Heald* (2005) the Court used the historical intent behind the Commerce Clause to strike down state regulatory schemes that gave preference to in-state companies at the expense of out-of-state companies.

However, the federal government does not always have widespread powers. Because the details of the electoral process (even for federal offices) was left up to the states by the Constitution, the federal courts are generally deferential to state politicians in these matters, even when they do review such cases. In *Georgia* v. *Ashcroft* (2003) the Court held 5–4 that Georgia's redistricting plan which spread out minority votes across many districts (thereby diluting several majority–minority districts) did not violate the 1965 Voting Rights Act. And in *Vieth* v. *Jubelirer* (2004) a plurality declined to intervene in a Pennsylvania redistricting plan that benefited the Republican Party. The Court's decision rested on the opinion that no judicial resolution could be found to the issue of partisan gerrymandering. This reflected the Court's decision in *Davis* v. *Bandemer* (1985), which held that partisan gerrymandering was not justiciable. Of course the justices will have ample opportunities to revisit these issues as the Court recently granted review in a series of cases involving the Republican redistricting plan in Texas. (*League of United Latin* v. *Perry, Travis County* v. *Perry, Jackson Eddie* v. *Perry, GI Forum of Texas* v. *Perry*). Still, it is also important to note that the Rehnquist Court is not uniformly deferential to state prerogatives. In *Tennessee* v. *Lane* (2004) the Court held that the federal Americans with Disabilities Act could be applied against states. The case involved a disabled woman who could not access the upper floors of a courthouse and its ruling could have widespread implications for the enforcement of other federal policies against the states.

In the past few years the Court made a number of decisions that were important to business interests. In *Aetna Health, Inc.* v. *Davila* (2004) a unanimous court held that individuals suing their health care companies must bring their case to federal court because of the Employee Retirement Security Act of 1974 (ERISA). This decision reinforces federal attempts to make the procedures for suing Health Maintenance Organizations (HMOs) uniform throughout the country. In *Eldred* v. *Ashcroft* (2002) the Court upheld the application of the Copyright Term Extension Act of 1998 (CTEA) applying copyright protection for 70 years after the author's death. Finally, in *Moseley* v. *V Secret Catalog, Inc.* (2002) the Court rejected a claim by V Secret Catalog (the owner of Victoria's Secret lingerie company) that the Federal Trademark Dilution Act would apply in a case absent evidence of actual economic injuries. This means that companies suing other companies for using their trademark must show evidence of actual harm from the dilution of their "famous" trademarks and cannot sue simply because the other company is trying to piggyback on the success of the better-known company's brand appeal.

Court decisions have also turned on interpretations of the *ex-post facto* clause of Article I, Section 9 of the Constitution. In *Smith* v. *Doe* (2003) the Court held that Alaska's Sex Offender Registration Act (passed after the defendants were convicted) did not constitute a violation of the *ex-post facto* clause because it did not impose a punishment. Consequently, people convicted of sex crimes have to register as sex offenders, even if this mandatory registration process was not required at the time of their conviction and sentence.

The Court has also made a number of decisions on issues of great political relevance. The case of *Kelo* v. *City of New London* (2005) provoked great interest and much criticism when the Court upheld the taking of private land by the city for economic redevelopment by a private developer. The decision continued a long line of precedent when the Court utilized a flexible interpretation of "public use" under the Fifth Amendment. The current controversy over gay marriage was intensified by the Court's decision in *Lawrence* v. *Texas* (2003), which held that a Texas law making sodomy a crime violates the Due Process Clause of the Fourteenth Amendment. In a 6–3 opinion the Court overruled *Bowers* v. *Hardwick* (1986) and held that laws criminalizing consensual sexual conduct done in the privacy of one's residence are unconstitutional. In *Pennsylvania State Police* v. *Suders* (2004) the Court held that an employee could file suit against an employer for sexual harassment in the workplace even though the employee had not followed the employer's procedures for filing harassment claims due to the overwhelmingly hostile nature of the work environment. Finally, in *General Dynamics Lands Systems* v. *Cline* (2004) the Court rejected a claim of reverse age discrimination filed by younger employees at a company which denied them retirement benefits because of their age. The Court relied on a narrow reading of the Age Discrimination in Employment Act (ADEA) finding that Congress did not intend to protect younger workers in its enactment of the act. The Court further refined its legal interpretation of the ADEA in *Smith* v. *City of Jackson* (2005) when it held that the provisions of the ADEA recognized claims of disparate-impact (superficially neutral practices that result in unequal burdens) but that these legal claims are limited in scope when compared to disparate-treatment claims under the ADEA.

Conclusion

The Rehnquist Court showed a remarkable diversity in its decisional outcomes, despite the fact that seven of the nine justices were appointed by

Republican presidents. Many would expect that a court so heavily dominated by Republican appointees would be quite conservative in its decisional outcomes. However, this has not necessarily been the case. The Court has actually shown a marked tendency toward politically moderate (and occasionally surprisingly liberal) decisions. The Court has been generally responsive to civil rights and liberties claims, has shown a strong tendency to protect free speech and religious freedom, and has even protected the essence of affirmative action. It is in the area of criminal defendants (notably individuals sentenced to death) that the Court has shown the most interesting pattern of decision-making. The Court has consistently taken a narrow approach to *Miranda* rights while taking a very strong stance on the rights of defendants during the trial phase. Finally, the Court's rulings restricting the application of the death penalty have been particularly noteworthy. Despite the fact that the death penalty enjoys widespread support in the United States the Court has reversed previous decisions and prohibited the execution of mentally retarded defendants and minors, increasingly recognizing the opprobrium which such practices incurred in other democratic countries.

While many of the decisions mentioned above have resulted in moderate to liberal policy stances (depending upon the classification criteria used), it must be made clear that the Court still shows a conservative bent in many cases. Part of the problem with classifying the political leanings of the Court is difficulty in defining what exactly constitutes a liberal or conservative decision. Nowhere is this difficulty more clear than in discussing judicial "activism." Commonly judicial activism is linked with politically liberal decision-making by judges. In fact, the term activism correctly refers to the degree of deference judges show to the elected branches of government. A politically conservative decision can be activist, if the outcome contradicts the will of another actor such as the legislature or a state government. The Court has exhibited a mixed record with respect to deferring to the other political branches. In presidential power cases the Court upheld the right of detainees to challenge their captivity, but did not actually resolve any of those challenges, instead leaving it up to the lower courts to make decisions in those areas. Also, the Court has generally deferred to the right of states to conduct redistricting plans.

Interestingly, the Court has shown a clear willingness to resolve issues of great political interest and controversy. While the Court's ruling on gay rights, sexual harassment, and age discrimination show a variety of ideological outcomes, it is clear that the Court is more than willing to resolve such issues in glare of the public spotlight. Such conflict is perhaps why Chief Justice Rehnquist spent so much of his *2004 Year-End Report* addressing the relationship between the legislative and judicial branches (2005). A degree of inter-branch conflict is inevitable, but it remains to be seen how the new Chief Justice will handle these concerns and whether he will continue to focus on these concerns. What is not in doubt is the likelihood of the Court hearing many more politically charged cases in the future.

Clearly many of the important decisions made in recent terms were the result of a closely divided court in terms of ideology. Because so many important issues have been decided with 5–4 decisions, the importance of new appointments cannot be underestimated. Rehnquist's replacement by Roberts is most likely to have an effect on decisional outcomes through leadership – not ideology. Rehnquist was reliably conservative and Roberts is expected to be the same, so the directionality of votes cast is unlikely to change. However, Roberts may be able to exert more effective leadership as Chief Justice, allowing the conservatives to attract Justice Kennedy's votes. Attracting Kennedy's vote is likely to be important now that Alito has replaced O'Connor. In many recent 5–4 cases O'Connor was often the swing vote – sometimes voting with the conservatives, sometimes voting with the liberals, and often carving out her own middle ground as the opinion writer in the most important cases. Replacing O'Connor with Alito will likely split the court evenly, with four justices (Breyer, Ginsburg, Souter, and Stevens) on the left and four justices (Alito, Roberts, Scalia, and Thomas) on the right. This means that Kennedy will be the pivotal justice, and his votes will most likely determine the outcome of closely divided cases in the future. While only time will tell in which direction the new justices will take the Court, the last few terms of the Rehnquist Court have provided Court watchers with an exciting show.

Chapter 8

American Federalism and Intergovernmental Relations

Robert B. Albritton

Federalism is the allocation of original authority (sovereignty), usually spelled out in constitutions, between national governments and subnational governments that distinguishes unitary from federal systems. Although there is little variation in this division of sovereignty among nations governed as unitary systems, there are considerable differences among federal systems in the relative allocation of authority between national levels and units of government below the national level. Switzerland, for example, is at one extreme, granting virtual autonomy to canton governments. Canadian provinces and German states (Lander) retain considerably more authority over their affairs than the American states.

A general theory of federalism suggests that a comparison of variances between unitary and federal systems would show significantly more variation across subnational governments in federal systems than in unitary ones, given appropriate controls for differences in population sizes and economic resources. In the United States, states vary widely in population structures and economic circumstances. Some state economies (e.g. California) are characterized by seacoasts and ports while others are landlocked; some, such as Iowa and Kansas, possess an abundance of rich farmland while others, such as Nevada and Utah, are arid plateaus unsuitable for farming; some states, for example Oklahoma and Texas, harbor rich resources of oil or other minerals uncommon to other states.

Demographically, states vary dramatically in population size and in the existence and influence of large cities, urban populations, and the peculiar mix of ethnic or racial factors that make up a state's population. Thus, for example, the white population is a minority in California, the ethnic mix in North Dakota consists largely of native Indians, while southern states have substantial populations of African-Americans. These variations all structure the different issues and opportunities that characterize states, as well as their relations with the national government. A redefinition of historically structured state boundaries could go a long way toward reducing these primary sources of variation, but, as they stand, the boundaries of most American states produce substantial variations in the context of politics across the United States of America.

As a result of some of the variations noted above, states vary widely in terms of political institutions through which they exercise their sovereignty. The size of legislative bodies varies from 40 in the Delaware and Alaska House of Representatives to 400 in New Hampshire's comparable legislative body. Governors are subject to varying term lengths and times for elections, as well as widely varying allocations of power and influence to the office. State judiciaries are even more varied in their arrangements with some states electing judges, others appointing judges by a variety of means, and some states using different methods for choosing trial judges from those at the appellate level.

Although the United States ranks substantially higher than other federal systems, such as Switzerland, Canada, and Germany, in its centralization of government discretion, authority, and responsibility, the history of intergovernmental relations indicates that relationships between national and state governments are dynamic, not only in the sense that they are always evolving; they also vary dramatically from one policy area to another. As a result, relationships between national and state governments in the United States seldom fit any one model of intergovernmental relations and, instead, incorporate a broad spectrum of theories about how national and subnational governments interact with each other.

As historical perspectives show, however, the trend of American politics continues around the shifting status and the relative importance of the federal-state connection. This same history also demonstrates that the exercise of sovereignty allocated to states by the Constitution does not emphasize state independence. Rather, American federalism is marked by the *inter*dependence of national and state levels on each other and among the states themselves, all within a federal compact. In this context, the study of special theories of federalism as they relate to the American states offers increasingly new perspectives on these relationships, as well as prospects and designs for the course of the nation's future.

The role of states in the federal system

Considerable diversity of subnational governments in the United States poses serious problems for coordinating national policies (see Table 8.1 on page 133). Why should there be states at all, given that they represent an enormous cost to citizens in expenditures for executive, legislative, and judicial functions alone, when these same citizens face financial constraints on education, housing, medical services, and welfare? From an analytical perspective, it is not satisfactory to say that the answer is because they were created by the Constitution and have always existed, nor is the idea that states represent economic and social communities of interest persuasive when confronted with cleavages between urban and rural populations that divide most of the states. California, for example, is often described as two political cultures of the North and the South, and, clearly, residents of the urban belt of Chicago, Illinois, Milwaukee, Wisconsin, and Gary, Indiana, have more in common with each other than with rural residents of those states.

A more compelling argument for the existence of states is that they represent decentralized administrative units of national policy. In this role, they serve the value of incorporating local citizen preferences that allow adaptation to unique characteristics of an area. States are in many respects, however, less effective administrative units of national policy than sources of variation across the United States in what constitutes crime and what the punishment will be, what will be the role of government in protecting citizens against communicable disease and unsanitary environments, and the mix of taxation and support for the poor – in addition to a wide variety of arrangements for political institutions often idiosyncratic to individual states. Those differences may, however, present problems for defining the real meaning of citizenship within the country as a whole.

As populations migrated into urban areas following World War II, defining the appropriate role for states becomes an increasingly challenging task. Traditionally, state governments have been controlled by rural or small town interests and the net effect of state governments has been to transfer resources disproportionately from cities such as New York or Chicago to the benefit of "upstate" or "downstate" interests, leaving America's major cities desperate for funds to maintain an acceptable quality of services. The apparent orphaning of New Orleans after the Katrina disaster makes this point in even more stark terms. The case for state government is hard to make on the basis of decentralized government control given the wide disparities in educational achievement, health, and poverty associated with states, often functions of local comparative advantages less characteristic of unitary systems. Nevertheless, the current system is not subject to modification now or in the foreseeable future. The massive interests of citizens in local advantages and the perquisites of state government and bureaucracy make it highly unlikely that residents would vote states out of existence – required by the Constitution before state boundaries can be changed.

Unlike states, residents of Washington DC, the national capital, experience political disadvantages as they have no representation in Congress. Although their votes do count in presidential elections, equal to the smallest states in the Electoral College, lack of representation with voting rights in either the House of Representatives or the Senate puts them at a disadvantage compared to residents of Wyoming and North Dakota, states with comparable populations. (Actually, state boundaries have been changed many times, usually by extension, but also western Virginia was excised to become WVA.).

Supremacy of the national government

American federalism, compared to more confederal systems, is heavily biased in favor of national supremacy derived from specific, constitutionally enumerated powers, such as the inter-state commerce clause, the general welfare clause, but, more especially, from the necessary and proper clause of Article I, Section 8, and the national supremacy clause in Article IV of the Constitution. All of these constitutional clauses now constrain state actions or give substantial powers to the national government. Perhaps most important has been the clause giving the federal government the power to regulate inter-state commerce, given that in 2006 there is little that is not in inter-state commerce.

In practice, this emphasis on central power was not always the case. Although the intention of the authors of the American Constitution was to increase the power of the central government and to limit the power of states in the name of "the people," the anti-federalist reaction to strong central government espoused reallocation of authority to the degree that states would have authority to nullify impacts of national laws on state populations by interposing their sovereignty between the national government and people of the states. Such political views gained popularity among agrarian populations in the southern states over the issue of slavery, based upon the "reserved powers" of Amendment X. Despite the Supreme Court ruling favoring national supremacy in *McCulloch* v. *Maryland* that states "may not retard, impede, or otherwise hinder" the national authority in its exercise of constitutional powers, as well as the vindication of national supremacy by the Civil War, state governments continued to adhere to a doctrine of "states' rights" through the middle of the twentieth century.

State governments are quite ready to relinquish their sovereignty to national control when confronted by severe stresses resulting from systemic shocks that transcend the capacities of states. Confronted with natural disasters such as flood, storms, or earthquakes, state governments are more than ready to defer to national action and most governors immediately appeal for national assistance from the Federal Emergency Management Administration (FEMA) after hurricanes, tornados, floods, or wildfires that characterize Florida during the hurricane season and western states during dry summer months. In the face of economic disasters, such as the Great Depression, states find themselves incapable of coping with the fundamental needs of their citizens. In seeking national support under these circumstances, states are, in essence, acknowledging the superiority of national sovereignty for citizens of the United States as the underlying reality of American federalism.

Decentralization of political authority

The strong bias in favor of the central government in the American constitutional system is in practice balanced informally by the highly decentralized politics in the United States. The power of states generally trumps that of the national government by holding national officeholders responsible to a constituency that is defined by state and local interests. The fact that small states are equal to large ones in the Senate enhances a focus on the politics of states whose populations may be small, but whose weight in policy-making is at parity with more populous states.

The role of states in administering elections makes these geographic units centers of political strength. It produces a wide variety of requirements for voter eligibility, so that states like North Dakota have no prior voter registration requirement at all, while other states have restrictive practices that reduce voter participation even in national elections. One of the most important sources of state control over national legislators is the authority of state legislatures to define legislative districts within their boundaries. It is little wonder that during consideration of legislative districting legislation, Members of Congress are often lurking in the halls, if not actually on the floor, of state legislatures paying deference to the acknowledged power of state governments over the tenure in office of these federal officials.

More importantly, perhaps, the process of electing the president provided by the Constitution also focuses political attention on the states. Because votes for electing the president are actually cast by state delegations of electors, presidential politics concentrates on winning pluralities in each state, rather than building national constituencies. The winner-takes-all system for allocating votes for president in the Electoral College simply discounts voters in the minority in most states, allowing a candidate to become president with less than a majority – or even a plurality – of the popular vote, as the election of 2000 illustrates. The practical effect, that an individual candidate may be elected President by obtaining pluralities in only nine states, means that candidates perceive, correctly, the importance of state politics and interests as paramount in the calculus of national elections.

The mechanism that drives American politics to an even more highly decentralized level is the dependency of political officeholders on their highly localized constituencies. State and local officials are central figures in turning out the vote and in using their personal influence to persuade voters to support their candidates for national office. States contribute to growing political decentralization by their determination to distance the operations of state political systems from national politics. This power of local political operatives is enhanced by severing ties between state politics and national political issues by the movement of states away from holding statewide elections during presidential election years. This trend since World War II of separating presidential from state elections means that even national candidates for political office, such as US Senators and Members of Congress, must have orientations to internal political issues of the states rather than national issues associated with presidential elections to determine their fate in their own elections. Holding elections for state governments in odd-numbered years (as in New Jersey, Kentucky, Virginia, and Mississippi) further distances the politics of states from national issues, so that the latter rarely intrude on the domestic politics of these states.

The combination of national supremacy and state diversity leads to a system of government that Samuel Beer calls "representational federalism" (Beer, 1978). Beer suggests that the American federal system offers citizens a dual system by which they can choose alternatives for the arenas in which they will express their interests before government. At one level, persons unsuccessful in the states can direct their pleadings to a national constituency, as in the case of the civil rights movement. It is also true, however, that failures at the national level may be transposed to state-level politics as, for example, enactment of state bans on firearms in state jurisdictions when gun-control advocates become frustrated over the political influence of the National Rifle Association at the national policy-making level.

For most purposes, the effect of the highly decentralized nature of American politics essentially reverses the flow of political influence proffered in the formal structures of the American Constitution. Although the superior power of the national government is always latent and sometimes exercised to adjust fundamental inequities such as in relation to voting rights or educational opportunity, political decentralization effectively means that policy-making flows from the grassroots, rather than from the top down. This bottom-up flow of political authority provides the essential structure of the American federal system and helps to explain evolution of the system into what most Americans experience today.

Intergovernmental relations in the American federal system

Putting aside issues of national supremacy, the doctrine of states' rights is also based upon a rather spurious claim that the United States had, from the beginning, operated under a model of "dual federalism" (sometimes called "layer-cake federalism") in which national and state governments existed and operated in distinct, clearly defined, and separate spheres. Scholars note, however, that the allocation of authority never followed such a model by showing that from its beginnings the nation operated as what they called "cooperative federalism." This latter concept (sometimes called "marble-cake federalism") defined intergovernmental relations as being so thoroughly intermingled that it is virtually impossible to define what functions are truly national and what are subject to the exclusive authority and control of states (Grodzins, 1966).

Most national initiatives respond to state and local needs. National government initiatives under cooperative federalism help to structure state policy initiatives by offering incentives when states adopt policies that coincide with national policy goals. This collaboration of national and state governments has the effect of reducing impacts of state variations in benefits and quality of life experienced by Americans. Involvement of the national government often has the impact of reducing disparities among the states. States' needs in some areas are often compensated by states that have needs and resources in quite different areas. For example, states with needs created by a disproportionate number of poor persons are compensated by states with burdensome demands for development of transportation resources and vice versa. The net effect of transfers among the states establishes a level of equity through a variety of collaborative efforts – with some additional benefits, of course, accruing to states with favored positions in national governmental bodies. As an incentive to states to undertake assistance to the poor, for example, the national government established a formula that awarded reimbursements to poor states of five times the state expenditures, while wealthier states were only reimbursed dollar for dollar.

Examples of cooperative relationships abound. Even before the Constitution was drafted, the national government used its authority to the advantage of states by establishing the forms and practices of new states in the Northwest Territories. Hamilton's plan to fund the national debt (i.e., for the federal government to assume the debts of bankrupt state and local governments) kept the nation afloat during dire circumstances for the new nation. In the early nineteenth century, the Homestead Act provided a basis for turning federal control of lands over to states and placing them on state tax rolls. In 1861, the national government used its authority to establish a system of land grants to states in return for state creation of agricultural and mechanical schools. Assistance to states was extended under the Hatch Act of 1887 which provided for financial support of state development of agricultural experiment stations, with the eventual effect of establishing extension services operated by state universities, but funded primarily by the national government. What is important to note is that all these actions by the national government represented direct assistance to states.

Samuel Beer also suggests another form of interaction between the national authority and state-local governments, the collaboration of state–local bureaucratic professionals with federal technocrats (Beer, 1978: p. 18), sometimes called "picket-fence" federalism. Similarly trained professionals who share a common discipline across levels of government facilitate cooperation that often transcends direction by coordinating authorities. This model of American federalism implies a series of vertical, policy bureaucracies uniting federal, state, and local levels of government across corresponding levels of representative governmental authority. Most scholars agree that this model of intergovernmental relations has descriptive merit. What is less settled is the degree to which technocratic interests are independent (or dependent) on outside interests, as recent revelations concerning cozy relationships between Food and Drug Administration researchers and corporations seeking approval of new drugs suggest, or to what extent the technocratic bias of "picket-fence" federalism contributes to corporate rather than personal representation.

Fiscal federalism

The most significant form of national–state interactions occurs in terms of "fiscal federalism." Faced with demonstrated incapacities of state governments at state and local levels to meet many of the needs of citizens, the national government undertakes a wide variety of activities from simple income assistance to regional economic development – as in the case of the Tennessee Valley Authority, a massive project to control flooding of the Tennessee River that proved to be of enormous economic assistance to industrial development of a poverty-stricken area through generation of electric power for industrialization. These "federal" actions rely on cooperation of the states, but the key to intergovernmental relations has been the primacy of fiscal federalism. In this regard, federalism can be viewed as cooperation of federal and state-levels of government in achieving common goals, a view in sharp contrast to political rhetoric suggesting that national initiatives pose a zero-sum game in competition with states; that is, that whenever the national government undertakes programmatic responsibilities in any area, it diminishes the authority and power of states to act in these areas.

Fiscal federalism implies use of superior taxing authority by the national government (notably after the Sixteenth Amendment in 1913 provided for direct taxation of individual incomes) and subsequent distribution of revenues for state purposes, that emphasizes collaboration of national and state governments in a variety of policy areas. No policy area is more representative of the cooperation of national and state governments than programs of assistance to the poor, beginning with the Social Security Act of 1935. This act provides for national government sharing of revenues with states in the form of poverty relief. Under its provisions, states that opt to participate in the program administer assistance to the poor in conformity with guidelines set by the national government. As the programs have developed, poorer states receive as much as five dollars reimbursement for every six dollars spent in poverty assistance, as long as they follow national standards for eligibility and access to the program. Assistance to the poor under this collaborative system expanded to include medical assistance under Medicaid in 1965, with a similar program of fiscal sharing and state administration.

A more familiar form of fiscal federalism is the inter-state highway system, a program initiated by a Republican administration during the 1950s. Once again, applying fiscal federalism, the national government provided 90 percent of the costs of new highway construction, but left the authority for implementing the actual construction to states in accordance with broad national planning. These were the general patterns of relationships for decades after the New Deal, extending into the present, with federal highway money still being a major source of funding for the states.

Growth of state governments under fiscal federalism

Development of American federalism as a highly cooperative and interdependent system is sharply at odds with political rhetoric that sees a necessarily competitive relationship between the national government and the states in a zero-sum game. According to this view, exercise of government authority by either level occurs at the expense of the other. That is, whenever the national government undertakes programmatic responsibilities in any area, such initiative diminishes the authority and power of the states to act in these areas.

Table 8.1   *Number and types of governments in the United States*

	1992	2002
Total	85,006	87,576
Federal	1	1
States	50	50
Local	84,955	87,525
of which		
County	3,043	3,034
Municipal	19,279	19,429
Township/Town	16,656	16,504
School District	14,422	13,506
Special District	31,555	35,052

Source: Bureau of the Census, *Census of Governments* (quinquennial).

Under cooperative federalism, the argument that federal activity implied a corresponding loss in state functions suggested a pattern of governmental interaction not supported by the data. A zero-sum game in federal–state relations would mean a decline in state government activity associated with increases in programmatic activity at the federal level. Instead, a pattern of increasing scope of state functions corresponded to increased federal activity under fiscal federalism. Figures 8.1 and 8.2 show corresponding increases in state and federal spending and employment since 1950. While federal spending increased steadily in constant dollars throughout the period, spending and employment by state and local governments increased at an even faster rate. Using measures of government spending and employment as indicators of government growth, it becomes clear that growth of government at the federal level does not dampen, but operates as a stimulus for even higher rates of growth at subnational levels.

Figure 8.1 shows that employment by state and local governments grew exponentially compared to federal employment growth during a 40-year period of federal stimulus to state activity. These data alone indicate the fact that growth in government during the last half of the 1900s has been at state and local, not at federal, levels. Figure 8.2 indicates that state and local spending not only was not affected by federal increases, but kept pace with spending by the national government over the past several decades even when defense expenditures are included.

134

Figure 8.1   *Ratio of state–local to federal employment, 1960–2000*

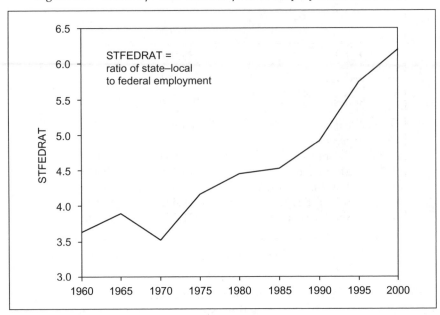

Figure 8.2   *Comparisons of state–local and federal spending, 1960–2000*

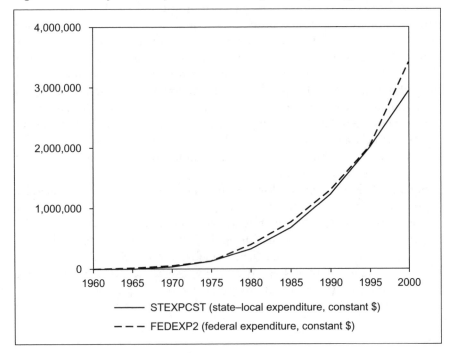

The zero-sum argument has validity only in areas in which state governments have, in the past, engaged in egregious violations of civil rights of citizens in ways that required intervention by the national government. In most other areas, the national government exercises exclusive authority only in areas in which the states have little or no interest. Where considerable programmatic activity by the federal government exists, it is almost always in collaboration with state governments. In these cases, the federal role is usually permissive and encouraging states to undertake efforts in housing, health, welfare, and transportation.

"New federalism"

Beginning with the Nixon administration in 1969, the federal government attempted new concepts of intergovernmental relations under the rubric of "the new Federalism." While the plan was a clear expression of Republican Party ideologies of decentralization, it coincided with efforts to restore capacities of state governments to govern. Beginning in the 1960s a movement to professionalize state governments, especially state legislatures, represented a solution to what the Citizens' Conference on State Legislatures called a "trend toward social disintegration," with the view that reform of state legislatures offered the best hope of reversing the trend (CCSL, 1971: xi). This movement was quite successful and state legislatures and even governors began to assert independence in policy initiatives from those of the central government.

The rise in importance of state governments had to do largely with modifications of fiscal federalism. The centerpiece of the Nixon "new federalism" was a shift away from grants-in-aid (reimbursements for specific state activities of intergovernmental cooperation), to a program of "general revenue sharing." Under this latter program, the federal government returned unrestricted funds to states and allowed them to set priorities for their use. In addition, states were given more control over welfare spending and other federal reimbursement programs enabling them to diversify priorities for poverty assistance and medical care. One result was that states quickly learned to shift the fiscal burden to the federal government in social services. California, under its then Governor Ronald Reagan, for example, transferred most of its developmentally disabled recipients to federal programs of rehabilitation, at one time receiving 38 percent of all funds expended by the federal government in this area.

General revenue sharing which operated in this form between 1972–80 is generally regarded as a failure. The overall evaluation of general revenue sharing was that it failed to accomplish objectives of social welfare programs previously operated jointly through cooperative relationships of state and national governments. Funds distributed to states often substituted for state-generated revenues or were used to fund operating costs of existing programs rather then providing surplus funds for state innovations. This experiment indicated that targeted aid and specific expense reimbursements as in grant-in-aid programs were more efficient than general aid to states. The political temptation to use unrestricted grants to states as substitutes for state-generated revenues proved too tempting, as former Chairman of the House Ways and Means Committee, Wilbur Mills, pointed out during a whirlwind campaign through the states in 1972.

The Reagan administration also used the slogan of a "New Federalism" to characterize intergovernmental relations during his presidency. This time, however, it meant transferring not only policy discretion from national to state levels, but a major portion of the fiscal burden, as well. Figure 8.3 shows the break from an overall trend in federal aid to states associated with the Reagan years, resumed in the early Bush administration and continued under President Clinton. Ironically, President Reagan's knowledge of the loopholes in federal funding schemes enabled him to close those avenues of support for states that he used so effectively during his terms as governor of California.

Figure 8.3   *Federal aid to states (constant $)*

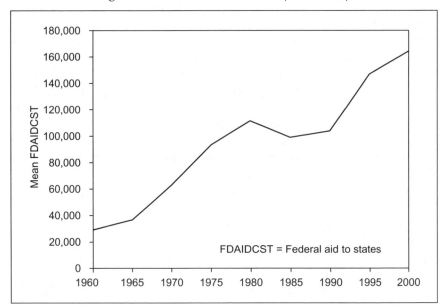

FDAIDCST = Federal aid to states

Despite these notable failures, formula block-grant programs in which the national government funds general programs of states (such as reduction of welfare dependency, rather than income assistance to poor families) have survived and have become the principal means of federal support to the states. Rather than offering matching funds to states by reimbursing their contributions to support for the poor, the federal government now relies on distributions of federal funds under fiscal federalism as bloc grants, allowing states greater discretion within policy areas. Decline in welfare caseloads associated with the shift from matching grants under Aid to Families with Dependent Children (AFDC) in favor of Temporary Assistance to Needy Families (TANF) block grants and the corresponding reductions in welfare expenditures associated with these policy changes encouraged reliance on the block grant form of federal assistance to states. The decline in needy families during the 1990s that coincided with the advent of TANF, however, may have been a result of the boom economy more than a specific policy shift. As the economy declined during the early 2000s, rises in state spending for the poor increased unexpectedly and in ways that make federal support inadequate. When block grants based upon previous year's performance remained relatively constant, but number of dependents increased as a result of downturns in the economy, states were stressed by unexpected costs of programs formerly within revenue flows from the federal government. Block grant programs also contribute to some of the problems of cities mentioned above, given that rather making grants directly to the cities, programs now come through state capitals, which are often still dominated by rural interests.

"Coercive federalism"

The trend of diminishing support for state governments during the 1980s was accompanied by movement away from longstanding federal-state "cooperative" relationships toward what Daniel Elazar has described as "coercive cooperation" (Elazar, 1990: 11–21). John Kincaid took a much more pessimistic view in suggesting that there has been a marked shift from traditional balances between federal and state power through a "coercive system of federal pre-emption of state and local authority and unfunded mandates on state and local governments" (Kincaid, 1990: 139). Contrary to previous history, the position of states relative to the national government has eroded as a result of perceived threats to national security and reduced revenues.

Although some states cut taxes during the 1990s "boom," growing revenues still exceeded expenditures. The mix of intergovernmental policy-making, however, has placed considerable strain on state resources. State income tax revenues, for example, are often calculated by individuals based upon their federal income taxes. The Republican tax cuts from 2001, at the federal level, have had consequences for state budget balances that, because of the pattern of revenue coupling, resulted in additional reductions in state taxes that were unanticipated by state governments.

The fiscal position of states has also declined as a result of a variety of other factors, the most prominent source of this decline being rapidly rising costs of health care, especially nursing home care funded by Medicaid. As state resources decline and liabilities increase, there has been an accompanying variety of initiatives by the national government coercing states into compliance with a variety of demands that states have found difficult to maintain. In late 2005 the federal government began to search for ways to constrain its own support for Medicaid, given severe budget problems at its own level.

Growth of federal mandates

Several initiatives by the federal government have increased stress in the relationship between federal policy and the ability of states to meet more decentralized policy goals. The general pattern of federal intervention in the affairs of states takes the form of assistance to states that exercise their own authority in collaboration with national policy goals; but defenders of state prerogatives now observe what they view as an alarming turn toward national dominance of policy arenas traditionally controlled at state and local levels. The instruments of this development have been a combination of federal mandates and pre-emption of state authority as interest groups discover that displacement of arenas of political conflict to the national level represents efficiencies of political action as a substitute for activity across 50 states. An increase in unfunded mandates and federal pre-emptive statutes has been accompanied by a shift from federal funding of geographic areas, such as states, to individuals. In FY 2001, roughly 60 percent of all federal domestic spending was distributed in programs to individuals (Keffer, 2003: 38). These figures mark a major shift in the objects of fiscal federalism – roughly $1 trillion in federal funds was directed to individuals, while only $340 billion was for grants to state and local governments.

A significant change in relationships between the national government and the states represented by this shift has been the punitive withdrawal of traditional grants-in-aid to states in order to coerce compliance with newly enacted federal mandates. During the Ford administration (1974–7), mandated minimum ages for consumption of alcoholic beverages at 21 allowed only putative discretion on the part of states, the penalty for noncompliance being the loss of federal highway funds. More recent mandates have been imposed on states without corresponding linkages to federal funding. The No Child Left Behind Act of 2001 imposes considerable costs on states for student testing, data collection, and higher teacher standards, but little of the promised $28 billion has been allocated in federal government appropriations. The Help America Vote Act of 2002 requires states to engage in major reforms of their administration of voting, including assuring voting access for persons with disabilities; however, Congress failed to appropriate any funding in support of this initiative. The federal government is obliged to fund 40 percent under the Individuals with Disabilities Education Act and its amendments, but, in fact, has provided only 18 percent of the required funding.

The rise in unfunded mandates to state governments and the coercive use of these mandates represents a departure from the enabling role the federal government played historically under cooperative federalism. FY 2006 budget proposals by the Bush administration shift the cost of federal mandates even more to the state-local level. The National Conference on State Legislatures estimates that these budget proposals represent at least $29 billion in new expenditures by state governments for federally imposed mandates. Local governments face the same problems, though local government often has even fewer economic resources than have the states.

Pre-emption of state authority

Even more threatening to collaborative federal–state relationships has been the growth of federal pre-emption in regulatory areas. When the national authority pre-empts state regulatory authority, there are often significant limitations placed upon state "concurrent powers," traditionally exercised by state and local governments. Preemption can often go so far as to remove all state regulatory powers in a field and assign responsibility to national governmental departments. The Atomic Energy Act of 1946, for example, effectively removed state authority from the regulatory process, but later experience showed that the US Nuclear Regulatory Commission lacked the capacity to protect public health and safety during a radioactive discharge and had to rely on state and local governments in this contingency. Other, less notable and less obtrusive pre-emption acts include the Bus Regulatory Reform Act of 1982 that prohibits states from regulating some economic aspects of bus companies such as fares and routes; the Occupational Safety and Health Act of 1970, authorized federal regulation of designated labor practices unless states enacted regulatory authorities that imposed standards at least equal to those of the national government. The Telecommunications Act of 1996 pre-empts all state barriers to inter-state communications, but even to intrastate service, and the Internet Nondiscrimination Act of 2001 forbids subnational governments from taxing internet sales. Federal pre-emption has also limited state authority over airlines, making it difficult for states to control deceptive practices, and over the financial securities industry. Although some actions have been taken to mitigate impacts of federal pre-emption statutes, one observer notes that "the sharp increase in...pre-emption statutes during the past four decades suggests states have been deprived of a significant portion of their reserved powers" (Zimmerman, 200: 36).

Homeland security

The traumas associated with 9/11 have also had a substantial impact on the restructuring of federal-state relations. Development of the Department of Homeland Security and corresponding portions of the Patriot Act mark a massive shift toward the federal government of duties and responsibilities traditionally left to states. Cooptation of state and local police and fire department functions by the national government pose as yet unforeseen implications for federal–state relations. Reliance on state-local agencies as "first responders," under the control of national authority, and the lack of sufficient fiscal provision for these agencies to assume their extended roles, promises to be a source of tension for the future. The greatly enlarged national control of domestic security, especially in areas of criminal justice, traditionally controlled by state and local governments, eliminates a great deal of the discretion in areas that previously have been left free of federal interference.

The federal government in the past has funded the states' costs of incarceration of undocumented aliens who are convicted of state crimes. This arrangement came about as a result of the federal government's unwillingness to prevent undocumented aliens from entering the United States and relying on state and local agencies to assume primary responsibilities for law enforcement. Funding of the State Criminal Alien Assistance Program by the federal government is in jeopardy, however, as the national government attempts to control its deficit by transferring costs to states. As a result, states joined to oppose federal legislation in 2005 requiring states to enforce federal immigration laws.

In general, the arena of Homeland Security promises to be a net drain on state resources. FY 2006 budget proposals to reduce funds for the Firefighter Grants program from $715 to $500 and earmarking even a proportion of what is granted for terrorism prevention activities, elimination of funding for Metropolitan Medical Response Systems, and other cost-shifting measures have been opposed by state organizations. The aura of a national emergency encourages a kind of sacrifice by all levels of government in favor of national security that falls particularly hard on states experiencing fiscal consequences of the national security environment they had not anticipated. The area of Homeland Security promises to be the most significant of adjustments in the federal system for the future (Wright, 2003: 21–3).

Federal interventions in the criminal and civil justice area

The Democratic Party in the United States (at least since the New Deal) has been associated with support of government nationalization, while the Republican Party has been seen as guardian of state and local government prerogatives in the federal system. Hamilton in Federalist 17 took the view that states would tend to dominate in the federal system by virtue of their control in areas of civil and criminal justice. Ironically, the current Bush administration and the Republican Congress have seriously undermined the role of states in the area of criminal law. Legislation in areas of civil and criminal justice at the federal level proves far more threatening to the balance of authority between federal and state governments than pre-emption. Preemptive legislation displaces the roles of states in their regulatory functions, but new initiatives in the civil and criminal area pose a threat to the last bastion of state authority under residual and concurrent powers of Amendment 10 to the Constitution.

Intervention by the national government in a variety of policy areas always left intact independent state sovereignty in most areas of civil and criminal justice, including domestic relations. One result of discretion exercised under state sovereignty has been widely varying definitions of what constitutes criminal behavior and what respective punishments might be for various criminal acts. For example, fornication in some states is a crime, although penalties are rarely enforced. During the 1970s, the penalty for possession of marijuana in any quantity was treated as a felony in Illinois punishable by up to 20 years in prison, while in neighboring Michigan, which relied on local option, possession of small amounts of this drug were considered a misdemeanor that, in some jurisdictions, carried a $25 fine.

Initiatives pursued under the Bush administration have usurped this traditional discretion under the sovereignty of state governments in areas of civil and criminal law. In most cases, these initiatives have (or would) invade state prerogatives in pursuit of what have come to be called a "moral" agenda. In other cases they pursue narrow interest agendas that benefit either specific economic groups that support the administration (for example eliminating some opportunities of consumers to sue businesses, or imposing specific moral codes).

Tort "reform"

In pursuit of campaign pledges of the 2004 presidential and legislative campaigns, legislation is before the Congress to limit awards for medical malpractice. The legislation includes caps on noneconomic damages ("pain and suffering"), waiving punitive damages against drug manufacturers if the drug has been approved by the Federal Food and Drug Administration, limits on attorneys' fees and other limiting provisions. What is significant is the provision specifically pre-empting all state laws not in conformance with these provisions and the inclusion of drug manufacturing interests in a protected status.

Unlike national security considerations, there is no obvious compelling reason for federal intervention in this area. Tort law has been almost solely the province of states. In addition, for the past several years, there has been considerable activity in state legislatures to address the issue of the level of damages awarded by juries within the states. Furthermore, states have strong motivations to deal with excessive medical malpractice awards. States with restrictions on such awards that sometimes result in lower medical malpractice insurance premiums are more attractive to physicians in what is developing as significant competition among states for medical personnel. Although such legislation is likely to fail in the United States Congress, campaigning by the Bush administration often appears as an unprincipled initiative for a political party traditionally identified with supremacy of state and local interests.

Late-term abortions

Congressional Republicans won legislation in recent years prohibiting third trimester or "late-term" abortions as part of their agenda on moral issues. Although *Roe* v. *Wade*, the Supreme Court decision that prohibits state limitations on abortions during the first trimester, specifically authorizes states to restrict or even ban third trimester abortions – and most states have done so – the United States Congress has enacted legislation that, again, overrides state preferences in favor of the nationalization of criminal laws related to this area of medical practice. Actions such as this that may actually have only marginally symbolic significance for the moral agendas, mark significant shifts in the traditional authority of states to pre-eminence in the area of criminal law and medical practice.

Same-sex marriages

The legal rights of same-sex couples is emerging as a major issue in federal–state relations. Inter-state variation as to how state populations regard same-sex couples ranges from recognition of marriages, or at least what are called "civil unions," to specific bans on recognition of same-sex marriages. The issue for the federal system is whether states are obliged to honor unions contracted in other states under the "Full Faith and Credit" clause of the Constitution. Some states have adopted legislation banning recognition of such unions from other states. There is political pressure for adding national legislation (or even a constitutional amendment) to the "moral agenda" as a way of creating uniform opposition to same-sex orientations, as well as unions that appear to sanction homosexual behavior.

The most blatant effort to invade state authority in recent years was the actions of the United States Congress in attempting to override not only acts of the state courts (in this case in Florida), but the discretion of a state legislature as well. In this case, the US Congress adopted legislation, signed by President Bush, to require that appeals from state courts regarding removal of feeding tubes from a patient that the courts decided was in a "permanent vegetative state" should be transferred to the federal judiciary. A disregard for state autonomy in favor of national authority indicates the precipitous nature of the movement toward nationalization of governmental functions in the current political atmosphere. Despite this congressional action, the federal courts exercised their discretion and refused to intervene, defending, in part, their own discretion under separation of powers.

Such efforts to invoke national authority in pursuit of "moral agendas" by invading traditional areas of state authority, such as issues of civil and criminal law, pose a significant threat to the balance of power between national and state governments that characterizes American federalism. Unlike economic and social cleavages that even James Madison in Federalist 10, believed could be translated into "positive-sum games" or "win-win" outcomes, moral issues are less amenable to political negotiation. They do, however, have significant implications for the future of the federal system. Significant pre-emption of state laws in the areas of civil and criminal justice chart a course for American federalism from which it may be difficult to return. Perhaps it is less the actual threat than the potential threat to the balance of federal–state relations that supporters of state sovereignty find most alarming.

Conclusion

The American federal system was born of a perceived need to strengthen the power of the national government and to limit the powers of the states. The dynamics of shared sovereignty in the United States, however, have been characterized by shifting balances of power between state and national governments. For most of the history of American federalism, there have been tensions and even conflicts, but, for the most part, relationships between national and subnational governments have been characterized by cooperation and collaboration. In most cases, each level of government performs where it is most competent, the national government developing national policies and states adapting them to fit more localized needs and conditions. In areas where rights of individual citizens are at stake or where constitutional guarantees and governing mechanisms are inadequate, the national government attains pre-eminence. In most other areas, discretion is left to states in the exercise of their residual sovereignty.

Recent years have been characterized by political initiatives that appear to break with traditions of cooperative federalism. Federal government transfers of fiscal burdens to states reverse the collaborative arrangements of fiscal federalism. Furthermore, the imposition of additional burdens of national policy without corresponding fiscal support creates crises in states whose constitutional requirements for balanced budgets make it difficult to adapt to external costs imposed by other levels of government. Mobilization of "first responders" in unconventional and unfunded roles by the new focus on "homeland security" is one example of stresses imposed upon the states.

Usurpations of state prerogatives in the areas of civil and criminal law represent the most significant threat to state sovereignty that has appeared in many years. This is not to suggest that issues of the "moral agenda" are not worthy concerns; what is at issue are the appropriate roles of state and national government in adjudicating and resolving cleavages among citizens that are not generally susceptible to negotiation. Moral questions are not generally subject to compromise and, indeed, previous forays into such waters by raising constitutional sanctions (as in the Eighteenth Amendment prohibiting the manufacture and sale of alcoholic beverages in the United States) hold stark lessons as to the limits of the political process. What is most clear is that there is a rather slippery slope toward nationalization of politics that seems capable of circumventing the balance of authority defined in the Constitution. The events of 9/11 have been instrumental in precipitating the nationalization of government authority in the United States and placed it on a track far more similar to unitary systems than to the other federal systems with which it is often compared.

The American federal system will always be characterized by complex and rapidly changing intergovernmental relations. Some scholars argue that virtually all government institutions at the national level have moved against the authority of states, primarily through pre-emption of policy areas formerly the province of states. One scholar suggests that "Congress in effect has become a unitary government in completely pre-empted regulatory fields and finances in part its policies in several other fields by imposing burdensome mandates on subnational governments" (Zimmerman, 2005: 378). The trend toward greater control of policy discretion by the national government represents a dramatic change in fundamental roles played by states in American federalism.

Chapter 9

The Rising Power of Minorities and the Deracialization of American Politics

Baodong Liu and Robert Darcy

Forty years after Martin Luther King Jr made his famous "I have a dream" speech, is race still important in American politics? Answering this question does not just involve assessing how the progress of the pursuit by minorities of material equality. At a much deeper level it touches on the different conceptions of the meaning of democracy within the United States.

There are three broad views on race and American politics. The first is the multicultural approach. According to this view, the growth of minority populations and the current record-level of elected minority officials have shown that race will continue to play a major role in American national politics, especially in presidential elections. On this view the influence of white voters will decline and the battle for support from minorities in general – and from Latino voters in particular –will become central to electoral competition. Thus Bruce Cain has suggested that multicultural-ism would become the main force in the new era of national politics, replacing the biracial politics of the civil-rights era (Cain, 1995). With the arrival of multicultural politics, Asian, Hispanic and Native-American issues and symbols would join those of African-Americans in the political dialogue.

The second view suggests that the country is being gradually taken over by minorities. As a result, they suggest, traditional white values are eroding. Some scholars used the concept of *symbolic racism* to describe and explain the modern white moralistic and abstract resentments toward blacks as a group. The subtle sentiments of symbolic racism are suggested as a reflection of the belief that "Blacks violate such traditional American values as individualism and self-reliance, the work ethic, obedience, and discipline" (Kinder and Sears, 1981: 416; Kinder and Sanders, 1996). Moreover, they see the white elites as not protecting white interests. Their solution is white separatism and a reinterpretation of white identity

(Swain, 2002; Winant, 2004). For them, immigration policy and language are central political issues.

The third view is grounded on majoritarianism. This perspective sees minorities continuing to be a secondary concern in American politics because white voters' retain plurality status. The current political system is still defined by a racial hierarchy for which there is no quick solution (Jennings, 1994). While minorities may dominate certain policy areas in a particular state or city, they are not likely to define the direction of future politics. Further, it is argued, the American melting pot historically works against minority-based politics. In the early nineteenth century the group defined as white Anglo-Saxon Protestants (or WASPs) dominated politics. The waves of Irish, Italian, Polish and other European immigrants threatened the WASPs demographically as Asians and Hispanics challenge today's whites. Rather than maintaining the nineteenth- and early twentieth-century conflict between WASPs and the European minorities, the WASP gradually became politically irrelevant. By the mid twentieth century the notion of "white" incorporated all European-Americans. That process is likely to continue as more and more Hispanics and Asians become defined as "white" or "American." Indeed it is interesting that Asians were defined as "white" as early as 1907 in the Oklahoma Constitution. Today the United States census allows persons to classify themselves into any number of racial categories alone or in combination. In addition to the racial categories, an individual can define his or her ethnicity as Hispanic. In all, the 2000 United States Census reports up to 63 racial combinations, which, if we include Hispanic or not, doubles to 126.

The danger is that this new assimilation, like the older version, will leave some, especially blacks, out. Black leaders, such as Al Sharpton, a presidential candidate in 2004, are aware of this threat. Many believe that the Democratic Party takes black support for granted and has ceased fighting for their interests (Brown, 2004). As political scientist Ronald Walters remarked the Democratic Party has been "running from race" (Coates, 2004). As this chapter will demonstrate, while elections can be won without the support of a majority of white voters, they cannot be won without substantial white support. Consequently, one of the most important defining features of American politics today is the paradox – the rising electoral potential of minorities is occurring simultaneously with the trend toward deracialized campaigns and policy-making.

Race in American politics today

In mid January of 2003, President Bush announced his opposition to the University of Michigan's program of racial preferences for minority applicants. Less than a month later, the *Los Angeles Times* published its first survey reacting to the President's position. This report found that a majority of Americans felt that the United States had "not even come close" to eliminating discrimination against racial and ethnic minorities (Richardson, 2003). The same survey also indicated, however, that 57 percent of Americans believed that "academic achievement should be used as the sole admission criterion for universities" (Richardson, 2003).

The irony of race relations in American politics is the lack of solution to African-American inequality. The problem is one Americans have always had difficulty facing. Thus, although in his second Inaugural Address President Bush celebrated equality, noting that from "the day of our founding" Americans had "proclaimed that every man and woman on this Earth" had "rights and dignity and matchless value, because they [bore] the image of the Maker of Heaven and Earth" (Delivered January 20, 2005), the original US Constitution reflected a different reality. It for long guaranteed and protected slavery, requiring escaped slaves be returned to their masters regardless of the laws of the state to which the escaped slave had fled. It also counted slaves as three-fifths of a person and prohibited interference with importing slaves and any amendments to the Constitution concerning importation of slaves until 1808. Many of the Founding Fathers owned slaves and the importation of more African slaves continued until 1808. It was not until December 18, 1865 and a civil war that the Constitution abolished slavery. It was another century before full civil rights for African-Americans were guaranteed in law.

Race and ethnicity have thus always been central to understanding the historical development of American democracy. In the United States "democracy" never referred to the political system of the ancient Athenians. Indeed, it typically did not refer to a political system at all. Rather, it contrasted the European and American social systems. In nineteenth-century Europe an individual's position was determined at birth; in America, at least in the popular mind, by "luck and pluck." A penniless immigrant orphan could become a corporate leader; a frontiersman born in a dirt-floored log cabin could become President of the United States. And, as the many Horatio Alger books illustrate, Americans born to privilege did not necessarily maintain that status in the absence of character. The nineteenth-century American concept of democracy was as much about social opportunity, and a chance for everyone to make good, as about legal rights.

The civil rights movement of the 1960s achieved an "ambiguous victory" in that open racism has been subjected to profound moral and political challenges (Winant, 2004). On the other hand, the integration policies of the federal government have failed so far to achieve the goal of complete integration. Segregation in schools is rising not shrinking, while affirmative action programs have less and less support among whites. African-Americans have made gains over the past half-century but remain marginalized in American society.

Marginalization is not restricted to a person's economic situation. Yet that is the simplest to measure and it has an impact on many other aspects of life. Table 9.1 shows blacks, American Indians and Hispanics are not benefiting from America's prosperity to the extent whites are. Politically, however, reactions of these minorities differ. African-American groups and elected leaders continue to push for more federal programs directed toward affirmative action and funding for the poor. American Indians see their opportunities through tribal sovereignty, especially tribally operated gambling facilities outside the limits of state regulation. Hispanics are focused on immigration and language issues. They want increased access to legal status within the United States and they resist pressures to further marginalize them through "English only" legislation that will restrict government functions to one language. Asian-Americans are generally prosperous and successful within the American social and economic system. They, as do many whites, resist any racial or ethnic limits that affirmative action programs may impose.

How has American politics responded to the continuing dilemma of racial inequality? The Bush administration has reached out to African-Americans through their churches. African-American churches play an enormous role in their community. Republicans favor channeling social program funding through churches, among other groups. This strategy creates a dilemma for Democrats. They favor the funding but want to keep state and church separate. Republicans generally favor opening borders to Hispanic workers. Democrats are uncomfortable with such a policy, however, fearing Hispanics lower wages and compete for jobs with their constituents. Tribal sovereignty does not fit neatly into either party's agenda. Republicans are uncomfortable with gambling while sovereignty claims bring tribes into conflict with Democratic constituencies.

Political scientists Edward Carmines and James Stimson argued events of profound importance, such as recessions and world wars, have come and gone with little effect on the nation's party system (Carmines and Stimson, 1989). Race, however, is not just a problem among many that have crowded onto the public policy agenda. It evolved and developed into the most significant difference between the major political parties.

Race in contemporary elections

Although African-Americans make up about 12 percent of the electorate, their overwhelming support for the Democratic Party, combined with the

Table 9.1 Some racial and ethnic demographic differences, 1997–2000

	Single-race households					Ethnicity	
	White	Black	American Indian	Asian	Other[1]	Hispanic	White non-Hispanic
1997 Population[2]	221,333,000	33,989,000	2,326,000	10,135,000		29,182,000	194,746,000
%	82.65	12.69	0.87	3.78		10.90	72.73
% Reported voting rates 1998[3]	43.30	39.60				20.00	46.50
1999 Median household income[4]	44,687	29,423	30,599	51,908		33,676	45,367
Housing[5]							
Owner	59,693,948	5,577,734	473,659	1,672,460	2,397,952	4,212,520	57,301,203
Renter	24,070,073	6,477,348	399,235	1,457,803	3,259,889	5,009,882	21,791,933
% Owner	71.26	46.27	54.26	53.43	42.38	45.68	72.45
% Renter	28.74	53.73	45.74	46.57	57.62	54.32	27.55
Total	100	100	100	100	100	100	100
Adults under correctional supervision 1997[6]	3,429,000	2,149,900	113,600				
%	60.24	37.77	2.00				
Prisoners under sentence of death 12/31/1997[7]	1,876	1,406	53		283		
%	56.25	42.16	1.59		8.49		

Notes:
[1] Includes two or more races.
[2] Authors' calculations from Resident Population of the United States by Sex, Race, and Hispanic Origin: April 1, 1990 to July 1, 1999 Population Estimates Program, Population Division, US Census Bureau, Washington, D.C. 20233.
[3] Jennifer C. Day and Avalaura L. Gaither, Voting and Registration in the Election of November 1998 Current Population Reports P20–523RV US Census Bureau, Washington, DC, August 2000.
[4] Authors' calculations from PS21 Median Household Income in 1999, Census 2000, Summary File, 3 (SF-3), Sample Data.
[5] Authors' calculations from US Census 2000, Summary File 1, Tables HO14001–HO14017, HO15H001–2, HO15H010, HO15I001–2, HO15I010.
[6] Authors' calculations from US Department of Justice, Correctional Populations in the United States, 1977 November 2000, NCJ 177613, p. 1, 3. American Indian–Asian category includes 'Other.'
[7] Authors' calculations from US Department of Justice, Correctional Populations in the United States, 1977 November 2000, NCJ 177613, pp. 131, 133. American Indian–Asian category includes 'Other.'

Table 9.2 *White and minority vote in presidential elections Gallup Polls, 1952–2004*

Election	Republican White	Non-White	Democrat White	Non-White	Other White	Non-White	Total White	Non-White	Winner
1952	57	21	43	79			100	100	R
1956	59	39	41	61			100	100	R
1960	51	32	49	68			100	100	D
1964	41	6	59	94			100	100	D
1968	47	12	38	85	15	3	100	100	R
1972	68	13	32	87			100	100	R
1976	52	15	46	85	1		99	100	D
1980	56	10	36	86	7	2	99	98	R
1984	66	13	34	87			100	100	R
1988	59	18	41	82			100	100	R
1992	41	11	39	77	20	12	100	100	D
1996	45	12	46	82	9	6	100	100	D
2000	52	12	39	78	9	10	100	100	R
2004	57	17	43	83			100	100	R

Sources: Authors' calculations from The Gallup Poll Monthly #374 November 1996 pp. 17–20; Jeffrey M. Jones, "How Americans Voted," November 5, 2004 Gallup Poll News Service; Gallup News Service "Candidate Support by Subgroup," November 6, 2000 and February 11, 2005 phone conversation with Eric Nielsen, Senior Director of Media Strategies, The Gallup Organization.

Democrats' inability to win the majority of white voters, has made minority and especially the African-American contribution to the Democratic Party enormous. In 1976 Jimmy Carter received 18 percent of his votes from non-whites. In 2000 Al Gore got 20 percent of his votes from non-whites. But the larger the percentage of the Democratic presidential vote that comes from minorities, the less the chance that candidate has of winning. That fact is because the bulk of the voters are white. A Democrat cannot win a two-candidate race with less than about 80 percent of his or her vote coming from whites. Both Republicans and Democrats are dependent on white votes. A Democrat can lose a majority of whites and still win, but to win Democrats still have to come close among whites.

In 2000 and 2004 George W. Bush won with the Southern, Mountain and most of the Midwestern states. The South, the eleven Confederate States, Alabama, Arkansas, Florida, Georgia, Louisiana, Mississippi, North Carolina, Tennessee, Texas and Virginia, has more than 84 million people, the largest geographic section in the country. Its 153 Electoral College votes are 57 percent of the 270 needed to elect the president; its 131 representatives are 60 percent of the 218 votes needed to control the House of Representatives; its 22 senators are 43 percent of the 51 votes needed to control the Senate. Today the South is solidly Republican in presidential elections.

In the early nineteenth century the South's great regional rival was New England with its six states. Today New England has only 34 electoral votes, 22 representatives and 12 senators. In the late nineteenth century the South's great rival was the block of eleven states which composed the Midwest. Today those states have only 113 electoral votes and 91 representatives. The five Pacific coast states, largely liberal and Democrat,

Table 9.3   *Race and vote in the 1976 and 2000 presidential elections*

| | Presidential vote % | | | |
| | 1976 | | 2000 | |
Race	Ford (R)	Carter (D)	Bush (R)	Gore (D)
White	96.60	81.70	97.07	79.24
Non-White	3.40	18.30	2.93	20.76
Total	100	100	100	100
(*n*)	(733)	(767)	(2,482)	(2,280)

Sources: Authors' calculations from Gallup Opinion Index #137 November, 1976 pp. 16–17; Gallup Poll News Service, "Candidate Support by Subgroup," November 6, 2000.

have only 80 electoral votes and 90 representatives. The three mid-Atlantic states, New York, New Jersey and Pennsylvania, are also liberal and Democratic but total only 67 electoral votes and 61 representatives. The remaining states, the 6 border states and the 8 mountain states, today are politically like the South, although together they have only 88 electoral votes and 60 representatives.

Between 1840 and 1960 the South was the region most loyal to the Democratic candidates. For much of that period the "Solid South" meant solid Democrat. After the Civil War the Republican Party in the South, with certain exceptions, was confined to blacks who, with limited voting rights and limited numbers, could not outvote white Democrats. The 1964 presidential election changed everything. Table 9.2 shows the racial breakdown of the Presidential vote, 1952–2004. While African-Americans began leaving the Republican Party during the New Deal (1933–1938), their desertion to the Democrats was not complete until 1964. Before 1964 Republicans did not get less than 20 percent of the non-white vote. After 1964, however, Republicans never got 20 percent.

The reason for the change is complex, but it certainly had a racial connection. In 1964 Lyndon Johnson pushed Democrats to racial liberalism. His party would be a party for civil rights legislation. Johnson knew that he was making a strategic decision to win the presidential election, and yet he might have paid a big price for the future. On the evening he signed the 1964 Civil Rights Act, President Johnson said to Bill Moyers: "I think we just delivered the South to the Republican Party for a long time to come" (Clymer, 2002). Senator Barry Goldwater, the 1964 Republican candidate, who was wedded to the principles of conservatism and small government, voted against Johnson's 1964 Civil Rights Act. Goldwater in 1964 won only his home state of Arizona, and more importantly, all five deep South states. Goldwater's vision changed the political future of the Republican Party, and laid a foundation for today's red and blue states.

Southern whites perceived the collapse of the New Deal coalition of Southern race-based politics with Northern liberal politics. The result was a swing of Southern whites to the Republicans and African-Americans to the Democrats. Republicans were able to campaign in the increasingly conservative South as conservatives without the race baggage of the old Southern Democrats, while Southern whites continue to view Northern liberal Democrats with suspicion.

Since 1964 the only Democratic presidents have been Southerners – Texas's Lyndon Johnson, Georgia's Jimmy Carter and Arkansas' Bill Clinton. Republicans have taken a majority of the white vote seven times since 1964, Democrats never won a majority of the white vote after 1964. While racial issues may not be vocalized, America is racially polarized in

154

Table 9.4 *Presidential vote by race and ethnicity, 1976–2004*

Year	Vote	Non-Hispanic White	Black	Asian	Hispanic	Total
1976	Democrat*	47	83		76	50
	Republican	52	16		24	48
	Total	99	99		100	98
1980	Democrat	36	85		59	41
	Republican*	56	11		33	51
	Other	7	3		6	7
	Total	99	99		98	99
1984	Democrat	35	90		62	40
	Republican*	64	9		37	59
	Total	99	99		99	99
1988	Democrat	40	86		69	45
	Republican*	59	12		30	53
	Total	99	98		99	98
1992	Democrat*	39	83	31	61	43
	Republican	40	10	55	25	38
	Other	20	7	15	14	19
	Total	99	100	101	100	100
1996	Democrat*	43	84	43	72	49
	Republican	46	12	48	21	41
	Other	9	4	8	6	8
	Total	98	100	99	99	98
2000	Democrat	42	90	54	67	48
	Republican*	54	8	41	31	48
	Other	3	1	4	2	2
	Total	99	99	99	100	98
2004	Democrat	41	88	58	56	48
	Republican*	58	11	41	43	51
	Total	99	99	99	99	99
Group % of total population		79	12	2	6	99

*Winner
Source: Marjorie Connelly, "Election 2004 How Americans Voted: A Political Portrait," *New York Times*, Sunday November 7, 2004, p. 4.

elections. There is little evidence the polarization is diminishing. Table 9.4 shows the racial-ethnic presidential vote breakdown between 1976 and 2004. In five of these eight elections, 1976, 1984, 1988, 2000 and 2004, the two major parties gained over 95 percent of the vote. In three, 1980, 1992 and 1996, minor parties gained between 6 and 10 percent of the vote. Looking only at the five elections dominated by the two major parties, we can see that Democrats won when they gained 47 percent or more of the white non-Hispanic vote and lost when they gained 42 percent or less. Likewise, Republicans won when they gained 54 percent or more of the white non-Hispanic vote and lost when they gained 52 percent or less.

This might vary a little by region (Black and Black, 2002). Because black voters have been extremely loyal Democrats, Republican presidential and congressional candidates in areas with substantial black populations, the South for example, need a massive landslide, about 60% of the white non-Hispanic electorate. Republicans have developed issues oriented toward religious whites and middle-class social and economic concerns. And they attempt to downplay race and issues directly connected to race.

Democrats cannot stress race as part of their strategy. To win elections Democrats need to build a coalition of moderate and liberal white non-Hispanics while energizing minority voters. Since the 1970s race has not worked well as a campaign theme for Democrats. The reason is simple. Democrats can already count on a disproportionate share of the minority vote. They need issues directed at whites. Thus, the United States has racially polarized politics while race, itself, is depoliticized.

Blacks are clearly the strongest Democrats, but this is both a strength and weakness for the Democratic Party. There are other minorities, however. Hispanics and Asians are growing as a result of immigration. Hispanics are not one race and, as noted earlier, can be classified white, Black, Asian or American Indian. Many Hispanics do not think of themselves in racial terms at all. Rather, they define themselves in terms of heritage and place of origin, Puerto Rico, Mexico, Cuba and Central America. Republican presidential candidates have not won a majority of

Table 9.5 *Race of American Hispanics, 2000*

Ethnicity	White	Black	American Indian	Asian	Other	Two or more races	Population
Hispanic	47.89	2.01	1.15	0.34	42.31	6.30	35,305,818
Not Hispanic	79.05	13.79	0.84	4.11	0.33	1.87	246,116,088
Total	75.14	12.32	0.88	3.64	5.60	2.43	281,421,906

Source: Authors' calculations from US Census Summary File 1 (SF 1), Tables P004001–11, P008010–17.

Hispanic voters in the last three decades but winning Republican presidential candidates have taken between 30 percent and 43 percent of the Hispanic vote. Losing Republicans have gained only between 21 percent and 25 percent of the diverse Hispanic vote.

Asians are another diverse minority, having origins in the Philippines, China, Japan, India, Pakistan, Korea and many other places. In 1992 and 1996 they supported Republican presidential candidates and in 2000 and 2004 they supported Democrats. Overall, Asians are the most evenly politically divided among American racial and ethnic groups. Generally Asians are a small minority although they are located throughout the United States. In two states, California and Hawaii, they are a substantial proportion of the population. Asian-Americans Daniel Inouye and Daniel Akaka, both Democrats, represent Hawaii in the Senate. Some of the electoral successes of Asian-Americans in California include the late Robert Matsui, re-elected to Congress as a Democrat from California in 2004. At the state level, for example, Wilma Chan, Leland Yee, Carol Liu and Judy Chu are Democrats, and Alan Nakanishi is a Republican elected to the California Assembly in 2004.

Oklahoma is the state with the largest number of Native Americans and Alaska has the largest Native-American population proportion. Native Americans live in all states and typically have tribal organizations recognized by states and the federal government as sovereign within the state. Oklahoma tribes, for example, have their own tribal governments and exercise their sovereignty by issuing their own motor vehicle license plates, collecting their own fuel and tobacco taxes on Indian-owned land and not collecting state taxes.

Tribes can enter into compacts with states by which the tribe can operate gambling facilities. In California 64 tribes have compacts according to one official publication (California Official Voter Information Guide, 2004). The compacts typically permit the tribe to operate gambling establishments in exchange for the state getting a share of the proceeds. Tribes have clashed with state governments on issues such as regulation of hunting and fishing, taxes and regulation of gambling. In 1837 Minnesota Chippewas agreed to a treaty by which they ceded land but retained the right to hunt and fish on that land. When, in the 1980s, Minnesota attempted to regulate hunting and fishing for conservation reasons without exempting the Indians, the Chippewas sued and, in 1999, won in the United States Supreme Court. As a result Minnesota was forced to negotiate with the Chippewas. Similar disputes occurred in Wisconsin and other states.

Today, Oklahoma Republican Congressman Tom Cole, a Chickasaw, is the only tribal member in Congress. The small numbers of Native Americans combined with tribal-based interests has led Native Americans

Table 9.6 Racial population California and Hawaii, 2000

Race	California Number	%	Hawaii Number	%	United States Number	%
White	20,170,059	59.55	294,102	24.28	211,460,626	75.14
Black	2,263,882	6.68	22,003	1.82	34,658,190	12.32
American Indian	333,346	0.98	3,535	0.29	2,475,956	0.88
Asian	3,697,513	10.92	503,868	41.59	10,242,998	3.64
Other	5,799,202	17.12	128,686	10.62	1756908	5.60
Two or more races	1,607,646	4.75	259,343	21.41	6,826,228	2.43
Total	33,871,648	100	1,211,537	100	281,421,906	100
White not Hispanic	15,816,790	46.70	277,091	22.87	194,552,774	69.13

Source: Authors' calculations from US Census Summary File 1 (SF 1), Tables QT-P4, P003001–9.

Table 9.7 Racial population Alaska, New Mexico, South Dakota and Oklahoma, 2000

Race	Alaska Number	%	New Mexico Number	%	South Dakota Number	%	Oklahoma Number	%
White	434,534	69.31	1,214,253	66.75	669,404	88.68	2,628,434	76.17
Black	21,787	3.48	34,343	1.89	4,685	0.62	260,968	7.56
American Indian	98,043	15.64	173,483	9.54	62,283	8.25	273,230	7.92
Asian	25,116	4.01	19,255	1.06	4,378	0.58	46,767	1.36
Other	13,306	2.12	311,385	17.12	3,938	0.52	85,270	2.47
Two or more races	34,146	5.45	66,327	3.65	10,156	1.35	155,985	4.52
Total	626,932	100	1,819,046	100	754,844	100	3,450,654	100

Source: Authors' calculations from US Census Summary File 1 (SF 1) Tables P003001–9.

to exert their political influence through lobbying and campaign support as opposed to depending on their voting numbers. They act politically more like corporations and business associations as opposed to the more usual minority politics model. In the 2003 California gubernatorial re-call election tribes contributed $6.7 million, about 20 percent of the total spent, making the tribes "the state's newest and biggest special interest" (Simon, 2003). Yet Native Americans can also organize protests and demonstrations. It makes a politically effective combination.

Minority political power and the implications of immigration and migrations

The US population has become increasingly diversified. However, with respect to the residential patterns, one still sees a segregated society. Immigrant minorities have tended to move to urban centers, while the waves of white flight from urban centers to suburbs continued during the last decades. For example, Tulsa, Oklahoma is a city largely within Tulsa County. In the period 1990–2000 there was a net movement of whites from the city into the growing suburbs of Jenks, Broken Arrow, Bixby, Owasso and Sand Springs. At the same time there was a net increase of blacks and other minorities in the city.

Many scholars have come to a conclusion that the migration pattern may overall benefit the Republican Party, because the growth of population in the sunbelt states (i.e., the South and the West) is within the stronghold of the GOP; the Northeast and Midwest, which have been critical areas of support for the Democratic Party, have seen out-migration. Moreover, middle-class whites are more likely to move to the South, and contribute to the growth of the Republican Party in those areas (Gimpel, 1999).

However, the growth of the minorities in the country has made many people speculate about the implications of America's changing demography. Table 9.9 shows the findings from the 2000 census. The African-American population share is 12.9 percent of the total population. The Asian-American population has grown because of the 1965 immigrations reform which ended a long history of discrimination against Asians; but their population share, at 3.6 percent, is still very small.

Hispanics have quickly become the largest minority in the country, and the 2000 census data show that they are more than 12.5 percent of the total. Their size will continue to grow because of their highest birth rate among the US populations and legal and illegal immigration. Many Hispanics are of Indian and African descent and thus people of color. Their assimilation will test America's absorbent power. Hispanics are

Table 9.8   *Tulsa City and County 2000 and 1990 racial groups*

	Total	White	Black	Other
Tulsa City				
1990 Number	367,302	291,444	49,825	26,033
1990 Proportion	100	79.35	13.57	7.09
2000 Number	393,049	275,488	60,794	56,767
2000 Proportion	100	70.09	15.47	14.44
Tulsa County suburbs				
1990 Number[1]	136,039	126,293	− 207	9,953
1990 Proportion	100	92.84	−0.15	7.32
2000 Number	170,250	147,093	862	22,295
2000 Proportion	100	86.40	0.51	13.10
Tulsa County				
1990 Number	503,341	417,737	49,618	35,986
1990 Proportion	100	82.99	9.86	7.15
2000 Number	563,299	422,581	61,656	79,062
2000 Proportion	100	75.02	10.95	14.04

Notes:
[1] A small portion of Tulsa City lies outside Tulsa County, subtracting Tulsa City from Tulsa County populations can leave negative numbers for the suburbs. The negative number is an indication of the small number of minorities living in the suburbs.

Source: US Census Bureau GCT-PL Race and Hispanic or Latino: 2000 Data Set: Census 2000 Redistricting Data (Public Law 94–171), Summary File Geographic Area Oklahoma-Place and Tula County, Oklahma; US Department of Commerce, 1992, 1990 Census of Population General Population Characteristics Oklahoma, Table 54, p. 140; Table 61, p. 262.

rapidly being taken into the political mainstream. The 2004 election brought two Hispanic senators, Florida Republican Mel Martinez and Colorado Democrat Ken Salazar, and 23 Hispanic representatives to Congress. In George W. Bush's second cabinet are Hispanics Carlos Gutierrez, the Secretary of Commerce, and Alberto Gonzales, the Attorney General.

With the growth of minority populations in the US, white population share has declined. The 2000 census data show that they represent about 75 percent of the US total population. White non-Hispanics are only 69 percent of the population. In California non-Hispanic whites are no longer the majority; they are only the largest minority. In Hawaii non-Hispanic whites are only the second largest minority.

Table 9.9   *United States race and ethnicity, 1990 and 2000*

| | 1990 | | 2000 | |
Race	Number	%	Number	%
White	199,686,070	80.29	211,460,626	75.14
Black	29,986,060	12.06	36,419,434	12.94
American Indian	1,959,234	0.79	2,475,956	0.88
Asian	7,273,662	2.92	10,242,998	3.64
Other	9,804,847	3.94	15,757,908	5.60
Two or more races			5,064,984	1.80
Total	248,709,873	100	281,421,906	100
Hispanic	22,354,059	8.99	35,305,818	12.55
Not-Hispanic	226,355,814	91.01	246,116,088	87.45
Total	248,709,873	100	281,421,906	100

Source: Authors' calculations from US Census 1990 Summary Tape File 1 (STF 1) Tables P001, P006, P008–9 and 2000 Summary File 1 (SF 1) Tables QT-P6 and QT-P9.

Minorities, especially African-Americans, have increasingly made their voice heard since 1964. The growth of their political power, thanks to landmark laws such as the 1964 Civil Rights Act and the 1965 Voting Rights Act, has been translated to enhanced political representation. In the 2004 elections, 42 blacks were elected to the House of Representatives and one, Barack Obama, to the Senate. This is a remarkable progress, giving blacks 9.7 percent of the total 435 members, although it is still below their 12.9% share of the population.

With the growing sizes of minorities and their increasing political representation at all levels of American government, the question is whether minorities can determine who will win the major elections? Are minorities even today's political battleground? It is certainly not correct to suggest that politicians do not pay attention to race when they design their campaign strategies. They do. In fact, right after the 2000 presidential election, Karl Rove, the top political strategy to President Bush, told the President that if he did not improve his 2000 minority vote (when he gained 9 percent from blacks and 35 percent from Hispanics), he would probably lose his re-election bid (Brown, 2005).

In June, 2001 President Bush, to solve a longstanding controversy among Puerto Ricans, ended military-training exercise on Vieques, a Puerto Rican island. Many believed that this step and Bush's proposal to introduce a new immigration policy for undocumented immigrants that would enable them to obtain temporary visas for stays of limited duration were designed to attract Hispanic votes. However, after President Bush introduced his proposals, politicians from his own political party, such as Dana Rohrabacher of California, launched a strong attack on him in the media. Eventually, the Republican's 2004 campaign decided to drop these issues. In the Republican national convention, Bush did not mention any policy proposals related to immigration or racial issues.

At the same time the Democratic Party does not want to draw too much attention to racial issues. As explained above, for the Democratic candidates, the main problem is how to attract more white votes, especially the votes of white men. Thus, the 2004 Democratic national convention featured John Kerry as a strong figure, a war hero in a way designed to appeal to white males. For sure, winning is the priority for the Democrats who lost control in all three branches of federal government.

Deracialization in American politics

The strategy that these politicians use to minimize the effect of race and focus on other issues in their campaigns is called "deracialization" in the political science literature. More specifically, deracialization is used when candidates try to:

- defuse the polarizing effects of race by avoiding explicit reference to race-specific issues while using racial symbolic black and Latino faces in their literature or advertisements;
- emphasize those issues that are perceived as racially transcendent;
- mobilize a broad segment of the electorate for purposes of capturing or maintaining public office (McCormick and Jones 1993).

Why do politicians want to adopt a strategy of deracialization? From the perspectives of politicians, it is imperative to analyze the strengths and weakness of all voting groups. To win an election, there are at least four elements candidates need to evaluate in relation to any given minority group: its size, its homogeneity, its distribution and its turnout level.

In terms of the sizes, Hispanics and blacks are more powerful than Asian-Americans, but none of these groups is big enough to guarantee a major party's success at the national, or even a state level. Blacks are the most homogeneous group among the minorities, thus the most powerful one. But their strongest regional location is in the South where Republicans are very strong among whites.

Hispanics are much less homogenous than blacks. There are mainly three groups that tend to live in the Southwest, Florida, and Northeast. Cuban Americans most likely live in Florida, and have supported Republican candidates. Mexican Americans are more loyal to the Democrats in the Southwest states such as New Mexico, but they may vote for GOP too, as occurred in Texas where they have supported Bush. Puerto Ricans, concentrated in New York, are more likely to support the Democrats. It should also be noted that blacks and Hispanics have supported the Democratic Party in those states with very big urban centers like California and New York.

Asian-Americans are only 3.6 percent of the US population. One limitation on their political power is that they are not homogeneous. There are many ethnic groups, such as Chinese, Japanese, Koreans, Indians, Pakistanis and Filipinos, and they are very different from each other culturally and politically. Another limitation is that they spread out among the states, and thus cannot form a big force in any states, except Hawaii and California.

No matter how large a group is in the population, its political power can only be realized when its members vote. Table 9.10 shows the reported turnout data in congressional and presidential elections from 1964 to 2000. Whites participate at the highest rate. They also have the largest numbers. In 2000 white non-Hispanics cast 83.8 percent of the votes and 84.2 percent in the 2002 election. In comparison, in a typical national election only

Table 9.10 *United States voting and registration in presidential elections by race and ethnicity, 1964–2000*

	Year	White	White Non-Hispanic	Black	Asian	Hispanic
			% of voting age who reported voting			
	1964	70.7		58.5		
	1968	69.1		57.6		
	1972	64.5		52.1		37.5
	1976	60.9		48.7		31.8
	1980	60.9	62.8	50.5		29.9
	1984	61.4	63.3	55.8		32.6
	1988	59.1	61.8	51.5		28.8
	1992	63.6	66.9	54.0	27.3	28.9
	1996	56.0	59.6	50.6	25.7	26.7
	2000	56.4	60.4	53.5	25.4	27.5
2000 Population proportion			78	12	3	7
% of all 2000 votes cast by group			83.8	11.4	1.4	3.4

Source: Authors' calculations from Amie Jamieson, Hyon B. Shin and Jennifer Day, "Voting and Registration in the Election of November 2000," Current Population Reports P20–542, US Census Bureau, Washington, DC, February 2002, p. 12.

11 percent of the votes were from blacks, 7 or 8 percent Hispanic, and about 1 percent Asian.

Given the limitations on the political power of minorities, it is "rational" for politicians to focus on the white majority, and to use deracialization strategy. More importantly, the deracialization strategy has been used not only in presidential elections, but also in many state and local elections where race is still one of the most dividing issues. The deracialization strategy has even been used by the new generation of African-American politicians. For example, one can see the increasing use of deracialization strategy in Memphis, a city that had been deeply divided along racial lines until 1991 when Dr Willie Herenton was elected as the first black mayor. Memphis was a black majority city, but black candidates had failed to attract white voters' support to win the mayoral office. In fact, in 1991 Herenton ran a very racialized campaign and won by 142 votes. He received more than 95 percent of the black votes, but less than 10 percent of whites.

What is intriguing is the change in Herenton's campaign and leadership style after his election when he became very popular among white voters. As a result he was re-elected three times largely because of white, instead of black, support, prompting black leaders such as Congressman Harold Ford to accuse him of being a black mayor for white interests. To defend his campaign and governing strategy, Herenton argued:

> I demonstrated that I had the ability to include the white members of this community to my administration...There were some blacks who thought that once they elected a black mayor, he could give everybody a job, regardless of their qualifications. I couldn't do that. I tried to select the most qualified people because I wanted people who had skills and knowledge. For some blacks, I wasn't black enough. (Dr. W.W. Herenton, authors' interview, July 17, 2003)

Indeed, American politics has entered into a new stage. Politicians at both national and local levels emphasize issues like jobs, the economy and foreign policy, not racial issues. Increasingly, race-based public policies have met challenges in the federal government and the fights of public opinions, especially among white population. For example, in 2003 a major test of affirmative action policies in college admissions ended with a 5–4 split decision from the Supreme Court. While the court upheld the individualized race-conscious admission policies of the University of Michigan's law school, in her pivotal opinion, Justice Sandra Day O'Connor called for racial preferences to end in 25 years.

The use of race in redistricting to create majority-minority districts has also been limited by recent Supreme Court decisions in *Shaw v. Reno* (1993), *Miller v. Johnson* (1995), and *Georgia v. Ashcroft* (2003). With respect to educational policy, mandatory busing has never been very popular in white majority areas. Furthermore, as Kennth Jost put it, "Whatever has or has not been accomplished in the past, the nation's changing demographics appear to be combining with law and educational policy to push ethnic and racial mixing to the side in favor of an increased emphasis on academic performance" (Jost, 2005: 194).

To understand the importance of deracialization in US public policy, as analyzed above, it is essential to examine the relationship between race and elections. Deracialization has been and will be a campaign strategy used by white as well as minority candidates to maximize their chance of electoral success. These politicians win elections based upon new coalitions which are very different from those we saw during the civil-rights era. In this context it is increasingly likely that minorities will have to struggle to get their concerns on America's political agenda and to find a coherent voice in the battle for equality.

Chapter 10

The Media

Robert Mason

A common observation about US politics at the start of the twentieth-first century involves the bitterness of the partisan conflict between the "red" Americans who support the Republicans and the "blue" Americans who support the Democrats. Some surveys indicate that differences among ordinary Americans are probably less stark than the concept of "red" and "blue" America implies, and some analysts argue that policy differences between many leading Republicans and their Democratic counterparts are less significant than their political rhetoric suggests. But the nation's news media do not foster the reconciliation of this apparent difference, instead often reflecting and even exacerbating conflict. Within this context of sharp political conflict, in recent years an old debate about media bias has received fresh attention, and both conservatives and liberals believe that they detect a partisan or ideological agenda within the output of supposedly nonpartisan and nonideological news organizations. At the same time, technological change has facilitated the development of new news sources – notably cable television and the Internet – that reduce the audience of older news sources such as newspapers and terrestrial television. As Americans face a fragmented and diverse media marketplace, evidence suggests that overall news consumption is in decline, especially among younger people. In search of an audience, the new news sources sometimes emulate the aspiration for objectivity of the old, but they also sometimes adopt a self-consciously subjective news agenda. This is especially true of weblogs, but according to its critics, Fox News, a cable news channel, has such an agenda, too. This chapter examines the arguments surrounding these recent developments within the American media and their implications for politics.

Bias

Scholars have generally concluded that mainstream reporting in television and newspapers has been free from political bias. Articles that advocate a particular viewpoint have been restricted to clearly labeled editorial and "op-ed" pages of newspapers and to opinion magazines of relatively small circulation, such as *The Nation, National Review* and *The New Republic*. According to surveys, most journalists are liberals and supportive of the Democratic party, but their profession's commitment to objectivity generally transcends any personal political agenda. A recent example suggests that liberals outnumber conservatives by five to one at larger organizations and by three to one in local news operations. Most media owners, by contrast, tend to be conservatives and supportive of the Republicans, but their concern to serve the public causes them on the whole to downplay political concerns for business as well as professional reasons. These analyses suggest that any bias among journalists is not of a partisan nature. Bartholomew Sparrow, for example, argues instead that professional reliance on established sources of news and on widely accepted experts about a particular topic creates a proclivity to ignore outsiders' testimony and stories that emerge from unconventional authorities (Sparrow, 1999). Many Americans continue to believe that journalism about politics is guilty of bias of a more conventionally partisan kind, however. During the 2004 campaign, for example, substantial numbers of Americans believed that news coverage of the candidates was unfair. In the case of Bush coverage, 37 percent thought it unfair, while the figure was 27 percent in Kerry's case (Pew Research Center, 2004). In another 2004 survey, 85 percent of respondents said that they detected media bias; of these, 48 percent considered it liberal, compared with 30 percent who saw conservative bias. Nevertheless, more than three-fifths said they generally found American journalism "credible." "Journalism may be slanted, but it's the best way to get the news," said one respondent. "If you take away journalism, you'd want it back with whatever flaws it has" (Missouri School of Journalism, 2005). The perception of bias is perhaps reinforced by the work of media watchdog organizations, such as the left-leaning Fairness and Accuracy in Reporting (FAIR) and the right-leaning Media Research Center, which carefully monitor reporters' treatment of politics.

Conservatives in particular have long harbored suspicions that bias existed among journalists who claimed to embrace objectivity as their professional goal. Richard Viguerie and David Franke, long-time activists on the right, claim that conservatives found it necessary to construct and to use alternative media in order to promote their message because of this bias. As the modern conservative movement started to coalesce during the 1950s and 1960s, mainstream journalists failed to take its ideas seriously, according to Viguerie and Franke. To disseminate their critique of liberal politics, they created alternative outlets, beginning with *National Review* during the 1950s. Viguerie himself was a pioneer of direct-mail campaigns in order to reach conservatives directly, and he helped a variety of interest groups to mobilize the "New Right" during the 1970s with this technique. The rise of talk radio during the 1990s, greatly dominated by conservative hosts, provided a platform for the Republican resurgence in that decade. (Talk radio remains a mostly conservative medium, and most popular in 2005 were the stridently populist right-wingers Rush Limbaugh and Sean Hannity. But Air America radio, launched in 2004, seeks to create a successful liberal alternative with shows featuring, among others, comedian and author Al Franken and actor Janeane Garofalo.) At the start of the twenty-first century, the diversity of media outlets that provide opportunities for the expression and discussion of conservative views means "that there is no conservative media monopoly today, the way that there truly was a liberal media monopoly in the 1950s and '60s," write Viguerie and Franke. "What we have today is just more of a level playing field" (Viguerie and Franke, 2004: 3).

Not all are satisfied with such a conclusion. A widely read book helped to reignite the decades-old debate about bias. *Bias* by Bernard Goldberg, a former television news correspondent, argues that liberal bias plagues the broadcast media. According to Goldberg, the liberalism of most journalists influences the selection of issues and stories to cover, the manner of their treatment on air, and the characterization of conservative ideas and concerns, even though his perspective acknowledges the lack of any concerted effort among journalists to promote liberals. Coverage of homelessness during the 1980s, for example, reflected liberal assumptions about the failings of conservative policy initiatives, and it ignored right-wing interpretations of the problem. He also argues that, as far as depictions on television news are concerned, homelessness "pretty much began the day Ronald Reagan was sworn in as president" and ended with the arrival of Bill Clinton, reflecting the tendency of journalists to present conservative politicians in a more hostile way than liberals (Goldberg, 2003: 78). Goldberg's view attracted some sympathetic support among journalists, though critics called the work excessively anecdotal. Paul Friedman, a former news executive for ABC and NBC, echoed some of Goldberg's criticisms. "I think the traditional broadcast media does have a slightly left-of-center bias," he said, on the grounds that they were more likely to cover "social-agenda stories ... rather than stories about the flag or religion" (Auletta, 2003: 270).

The tendency of the American media to adopt a cosmopolitan and arguably liberal approach to key social issues is a claim that attracts a rare degree of agreement within the generally contentious debate about bias. In arguing that the idea of leftist bias represents a tactic by conservatives to secure more favorable coverage, Eric Alterman nevertheless supports the view that media treatment of topics such as abortion, environmental issues, gay rights, and race is often friendly to liberal perspectives. He draws a contrast with coverage of economic issues, which consistently takes a nonliberal approach, reflecting in part the interests of the media conglomerates that increasingly dominate ownership of the sector. According to Alterman, however, what is politically much more significant is conservative success in "working the refs" over a number of decades. "Much of the public believes a useful, but unsupportable, myth about the [so-called "liberal media"] and the media itself has been cowed by conservatives into repeating their nonsensical nostrums virtually nonstop," he writes (Alterman, 2003: 13). When in 2005 House Majority Leader Tom DeLay (R-TX) faced accusations of ethics violations, he singled out the "legion of Democrat-friendly press" as a reason for his problems. For Alterman, the coverage of the Clinton administration was generally more critical than that of George W. Bush's presidency, and his explanation largely lies in the desire of media outlets to avoid the liberal tag. Further weakening any vestiges of liberal tendencies within the media, according to Alterman, is the greater prominence of conservative voices in both print and broadcast outlets within discussions of current events.

Deregulation has encouraged a trend toward the concentration of media outlets in the hands of a smaller number of large corporations; this is the ownership issue that Alterman sees as a contributory factor in explaining his observation of a nonliberal emphasis in much coverage of economic issues. A significant revision of telecommunications law in 1996 relaxed limits on media ownership, historically justified as a way to promote diversity within the sector. But when in 2003 Michael Powell, chair of the Federal Communications Commission (FCC), the agency that regulates the nation's airwaves, announced a further planned relaxation, he faced criticism from both liberals and conservatives, all concerned about its implications for the American media (Beckerman, 2003). Justified as part of the Bush administration's deregulatory agenda and as a response to the arrival of new technologies, the proposal was described by former FCC chair Reed Hundt as an effort to consolidate the political right's friendship with large media companies (Hickey, 2003). Especially controversial was a proposal to allow networks to own television stations covering 45 percent of the national audience, in place of the former maximum of 35 percent; Congress fixed the proportion in law at 39 percent in early 2004. Opponents successfully challenged the FCC in the courts over other proposals, such as those allowing a single company to own multiple media outlets in the same city, and in early 2005 the administration decided not to appeal the matter to the Supreme Court.

The bias debate also won fresh impetus because of controversy surrounding a new news organization. The Fox News Channel, founded in 1996 by Rupert Murdoch's News Corporation, harnessed suspicions about political bias in pursuit of commercial success. Its slogans emphasized the point. Promising "fair and balanced" coverage, the channel affirmed, "We report, you decide." But it gained its own critics who claimed that Fox News, rather than its rivals, was responsible for introducing bias to television news. Expectations of Fox News were low on its arrival as a competitor in cable news with the well-established CNN and another new operation, MSNBC. But in the aftermath of the 9/11 attacks and with the start of the "war on terror," Fox News secured notable ratings success that overshadowed its rivals. Analysts identified the patriotic emphasis of its news coverage as important in accounting for this success; the output of Fox News featured the American flag in the screen's corner, and its journalists straightforwardly identified themselves with their nation's cause. During the early months of the war, one television critic called it "a smart bomb of a channel that speaks, alone among American TV news outlets, to those who want their news to resemble a Washington shout show and to include open sneering at ... the *New York Times*, Europe, Turkey, the United Nations and, of course, the former and current military men who were questioning the US battle plan and the media who reported on such questions" (Johnson, 2003). In response to such criticisms of the channel's objectivity, Shepard Smith of Fox News observed, "[The vast majority of Americans] understand that we can be credible journalists, fair and balanced about everything that we do, and still be on our side" (Collins, 2004: 213). Whether bias exists at Fox News or other news organizations, or whether there is merely a perception of bias, viewers of different political stripes are choosing to watch different cable news channels. According to a Pew survey during the campaign, 70 percent of voters for whom Fox News was the main source of election news intended to vote for George W. Bush, while 67 percent of those who turned to CNN for most political information preferred John Kerry (Pew, 2004).

Film

Film has a fresh and direct relevance as a medium of political communication. It is a medium that is openly and avowedly subjective; the role in politics of film is not, therefore, an example of bias but instead of a fresh battleground for political ideas, one that casts aside objectivity in favor of advocacy. Most notable is *Fahrenheit 9/11* (2004) by director Michael Moore, which presents a harshly critical interpretation of George W. Bush's response to the 2001 attacks and his foreign policy. The film achieved a large audience at cinemas in the United States and elsewhere, and a speedy DVD release and a debut on cable television just days before the November elections sought to maximize its impact. The nature of its impact is open to question. Michael Moore aimed to boost antiwar sentiment, but his critics argued that the film deepened the convictions of Bush opponents rather than making converts.

A cluster of films, all released in 2004, emulated *Fahrenheit 9/11*'s engagement with current politics, even while they did not achieve the same degree of commercial success. On the left, *Bush's Brain* is a critical evaluation of political strategist Karl Rove and *Going Upriver: The Long War of John Kerry* offers favorable coverage of Kerry's Vietnam service. On the right, *Stolen Honor* attacked Kerry's war record, while *Michael Moore Hates America* attacked *Fahrenheit 9/11* and its techniques. The cinematic release of these documentaries was limited, while still other political films were mostly reserved for DVD release, such as Robert Greenwald's *Outfoxed*, which charges that the Fox News Channel deploys an array of surreptitious techniques to promote a conservative agenda. On its release in July 2004, the Internet-based organization MoveOn.org, which helped to finance the documentary, worked with other liberal groups to organize about 3,500 house parties to show the film.

Judged by its political contributions, the television, film and music industry is almost as supportive of Democrats as the oil and gas industry is of Republicans. According to the nonprofit and nonpartisan Center for Responsive Politics, the industry made political contributions totaling more than $32 million, and 69 percent of this money went to the Democratic cause; of this number, the film production industry contributed $8.3 million, of which 86 percent went in support of Democrats. By comparison, the figure for the oil and gas industry was $25.5 million, 80 percent of which went to Republicans. Although the most prominent member of the industry in politics, Arnold Schwarzenegger, won the California governorship as a Republican in 2003, much of Hollywood instead is associated with the Democratic party. The implications of the entertainment industry's connection with the Democrats are less clear. Some believe that the industry's product is often culturally liberal, and conservatives criticize the Democratic party for its association with a cultural elite whose values are out of step with those of many Americans. Others believe that the commercial imperative ensures that Hollywood does not usually promote liberalism in this way.

The Internet

The Internet has achieved maturity both as a news medium and as a tool for political mobilization. According to a Pew survey, in 2004, 29 percent of Americans read on-line news at least three times weekly, as opposed to 42 percent who regularly read a newspaper and 34 percent who regularly watch nightly network news on television. It is especially popular among

Table 10.1   *Most important source of news for young Americans (between 18 and 34)*

	%
Local television newscasts	31
The Internet	25
Newspapers	14
Cable television general news programmes	9
National network television newscasts	7

Question: Which source is most important for learning about news in your daily life?

Source: Carnegie Corporation of New York, May 2004.

younger Americans. As Table 10.1 shows, a 2004 Carnegie survey revealed that the Internet was the most important source of news for a quarter of Americans between the ages of 18 and 34. It found a significant gender difference; the figure was as high as 31 percent among men, while women were more likely to turn to local television news.

The Internet provides an alternative and increasingly popular mode of content dissemination for existing news organizations. Among the more visited news sites are those of newspapers, such as *The New York Times* and the *Washington Post,* and those of television news organizations, such as ABC News and CNN. The news sites of Internet companies such as Yahoo and Google are also successful. MSNBC, launched in 1996 as a joint venture between Microsoft and the television network NBC, explicitly sought to create cross-media synergy between its website and its cable channel. The Internet also offers a platform for the development of a more partisan approach to the delivery of news, in sharp contrast to the nonpartisan intent of newspapers and television news in recent American history. NewsMax.com and WorldNetDaily are websites that provide overviews of the news from a conservative perspective, and in 2005 both numbered among the ten most-visited sites about politics.

A new source that provides information about and interpretation of political developments are weblogs, or blogs. By early 2005, according to Pew polls, there were 4 million active blogs and 32 million Americans who regularly read them. Among these blogs are those that offer political comment and feature political debate, and a few have achieved a large audience. "Daily Kos," by Markos Moulitsas Zuniga, achieved around 200,000 hits each day during 2004. A signal of their importance was the decision of the Republican and Democratic parties in 2004 to provide bloggers with official credentials to cover the national conventions –

about 20 when the Republicans gathered in New York and about 30 when the Democrats met in Boston. But their current importance should not be overstated. After the 2004 election, no more than about one in ten Internet users said they had read political blogs "frequently" or "sometimes" during the campaign.

Bloggers have achieved some influence thanks to prominent cases where blogs shaped the news agenda. When in 2002 Trent Lott (R-MS) made comments in praise of Strom Thurmond's racist 1948 third-party candidacy for the presidency, a blogger's investigation of Lott's record on race helped to create the conditions under which Lott stepped down as Senate majority leader. During the 2004 presidential campaign, some bloggers questioned the authenticity of documents used as part of a critical report on CBS's *60 Minutes Wednesday* about George W. Bush's military service, forcing CBS News to admit errors.

Political organizations and politicians are eager to harness the power of the Internet. As a medium free from the mediation of journalists, the Internet provides them with a rare opportunity to communicate directly with voters through their own websites. One response by candidates to this opportunity is to include commercials – free from the regulations governing television ads – that visitors are able to download; campaigns hope that the news media report their content, providing free coverage of their claims. They also seek to mobilize a virtual community of activists on line and to raise funds. The Internet is not only offering established organizations with another way to reach out to supporters, but it is also providing a platform for the creation of new groups. MoveOn.org, created in September 1998 with an on-line petition to "Censure President Clinton [over the Monica Lewinsky scandal] and Move On to Pressing Issues Facing the Nation," campaigned in 2000 against Republicans for their support of impeachment, raising more than $2 million. By 2004, MoveOn.org claimed a membership of more than two million, who participate in "electronic advocacy groups" on a range of issues. Meetup.com, founded in 2002, allows people to find others with similar interests, involving a large array of topics, in their area. The site is not explicitly political, but in 2003 and 2004 like-minded activists coalesced there in support of various candidates.

The Internet was especially significant to the candidacy of Howard Dean for the presidential nomination of the Democratic party. Meet-up.com provided a starting-point for supporters of this dark-horse candidate to gather and to begin work for his candidacy. The Dean campaign emphasized the importance of active participation in voter mobilization by large numbers of volunteers, and it made innovative use of the Internet in recruiting these volunteers and in raising money to fund the effort, reaching a record-setting sum of $15 million in one quarter.

Together with his appeal as an early and outspoken critic of the war in Iraq, it briefly helped to elevate Dean to the front ranks of the party's contenders, though Dean soon suffered a decline, leading to his withdrawal from the race, after disappointing results in the Iowa caucuses. Joe Trippi, who managed it, claims that the Dean campaign was "the opening salvo in a revolution, the sound of hundreds of thousands of Americans turning off their televisions and embracing the only form of technology that has allowed them to be involved again, to gain control of a process that alienated them decades ago" (Trippi, 2004: xviii–xix). Some critics charged that the enthusiastic commitments of the volunteers did not equip Dean well to secure a broad-based coalition of voters, because the out-of-state, orange-hatted "Deaniacs" were not successful advocates of their candidate in rural Iowa. But in his book about the campaign and about the Internet as a political tool Trippi finds no connection between the Web-based nature of the Dean effort and its failure, as opposed to its successes.

Some bloggers were successful in raising funds for candidates. In 2004 Zuniga's DailyKos.com, for example, advocated support of the "Kos Dozen," a group of Democrats, providing web links to campaign sites. Its appeal for financial assistance for candidates secured more than $574,000. Activity of this kind potentially creates conflicts between blogs as a new form of news media that requires First Amendment protections and blogs as a type of campaign advocacy that is subject to government regulation. In 2004 Reps. Christopher Shays (R-CT) and Martin Meehan (D-MA), House cosponsors of the 2002 Bipartisan Campaign Reform Act, sued the Federal Election Commission over its implementation of the legislation, which viewed generously certain exemptions for on-line activity. Their lawsuit was an early act in what promises to be a long-running controversy about the appropriate regulation for bloggers when they turn from news comment and interpretation to political advocacy and activism.

Political commercials

Political commercials on television are a controversial form of communication between politicians and voters. Observers see commercials as contributing to the trivialization of political debate, because they encourage politicians to oversimplify complicated issues and arguments. At the same time, because many commercials involve attacks, often of an aggressive nature, on an opposing politician or perspective, they seem to foster public cynicism about the political process. Moreover, the cost of television commercials helps to ensure that raising money is especially important in American politics. This money is a significant source of income for television stations during election years, and some critics see these ads' lucrative nature as an encouragement for station owners and managers to avoid any real increase in on-air political coverage, which might diminish the need for so much investment by the candidates in commercials. There are, in any case, formidable obstacles to any wholesale reform of the system. First, prevailing interpretations of the speech freedoms that the First Amendment protects suggest that the Constitution permits relatively little regulation of political communication. Second, politicians are in general unlikely to oppose a system that facilitated their election to Congress and that usually seems to provide advantages to incumbents as opposed to challengers, especially because they tend to experience fewer difficulties in raising the large sums of money necessary for television advertising.

Despite the significance of these obstacles to change, in 2002 Congress passed landmark legislation, the Bipartisan Campaign Reform Act, which among other provisions subjects to new controls television advertisements by political candidates. The most noticeable feature of the reformed regime is the inclusion in commercials of a line, spoken by the candidate, confirming their approval of the content. Among the more persistent criticisms of the old system involved the candidates' ability to distance themselves from the attacks orchestrated by their own campaign apparatus and therefore from the public's disapproval of negative politics; the new formula seeks to ensure that a candidate takes direct responsibility for the contents of an ad.

The legislation also placed new restrictions on "issue ads" during an election campaign. Before the act, political parties, businesses, unions, advocacy organizations, and others were able to escape the limitations of existing election law on campaign fundraising and spending when they aired legislative issue advertisements, which mentioned a candidate only indirectly and were not officially connected with a candidate's campaign. Although the act toughened the definition of what permissibly constituted a genuine issue ad, distinctive from a candidate ad, the new regime created by the legislation allowed unregulated activity by 527 groups, a name that refers to the relevant section of the tax code. The 527 groups are supportive of a candidate but unconnected with a candidate's official campaign; in fact, in 2004 there were clear connections between the parties and 527 groups, but the Federal Election Commission ruled that they were outside the range of the new law's regulation. During the 2004 presidential campaign, the 527 organizations were responsible for raising more than $350 million and for televising some of most aggressive commercials. Most prominent among them was the Swift Boat Veterans and POWs for Truth, which ran a series of harshly worded ads that questioned John Kerry's conduct during his military service in Vietnam. Kerry himself identified these commercials as successful in undermining his campaign, especially because he was slow to respond to the attacks. But overall there was more 527 activity in support of his party than the Republicans; 527 groups favorable to Democrats, such as America Coming Together and the MoveOn.org Voter Fund, raised twice as much money as their rivals, and this money funded attacks on Bush and voter-mobilization efforts. Among other advocates of 527 control, Senator John McCain (R-AZ), who cosponsored the 2002 act, argues in favor of further regulation as the next step of campaign reform; during the campaign George Bush spoke in opposition to their use.

Public information

Many analysts of the relationship between the media and politics in the United States have voiced concerns about the implications of long-term trends toward the trivialization of news content. According to this perspective, commercial pressures have encouraged the reduction of serious attention to political developments, and in time this inattention poses a threat to the maintenance of an adequately informed citizenry. According to Robert Entman, there is no straightforward way to reverse these trends within the media marketplace. "[N]ews organizations have to respond to public tastes," he writes. "They cannot stay in business if they produce a diverse assortment of richly textured ideas and information that nobody sees. To become informed and to hold government accountable, the general public needs to obtain news that is comprehensive yet interesting and understandable, that conveys facts and outcomes, not cosmetic images and airy promises. But that is not what the public demands" (Entman, 1989: 17). Table 10.2 suggests that overall interest in news is in decline, though it does not reflect the growth of the Internet as a news source. Scholars have expressed concern about the nature as well as the amount of political news that most citizens consume. Thomas Patterson notes that, since the 1960s and 1970s, journalists have increasingly taken an analytical rather than descriptive approach to their reports on politics. This analytical emphasis often involves scrutiny of political actors' strategic goals, rather than a straightforward account of their public statements. This scrutiny in turn has fostered among the electorate disillusionment with and disengagement from the political system (Patterson, 1993). The theory secures support among politicians as well as academics. Karl Rove, Bush's political strategist, echoed these insights in a 2005 speech, for example. He said that journalists over-emphasize polls and the "horse race" between competing politicians, and they adopt an approach that is "less liberal than it is oppositional."

Table 10.2   *Americans' news consumption*

Did yesterday	Jan. 1994 %	April 1998 %	April 2000 %	April 2002 %	April 2004 %
Watched TV news	72	59	56	55	60
Read newspaper	49	48	47	41	42
Listened to radio news	47	49	43	41	40
Consumed any news	90	85	83	80	82

Source: Data from Pew Research Center for the People and the Press, *Trends 2005*, 44.

"Reporters now see their role less as discovering facts and fair-mindedly reporting the truth and more as being put on the earth to afflict the comfortable, to be a constant thorn of those in power, whether they are Republican or Democrat," he explained. A compelling alternative to those who posit a causal connection between "oppositional" journalism and public cynicism is Pippa Norris's. Her comparative work suggests that those who consume more news tend to be less disaffected with politics than those who consume less (Norris, 2000).

The attacks on the United States and the launch of "the war on terror" posed a challenge to the long-term trivialization of the news media. The developments invited a return to more substantial coverage of domestic politics and international news. But the evidence suggests that there was at most a minor increase in news interest among the public except during the immediate aftermath of the 9/11 attacks and during the opening months of the Iraq war. The increase in media outlets' political and foreign coverage was similarly short-lived. While interest remains in the specific topics of terror and Iraq, coverage of world affairs remains thin. A book by Tom Fenton, a veteran television reporter who specialized in foreign affairs, argues that the news media do not equip Americans with the information they need about the wider world. Fenton notes, for example, that despite a realization among journalists about China's global importance, during the first ten months of 2004 the *CBS Evening News* ran a total of four reports about China – one about a fake edition of Bill Clinton's autobiography, one about stem-cell research, and two about pandas (Fenton, 2005: 144).

A series of University of Maryland polls, conducted during the campaign season, suggested that misperceptions about the Iraq war were common. Among respondents, almost a half believed that there was evidence of links between the Saddam Hussein regime and Al Qaeda, for example. Those who primarily watched Fox News – which was self-consciously attentive to US interests in its coverage – for information were most likely to have such misperceptions. In terms of electoral choices, people with misperceptions about the war were much more likely to be supporters of George W. Bush than John Kerry in 2004; Kerry supporters generally held more accurate beliefs about such issues as the extent of international support for US policy and the nondiscovery of mass-destruction weapons in Iraq. One interpretation of the findings is that most Bush voters were startlingly misinformed about the war and its geopolitical context (PIPA, 2003; 2004). The existence of these differences perhaps reflects their confidence in the administration's foreign policy and their optimism about its likely outcome, however.

News consumption is particularly low among younger Americans. Pew figures suggest that in 2004 Americans between the ages of 18 and 24 spend only 35 minutes daily watching television news, listening to radio news, or reading newspapers, compared with 51 minutes in 1994. By contrast, the figure for Americans between the ages of 35 and 49 fell from 74 minutes in 1994 to 66 minutes in 2004. (The survey did not include Internet news.) According to David Mindich, Americans have an increasingly large array of entertainment options, and among younger people newspapers and broadcast news are failing to secure a sizable audience in competition with these alternatives. "What journalism is facing now is that fewer people understand the importance of being politically informed and more people are judging journalism's entertainment value against that of *Friends*," Mindich observes. "It's a losing proposition" (Mindich, 2005: 48). Mindich argues that the growth in Internet use does not adequately meet the problem of declining audiences for traditional forms of news, because news sites are not the most favored; the overall impact of the Internet is to provide still more entertainment options that are a distraction from the news.

But others are more optimistic about future trends. Rupert Murdoch of News Corporation, for example, identifies enterprising and innovative use of the Internet as a good way to boost news consumption, and challenges Mindich's assumptions about the level of interest in news among younger Americans. "In fact, they want a lot of news," he told a meeting of newspaper editors in 2005, "just faster news of a different kind and delivered in a different way" (Murdoch, 2005). To tackle the problem of declining circulations, especially among young people, newspapers are not only developing an Internet presence. In 2002, the two major Chicago newspapers launched cheaper tabloid versions, featuring shorter news reports and more entertainment pieces, the *Chicago Tribune*'s *RedEye* and the *Chicago Sun-Times*'s *Red Streak*. Other cities have seen similar developments, such as Washington, DC, where there are two free tabloids, the *Washington Post*'s *Express*, established in 2003, and *The Examiner*, which arrived the following year.

The different way to deliver the news frequently involves comedy. About a fifth of Americans between 18 and 34 reported that television comedy shows were an important source of information for them about the 2004 campaign, roughly the same proportion as those who used the Internet for such news. *The Daily Show with Jon Stewart*, shown on cable channel Comedy Central, has gained a larger audience among Americans between 18 and 34 than any of the three network news programmes, ABC's *World News Tonight*, the *CBS Evening News*, and *NBC Nightly News*. According to some critics, *The Daily Show* trivializes news, but its defenders argue that its satire is a healthy aspect of democratic debate and note studies suggesting that it draws an audience well informed about politics.

The Bush administration

An effective relationship with the news media is a priority for all politicians, because their fortunes to a lesser or greater extent depend on the way they communicate their message with the electorate. George W. Bush has won admiration for his administration's success in winning favorable coverage for many of his initiatives, even while its strategies of news management have also attracted criticism. According to many White House correspondents, one element contributing to this success is the President's personality. Alexandra Pelosi's documentary *Journeys with George* (2002) depicts Bush during the 2000 campaign as maintaining a wary distance from reporters but simultaneously developing friendly relations with them.

The discipline of the Bush White House is also important. Senior administration figures have managed to maximize control over the dissemination of its message thanks to an environment where staffers do not speak freely to reporters, where leaks are not tolerated, and where lists of "talking points" ensure that aides understand communication priorities. The goal of a consistent message is much less unusual than the extent of the administration's success in achieving it. One of the first aides to leave the Bush administration, speech-writer David Frum, did so when his wife publicized his authorship of the phrase "the axis of evil," with which Bush described hostile nations. For the White House, this leak represented an ill-disciplined and disloyal action of the kind that undermined the overall communications strategy.

The disinclination of the administration to provide easy access to reporters generated some criticism. During his first term in office, Bush held only 14 news conference, by contrast with Bill Clinton's 44 and

George H. W. Bush's 83. Helen Thomas, a White House reporter for more than 40 years, claims that this example of discipline represents secrecy of a dangerous kind. "The presidential news conference is the only institution in our society where the president can be questioned openly, the only form where he can be held accountable," she has commented. "Otherwise he can rule by edict and live like a king." The administration has made reporters' access even more difficult in cases where it is considered that the coverage by individuals or organizations is unfair. Because the White House considered that a report by CBS's Dan Rather during the 2004 campaign treated Bush's military service in a misleading way, its response was a non-cooperative approach to the CBS journalists. Only when Rather stepped down as *CBS Evening News* anchor in 2005 did the network's White House correspondent discover that administration figures were once again prepared to speak with him. To some, such actions suggest a disrespect for the role of the press in maintaining an informed citizenry and in ensuring the accountability of elected officials. Others argue that the Bush first-term record in securing favorable coverage is simply a successful example of a conventional approach to media relations.

New techniques of political communication

In seeking support for their proposals, politicians look for new ways to do so. Some innovative and unconventional publicity strategies of the Bush administration have garnered controversy as representing forms of government propaganda. First, it emerged in early 2005 that a public relations consultancy working for the Department of Education made payments of $240,000 to Armstrong Williams, a conservative columnist and television host, for his work in support of the No Child Left Behind legislation of 2001. Although two other columnists received payments for similar advocacy work, the practice is an unusual one, and the administration condemned it once uncovered.

Second, the federal government has made increasing use of video news releases that mimic the style and format of television reports. This practice is not new, but its scale has grown; during the first term of the Bush administration, 20 federal agencies were responsible for spending $254 million on such releases, twice as much as during the Clinton administration. Some local stations have screened unedited versions of these releases on subjects such as Medicare reform, Iraq, and farm policy without indicating their origins. The nonpartisan Government Accounting Office suggested that some of the reports amounted to "covert propaganda," but the Department of Justice affirmed that they were not and were thus legal.

George W. Bush emphasized that it is the responsibility of television stations to use video news releases appropriately.

Third, the White House issued press credentials to Jeff Gannon, a reporter for Talon News, an openly partisan website of limited readership, owned by a Texas Republican activist. Some observers thought that Bush and others turned to Gannon in news conferences for sympathetic questions, and that Gannon operated as a political supporter of the administration rather than as a journalist. To critics, Gannon represented another part of a White House strategy to evade press scrutiny and to manipulate coverage. But to others, the creative use of the "blogosphere" did not have sinister implications. "The White House is not waging war on the press any more than the Democratic National Committee or MoveOn.org are," said one journalist. "All these institutions now employ the black arts of public-relations newspeak, factual misrepresentation and take-no-prisoners rhetoric to advance their causes.'

Conclusion

The past decade has been a period of great change for the news media, particularly because of technological innovations. The once-dominant evening news programs on ABC, CBS, and NBC are losing viewers, while a long-term trend of declining newspaper readership continues. Some of this decline is balanced by an increasing audience for cable and on-line news, which is sometimes of a more subjective nature than the output of more traditional media. But there is also evidence that overall consumption of news is in decline, especially among young people. The diversity of news outlets has further boosted the already formidable competitive pressures of the marketplace, and these pressures often discourage editors from substantial coverage of domestic politics and international affairs. For pessimistic observers, it is increasingly difficult to achieve the important normative goal of a well-informed citizenry, even at a time of tumultuous developments for the nation and for the world. For optimistic observers, the new media create new opportunities, and the Internet in particular seems to carry great promise as a medium that might both revitalize debate about politics and expand participation in political activism.

This change has had implications for politicians, who now deal with this array of journalistic outlets across a 24-hour news cycle. Sometimes operating without journalistic experience of any conventional kind, some political bloggers, an unknown phenomenon as recently as the mid-1990s, have enjoyed influence over the news agenda. In some cases, they have also provided support to the efforts of politicians to master the Internet's potential to mobilize activists and to raise funds. Within this new media framework, the Bush administration has achieved some remarkable success in securing effective coverage of its initiatives. In the eyes of some critics, this coverage is too deferential and in part reflects a long-term campaign by conservatives to stigmatize critical reporting as biased. The arguments about the administration's press strategies and about the nature of media bias are a key example of the tense political differences of the Bush years.

Chapter 11

Values, Lifestyles, and Politics

Christopher J. Bailey

A striking feature of contemporary American politics is the salience of lifestyle issues at federal, state, and local level. Concern about homosexuality, reproductive rights, drug taking, smoking, obesity, and even fashion have propelled issues involving lifestyle choices onto the political agenda and opened up complex fissures in the polity. Bitter battle lines and unusual alliances have characterized the politics surrounding these issues as groups have sought to define the boundaries both between the public and private spheres, and among the appropriate remit of different levels of government. Recent debates have seen opponents of big government support an expansion of the public sphere into areas traditionally viewed as private, champions of states' rights act to pre-empt state authority, and the Christian right make occasional common cause with a generally liberal medical establishment to tell people how to live their lives.

Two impulses underpin this growing concern with lifestyle issues. First, demographic and social changes, amplified by the events of 9/11, have reinvigorated debate about what it means to be American (White, 2003; Huntington, 2004; Kaufman, 2004). Growing population diversity, changes in family structures, and challenges to national security have undermined agreement on core values and generated conflict about how Americans should live their lives. At the heart of this conflict is an effort to distinguish the American "us" from the non-American "them" (Morone, 2003). Such battles are not a new phenomenon in America. Persistent religious fervor and frequent social chaos have ensured that battles over belief systems have been an episodic feature of American politics since the Puritan landings. Second, growing affluence, medical advances, and improved knowledge have changed the focus of public health from controlling infectious diseases to regulating risky behavior. Proponents of this "new public health" have argued that promotion of healthy lifestyles is essential to tackle such modern epidemics as heart disease and cancer (Fitzpatrick, 2001: 3). The result is that government and the medical establishment have increasingly sought to tell people what to eat, how to exercise, and what activities to avoid.

A moral dimension is common to both impulses. Efforts to define what it means to be American have an overt moral cast while the promotion of healthy lifestyles places an emphasis on virtuous living. These moral dimensions mean that lifestyle politics has a particular set of characteristics (Mooney, 2001). First, debate is about first principles. At issue are core values not instrumental policy concerns. This means that almost anyone can claim to be well informed about the issue. No technical policy expertise is required, for example, to participate in the controversy over same-sex marriages. Second, the focus on core values means that lifestyle issues resonate strongly with the general public. Issues such as abortion, the death penalty, or smoking are more immediately meaningful to people than complex changes to the tax code that are difficult to interpret on an individual basis. People may not know with any certainty how tax changes will affect their disposable income but they do know whether they are aggravated by cigarette smoke in a restaurant. Third, conflict over first principles and strong resonance among the public generates greater civic engagement with these issues than many other policy concerns. People listen to debates, form opinions, and participate more readily than usual in the policy-making process.

Contested values

The contemporary battle over core values is driven by changes in American society that have stimulated debate about what it means to be American. Demographic changes caused by new patterns of immigration, uneven population growth, and the breakdown of traditional social structures, have kindled a "culture war" in American society (Hunter, 1991). Ranged on one side of the battlefield are those who stress a progressive, multicultural, and largely secular view of what it means to be American. Organizations such as People for the American Way (PFAW) promote a set of values that emphasize "pluralism, individuality, freedom of thought, expression and religion, a sense of community, and tolerance and compassion for others" (PFAW, 2005a). Ranged on the other side of the battlefield are those who stress an absolutist set of values based on religious belief. Organizations such as Citizens for a Better America (CFABA) argue that "America is dying from the inside out as functional values like honor, truthfulness, respect and responsibility for action are cast aside for a valueless society. We believe there is a place for Morality and Values in America" (CFABA, 2005). Each side believes it has the answer to de Crèvecoeur's famous question "What is an American?" (1986 [1782], Letter 3).

Demographic and social changes

Over the last 30 years the population of the United States has grown faster than most other comparable industrialized countries. Between 1970 and 2003 the population of the country increased by 42 percent from 205 million to 291 million (US Census Bureau, 2004: table 2). In comparison the population of Britain increased by 7 percent in the same period (Council of Europe, 2003: T1.1). Both high natural increases and immigration account for this growth in the American population. The rate of natural increase of the population in the United States (a measure of the difference between a country's birth and death rates) has remained higher than virtually all European countries over the last 30 years. The United States' rate of natural increase declined from 0.89 in 1970 to 0.59 in 2000 compared to a fall in Britain's rate of natural increase from 0.45 to 0.12 in the same period. Countries such as Germany, Italy, and Russia have frequently experienced negative rates of natural increase in recent years. Natural increases account for almost three-quarters of the population growth in the United States over the last three decades. Immigration accounts for the remainder of the population growth. Between 1970 and 2002 approximately 23 million legal immigrants entered the United States (US Census Bureau, 2004: table 5). Immigration totals were higher in the 1990s than in any other decade in American history. Estimates of illegal immigration suggest that a further 7 million people were living in the United States in 2000.

New patterns of immigration and variation in birth rates between ethnic and racial groups means that this population growth has transformed the composition of the American population. Over the last two decades the number of immigrants arriving from former Soviet bloc and developing countries has increased considerably (US Census Bureau, 2004: table 8). Between 1980 and 2000 the United States admitted more people from Mexico than any other country, while the number of immigrants from countries such as China, India, the Philippines, and Vietnam exceeded the numbers from Western Europe as a whole. The increased population diversity resulting from this pattern of immigration has been reinforced by differential birth rates between the various racial and ethnic groups in the United States. Between 1990 and 2002 the number of births to women of Asian or Hispanic origin rose while the number of births to women of white or African-American origin fell (US Census Bureau, 2004: table 71). In 2002 there were 8.8 million children born to Hispanic women compared to 5.9 million born to African-American women. The number of white births fell from 32.9 million in 1990 to 31.7 million in 2002.

Immigration and differential birth rates have produced a less white, less black, less homogenous, less Christian, and more foreign population over the last three decades. Although whites still constitute a majority, Hispanics have overtaken African-Americans as the second largest racial or ethnic group. In 2003 Hispanics constituted approximately 14 percent of the population while African-Americans made up just under 13 percent. To take account of the growing heterogeneity of the population the US Census Bureau provided Americans with 19 racial categories to choose from in the 2000 census. The influx of immigrants from Africa and Asia over the last three decades has also altered the religious complexion of the United States. Between 1990 and 2001 the number of Americans identifying themselves as Muslims or Buddhists doubled while the number of Hindus more than trebled (US Census Bureau, 2004: table 67). In 2001 there were just over 1.1 million Muslims, just under 1.1 million Buddhists, and 766,000 Hindus in the United States. Large-scale immigration has also increased the number of foreign-born Americans. In 2000 11.1 percent of the American population was foreign-born compared with 6.2 percent in 1980 (US Census Bureau 2004: table 42). Unequal settlement patterns means that the foreign-born population of the individual states varies considerably. While 26.2 percent of Californians and 20.4 percent of New Yorkers were born overseas, a mere 1.8 percent of Montanans and South Dakotans and just 1.1 percent of West Virginians were foreign-born.

A consequence of these population changes has been the undermining of traditional notions of the American "us" and the non-American "them." Stereotypical white, Protestant, English-speaking America still exists, but so does a Hispanic, Catholic, Spanish-speaking America, a North African, Muslim, Arabic-speaking America, and an Asian, Buddhist, Chinese-speaking America. Compounding this identity crisis has been a number of social changes. Between 1990 and 2003 the number of Americans who had never married increased from 40.4 million to 51.9 million while the number who had divorced rose from 15.1 million to 21.6 million (US Census Bureau, 2004: table 51). According to some estimates the divorce rate in the United States reached 50 percent by the start of the twenty-first century (ADR, 2005). During the same period there was a 17 percent increase in the number of births to unmarried white mothers as the stigma of illegitimacy declined. The net effect of these social changes has been to undermine traditional family structures (US Census Bureau, 2004: table 56). In 2003 married couples constituted just under 52 percent of American households. A wide variety of household forms made up the remainder. Just over a quarter of American adults lived alone, about 18.2 percent in one-parent family groups, approximately 5 percent cohabited with a partner of the opposite sex, while just under 1 percent cohabited with a partner of the same sex. By the start of the twenty-first century the traditional two-parent family that had been central to American cultural values was in decline.

The demographic and social changes that have occurred in the United States have stimulated a debate about what it means to be American. Huntington (2004: 9) summarizes the central questions of this debate as follows: "Are we a "we," one people or several? If we are a "we," what distinguishes us from the "thems" who are not us? Race, religion, ethnicity, values, culture, wealth, politics, or what?" To some the answer to these questions lies in a vision of a multicultural America that tolerates diversity. The American "we" is defined by a commitment to individual rights and self-fulfillment. To others the answer lies in a vision of a Christian America that promotes a set of absolute moral truths. The American "we" is defined by a commitment to traditional values. Both sides in this debate seek to portray the other as radical and "un-American" (Nolan, 1996: 162–4). Advocates of diversity typically use language such as "hate-mongers" or "Nazis" to describe their opponents while proponents of traditional values use phrases such as "immoral" or "godless." Nuanced arguments count for little in what James Dobson, head of Focus on the Family, has described as "a civil war of values and the prize to the victor is the next generation" (quoted in Hunter, 1991: 64).

This debate over what it means to be American is not simply an arcane rhetorical battle over the meaning of the words in texts such as the Declaration of Independence, but informs policy-making across a range of issues. A contest over core values is evident in contemporary debates about immigration, education, pornography, funding for the arts, affirmative action, the death penalty, gun control, and foreign policy. The contest is most intense, however, in debates over sexual issues such as homosexuality and reproductive rights. Not only is the moral divide over these issues stark, but they also impinge directly upon how people live their lives. Sexual issues generate conflict over different visions of what constitutes appropriate behavior for Americans.

The politics of sexual behavior

The contest over core values is intense in debates about sexual behavior. Issues such as homosexuality, abortion, adultery, divorce, and childbirth outside marriage raise profound questions about the nature of families, gender roles, and the sanctity of life that accentuate a deep moral divide among Americans. Progressives argue that individuals should make their own decisions about these matters and that government has no role intruding into bedrooms. Women's rights groups such as the National Organization of Women (NOW), gay rights groups, and progressive organizations such as People for the American Way (PFAW) promote a vision of America that tolerates different lifestyles and accepts non-traditional family structures. Traditionalists counter that sexual liberation has undermined families, promoted hedonism, and ushered in an era of immorality. Organizations such as Focus on the Family, the Family Research Council, and the Traditional Values Coalition argue that government has a duty to regulate sexual behavior in order to protect society, families, and children. Based on different moral perspectives these two positions are non-negotiable and produce a politics characterized by vitriolic exchanges and occasional violence.

The structure of contemporary sexual politics dates from the US Supreme Court's 1973 decision in *Roe* v. *Wade* that women have a constitutional right to abortion in the first trimester of a pregnancy (Saletan, 2004; Critchlow, 2001). Predicated upon a woman's right to privacy the court's decision confirmed the progressive position that the state has no right interfering in private affairs. Largely welcomed by feminists, who argued that birth control was essential to gender equality, the case provoked a passionate response that still reverberates. Not only did the case prompt the mobilization of various pro-life groups, but opponents of the permissiveness of the 1960s also used the decision to portray "the culture of easy sexuality" as "a cult of mass murder" (Morone, 2003: 488). The case offered traditionalists an opportunity both to create an institutional structure to promote their goals, and also to infuse concern about changing family structures and gender roles with a powerful moral message that could be applied to issues such as homosexuality and divorce. As Peele (1984: 94) notes: "The abortion question ... reminded American politicians and the electorate of the recurrent power of moral questions in American politics."

Abortion remains a central issue in sexual politics. Efforts to overturn *Roe* v. *Wade*, enact legislation to ban "partial-birth" abortions, and prohibit federal funding for abortions both in the United States and overseas, have been a constant of American politics over the last 30 years. Judicial rulings have restricted the availability of abortions with rulings on the need for spousal consent and parental approval for minors, but in *Planned Parenthood* v. *Casey* in 1991 the Supreme Court took the important step of affirming the precedent established by *Roe*. Legislation has also restricted the availability of some forms of abortion. Congress passed measures banning "partial-birth" abortions twice during the 1990s but President Clinton vetoed both measures. Legislation was finally enacted in 2003 when President Bush signed the Partial-Birth Abortion Act. Bush described the law as "very important legislation that will end an abhorrent practice and continue to build a culture of life in America" (Bush, 2003). The law was declared unconstitutional by US District Courts in California, New York, and Nebraska in 2004 because it lacked provisions to preserve women's health. The US Supreme Court in *Stenberg* v. *Carhert* had previously struck down a similar Nebraska law on these grounds in 2000. In 2001 President Bush reinstated a ban on federal funding for overseas organizations that advocated abortions as a method of population control, and in 2002 approved final regulations making fetuses but not pregnant women eligible for health care coverage under the State Children's Health Insurance Program (SCHIP). Legislation prohibiting the use of federal funds for abortion has been renewed every year since the passage of the Hyde Amendment in 1976.

Homosexuality has emerged as a further touchstone issue in contemporary sexual politics (Rimmerman, 2002). The spark that ignited debate over gay rights was the 1993 decision of the Hawaiian Supreme Court in *Baehr* v. *Miike* that rules prohibiting same-sex couples from marrying violated the state constitution's equal protection clause (Goldberg-Hiller, 2002; Eskridge, 2002). Concerned that other states would be required to recognize same-sex marriages performed in Hawaii, the Congress passed the Defense of Marriage Act (DOMA) in 1996 that prohibited any state from recognizing a marriage ceremony involving couples of the same sex. A number of states also passed "mini-DOMAs" stating that they did not recognize same-sex marriages. Two court decisions in 2003, however, cast doubt upon federal and state restrictions on same-sex marriages. In *Lawrence* v. *Texas* the US Supreme Court ruled that state homosexual sodomy laws were unconstitutional, and in *Goodridge* v. *Department of Public Health* the Supreme Judicial Court of Massachusetts ordered state officials to issue marriage licenses to same-sex couples. President Bush responded by calling for a constitutional amendment to define marriage as a union between heterosexual couples, claiming that "activist courts have left the people with one recourse" (Bush, 2004b). The Federal Marriage Amendment (FMA) was debated in the Senate in July 2004 but not enough votes were available to invoke cloture. Propositions to ban same-sex marriages were passed by 11 states in the 2004 elections.

Agitation for the recognition of same-sex marriages propelled homosexuality onto the political agenda and reinvigorated debate about the fate of American families. "The flames of hedonism, the flames of narcissism, the flames of self-centered morality are licking at the very foundation of our society, the family unit," declared Rep. Bob Barr (R-GA) during the debate on DOMA in 1996 (quoted in White, 2003: 110). In the debate over FMA in 2004 Republican senators continued to claim that same-sex marriages threatened the existence of the traditional family unit. Senator James Inhofe (R-OK) predicted that marriage would become "little more than an optional arrangement, not the presumptive locus of family life" (quoted in Liu and Macedo, 2005: 212). Concern that the traditional family unit was already in crisis had previously led to proposals to make divorce harder to obtain and to change the tax code to provide financial advantages for married couples.

Abortion and homosexuality deeply divide the American public. Opinion polls conducted since 2001 reveal that a slender majority of Americans believe that abortion and homosexual relations are morally wrong. Over the last four years the percentage of Americans who believe that abortion is morally wrong has ranged from 45% to 53%, and the percentage that believe that homosexuality is morally wrong has hovered between 52% and 55% (Gallup Organization, 2005). These headline figures, however, disguise a complex range of attitudes towards the two issues. When questioned about their attitudes towards abortion in May 2005, 48% of Americans described themselves as pro-choice while 44% characterized themselves as pro-life (Saad, 2005a). Public opinion on homosexuality is equally ambiguous. Although 87% of Americans in 2005 believed that homosexuals should have equal job opportunities, only 51% regarded homosexuality as an acceptable alternative lifestyle (Saad, 2005b). When questioned about same-sex marriages, only 39% of those polled believed that marriages between homosexuals should be legally valid.

The differences between Republican and Democrat identifiers on these two issues are marked. An opinion poll conducted in May 2005 found that 36% of Republicans believe that homosexual relations are morally acceptable compared with 51% of Democrats (Carroll, 2005). The same poll revealed an even larger difference over abortion. Just 29% of Republicans regard abortion as morally acceptable compared to 51% of Democrats. With a similar divide evident on other sexual issues, the evidence from this poll suggests that the battle over core values currently being waged in the United States has a partisan edge. Republican identifiers attend church more frequently than their Democrat counterparts, and tend to espouse traditional rather than progressive values as a result (Newport, 2005).

Evidence of a partisan divide on sexual issues was evident in the 2004 elections. While the Republican Party adopted a "faith and family" platform that advocated passage of constitutional amendments to ban abortions and same-sex marriages, the Democratic Party's platform contained statements in support of *Roe* v. *Wade* and homosexual rights. President Bush's campaign faithfully mirrored his party's platform. He stressed his support for traditional family values, promised to appoint federal judges opposed to *Roe,* and stated that he would introduce constitutional amendments on abortion and same-sex marriages. Senator Kerry's campaign also reflected his party's platform. He declared support for abortion and homosexual rights, but expressed opposition to same-sex marriages. Similar partisan divisions on sexual issues were also apparent in campaigns at the sub-presidential level. Although the position of individual candidates varied depending on personal preferences and constituency characteristics, Republican candidates tended to promote traditional values more vigorously than Democrats. Extreme examples can be found in the campaign speeches of Republicans Tom Coburn in Oklahoma and Jim DeMint in South Carolina (Gumbel, 2004). Coburn advocated the death penalty for abortionists while DeMint argued that homosexuals and unmarried pregnant women should not be allowed to teach in schools. Both were elected to the US Senate.

The campaign activities of abortion and homosexual groups in the 2004 election reflected this partisan divide. Pro-choice groups such as Planned Parenthood and the National Abortion and Reproductive Rights Action League (NARAL) donated funds overwhelmingly to Democrat candidates, and pro-life groups such as National Right to Life and the National Pro-Life Alliance donated funds almost exclusively to Republican candidates. Democrats received 87% of the direct contributions made by pro-choice groups while Republicans received 99% of the funds distributed by pro-life groups (OpenSecrets, 2005). Democratic candidates also received 92% of the direct contributions made by homosexual rights groups. Independent expenditures and voter mobilization drives by these groups provide further evidence of the partisan divide in sexual politics. Issue advertisements, Internet advocacy, and direct mail campaigning saw progressive groups promote the election of Democrat candidates while traditionalist groups sought to secure the election of Republican candidates. Even mainstream churches entered the fray, with some Roman Catholic bishops publicly expressing their unwillingness to allow Senator Kerry take communion because of his position on abortion (Kuhn, 2004).

Initial explanations of the 2004 elections emphasized the importance of moral issues such as abortion and homosexuality to the outcome. With voters rejecting same-sex marriages by significant majorities in propositions in 11 states, and an early exit poll reporting that 22% of voters viewed "moral values" as the most important issue in the campaign, commentators were quick to conclude that President Bush's re-election and Republican victories elsewhere were a consequence of the GOP's advocacy of traditional values. "Three days after the presidential election, it is clear that it was not the war on terror, but the issue of what we're calling moral values that drove President Bush and other Republicans to victory this week," claimed Tucker Carlson, co-host of CNN's *Crossfire* (quoted in Meyer, 2004). Although subsequent analysis has cast doubt upon the importance of issues such as abortion and homosexuality in determining the outcome of the election (see Chapter 2), the perception that these issues were important was immediately used by traditionalist groups to push their agenda. Peter Sprigg of the Family Research Council claimed that: "We're seeing from the exit polls that conservative Christian voters turned out in record numbers ... so we certainly will be pressing for action on key items of our agenda" (Burkeman, 2004).

In his acceptance speech on November 3, 2004 President Bush promised that his Administration "will uphold our deepest values of family and faith". Bush subsequently reaffirmed his opposition to abortion and same-sex marriages. In an early action he issued a proclamation declaring January 16, 2005 as National Sanctity of Human Life Day in which he spoke of the need to "build a lasting culture of life and a more compassionate society." He employed the same rhetoric when addressing "March for Life" participants onJanuary 24, 2005. At that meeting Bush spoke of the need "to promote a culture of life, to promote compassion for women and their unborn babies," and promised to continue efforts to restrict abortion. A week later he re-iterated his opposition to same-sex marriages. In his State of the Union address on February 2, 2005 Bush declared: "Because marriage is a sacred institution and the foundation of society, it should not be redefined by activist judges. For the good of families, children and society, I support a constitutional amendment to protect the institution of marriage."

Legislation to amend the Constitution to define marriage as between one man and one woman was introduced in the US Senate by Majority Leader Bill Frist (R-TN) on the first day of the 109th Congress (2005–2006). "We have made the Marriage Protection Amendment S.J. Res 1. This is significant. It shows we will continue to defend marriage against activist judges," Frist declared (Perkins, 2005). Companion legislation was introduced in the House of Representatives on March 3, 2005 but neither chamber took early action on the measure. Instead the primary focus of Republican efforts to ban same-sex marriages and abortion turned to appointments to the federal courts. A Democratic filibuster of seven of President Bush's appellate court nominees brought tensions about the role of the federal courts in shaping policy on abortion and homosexuality into stark relief. Democrats and progressive groups argued that the seven nominees were outside the mainstream of judicial opinion. Typical was the statement of People for the American Way that the nominees "have an appalling record in the important areas of civil rights and civil liberties, privacy and reproductive choice" (PFAW, 2005b). Most Republicans and traditionalist groups argued that the appointment of these judges was necessary to counter the activism of liberal courts. Typical was the claim by the Family Research Council that "many of these nominees to the all-important appellate court level are being blocked ... because they are people of faith and moral conviction. These are people whose only offense is to say that abortion is wrong or should be between one man and one woman" (FRC, 2005). The filibuster was eventually ended by an agreement brokered by Senator John McCain (R-AZ) and a bipartisan group of centrist Senators that allowed a majority of the nominations to proceed to a vote but blocked those viewed as most extreme.

Outside Washington DC the controversy over issues such as same-sex marriages and abortion continued unabated. The most important development occurred in May 2005 when a federal court ruled on same-sex marriages for the first time. In *Citizens for Equal Protection, Inc, et al. v. Attorney General Jon Bruning, et al.* US District Judge Joseph Bataillon ruled that Nebraska's constitutional marriage amendment violated the US Constitution's 1st Amendment right to petition the government and the 14th Amendment's due process and equal protection clauses. Traditionalist groups seized upon the ruling to press for action on a constitutional amendment. Richard Land, president of the Southern Baptist Ethics and Religious Liberty Commission, stated that the ruling destroyed the "myth" that "gay rights" was a states' rights issue. "The only remedy for this kind of imperial judiciary is a federal Marriage Protection Amendment," he continued (Foust, 2005). James Dobson of Focus on the Family agreed with this view. "Federal protection of marriage is more necessary now than ever before," he stated. "Those who have argued that the definition of marriage is a states' rights issue have nowhere to hide. Defense of marriage acts are not sufficient. Either marriage will be enshrined in the US Constitution, or we will see an untenable patchwork of marriage definitions" (Winn, 2005).

These recent developments over abortion and same-sex marriages reveal a political landscape in a state of flux. Variation in policy can be seen between different states, between federal and state governments, and between legislatures and the courts. This flux is a consequence of the intense contest over core values that is raging in the United States. Differing views of what constitutes acceptable behavior are driving policy in different directions at different times across the country. With neither side in the debate currently able to impose their values on the other, the politics of sex will continue to be characterized by uncertainty and instability in the foreseeable future.

The public health crusade

A major element of contemporary lifestyle politics is a public health crusade that seeks to reduce risky behavior. Increased affluence, medical advances, and improved knowledge have led to a greater emphasis on the promotion of healthy lifestyles as a means of combating modern epidemics such as heart disease, cancer, and diabetes. Proponents of the "new public health" argue that this focus on changing personal behavior is the best way of improving the population's quality of life and reducing deaths. C. Everett Koop (US Surgeon General 1982–1989) summed up this position with his remark: "I think that the government has a perfect right to influence personal behavior to the best of its ability if it is for the welfare of the individual and the community as a whole" (quoted in Sullum, 1998: 275). Opponents counter that telling people how to behave for their own good is paternalistic and runs counter to the traditional American libertarian ethic: "It's my body and I'll do with it as I choose" (Brandt, 1990: 167). The emphasis on healthy lifestyles is characterized as a "hygienic ideology" in which the "good life" is a long life lived healthily (Whorton, 1982; Fitzpatrick, 2001).

The new public health

Over the last forty years the focus of public health has shifted from controlling infectious diseases to the promotion of healthy lifestyles. Public health traditionally involved activities such as quarantining people with infectious diseases, vaccination programs, and providing clean water (Mullan, 1989). A goal of protecting people from harmful contagions underpinned these efforts. Contemporary public health campaigns, however, have a different emphasis. Richard Carmona, the current US Surgeon General, has identified obesity, inadequate physical activity, HIV/AIDS, tobacco use, birth defects, and personal injuries as the main public health problems facing the nation (US Surgeon General, 2005). Eating healthy food, taking more exercise, not smoking, limiting alcohol intake, and avoiding drugs is the advice offered to address these problems. The purpose of the "new public health" is to reduce risky behavior. "Public health officials used to protect people from external threats. The new enemies of public health come from within; the aim is to protect people from themselves rather than each other," notes one critic of this approach (Sullum, 1998: 269).

An indication of this emphasis on reducing risky behavior can be seen in the contents of the reports issued by the US Surgeon General over the last 40 years. The overwhelming majority of the 44 reports published between 1964 and 2004 addressed behavioral issues. There have been 31 reports on smoking, 3 reports on HIV/AIDS, 2 reports on youth violence/sexual abuse, 2 reports on nutrition/physical fitness, and a general report on health promotion. The latter report, *Healthy People – The Surgeon General's Report on Health Promotion and Disease Prevention* (US HEW, 1979), was particularly important in shifting the direction of public health in the United States. The report stated that "Prevention is an idea whose time has come," and asserted that "We are now able to identify some of the major risk factors responsible for most of the premature morbidity and mortality in this country." Cigarette smoking, alcohol and drugs, occupational risks, and injuries were identified as leading causes of preventable death, and "modest lifestyle changes" were recommended "to substantially reduce risk for several diseases." These included stopping smoking, reducing alcohol intake, dietary changes, moderate exercise, obeying speed limits, and use of seat belts.

Publication of the 1979 US Surgeon General's Report sparked a "healthy people" initiative that placed prevention at the heart of public health strategies in the United States. In 1990 the US Department of Health and Human Services issued a report *Healthy People 2000* that established a set of national health promotion and disease prevention targets to be achieved by 2000 (US HHS, 1990). The report identified 22 "priority areas" for action with physical activity, nutrition, tobacco, substance abuse, and family planning occupying the top five places. Immunization and infectious diseases ranked 20 in the list. In 2000 the Department of Health and Human Services issued a further report *Healthy People 2010* that built upon the initiatives of the previous two decades (US HSS, 2000). The report contained 467 objectives organized in 28 focus areas. Donna E. Shalala, Secretary of Health and Human Services in 2000, claimed in a foreword to the report that it "represents an opportunity for individuals to make healthy lifestyle choices for themselves and their families." President Bush continued in this vein when he launched a *HealthierUS* initiative in 2002. The initiative urged Americans to take more exercise, eat a nutritious diet, get preventive screenings, and avoid risky behaviors. "Behavioral changes reduce the chance of illness or injury; even washing one's hands regularly prevents the spread of many common illnesses and infections," concluded *HealthierUS*.

The idea that government should promote health through public education programs is relatively uncontroversial as "informed choice" is central to notions of rational behavior. Few Americans would challenge the idea that people should be told of the dangers associated with particular behaviors or actions in order to make informed decisions about how to live their lives. Controversy begins to emerge, however, when public education programs fail to change behavior. The problem is what to do when people continue to smoke, drink, lead sedentary lives, engage in unsafe sex, fail to wear seatbelts, ride motorcycles without helmets, and leave their hands unwashed. The 1979 US Surgeon Generals' Report *Healthy People* noted that "individual attitudes toward the changes necessary for better health" are "formidable obstacles" to improved public health (US HEW, 1979: 11–12). Other health professionals have been less diplomatic. One New York lung surgeon told a talk show in 1997 that "people who are making decisions for themselves don't always come up with the right answer" (quoted in Sullum, 1998, 271).

One response to the fact that informed individuals may continue to engage in risky behavior is regulatory action that prohibits or restricts particular behaviors. Laws have been enacted, for example, that require motorcyclists to wear helmets or mandate the use of seatbelts in cars. Such laws are controversial. Critics argue that the use of the government's regulatory power to promote healthy behavior not only represents a willingness to impose a particular set of values on a recalcitrant population, but also threatens to erode civil liberties. Public health campaigners respond to such concerns by emphasizing the social costs that may arise from individuals engaging in risky behavior. "Motorcyclists often contend that helmet laws infringe on personal liberties", noted the 1979 Surgeon General's Report *Healthy People*, "and opponents of mandatory laws argue that since other people usually are not endangered, the individual motorcyclist should be allowed personal responsibility for risk. But the high cost of disabling and fatal injuries, the burden on families, and the demands on medical care resources are borne by society as a whole" (US HEW, 1979: 18). Critics point out that as virtually all lifestyle choices have an effect on "society as a whole" such arguments could be used to legitimize government regulation of all personal behavior regarded as posing a risk to health (Fitzgerald, 1996).

This debate over the "new public health" is similar in some respects to the contest over core values that is currently raging in the United States. Ranged on one side of the battlefield are those who stress a commitment to individual rights and self-fulfillment. Numerous single-issue groups ranging from opponents of helmet laws to drug legalization groups argue that individuals should be free to choose how to live their lives. Ranged on the other side of the battlefield are those who stress the need to live in a particular way in order to promote health. Public health groups advance a vision of a virtuous life that has health as its goal. The presence of powerful economic groups with an immediate vested interest in the outcome of this debate, however, differentiates the politics of the "new public health" from that generally found in the contest over core values. Big businesses have an important role in shaping and determining the outcome of the debate about individual rights and collective well-being. This is seen most starkly in the politics of smoking and eating where corporations such as Phillip Morris and McDonalds have played a prominent role in determining policy outcomes.

The politics of smoking and eating

Efforts to reduce smoking and combat obesity dominate public health campaigns in the United States. Physical activity, overweight and obesity, and tobacco use, for example, constitute the three main priorities for action in the *Healthy People 2010* initiative. This focus on smoking and obesity flows from general acceptance that they are the two leading causes of morbidity and death in the United States. Smoking is widely regarded as increasing the risk of various cancers, heart disease, strokes, and a number of other health problems. Obesity has been indicted as increasing the risk of heart disease, type 2 diabetes, various cancers, and a number of musculoskeletal disorders. Mortality rates confirm the seriousness of these health problems. Estimates of causes of death in the United States reveal smoking and obesity to be the two leading causes of death. In 2000 approximately 435,000 deaths were attributed to tobacco use and 365,000 deaths to obesity (Mokdad *et al.*, 2004).

Publication of the 1964 US Surgeon General's report on "Smoking and Health" marked the beginning of contemporary government efforts to restrict smoking (US HEW, 1964). The report identified a link between smoking and lung cancer and recommended "appropriate remedial action." Early efforts at "remedial action" focused upon public education initiatives that sought to persuade people not to smoke. Warning labels were required on cigarette packages, restrictions placed on advertising, and Public Service Announcements used to promote an anti-tobacco message. Calls for greater government regulation of smoking foundered against the power of the tobacco industry, their allies in Congress, and a widespread feeling that individuals should make up their own minds about whether to smoke or not. The discovery of a link between environmental tobacco smoke (ETS) and ill-health in the early 1970s, however, fundamentally altered the politics of smoking. The possibility that non-smokers might be harmed as a result of exposure to ETS undermined completely notions of "informed consent" and acceptance of risk.

Public concern about ETS produced a flurry of legislative activity at the state and local level to restrict smoking. The first restrictions on public smoking were introduced in the 1970s. In 1973 Arizona became the first state to restrict smoking to designated areas in public places, and in 1977 Berkeley, California, became the first community to introduce restrictions on smoking in restaurants. Publication of a Surgeon General's Report on *The Health Consequences of Involuntary Smoking* in 1986 (US HHS, 1986), and the release of a report by the US Environmental Protection Agency (EPA) in 1992 that identified ETS as a "Class A" carcinogen sparked further activity (US EPA, 1992). Between 1993 and 2005 104 municipalities enacted laws prohibiting smoking in all workplaces, restaurants, and bars (ANR, 2005). Four states (Delaware, Massachusetts, New York, and Rhode Island) have imposed similar statewide bans on smoking while seven states (California, Connecticut, Florida, Idaho, Maine, South Dakota, and Utah) have laws that prohibit smoking in workplaces or restaurants. Wyoming is the only state that has not legislated against public smoking in any form. Federal action to restrict smoking began in 1971 when the Interstate Commerce Commission required designated smoking sections on inter-state buses and trains. In 1973 the Civil Aeronautics Board followed suit and ordered all US airlines to provide non-smoking sections. In 1986 Congress banned smoking on domestic flights lasting two hours or less, and two years later extended the ban to cover all domestic flights. Bans on smoking in federal buildings began to be introduced in the late 1980s, and President Clinton finally issued an executive order that banned smoking in all federal facilities in 1997.

The widespread adoption of restrictions against public smoking at all levels of government is testimony to the success that anti-smoking campaigners have had in changing the terms of debate about smoking. An opinion poll conducted in 2004 revealed that 58% of Americans, and 66% of non-smokers, favoured legislation banning smoking in public places (Carlson, 2004). ETS provides campaigners with an opportunity to avoid arguments about personal choice and to focus instead on the harm that smokers do to others. This tactic also underpins arguments that emphasize the social costs of smoking. Anti-smoking campaigners argue that smokers take more sick leave and generate higher medical expenses than non-smokers. The Center for Disease Control (CDC) estimates, for example, that the annual health bill associated with smoking is $75 billion, with another $80 billion per year resulting from lost productivity (CDC, 2005). The purpose of such claims is to show that smoking is not simply a matter of personal choice but that it imposes a burden on others.

Obesity has emerged in recent years to challenge smoking as the main priority of public health campaigners. The cause of this concern is a dramatic increase in the number of Americans who are overweight or obese. Results from the US Government's 1999–2000 National Health and Nutrition Examination Survey (NHANES) indicate that 64% of adult Americans, approximately 127 million people, were overweight with a Body Mass Index greater than 25 (BMI > 25) compared to 47% in 1980 (NHANES II). Even more dramatic has been the increase in the number of Americans who are obese. Approximately 31% of adults, nearly 60 million Americans, are obese with a BMI > 30. Significant disparities exist in the prevalence of obesity among different sections of the population. Obesity is particularly common among minority groups and those with a lower family income. NHANES suggests that 50.8% of African-American women and 38.1% of Hispanic women are obese compared with 30.9% of white women. Women with low incomes are especially prone to obesity. Low socio-economic status women of all racial/ethnic groups are approximately 50% more likely to be obese than those of a higher socio-economic status. Health surveys also reveal that children and adolescents gained weight during this period. Between 1980 and 2000 the percentage of children (ages 6–11) who were overweight doubled, while the percentage of adolescents (12–19) who were overweight tripled.

Concern that obesity posed a growing public health problem led the US Surgeon General to issue a *Call to Action to Prevent and Decrease*

Overweight and Obesity in 2001 (US HHS, 2001). This *Call to Action* claimed that "Overweight and obesity have reached nationwide epidemic proportions" and stated "Both the prevention and treatment of overweight and obesity and their associated health problems are important public health goals." The Surgeon General recommended government action to publicize the dangers of obesity, provide Americans with advice on nutrition and exercise, identify treatments for obesity, and encourage environmental changes that help prevent obesity. "Americans need to understand that overweight and obesity are literally killing us," HHS Secretary Tommy Thompson told a press conference in March 2003, "To know that poor eating habits and inactivity are on the verge of surpassing tobacco as the leading cause of preventable death in America should motivate all Americans to take action to protect their health" (US HHS, 2004).

The problem for public health campaigners is legitimizing government intervention in an area widely regarded as private. Government may seek to provide individuals with the means to make an "informed choice" about their lifestyle, but support for regulatory action is limited by a general belief that obesity is a personal matter. Whereas ETS may harm a non-smoker, no similar harm is done to others if an individual overeats or does not exercise sufficiently. An individual does not get fat if someone else consumes more calories than they need. This view of obesity as causing harm only to the person involved acts as a powerful bulwark to government action. In an effort to overcome this bulwark, public health campaigners have started to emphasize the social costs of obesity. The central message of such "stories" is the economic cost to society arising from the "obesity epidemic" in the form of medical expenditures and lost economic activity. Studies suggest that the direct health care costs associated with obesity are approximately $61 billion per year (US HHS, 2003). Approximately half of these costs fall on the government in increased Medicare and Medicaid payments. An obese Medicare recipient, for example, spends approximately $1,500 more on medical care each year than a non-obese counterpart. The indirect costs of obesity resulting from factors such as lost productivity have been estimated at $56 billion each year.

Public health campaigners argue that the size of these direct and indirect costs means that obesity should be viewed as a societal problem. "The economic and personal health costs of overweight and obesity are enormous and compromise the health of the United States," concluded a study published in *Obesity Research* (Wolfe and Colditz, 1998). "There has been a debate about whether obesity is a personal or societal issue and whether the government has any business being involved," another prominent public health campaigner noted. "The fact that the government, and ultimately the taxpayer, is financing half the economic burden of obesity suggests that the government has a clear justification to try to reduce obesity rates" (quoted in Connolly, 2003). Opinion polls suggest that few Americans concur with this view (McMurray, 2004). A widely held view that obesity is a matter of personal responsibility dominates the politics of obesity with the result that support for greater government action to tackle the problem is limited. Federal and state legislators have introduced bills to require the "fast food" industry to provide nutritional information, restrict the sale of junk food in schools, regulate food advertising, tax specific foods, and impose physical education standards in schools, but with little success.

Recent developments in the campaign against smoking and obesity reveal the willingness of public health campaigners to tackle problems traditionally viewed as private rather than public. The nature of government action in such cases, however, is shaped by the way that the problem is defined. The discovery that ETS posed a health threat to non-smokers allowed the problem of smoking to be defined as an environmental issue involving broad social concerns rather than a matter of personal behavior. Public health campaigners have so far failed to persuade Americans that obesity raises similar concerns, but the scale of the problem means that agitation for greater government action will continue.

Conclusion

Lifestyle issues play an important part in contemporary American politics. Efforts to define what it means to be American and improve public health have focused attention on personal behavior and questioned the boundary between the public and private spheres. The battle over "core values" has been most intense. Issues such as abortion and homosexuality divide the population, generate conflict, and are not easy to resolve. Pending court cases, and uncertainty about judicial politics, mean that they are likely to remain hot issues for the foreseeable future. The battle to improve public health has been less intense. Although smoking arouses strong passions, few Americans currently feel the same way about obesity. The commitment to reduce "preventable deaths," however, means that government will continue to take action to change people's lifestyles. In the short term this may be done through public education initiatives, but the logic of the "new public health" suggests that regulatory powers may be used if health targets are not met.

Chapter 12

Economic Policy

Andrew Wroe

The United States' economy dwarfs that of even its closest competitors. Its 2003 gross domestic product (GDP) was $11 trillion compared to Japan's $4.3 trillion, Germany's $2.4 trillion and the United Kingdom's $1.8 trillion. The US economy is the same size as that of all members of the European community combined, and is responsible for a nearly a third of the gross world product of $36 trillion. In addition to its size, the US economy is also remarkable for its continued high levels of growth at a time when the economies of most of its key competitors and trading partners have fallen on hard times. Despite a recession in 2001, it grew by 10 percent between 2000 and 2004, twice the average of the Eurozone countries and considerably better than Germany and Japan, which grew by just 2.4 and 4 percent respectively over the same period. It has by far the largest services output of any nation, and yet it is also the world's largest industrial producer and second largest agricultural producer. It leads the world in information technology, in communications systems, and new start-ups. It drives the world economy, and it will continue to do so for some time. The old adage that "when the United States sneezes, the rest of the world catches a cold" remains true today. One key reason for this is that the US imports about $1.5 trillion of goods and services each year. If the US slides into recession, demand for imports declines, thus tipping its trading partners' economies into recession too.

While it is impossible to quantify precisely the reasons for America's economic strength, many economists point to a combination of factors revolving around its culture of hard work, large-scale immigration, abundant natural resources and high efficiency and productivity. A further explanation is that it has a business-friendly political system that pursues a low-tax regime and does not interfere with market mechanisms. As Ronald Reagan argued, the business of government is not the government of business. Despite periodic howls of protest from Americans that they are overtaxed, the federal government takes only 16 or so percent of GDP in tax, and the state governments another 10 percent, while most European governments take double this. America's low-tax regime is in part a consequence of its enterprise culture and *laissez-faireism*, but it also means in turn that government is much less involved in the life of its citizens and corporations in a whole host of ways. The Americans do not enjoy the same level of protection as Europeans from William Beveridge's "Giant Evils" of Want, Disease, Ignorance, Squalor and Idleness. Health care, for example, is fully privatized. Even Clinton's ambitious but ultimately failed 1994 reforms offered a market-based solution. The government does buy some basic medical services in the private marketplace on behalf of the very poorest and elderly (Medicaid and Medicare), but the vast majority of Americans are left to fend for themselves. Indeed, such is the high cost of medical care that an estimated 45 million Americans have no medical insurance and millions more are underinsured. Moreover, able-bodied unemployed persons cannot look to government for benefits and sustenance. The homeless cannot look to government to provide shelter. And the mentally ill cannot look to government for treatment and protection. While this may seem like wanton cruelty to some European observers, it is the flip side of America's culture of rugged individualism, freedom and capitalism. Indeed, the absence of a well-woven safety net reinforces the entrepreneurial spirit that drives the American economy forwards and upwards.

The economy provides the foundation for America's military and political dominance. A much quoted but instructive statistic is that the US spends as much each year on its armed forces as the next ten biggest spending nations *combined*. While it does not have the biggest army in the world in terms of manpower (China does), it has the most sophisticated and effective military, which can fight two major wars simultaneously. The invasion of Iraq and its aftermath had cost the US about 200 billion dollars by the end of 2005 – a cost no other nation could bear without disastrous economic consequences. As well as underpinning America's "hard" power, its wealth is key to its "soft" power, too. The United States is, for example, the biggest donor to the United Nations and thus its most important member. It is also one of its most reluctant members, with conservative and neo-conservative Republicans in Congress and the White House expressing open hostility. Bush's warning that the UN must become more "relevant" in the post-9/11 world is code for more supportive of US positions. The United States also uses soft power to influence outcomes in forums such as the WTO, World Bank and IMF. The United States' delegations to WTO negotiations on free trade include hundreds of specialist lawyers, while many poor nations have no or little legal representation. It is little wonder that the terms and conditions of free trade agreements often favor already wealthy nations and in particular the United States. Developing nations complain that they are forced to open up their markets to American goods, only to find their domestic producers undercut by cheap American imports. This situation is particularly iniquitous when the keen price of the import is itself partly a product of government subsidy. American farmers in particular receive considerable help from the government in the form of subsidies, price supports and tax breaks – advantages not enjoyed by their competitors in less developed countries. Individual American corporations also have considerable power, both outside and within the United States. Wal-Mart's turnover of $258 billion in 2005 makes it the world's largest retailer, and the world's 21st largest economy. It has 1.6 million employees and 138 million customers per week visiting over 6,000 stores.

The US economy today

The economic story of the Bush presidency is complex and mixed. The economy under President Bill Clinton performed spectacularly well during the latter part of the 1990s. Growth was high, tax revenues up, and the budget balanced for the first time in 30 years. However, the economy began to slide between the November 2000 presidential election and Bush's inauguration in January 2001 and by mid 2001 was firmly in the grip of recession. Growth in GDP fell from nearly 2 percent in the first quarter of 2001 to just 0.8 percent in the last quarter (OECD, May 2005). Other economic indicators tell a similar story. While unemployment fell steadily between 1995 and 2000 from nearly 6 percent to 4 percent, these gains were lost during 2001. Unemployment increased again in 2002 before reaching a peak in mid 2003 (see Figure 12.1). Share prices also suffered. The great American bull market saw the Dow Jones Industrial Average rise exponentially from under 1,300 in 1983 to its all-time high of 11,723 in January 2000. By the end of the year, however, the DJIA dropped back 8 percent, fell 7 percent in 2001 and a further 17 percent in 2002 (see Figure 12.2). While nearly all stocks suffered, a good proportion of the decline was due to the bursting of the dot.com bubble. NASDAQ, the stock index which includes many IT stocks, rose sharply in the late 1990s as corporate and private investors piled money into established companies like Microsoft and new start-ups – many of which had never made a profit and some of which had no product to sell. In March 2000 the NASDAQ index peaked at 5,000 but tumbled to 3,200 in mid 2000 and 1,600 in early 2001. By late 2002 the index stood at 1,100, the same level as in 1996 when nobody had heard of dot-coms and high-tech bubbles (see Figure 12.3).

The largest technology failure was the established communications corporation WorldCom, which had merged with MCI, another communications specialist, in 1997 in a huge $37 billion deal. In June 2002 an internal audit revealed that $3.8 billion had been "miscounted', a total

Figure 12.1 *Unemployment rate 1983–2005*

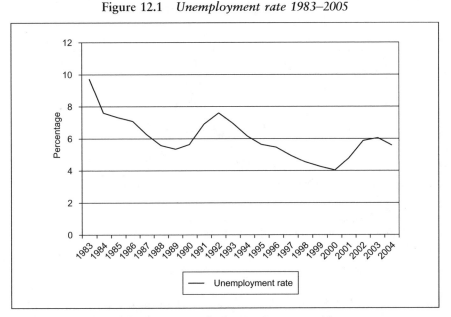

Source: US Department of Labor, Bureau of Labor Statistics < www.bls.gov > .

Figure 12.2 *Dow Jones industrial average, 1983–2005*

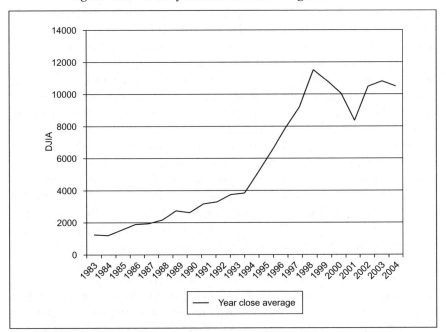

Source: Dow Jones Indexes < www.djindexes.com > .

Figure 12.3 NASDAQ

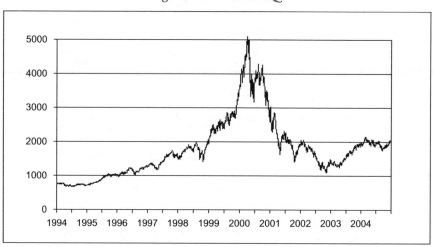

Source: <Nasdaq.com>.

later raised to $11 billion. The corporation had been inflating its profits and assets in order to increase its share price. In July 2002 WorldCom filed for bankruptcy in the biggest corporate collapse in US history and three years later its founder Bernie Ebbers and many top executives were found guilty of fraud. The 63–year-old Ebbers was sentenced in July 2005 to 25 years in prison. WorldCom's demise was triggered by the collapse of Enron. Based in Houston, Texas, and led by the charismatic Kenneth Lay, a personal friend of and financial contributor to George W. Bush (who used to refer to him as Kenny Boy), Enron was the darling of the corporate world due to its fast growth, high stock prices and large dividends. *Fortune* magazine labelled it "America's Most Innovative Company" five times in the mid-to-late 1990s, but the edifice crumbled in 2001. It was alleged that Enron had bribed and misused political connections to win contracts; that it in part caused California's energy blackouts by reducing supply to increase prices and thus its own profits; and that it used creative and fraudulent accounting to inflate its profits and share price. As the scandal unfolded, with its share price collapsing from $85 to just 30 cents, Enron filed for bankruptcy in December 2001 in the then biggest corporate collapse in US history. It triggered a wave of further scandals and bankruptcies, and for a short time the foundations of corporate America looked to have been built on sand. Congress reacted quickly by passing the Public Company Accounting Reform and Investor Protection Act in July 2002 (commonly referred to as Sox after its congressional sponsors Senator Paul Sarbanes and Representative Michael G. Oxley). The law increased protection for stockholders by updating corporate accounting procedures to ensure transparency and accuracy. The unusual speed with which Congress reacted to the scandals and the law's thoughtful changes did much to help stabilize the situation.

While the stock market and corporate America have experienced many ups and downs in recent years, inflation has remained steady and low. In the 1970s and early 1980s, inflation was regularly at or above 10 percent, but has been below 4 percent for the last two decades. The success in defeating inflation is largely attributed to the Federal Reserve Board, the United State's truly independent central bank, established by the Owen-Glass Act of 1913. While the Bank of England is often described today as independent after Gordon Brown freed it from government control in 1997, in truth the bank only enjoys "operational independence'. This means that Gordon Brown sets the inflation target (say 2.5%) and the bank's monetary policy committee sets interest rates to meet the target. In contrast, the Federal Reserve has free rein over monetary policy; it sets inflation targets and interest rates. Increasing interest rates tightens the money supply and should dampen inflationary pressures; conversely, reducing rates expands the supply and should encourage economic growth. The problem is that low interest rates engender inflation as well as growth, while high rates constrain both. The Board's tricky job is to strike a delicate balance between keeping inflation under control and allowing the economy to expand.

The underlying inflation rate was 3 percent in 1995. It declined to 2 percent between 1995 and 1999, rose three-quarters of a point during the 2000 and 2001 and dropped back one-and-half points to only 1 percent in late 2003, before rising again during 2004. While the Board has done a good job over the last quarter century of reducing inflation without tipping the economy over into a serious recession, economic commentators often single out one person in particular as responsible for this success: Alan Greenspan, Chairman of the Federal Reserve. Often referred to as the "maestro', he was appointed chair in 1987 by Ronald Reagan and reappointed by Presidents George Bush, Bill Clinton and George W. Bush. His tenure as America's and therefore the world's chief monetary policy-maker is widely regarded a great success, but his vast experience, steady hand and impressive record make him a difficult act to follow after his retirement on January 31, 2006. His successor, Ben Bernanke, previously a Federal Reserve governor and chair of Bush's Council of Economic Advisers (CEA), is an academic economist rather than a Wall Street practitioner. While news of his appointment was warmly received by the financial markets and easily confirmed by the Senate, it remains to be seen whether his tenure will be judged as successful as Greenspan's.

The Board's tricky job of using interest rates to balance inflation and growth is made more problematic still because rates also impact on the trade deficit and exchange rates. High interest rates, for example, help push up the price of the dollar (more people buy dollars as the return increases), thus making American exports more expensive and imports cheaper. This in turn has both positive and negative effects. Cheaper imports help dampen inflation but expensive exports make it more difficult for US firms to sell goods abroad, possibly leading to economic contraction at home and a trade deficit as imports grow relative to exports. Indeed, the United States' trade deficit – defined simply as the difference between what America sells to and buys from foreign nations – has increased markedly in recent years. The United States now imports half as much again as it exports, with the current deficit at about $700 billion per year and rising. The conundrum is that the deficit has worsened at the same time as the dollar has fallen in value by roughly a third against a basket of major currencies. Some economists explain the puzzle by pointing out that the benefits of a weak dollar and low export prices have been outweighed by a drop in demand in key American markets in Asia and Europe. Unsurprisingly, the trade deficit and international trade is a hot political issue in the US today, and we will return to this below.

Another deficit of great concern to some Americans is the budget deficit. This is the yearly difference between what the federal government spends and what it raises in taxes – a difference the government must make up by borrowing money. The accumulation of all budget deficits (and, less often, surpluses) over time is the national debt. After years of rising deficits from the mid 1970s onwards, the budget deficit was placed firmly on the political agenda with the quirky, populist candidacy of Ross Perot in the 1992 presidential election. Bush lost the 1992 election in large part because he raised taxes having promised not to ('read my lips: no new taxes'), but it was his tax rise combined with sustained economic growth during the Clinton presidency that finally facilitated the first budget surplus in more than a generation in 1998. The government raised $200 billion more than it spent in 2000 alone, and managed to reduce the national debt by $360 billion during the last three years of the Clinton presidency. In contrast, the first term of George W. Bush has been marred by large budget deficits, a corresponding steep rise in the national debt and, as outlined above, general economic malaise. This does not necessarily mean that Bush is a poor custodian of the largest economy in the world. While the recession of 2001 unquestionably happened on Bush's watch, it is probable that it took root during the last months of the Clinton presidency. The interesting question is: how has Bush responded to America's economic difficulties? Before answering this, it is necessary to review briefly how economic policy is made in the United States.

Making economic policy

The Constitution of the United States gives Congress the "power of the purse." Specifically, it is given power to set and collect taxes, to borrow money, to print money, and to regulate commerce between the US and foreign nations and between the individual states. However, Congress has delegated much of its authority in matters of the purse to other actors. As we saw above, it gave control of monetary policy to the Federal Reserve in 1913. The "Fed" as it is known sets its own inflation and money supply targets and moves interest rates up or down to meet these targets without congressional or presidential approval. Under the provisions of the 1978 Humphrey-Hawkins Act, the Fed's chair must from time to time testify before Congress on monetary policy and the general state of the American economy, but Mr Greenspan was always treated with great reverence and afforded great respect and little effort was made to influence him. Congress does though have the authority to change the role and power of the Federal Reserve. It created the bank and gave it control over interest rates, and it could legislate once more to curtail its powers or even abolish it. This is, however, little more than a theoretical power. The bank's independence survived the Great Depression of the inter-war years and the economic difficulties of the 1970s, and it is difficult to see what circumstances could lead Congress to attempt such an audacious power grab, and even more difficult to imagine that it would succeed.

As well as delegating control of monetary policy to an independent central bank, Congress delegated some, but by no means all, control over fiscal policy to the executive branch with the passage of the Budget and Accounting Act in 1921. Fiscal policy refers to issues surrounding taxation and government expenditure, and the president must under the terms of the 1921 Act submit to Congress an annual budget. To advise the president on budgetary measures, the act established a Bureau of the Budget, later named the Office of Management and Budget (OMB). The budget is key to the governmental process because it sets the parameters for all federal spending on health, education, defense, pensions, and so on. The Employment Act, passed by Congress in 1946, set the goal of full employment and gave the president further powers to manage the economy to meet the new goal. The act also established the Council of Economic Advisers to advise the president on the best ways to achieve his goals. Further advice and information is provided by the Treasury and independent experts in academia and think-tanks. Some presidents establish further layers of bureaucracy to coordinate, order and filter the mass of data, interpretations and policy options. Clinton, for example, set up and chaired the National Economic Council, a large, unwieldy advisory body designed to bring together the many economic policy-makers in his administration, whereas George W. Bush relies on informal discussions with a few trusted aides. However individual presidents organize their staff, they all need good advice to achieve their policy and persuasive goals (Neustadt, 1990), and the OMB, CEA, Treasury and more informal channels give the president an important institutional advantage over Congress in making fiscal policy. While individual members of Congress may receive advice from independent experts and congressional committees can call experts and bureaucrats to testify before it, for many years Congress the institution had no formal bureaucracy to advise on fiscal policy. The situation came to a head in the early 1970s when President Richard Nixon refused to spend money specifically appropriated by Congress to certain projects. In response, Congress passed the Budget and Impoundment Control Act in 1974 to prevent presidents "impounding" funds. The act also attempted to redress the executive branch's institutional advantage by establishing the Congressional Budget Office (CBO), a nonpartisan public-sector think-tank. It produces a Budget and Economic Outlook Report in January, which serves as Congress's starting point for budget deliberation, an independent estimate of the president's budget each February, and economic forecasts and expenditure and revenue projections throughout the year.

Congress and the president also share responsibility for regulatory policy and trade policy. The former includes such issues as safety standards for automobiles and planes, air or water purity, CFC emissions, drilling for oil in sensitive environments and protecting eco-systems. The main focus of the latter is the United States' trade with other nations, but it also refers to the federal government's role in regulating trade between the individual states. While the federal government undoubtedly plays a larger regulatory role today than ever before, much economic activity and policy-making is under the control of the 50 state governments, whose economic policies vary dramatically. While most have a state income tax, some do not (Alaska, Florida, Nevada, New Hampshire, South Dakota, Tennessee, Texas, Washington and Wyoming). Similarly, most have a sales tax, while a few do not (Alaska, Delaware, Montana, New Hampshire and Oregon). Tax levels for business also differ across states, as do environmental standards. Some states have stricter standards than the federal minimum (especially California) while others operate a fairly lax regulatory regime. The differing tax and regulatory regimes in part reflect the states' different histories and cultures. California's relatively high taxes, for example, helped support an excellent infrastructure that in turn helped attract immigrants and migrants to the Golden State. Unfortunately, California's roads and education system, which includes some of the world's great universities, are crumbling through lack of investment. Rules adopted through direct democracy procedures have made it very difficult for the state, county and local governments to increase taxes without the authorization of a supermajority of the electorate (Schrag, 1998). Other states face similar problems brought on by a "race to the bottom" as each offers lower taxes, subsidies and lower environmental standards to encourage new investment and to lure firms to relocate from other states. Investors may bring jobs, but they also increase the pressure on the existing infrastructure and increasingly provide few tax dollars to improve it.

Bush's first term

With the economy booming and the budget in surplus, Bush argued during the 2000 presidential election campaign that middle-class Americans should share in the country's economic good fortune in the form of an unprecedented $1.3 trillion tax cut. Al Gore also promised to cut taxes, but by a third as much as Bush. Gore proposed instead to spend the rest of the surplus on paying off some of the national debt and increasing spending on public services. It is difficult to argue that Bush's policy plans were the crucial difference between the candidates – in part because Gore actually won more popular votes than Bush and in part because the economy was for once not a key election issue. It looked as if economic good times had returned, whoever won the election. Such optimism was soon dashed, however. The economy began to slide into recession in late 2000, and the president-elect's huge tax cut appeared doomed. In what some commentators regard as a deft political move and others as astonishing effrontery, Bush stopped arguing that a tax cut was necessary to give over-taxed Americans their money back and started arguing, using the language of Keynes, that a tax cut was necessary to stimulate demand and get the economy back on its feet again. Critics pilloried Bush for his "one solution fits all problems" approach, argued that people saved rather than spent tax rebates during difficult economic times, and pointed out that the vast majority of the tax cut would go not to ordinary Americans but to the very wealthiest. Despite the opposition of many professional economists, Bush succeeded in steering his tax cut through difficult congressional waters – a political victory that should not be underestimated. While presidential scholars tell us that it is increasingly difficult for presidents to get their policy proposals through Congress (Rose, 1991), Bush did so only seven months after receiving fewer popular votes than Al Gore, only six months after the Republican-dominated Supreme Court awarded him Florida's Electoral College votes and thus the presidency, and with a Senate split 50–50 along party lines. Bush's much underestimated persuasive talents are the key to his success in this and other policy areas. His new defense of the tax cut as a stimulus package appealed to the few centrist Democrats in the Senate whose votes would be necessary to pass the budget resolution and head off a later filibuster on the tax bill proper.

Bush's advisers claim that "substantial tax relief together with expansionary monetary policy provided stimulus to aggregate demand that softened the recession and helped put the economy on the path to recovery" (CEA, February 2005). It may well be true that "without the boost to disposable income from tax relief, the recession would have been deeper and longer" (CEA, February 2006), but the debate among economists concerns how much deeper and longer and whether alternative measures, such as a $1.3 trillion injection of government spending, would have proved more effective. Moreover, data show that Americans squirreled away much of their tax cut in savings accounts or used it to pay off debt. As 2001 progressed, the economy dipped further into recession as the dot-com bubble deflated and the 9/11 terrorist attacks dented consumer and producer confidence. The response of the Bush administration was more of the same. Signed into law in May 2003, the Jobs and Growth Tax Relief Reconciliation Act reduced taxes by a further $350 billion, the third largest cut in US history. It sought to stimulate capital investment, private spending and consumption. To do so it allowed firms to claim larger tax deductions for depreciation, reduced capital gains tax and tax on dividends, accelerated the introduction of lower income tax bands, and increased child tax credits.

Democratic presidential candidate John Kerry tried to turn America's faltering economy to his advantage early in the 2004 presidential election campaign. In March and April 2004 he criticized Bush's "failed economic policies that have steadily led America into economic decline ... There is not a single month of this administration that has seen the creation of a single manufacturing job" (*USA Today*, July 2, 2004). However, as the election approached, economic performance improved. While it would not match the formidable expansion of the late 1990s, GDP began to grow more strongly and unemployment declined. According to Gallup, perceptions of current economic conditions improved during 2004, the first time for three years. Perceptions about how the economy would perform in the future also improved after a small fall in 2003. In response, Kerry and his team changed tack, and started arguing that although things were getting better, they were not doing so quickly enough. "Are you really satisfied with the president's economic performance? Is the improving economy actually lifting all boats? And has President Bush addressed the biggest short-term and long-term economic challenges facing us – health care, energy costs, education and the deficit – the way he should have?" asked Kerry economic adviser Gene Spelling. A Bush spokesperson in turn attacked the Kerry camp for taking "good news about the fastest-growing economy in 20 years and try[ing] to spin it into bad news. His strategy relies on gross misinterpretations of reality and the manipulation of statistics" (*USA Today*, July 2, 2004).

The Kerry campaign lost ground in August when an organization called Swift Boat Veterans for Truth accused Kerry of lying about his Vietnam record. The allegations dominated media coverage and Kerry began to slip in the polls. Kerry shook up his campaign team in response, bringing in some old faces from the Clinton administration. James Carville, Stanley Greenberg, Joe Lockhart and others had helped Clinton win in 1992 and 1996 by focusing on the economy – Carville authored the famous "It's the economy, stupid!" memo – and thought that Kerry should do the same. Clinton himself spoke to Kerry and urged him to hit Bush harder on economic issues, and especially jobs, in swing states. While Gallup polls showed that Americans were more optimistic in 2004 than 2003, the increases were from a very low base. During 2004 only a net 14 percent felt positive about the country's current economic performance and a net 5 percent were positive about the future. According to political scientists (MacKuen, Erikson and Stimson, 1992), incumbent presidents struggle to win elections when voters are worried about future economic prosperity. Worryingly for Bush, only a small minority of Americans felt confident in early 2004 and many actually became less confident during the four months preceding the November presidential election. Indeed, in the final Gallup poll before the election only a net 12 percent were positive about current economic performance and a net 11 percent were negative about future prospects. Given this context, it seems that Clinton and his former advisers were right to try to persuade Kerry to push the economy up the agenda. Kerry certainly thought so, and took their advice, arguing, "if you believe that losing good paying jobs and replacing them with ones that don't pay the bills means that America is heading in the right direction, you should vote for George Bush and his policies of failure" (*The Guardian*, September 6, 2004). Kerry also promised to repeal the portion of Bush's tax cuts for America's wealthiest 2 percent.

Despite Gallup's evidence that many Americans felt uneasy about their own and the country's prospects, Kerry's refined strategy to run hard on the economy did not ultimately deliver him the office of the presidency, largely because the economy was not the defining issue of the campaign. In a closed NEP exit poll in which respondents were asked to choose from a predetermined list of seven issues, 20 percent said the economy was the most significant issue, while 22 percent said moral values, 19 percent terrorism and 15 percent Iraq. Kerry won most votes among those who said the economy and Iraq were the key issue, but Bush won comfortably among voters who placed moral values or terrorism top of their list. In an open-ended Pew Research Center poll, only 12 percent identified the economy as the top issue, while 14 percent said moral values, 9 percent terrorism and 25 percent Iraq. In the post-election post-mortems, some commentators and many of Clinton's advisers argued that Kerry should have made the economy more central to his campaign. Others rejected this view, arguing he should have focused more on the deteriorating security situation in Iraq. Whatever the rights and wrongs of these interpretations, it should be remembered that if just 60,000 voters in Ohio had switched from Bush, Kerry would be President of the United States and his campaign team lauded as political geniuses. Such is the difference between success and failure.

Bush's second term challenges

Bush argued in his February 2, 2005 State of the Union Address that his stewardship of the American economy over the previous four years had been a great success: the recession was over, growth strong, taxes cut, corporate criminals prosecuted, home ownership at record levels, and 2.3 million jobs created in 2004 alone. In his vision for the next four years, Bush promised to restrain federal spending and cut the deficit, reform education and training, cut red-tape for entrepreneurs and small businesses, reform "the archaic, incoherent federal tax code" and make permanent his first-term tax cuts. In addition, he proposed fundamental reform of the immigration system to allow immigrant "guest workers" to fill jobs Americans won't do, and of the social security system (pensions) which "is headed towards bankruptcy." Bush fleshed out the basic ideas set out in the State of the Union Address a few days latter in his Budget Message of the President that accompanies the OMB-authored Budget of the United States Government and also in the Economic Report of the President accompanying the Annual Report of the Council of Economic Advisers.

The 2006 budget proposed a 4.8 percent increase in funding for America's armed forces to guard against security threats at home and abroad, including $35 billion to reorganize the structure of the armed forces, an extra $1.5 billion for the Millennium Challenge Account to promote good economic and governance policies in less developed nations, and $555 million more for the FBI. Bush has increased defense spending by some 40 percent since taking office in 2001, but the extra money promised for the war on terror and other security threats makes it more difficult to achieve his other key objectives of reducing federal spending and cutting taxes. His task is made more problematic still because most federal spending is difficult to cut – it is in the language of budget politics *non-discretionary*. Moreover, a good chunk of *discretionary* spending, that which is ripe for cuts, is actually constituted by defense and security expenditure, which Bush increased. In the event, Bush's budget proposed to increase total discretionary spending by a below-inflation 2.1 percent and reduce non-security discretionary spending by 1 percent. These savings, albeit small, combined with increased tax revenues from a slowly expanding economy should, according to Bush's projections, permit a decline in the budget deficit from 3.5 percent of GDP in 2005 to 3.0 percent in 2006 and eventually down to 1.5 percent in 2009. Of course, the US government still spends more than it raises in taxes each year, but the overspend is declining relative to the size of the overall economy. Nonetheless, Bush inherited from Clinton a budget in surplus and a declining national debt. Today the budget is in deficit and the national debt is rising.

Lower tax rates, according to the OMB, "reduce obstacles to growth by increasing the incentives to work, save, invest, innovate, and start new businesses," but low taxes on their own are not enough. The American tax code itself "is not just a complicated mess; it is also a maze of special-interest loopholes that cause America's taxpayers to spend more than six billion hours every year on paperwork. Work, entrepreneurship, investment, ownership, and even education are discouraged by our tax system" (OMB, February 2005). One radical reform advocated by some Republicans and *laissez-faire* economists is to abolish the federal income tax altogether and replace it with a "consumption" tax – very much like VAT in the UK. Doing so would make the tax system less progressive and more regressive; it would in other words shift the burden of taxation away from richer Americans and towards poorer ones. For this reason, it will likely to be opposed by most congressional Democrats and perhaps some centrist Republicans, and thus unlikely to become law. Bush will probably have more success reforming the tax code to encourage Americans to save more. Historically, ordinary American citizens saved about 10 percent of their income, but since the 1990s the figure has fallen precipitously, dwindling to just 1 percent in 2004. Savings are important because they provide stability during recessions and engender economic growth when loaned by financial institutions to entrepreneurs. To promote a culture of saving and thus promote prosperity, Bush has proposed three new programs – Retirement Savings Accounts, Employer Retirement Savings Accounts and Individual Development Accounts.

Bush also hopes to reform the litigation system, which he believes places an unwarranted burden on businesses, often does little for the victim, while lining the pockets of lawyers. For example, according to the Bush administration, asbestos lawsuits have forced 74 companies into bank-ruptcy, resulted in 50,000 lost jobs, and will cost up to $265 billion. Lawsuits against medical practitioners are also destructive because they force doctors to practice defensive rather than preventive medicine and to take out expensive insurance policies to cover against sometimes-malicious claims, thus increasing the overall cost of health care. A key problem for Bush's reform agenda is that lawyers are a significant force in the corridors of power in Washington. They are well organized, have top lobbyists working on their behalf, and donate large sums of money to both political parties (especially the Democrats).

Powerful special interests also pose a barrier to Bush's professed desire to promote free trade in an interdependent and globalized economy. Economists argue that free trade allows countries to specialize in products they produce most efficiently. This pushes down prices and/or increases quality and, when traded freely in the global market, enriches everyone. Bush and his economic advisers argue that free trade is good because it opens up new markets for many American goods, helps push down prices and expands choices for consumers, and encourages foreign investment in the US economy. All this adds up to more and better jobs and a vibrant economy. Whatever aggregate benefits free trade may bring, however, it unquestionably imposes individual-level costs and thus engenders well-organized opposition.

Opposition to free trade almost derailed Bush's proposal to augment the North American Free Trade Agreement (NAFTA) between the US, Canada and Mexico with the Central American Free Trade Agreement (CAFTA) between the US, Costa Rica, El Salvador, Guatemala, Honduras, Nicaragua and the Dominican Republic. The seven nations signed the pact in May 2004 but Congress only ratified it in July 2005 after vigorous lobbying by Bush and his officials. Pro-labor Democrats thought the agreement did too little to protect workers' rights and worried about the threat posed to American workers' jobs and wages by cheap foreign labor and imports; environmentalists feared the damaging effects of unbridled development; and American farmers and some of their Republican supporters didn't want government subsidies cut and tariffs abolished. For example, US sugar producers were protected by a quota system that limited the amount of (cheap) foreign sugar imported each year. The quotas pushed up the price of sugar for producers of goods containing sugar, and in turn raised prices for consumers. They also artificially constrained the potential market of more efficient foreign producers. While US sugar producers employ relatively few people nationwide, many producers are located in Florida where they are an important employer and contributor to the state economy. They are also well organized and very influential. Thus, many of Florida's congressmen and women opposed CAFTA, and politicians with national ambitions must take care to listen carefully to this key presidential election state. While Bush ultimately was able to secure CAFTA's passage, one observer noted that "the last-minute negotiations for Republican votes resembled the wheeling and dealing on a car lot. Republicans who were opposed or undecided were courted during hurried meetings in Capitol hallways, on the House floor and at the White House. GOP leaders told their rank and file that if they wanted anything, now was the time to ask ... Many of the favors bestowed in exchange for votes will be tucked into the huge energy and highway bill" (Blustein and Allen, *Washington Post*, July 28, 2005). Bush hopes to follow CAFTA with an ambitious plan to establish a Free Trade Area of the Americas, a hemispheric free-trade pact among 34 nations in north, central and south America. Negotiations to create the world's largest free-trade area began in 1994 but are stalled due to the opposition of some countries, notably Brazil, Argentina and Venezuela, which recently elected more left-wing leaders opposed to the US version of free-market capitalism.

Globalization and the move toward free trade in goods and capital pose other problems for the Bush administration. Economic interdependence further loosens the already weak control of policy-makers over national economies and is undermining established macro-economic models used to predict trends in growth, employment and so on. For example, recent increases in short-term interest rates by the Federal Reserve have not produced a rise in interest rates on mortgages and long-term bonds, as economic models predict. Indeed, rates on the latter two have actually fallen, much to the bemusement of many economists, including the "maestro" himself, Alan Greenspan. Another example, noted above, is that consumers are spending more and saving less, while increases in spending seem no longer tied to increases in income. It appears instead that a "wealth effect" – that is money tied in homes and shares – now drives spending. Economists worry that future recessions may be deeper and longer if consumers respond to potential falls in share and house prices by reining in spending. Economists also worry that the internationalization of financial markets makes national economies more sensitive to problems in other economies. Could this interconnectedness produce a worldwide domino effect as recession in one tips all others into recession, ultimately producing a global depression to rival that of the early 1930s? While this is a serious concern for policy-makers, it is not at all clear what they could do about it or even whether they truly understand the complexities of the modern global economy. However, as Robert Samuelson of the *Washington Post* (June 22, 2005) notes, while "change has outpaced comprehension ... the less we understand the economy, the better it does." Moreover, while the US economy is constantly being written off by pessimistic commentators, it continues to perform well, especially relative to its major competitors in Europe, and has during Bush's tenure survived the shocks of 9/11, a war on terror and Hurricane Katrina. The US will undoubtedly face further shocks, but it is unlikely that any other country will threaten America's economic and therefore political and military dominance in the foreseeable future.

Chapter 13

Social Policy

Alex Waddan

Social policy issues were not at the forefront of the 2004 election campaign. The Iraq war and security against terrorism were the dominant themes. In the immediate aftermath of winning re-election, however, President Bush declared that he intended to use his renewed political capital purposefully. To this end he announced that he would proceed with reform of the US's public pension system, commonly known as Social Security. The aim was to introduce legislation that would allow individuals partially to opt out of the existing, compulsory, Social Security payroll tax and put that money into an individual retirement account. In terms of social policy reform this was the equivalent of lighting the blue touch paper to one of the most explosive issues in American politics.

In addition, President Bush pledged to articulate further the philosophy of "compassionate conservatism" developed in the 2000 campaign; and the first term of the Bush presidency had seen action on several social policy fronts. There was significant reform in education policy and a new benefit helping the country's seniors pay for prescription drugs was legislated. The White House also made efforts to get its new faith-based initiative up and running, allowing religious groups to receive federal grants to provide local services. Further to these new programs there was continuing monitoring of the radical reform in welfare policy that had been enacted in 1996. Although this reform had been signed into law by President Clinton its content was largely devised by the Republican majorities in Congress and it was praised by Bush as an example of compassionate conservatism in action.

This chapter explores these recent developments in US social policy in the context of the nature and purpose of the American welfare state. In comparison to most other industrialized Western states the US government plays a lesser role in providing benefits and services. Furthermore, since the start of the 1980s there has been a growing ideological attack on collective social welfare provision. On top of this, economic, fiscal and demographic changes have combined to undermine the long-term sustainability of established programs. On the other hand, the extent of government involvement in the social welfare arena in the United States should not be understated and what might be described as the big-ticket items of the American welfare state – Social Security, Medicare and Medicaid remain popular. This makes for a complex and at times contradictory politics when social policy issues are under discussion. The chapter will consider how the Bush administration, with its ideological preference for down-sizing the role of government, pursued its goals while coping with these contrary pressures. The chapter will conclude by reflecting on continuing problems in the social welfare field such as the rising number of Americans lacking health care insurance.

The American welfare state

It was in the New Deal era when the federal government first intervened in the social welfare arena in a substantive fashion and established the contours of the modern American welfare state. There has, of course, been much change since the 1930s, but it is still the case that the New Deal laid in place a welfare state settlement which has a continuing legacy in the early twenty-first century. What was done at this time and, equally, what was *not* done critically affected future development (Hacker, 2002). Most significantly the 1935 Social Security Act established the Old Age, Survivors and Disability Insurance (OASDI) program that provided cash benefits to retirees, the disabled and their dependants. This legislation also created the Aid to Families with Dependent Children (AFDC) program that gave benefits, on a means-tested basis, to single-parent families. For much of the following 40 years various initiatives were designed to build on the New Deal programs with a steady process of incremental adjustment and expansion. The most identifiable period of growth came in the 1960s with the Great Society and War on Poverty. In 1965 the public health care programs Medicare and Medicaid were founded and through the decade and into the 1970s there were a series of expansions of the food stamp program. Furthermore, in the early 1970s there were a sequence of *ad hoc* increases in the level of Social Security benefits before payments were tied in to rise automatically with the cost of living.

This period of relatively consensual social welfare expansion came to an end, however, in the late 1970s. Indeed the political discourse of the 1970s shifted rapidly from assumptions about consensus to assumptions about crisis as the US economy, along with the economies of other leading industrial nations, went into reverse. In 1976 the Democrat presidential candidate Jimmy Carter invoked the concept of the "misery index" in order to attack incumbent Republican Gerald Ford. The misery index was an aggregate of the rates of unemployment and inflation. In 1976 this added up to 13.5. Unfortunately for Carter, and the United States, in his fourth year in office in 1980 it stood at 20.6. This economic downturn gave extra credence to conservative arguments that the welfare state was an excessive burden on the economy.

In political terms this change in mood was marked most manifestly by the election of President Reagan who, in his inaugural address, famously proclaimed that government was in fact the problem rather than part of the solution. There is still disagreement about the extent to which Reagan succeeded in rolling back the American welfare state; but over the last quarter century both the principles and practices of public social welfare provision have come under much greater critical scrutiny.

Indeed, even prior to Reagan's explicit attack on the welfare state, the US was widely perceived as having a deep-rooted skepticism about the value of government-organized collectivism; and, in an international context, the US does have a relatively modest publicly funded and government-organized social welfare sector. For example, comparative data show that the US government spends a smaller proportion of the country's Gross Domestic Product on social welfare. According to OECD figures, in 1998, the US spent 14.6 percent of GDP on cash benefits, health care and social services. This compared with figures such as 31 percent in Sweden, 26 percent in Germany and 20.8 percent in the UK. The average figure for the then member states of the European Union was 24.2 percent and the average for the OECD countries was 20.8 percent (Barr, 2004: 9).

In his seminal study of welfare states Gosta Esping-Andersen identified three types of welfare regime in capitalist economies (Esping-Andersen, 1990). First, in "social democratic" welfare states, government uses its authority to promote redistributive public policies. Furthermore, social assistance programs are likely to be inclusive and universal. Second, in "conservative" or "corporate" welfare states governments try to maintain traditional social structures but are still actively engaged in organizing a wide array of social benefits. Finally, in liberal regimes it is individuals who are primarily responsible for their own economic fate and it is therefore a characteristic of liberal social policy arrangements that there is a reliance on residual and means-tested, rather than universal, assistance programs. In short, the government's role is a relatively small one with the emphasis on providing a safety net rather than a comprehensive system of benefits and services. While Esping-Andersen's work can be criticized for trying to squeeze too much variety into too narrow categories this is a widely used typology and the United States is regularly cast as the definitive exemplar of a "liberal" welfare state (Goodin *et al.*, 1999).

This portrayal of the US government as a relatively low-key player in the social policy arena has, however, been disputed. Some scholars have questioned the extent of this American exceptionalism and have pointed to

America's "hidden welfare state.' The argument focuses on the methodology of measuring welfare state "effort'. Neil Gilbert notes that assessing "the generosity of welfare states" by calculating a government's direct public expenditure on social welfare as a percentage of GDP is "deeply flawed" (Gilbert, 2002: 48). The point is that measuring only government outgoings does not take account of policies which do cost the government money, but in terms of revenues forfeited through the extensive use of tax credits and rebates rather than through explicit spending. The US tax system has a variety of what are effectively tax give-backs but the most significant are in the social welfare field. In particular there are significant tax subsidies to employers who provide their workers with retirement pensions and health insurance (Howard, 2003). Furthermore, the US is a relatively low-tax economy in terms of both direct and indirect taxation; for example, there is no national consumption tax (or VAT). This implies that the government has less revenue to spend on social policy but it also means that fewer of the benefits that are paid out are clawed back. Howard concludes that if all these features are factored into the equation then the gap between the generous welfare states and the US in terms of welfare state effort is less significant than the raw spending data suggest (Howard, 2003).

Hence proper consideration of this "hidden welfare state" does reveal the US government to be a more active player in shaping American society and, through tax credits encouraging work such as the Earned Income Tax Credit, moulding the behavior of individual Americans to a greater degree than is sometimes appreciated. On the other hand, reimbursements or credits paid through the tax system do only apply to those that are in work and therefore do not help the poor outside the labor force. Moreover, there are still significant gaps in the US welfare state – most immediately represented by the inadequacy of the public health care system and the lack of a family allowance benefit – that "remain startling to many European observers" (Ross, 2002: 203).

Party politics and social policy

According to Goodin *et al.* (1999: 58) "the basic ethos of US social policy has long been dominated by rugged *laissez-faire* individualism and liberal notions of self-help." Seymour Martin Lipset maintains that this distinctive feature of the US polity reflects the fact that Americans have distinctive beliefs about the balance of responsibility between the individual and the government (1996). Everett Carl Ladd's study of the "American ideology" led him to conclude "American policy on social welfare reflects national insistence on a large measure of individual, rather than government responsibility" (Ladd, 1994: 35). This conclusion, he noted, came from surveys showing "the US public consistently less inclined than citizens of most other industrial nations to turn to government for various guarantees and assistance" (Ladd, 1994: 40–1). According to this version of American culture the US welfare state broadly reflects what most Americans want and expect from government.

There is considerable evidence, however, that public opinion towards welfare state structures is more complex than these statements of American exceptionalism might suggest. At times majority popular belief clearly does reflect the values of classical economic liberalism, particularly with regard to cash benefits to able-bodied, working-aged Americans. Hence in the mid-1990s Weaver *et al.* concluded that AFDC, the monthly welfare benefit paid to poor single-parent families, had fallen into such disrepute that it was "perceived as being at odds with the widely shared American values of individualism and the work ethic" (Weaver *et al.*, 1995: 607). This was despite the fact that in 1994, the peak year for AFDC enrolment, the average monthly benefit per family was only $386 for an average family size of 2.8. The popular antipathy toward "welfare" meant that there was widespread public support for dramatic reform in 1996 when the Personal Responsibility and Work Opportunity Reconciliation Act (PRWORA) abolished AFDC and replaced it with a time-limited benefit with strong work requirements attached. Ironically, however, the US's big welfare state programs, notably Social Security and Medicare that provide for the elderly, have strong political support from both the general public and from well organized interest groups, notably the American Association of Retired People (AARP), which makes retrenchment politically difficult.

Recent polling evidence in fact suggests that even when people express a general skepticism about the role of government they are protective towards existing government programs from which they expect to benefit (Jacobson, 2003: 210–13). Thus Democrats are keen to portray themselves as the champions of the popular government programs, but are wary of being seen as the party that advocates Big Government solutions in a knee-jerk fashion leading to unsustainable tax and spend policies. Conversely, Republicans wish to establish their credentials as the party of low taxes and smaller government without alienating voters by appearing to threaten popular programs.

The contradictory impulses of the public and the contrary politics this produces were well illustrated during the Clinton era. In his 1996 State of the Union address Clinton declared that "The era of big government is over" (Baer, 2000: 241), but the administration remained happy to make political capital out of defending the biggest existing government programs. These tensions were illustrated by the politics of health care policy in the administration's first term. In 1992 one of Clinton's campaign themes was the need for dramatic reform of the American health care system but the effort in 1993 and 1994 to push through legislation expanding government intervention and regulation flopped. In November 1994 the health care debacle was perceived as one of the key factors helping the Republicans capture Congress in the midterm congressional elections. On the other hand, Clinton's subsequent political rehabilitation came about largely because of the budget battles with the Republican-controlled Congress through 1995 when the President insisted that proposed Republican budget cuts and structural changes to Medicare and Medicaid threatened the integrity of these programs. This time public opinion rallied to the cause of big government.

The next twist in this narrative came in August 1996 when Clinton signed PRWORA which was the first time an entitlement program established by the 1935 Social Security Act had been repealed. Clinton had never defended the old AFDC program – indeed his pledge to "end welfare as we know it" in the 1992 campaign was a primary basis of his claim to be a "different type of Democrat" – but the plan advanced by Republican leaders did go well beyond his own reform agenda. PRWORA imposed a five-year lifetime limit on adults receiving welfare benefits (the new benefit was called Temporary Assistance to Needy Families) and declared that adults in households receiving welfare, predominantly single mothers, would have to engage in a work effort within two years of starting to receive welfare. Furthermore, this two-year period of grace for new welfare recipients could be reduced at state discretion (for a full discussion of PRWORA see Ross, 2002). The decision as to whether President Clinton should sign or veto PRWORA caused one of the biggest rifts in the Clinton White House. In the end, Clinton's distaste for the existing system and the desire not to give the Republicans a so-called wedge issue in the forthcoming elections proved decisive (Waddan, 2002: 122–6).

If, however, ending AFDC was a popular move, the enduring strength of the US's largest social welfare program was illustrated toward the end of the Clinton era. Through the 1990s there had been a growing conventional wisdom that the Social Security system needed reform and towards the end of his presidency Clinton flirted with reform ideas. In the end, though, Clinton settled for scoring political points by emphasizing that he would protect the traditional Social Security program. The overall story of the Clinton years, therefore, illustrates the elaborate interaction between politics, social policy and public opinion. Thus President Bush, with his brand of "compassionate conservatism," stepped into a complex environment.

Bush and social policy

Through the 2000 campaign Bush attempted to ameliorate concerns that Republican attitudes on social welfare issues were too hard-faced through the doctrine of "compassionate conservatism'. Although something of an intangible concept, compassionate conservatism did promise a scaling back of government's role and a greater emphasis on nongovernmental agencies stepping into the breach, but it did acknowledge a legitimate role for government and was not a conservatism dedicated simply to "benign neglect" and shrinking the state. Speaking in April 2002 Bush explained:

> Government cannot solve every problem, but it can encourage people and communities to help themselves and to help one another. Often the truest kind of compassion is to help citizens build lives of their own. I call my philosophy and approach "compassionate conservatism." It is compassionate to actively help our fellow citizens in need. It is conservative to insist on responsibility and on results. (Bush, 2002)

During the 2000 campaign Bush enthusiastically promoted two policy ideas which indicated the distinctive nature of this compassionate conservative agenda. First, reform in education, and second plans that government provide financial support to faith-based groups which would allow these groups, rather than government agencies, to deliver social services at a local level. Polls showed that these were popular proposals which was particularly significant in the education arena as this was normally a policy domain where the Democrats would expect to have the political edge (Jacobson, 2003: 199).

Education reform: No Child Left Behind

According to Joel Aberbach education reform and specifically the passage of the No Child Left Behind legislation (NCLB) was "a signature accomplishment of the Bush administration" (2005: 131). Education reform had been a priority for Bush during his time as Governor of Texas and through the 2000 campaign he championed the Texas model as evidence of both how it was possible to improve educational standards and also of his own capacity to work across party lines. Certainly, as Fortier and Ornstein point out, the NCLB "was bipartisan, cutting across ideological lines ... It reinforced Bush's image as a compassionate conservative and appealed to moderate voters" (2003: 147). Through the development of the bill the White House sought the cooperation of leading Democrats, and the legislation's final congressional passage in December 2001 was accomplished with big majorities in both parties voting in favor.

The policy focus of the new law was to provide more money to states and more flexibility in terms of how they spent it, but in return it required greater accountability through more rigorous student testing, with schools obtaining unsatisfactory results required to take appropriate remedial measures. In its final form the NCLB in fact disappointed some conservatives who felt that it had been watered down in order to gain wider support. In particular conservatives were frustrated that proposals that parents of children at failing schools be given vouchers to use at any school, even a private school, were not included in the final bill. Furthermore, conservatives felt that the discretion given to states and local government in terms of how to spend federal money was insufficient. Indeed, in an important fashion the NCLB broke with traditional conservative preferences in education policy and politics by extending rather than reducing the scope of federal government. As Gillian Peele states the NCLB represented "a major and novel extension of federal power into state and local control of education" (2005: 160).

After its enactment and implementation, however, the NCLB fell into some disrepute. Critics lamented what they saw as the over-emphasis on testing and charged that in many areas the promise that students could move schools if they attended a failing school was not a practical possibility. Furthermore, state governments, which came under increasing budgetary strain after 2000, complained that the requirements on them to institute improvements in failing schools effectively constituted an unfunded mandate as the extra moneys provided under NCLB were inadequate for the task. Nevertheless, it is difficult to argue against improving educational standards and, whether or not the testing regime instigated by NCLB is the best way to achieve this, Bush's political opponents have shied away from attacking the principles of the law and have focused on the manner of its implementation. For example, in 2004 John Kerry promised to pursue the goals of NCLB by providing sufficient funding.

Faith-based initiatives

One of Bush's early actions as President was to issue an executive order establishing the Office of Faith-Based and Community Initiatives (OFBCI). The aim was to increase the role of religious organizations in providing street-level social services by allowing religious groups to compete for government grants. According to the President locally organized faith-based groups were often better placed than government agencies to deliver on "valid public purposes such as curbing crime, conquering addiction, strengthening families and neighborhoods, and overcoming poverty" (quoted in Aberbach, 2005a: 142). In the first term, however, there was more rhetoric than action. Bush did issue a further executive order in December 2002 that allowed religious groups to secure government grants even if they discriminated on a religious basis when hiring employees but there was not a vigorous undertaking to get legislation through Congress that would have significantly expanded the overall initiative. Indeed the first director of the OFBCI, John DiIulio, has written: "faith initiatives got on the president's policy agenda and remained there without a concerted effort to draft proposals that could pass and, once passed, effect administrative and funding changes in keeping with the president's public positions on the issue" (DiIulio, 2003: 256).

In a speech to the leaders of various faith-based groups in March 2005 President Bush did celebrate the fact that there had been an increase in the amount of federal grants being distributed through the faith-based initiative through 2003 and 2004. He announced: "about $2 billion in grants were awarded last year to religious charities." He acknowledged, however, that there were still problems in persuading government bureaucracies of the merits of the faith-based initiative, but he reiterated his own belief that "armies of compassion" and "social entrepreneurship" were often a more effective way of providing services than bureaucrats (Bush, 2005b).

Welfare reform

One example of compassionate conservatism in action in fact pre-dated the Bush administration. That is, despite being signed into law by President Clinton, the PRWORA has consistently been hailed by Bush as an example of government encouraging personal responsibility and hence helping people to help themselves. Advocates of the 1996 reform have pointed to the subsequent significant drop in the welfare rolls and declared that PRWORA was an undebatable success. Between August 1996 and September 2001 the number of families receiving welfare dropped from 4.4 million to 2.1 million, a fall of 52 percent. By June 2003 the number of families on the welfare rolls had fallen again to just over 2 million. In addition, supporters of reform have pointed out that an increased number of former welfare recipients were engaged with the labor force. For example, between 1993 and 1999 there was a 50 percent increase in the number of never-married mothers, traditionally the least likely of all women to do paid work, who had a job (Haskins *et al.*, 2001). Critics, on the other hand, worry that some of those no longer on welfare have fallen into deep poverty and that even those who do find work are in jobs paying low wages. Overall, nearly a decade on from its enactment the jury is still out on PRWORA as, despite intensive research efforts by the social science community, there is not yet a full and coherent picture of what has happened.

It is very clear, however, that whatever evidence the research community comes up there will be no repeal of the workfare principles embodied in PRWORA. Arguments continued in Washington about how the original legislation might be amended but these focused on the Bush White House's desire to toughen the existing work requirements and place a greater emphasis on discouraging single parenthood. These disagreements did prevent the reauthorization and updating of the 1996 law that was due in 2002; and through to the end of 2005 PRWORA continued to operate under its original remit.

Health care reform

The most controversial piece of social policy legislation enacted during the Bush first term was the Medicare Modernization Act (MMA) which was signed into law by the President in December 2003. Medicare is the government-run health care program for America's seniors and is the second biggest welfare state program in the US. The centerpiece of the MMA was the addition of a new prescription drug benefit to the Medicare program. At the time of the bill's passage it was estimated that this new benefit would cost $410 billion over ten years. Less than two months after the law was enacted, however, the administration upped this estimate to $534 billion – and a story then unfolded about how this latter figure was deliberately suppressed by officials during debate over the law so as not to jeopardize its chances in Congress, where many fiscally conservative Republicans were anxious about the long-term expense (Aberbach, 2005a: 141). A year later the revised estimates put the likely cost at $724 billion.

Whatever the true cost of the new benefit the MMA represented the largest benefits expansion to the Medicare program since it was created in 1965. What is so surprising about this is that the MMA was crafted by a Republican President working with a Republican Congress. It seems counterintuitive that these forces of conservatism would so expand the American welfare state, especially since congressional Republicans had aggressively attempted to restrict Medicare expenditures in the mid-1990s. The explanation of this apparent conundrum lies in two parts.

First, the MMA was in part a response to electoral exigency. The idea of extending Medicare to cover prescription drugs was pushed to the front of the political agenda by President Clinton in his 1999 State of the Union address. By 2000 the issue had gained real political traction and Al Gore, the Democrat presidential candidate, attacked Bush for his initial apparent ambivalence on the matter. Bush responded by promising that he too would introduce a benefit if elected. Indeed in January 2001 the White House put forward a proposal called Immediate Helping Hand that would have helped pay for prescription drugs for seniors on a means-tested basis via $48 billion distributed in block grants to the states over four years. This plan made no legislative progress but the congressional parties and the administration then engaged in something of a bidding war as they offered up more expensive proposals. Congressional Democrats always outbid their opponents but the Republican leadership in House and Senate along with the White House did increase the amount that they were prepared to spend to fund the new benefit. With the matter still unresolved the Democrats made the issue of prescription drugs central to their campaign in the 2002 midterm elections as polls showed that this was an issue where the public trusted the Democrats over the GOP (Serafini, 2002). Republicans again responded by promising that they too would act; and, ironically, the advent of unified Republican government as a consequence of the 2002 elections increased the pressure on the White House and congressional leadership to fulfill their promise. Their determination to deliver was made clear by the extraordinary scenes in the House of Representatives when the final floor vote on MMA was taken. At this point, in an unprecedented move, House Republican leaders held the vote open for nearly three hours as they worked to change a vote of 219 to 215 to defeat the bill into a 220 to 215 majority to pass it.

The second part of the explanation for why the MMA was supported by the vast majority of Republicans and opposed by the vast majority of Democrats was that there was considerably more to the MMA than the new drugs benefit; and, these extra elements had a distinctively conservative twist. One aspect that was particularly revealing of the direction conservatives would like future health care reform to take was the decision to increase the availability of so-called Health Savings Accounts (HSAs). Individuals who start such a savings account, to be used to pay for health care as necessary, benefit from the fact that any contributions they make to their HSA are tax-deductible and the interest generated in the account is tax-exempt. Previously, HSAs had only been authorized for limited groups and debate about them had caused considerable friction between the two parties. Supporters see HSAs as a means of improving choice by giving individuals more scope to devise a plan to suit their own health care needs. They are controversial because critics allege that the tax advantages mean that HSAs offer the most benefits to the wealthy who can afford to put more money into savings. The worry is that this will lead to a further segmentation of the health insurance market with the healthy and wealthy investing in HSAs and opting for cheaper insurance plans that have high deductibles. This will leave behind those with poor health and those who cannot afford to save to pay for potential health problems. This latter group will constitute an unattractive proposition to health insurers who will raise their premiums as a result (for a full discussion of the MMA see Jaenicke and Waddan, 2005).

Illustrating conservative enthusiasm for HSAs, Newt Gingrich, the former Speaker of the House, was instrumental in persuading some Republicans, who were nervous about the cost of the MMA, into voting for the law on the basis of the HSAs. Indeed Gingrich called HSAs the "single most important change in health care policy in 60 years" (quoted in Dreyfuss, 2004: 26). This is an exaggeration and the initial take-up of HSAs was slow. Nevertheless, it is indicative of how conservatives see the use of tax and market incentives as the basis for future health care reform.

There were further aspects of the final bill that reflected both conservative preferences and also the influence of the pharmaceutical industry. The law stipulates that the new drug benefit must be provided, whenever possible, by private insurers and not directly by the Medicare program. In addition the MMA prohibited Medicare from using its bargaining power to negotiate with pharmaceutical companies to get discount prices on prescription drugs despite the fact that this was a practice already employed by the Veterans Administration to keep its cost down when buying drugs. One feature of the long political saga before the enactment of the MMA was the intensive interest group activity. In particular the Pharmaceutical Research and Manufacturers of America (PhRMA) stepped up its lobbying capacity in Washington and its member companies made hefty campaign contributions, overwhelmingly to the GOP. PhRMA did not oppose a prescription drugs bill in principle but was anxious that it did not impose new regulatory burdens on the industry nor use the power of government to lower drug prices. Actively organizing for a comprehensive and generous benefit in terms of both coverage and price was the powerful seniors organization, the AARP (Stone, 2002). In the end there was considerable surprise when the AARP expressed its support for the MMA in its final form as many analysts felt that PhRMA had got more of its wish list than AARP had achieved.

One reason for the surprise at the AARP's approval of the MMA was that the new benefit is not comprehensive and leaves seniors to continue to bear much of the burden for the cost of prescription drugs. For example, according to details of the legislation, an elderly American with annual prescription drug costs of $1,000 would still pay approximately $857 of their own money with the new benefit covering only $143. The individual's expenses would consist of an estimated $35 per month in premiums, a $250 annual deductible and a 25 percent co-payment. Moreover, the benefit is subject to a gap in coverage – or the so-called doughnut hole – such that there is no government help once someone's annual bill exceeds $2,250 until total out-of-pocket costs hit $3,600.

When Bush entered the White House the question of prescription drugs for seniors shared the health care spotlight with the issue of "patients rights." This had become a high-profile cause through the 1990s as more and more Americans with employer-related health insurance found that they were enrolled in managed care plans. These plans were more concerned with containing costs through methods such as regulating access to specialists than was the case with the more traditional fee-for-service type of health plan. Hence, there was a growing concern that people were being denied necessary treatment because of the emphasis on cost containment and aggrieved patients were increasingly turning to the courts as a means of restitution.

As with prescription drugs it was the Democrats who made the political running in terms of putting forward legislative proposals for a comprehensive Patients' Bill of Rights. Again the Republicans responded by advancing alternative plans which they described as offering more calibrated and moderate answers to the problem. The two parties disagreed most vehemently over the extent of liability for insurers and employers. Democrats argued that patients should have an unrestricted right to sue if they were denied necessary treatment. Republicans worried that such an unrestricted right would lead to a major burden on insurers who in turn would pass on their costs to employers. As President, Bush said that he would veto a bill that had no restrictions on insurer and employer liability. For a time in the summer of 2001 it looked as if the President might have to carry out this veto threat, but in the end the bill died in conference committee as the separate versions passed in the House and Senate could not be reconciled. As it was, this left Bush "able to stake out the position that he supported a version of patients' rights without having to sign a bill that would have alienated many of his conservative supporters" (Fortier and Ornstein, 2003: 155). At this point the issue of patients' rights rather lost its momentum and retreated from the political headlines.

Continuing issues in social policy

One aspect of the two health care issues discussed above is that they both reflected the fears of the relative "haves" in the US system. Since the failure of Clinton's effort at comprehensive health care reform there has been little serious effort at dealing with the problem of uninsured Americans. The creation of the State Children's Health Insurance Program, enacted in 1997 as part of the Balanced Budget Act, did extend government health care to children in low-income households but this has not stopped an increase in the overall numbers of uninsured. In 1993, when President Clinton advanced his reform plan, 39.7 million Americans, amounting to 15.3 percent of the population, lacked health insurance. Ten years later very nearly 45 million Americans, amounting to 15.6 percent of the population, were without insurance. In addition many more had inadequate insurance coverage. All this is despite the fact that the US spends a higher percentage of its GDP on health care than other industrialized nations do. In 2001 the US spent 14.1 percent of GDP on health care compared to 10.9 percent in Switzerland, 10.7 percent in Germany, 9.5 percent in France and 7.6 percent in the United Kingdom (OECD, 2003).

The majority of this health care spending takes place in the private sector and for most able-bodied, working-aged adults, access to health insurance comes as a perk of employment. The decline in the percentage of private sector workers receiving employer-provided health insurance is, therefore, particularly worrying. In 1979, 70.2 percent of private sector workers were insured through their employment. In 2000 this figure stood at 63.1 percent (Mishel *et al.*, 2003: 144). Furthermore, in many cases where employers have maintained coverage for their workforce they have shifted more of the cost onto workers by increasing co-payments as health care inflation constantly raises costs for all players in the insurance chain. That is, insurers, who are paying out more, raise their premiums to employers. Employers are then faced with the choice of absorbing these costs themselves or passing them on to their employees.

For all this, however, health care was a dog that did not bark in the 2004 election. Exit polls showed that 8 percent of voters prioritized health care as the key issue and of these 77 percent voted for Kerry; yet, the broad-ranging health care plan advanced by Kerry did not capture the popular imagination and Bush was put under relatively little pressure to explain the significant increase in the numbers of uninsured during his first term.

As well as the increase in the numbers of uninsured, the Bush first term also witnessed a rise in the number of Americans living below the poverty line. This fact, however, also received minimal comment during the 2004 presidential election. The Kerry campaign did talk about those who it said had missed out during the Bush years, but the focus was relentlessly on middle-class Americans rather than on the poorest (Peele, 2005: 152). Table 13.1 illustrates the patterns of health care uninsurance and poverty in the years since Bill Clinton became President.

The rise in poverty has been accompanied by rising economic inequalities. American society has traditionally tolerated higher levels of inequality than have other developed nations but over the last 30 years income inequalities have grown sharply, with little public policy effort to

Table 13.1   *Indicators of need: Americans below the poverty line and lacking health insurance, 1993 to 2004*

	% below poverty line	% without health insurance
2004	12.7	15.7
2003	12.5	15.6
2002	12.1	15.2
2001	11.7	14.6
2000	11.3	14.2
1999	11.9	14.5
1998	12.7	16.3
1997	13.3	16.1
1996	13.7	15.6
1995	13.8	15.4
1994	14.5	15.2
1993	15.1	15.3

Source: US Census Bureau 2005: 53, 67.

counter this trend. Bartels offers the following evidence: "the share of income going to the top one-tenth of one percent quadrupled between 1970 and 1998, leaving the 13,000 richest families in America with almost as much income as the 20 million poorest families" (Bartels, 2005: 16). Income inequalities have simultaneously grown in other countries too, but a report sponsored by the American Political Science Association found that the increase in income disparities in the US outstripped that of other nations and that this was at least in part a result of public policy decisions (Taskforce on Inequality and American Democracy, 2004: 2–3). The APSA taskforce noted that the causes of rising inequality were various, "including changes in technology, new forms of family life, and market forces promoting global integration." These factors, however, also applied elsewhere but governments had chosen to respond through policies designed "to buffer" against the inequitable consequences of these pressures. Thus, "Policies pursued – or not pursued – help to explain sharper socioeconomic disparities in the US compared to more muted inequalities in ... other advanced industrialized countries" (Taskforce on Inequality and American Democracy, 2004: 4). Along with the increases in poverty and health uninsurance, however, this increase in inequality has not yet produced a significant political backlash. Indeed the Bush administration exacerbated these inequalities through its tax cuts in 2001 and 2003. According to Hacker and Pierson the distribution of the 2001 legislation was such that "36 percent of the cuts accrued to the richest 1 percent of Americans – a share almost identical to that received by the bottom 80 percent" (2005: 33).

The future and social policy

One concern of this chapter has been to examine the factors that drive change or encourage inertia in US social policy. One helpful way of thinking about when things happen and when they do not is to utilize Kingdon's account of agenda-setting (Kingdon, 1995). In 1996 welfare reform was enacted when there was a convergence of the problem stream (perceived as excessive welfare dependency) and the policy stream (a consensus on time-limits and work requirements as a solution for dependency) at an opportune political moment. The question is why there has not been a similar convergence elsewhere, particularly in health care where the problems are obvious and pressing. Clearly there are many features at work, including; ideological preferences; the balance of political power in Washington (and also in state governments); popular opinion; the relative strengths and weaknesses of relevant interest groups and the wider economic and fiscal context. It is also evident that these features often work at cross-purposes. Consequently sometimes there is dramatic change, such as with PRWORA, while other problems, such as the number of Americans lacking health insurance coverage, fester on.

What is certain is that over the last 25 years elite debate about social welfare provision in the US has tilted in a conservative direction. This has not resulted in across-the-board conservative policy innovation but, regardless of ideological conviction, even commentators sympathetic to government activism in social policy have questioned the long-term viability of programs continuing in their traditional format. One leading social policy analyst, Paul Pierson, has pointed to a series of factors which have squeezed the capacity of government to maintain expansive welfare benefits and services. These factors include; demographic trends, primarily the increase of the proportion of the population who are elderly; changing household structures such as the increasing number of single-parent and single-person households, and the shift from manufacturing to service-based industries which has slowed economic growth and therefore real wage growth. Hence, Pierson has concluded that the welfare state is now in an era of "permanent austerity" (Pierson, 2001). Nevertheless, even with a combination of ideological and objective factors pressing for reform, major restructuring of social policy remains difficult to accomplish. First, big programs have big constituencies which may well oppose change. Second, reform is often technically complex. This combination of features makes reform proposals particularly vulnerable to being derailed from the legislative track in the US's multi-layered institutional context.

The difficulties inherent in achieving major reform did not, however, deter President Bush from accelerating reform of the Social Security system to the top of the political agenda after his re-election. According to different perspectives this was either a brave or foolhardy political maneuver. Social Security had developed a reputation as the "third rail" of American politics – that is, "touch it and die" – and so any effort at significant restructuring would involve a major political contest setting the administration against powerful interests, notably the AARP. On the other hand, there was a general acknowledgment that some reform of the pensions system was needed as there was a real concern about the long-term viability of the program.

The existing Social Security system was funded through its own trust fund which in turn was funded by a specific payroll tax split between employer and employee (12.4 percent in 2005). In 2005 the trust fund was in surplus but in 2004 the Social Security Board of Trustees predicted that the fund would be exhausted by 2042, at which point the program would only be able to pay out 70 percent of scheduled benefits. These long-range projections are clearly a little hit-and-miss (for example, in 1997 the predicted exhaustion date for the fund was 2029), but there was a genuine long-term problem to be faced with people living longer and the first of the baby-boom generation not far from retirement. Hence, even in 2005 there was a real question of how to ensure that those at the beginning their working lives would have access to a reasonable pension.

While, however, there was consensus on the need for change this did not extend to agreement on what form change should take. Critics of the administration argued that Bush's plans were driven more by his ideological preferences than by a real desire to put the pension system on a sound fiscal footing. Thus supporters of the traditional Social Security program argued that the system could be shored up through modest adjustments to the established arrangements. That is, incremental rises in the retirement age and marginal increases in the payroll tax would be sufficient to defuse the fiscal time bomb. Conservatives, however, maintained that the time was ripe for a more fundamental reform. Hence the administration wanted to change not just the fiscal dynamics of the program but also its organizing principles. In particular it called for individuals to be given more say in determining their own long-term financial fate by allowing people to divert some of the money they had been putting into the Social Security trust fund into their own individual retirement savings account. Advocates of this type of partial privatization insisted that people would benefit from wise investment in private stocks and bonds and therefore have a higher income in retirement. Private savings accounts, as distinct from government-organized collective saving, do increase the amount of risk borne by individuals but conservatives argued that this would encourage people to think more carefully about their financial decisions.

Clearly the battle over Social Security had significant policy implications and involved high political stakes. If the Bush administration had succeeded in its effort in 2005 to push through a reform that at least partially privatized the existing Social Security system then this would have been a major triumph for advocates of a conservative approach to social policy. By the middle of 2005, however, it was evident that Social Security had lived up to its reputation as the "third rail" in American politics as the reform efforts floundered. President Bush did not formally give up on the reform agenda, but his claim that his November 2004 re-election provided a mandate to restructure Social Security proved hollow. Hence within months of re-election the President had expended considerably of his renewed political capital to no avail.

More generally US social policy is likely to continue to be subject to pressures for downsizing the role of government shaped by conservative values and fiscal strains set against demands that existing programs be maintained. It is not easy to predict how these conflicts will be resolved, but the shift through the Bush first term from federal budget surplus into deficit did increase the pressure to cut spending. Indeed, some commentators (Schick, 2003) have portrayed the tax cuts and the consequent exaggeration of the deficit as a stealthlike conservative strategy to force a reduction in the federal government's social welfare spending. There is a logic to this argument and state governments have been forced to limit spending on key social welfare items such as Medicaid and the SCHIP program; but Washington politicians have not always proved to be slaves to fiscal responsibility and sometimes welfare state programs prove more resilient than might be anticipated. Hence, while further conservative reform is possible it will not necessarily come easily. The recriminations in the aftermath of Hurricane Katrina illustrated the different ideas on offer. Liberal advocates of a significant role for government in social policy maintained that the inadequate response to the disaster demonstrated the need for an activist government role in helping the most vulnerable in the community. Conservatives answered that the disaster had exposed the ineptitude of government and that community groups and nongovernment agencies had provided the most effective response to the calamity.

Chapter 14

Foreign and Security Policy

Jonathan Herbert

The "end of history" seems a long time ago. When Fukuyama coined this phrase in the early 1990s, he was referring to the end of the ideological conflict between communism and capitalism that had underpinned nearly 50 years of Cold War (Fukuyama, 1993). He believed that history's central narrative had ended. Recent events suggest that reports of history's demise were greatly exaggerated. The historical narrative observed by Fukuyama may have faded, but a replacement has emerged, describing a conflict between the US and radical Islamic terrorists. Under Bush, US power has been asserted in new arenas, and in new ways, generating a distinctive foreign policy. The US has embarked upon a "War on Terror" with an accompanying Bush Doctrine, a war in Iraq, and an attempt to reinvent political systems across the Middle East.

However, the pursuit of these interests through a new US foreign policy has proved problematic, as US power has not achieved everything that the Bush administration had hoped. Indeed, some claim that Bush's second term has witnessed a reinvention of Bush's foreign policy that takes more account of the realities of the international system, and America's limited power within it.

US power

America is the world's sole superpower. It derives its power from military strength, economic might and "soft power."

The US military is vastly superior to the armed forces of other nations. With a budget of $419 billion in 2004, America spends more than the next 15 military spenders put together (Center for Arms Control and Non-Proliferation, 2005). Not only is spending high, but the US military is by far the most technologically advanced fighting force. The advantage is so great that Americans have found it increasingly difficult to integrate willing allies into US military missions. And because the United States has embraced network-centric warfare, allowing more central control of the battlefield, the addition of allies without suitable technology can be a force for chaos rather than a help.

The US also has massive economic power. It produces more than $11 trillion gross national income, just under one third of the world's total. Japan's economy, second in the world on this measure, produces only $4.3 trillion (World Bank, 2005). America is also the leading trading state, with annual exports worth $1 trillion in 2003 (15% of the global total) and imports of $1.5 trillion (20% of the global total). America's economic and trading strength gives her enormous influence over the operation of other countries' economies, and therefore significant political leverage over their governments.

America also has "soft power," that is, it can "attract others by the legitimacy of American policies and the values that underlie them" (Nye, 2004). Nye argues that the United States has an ideology and culture that is intrinsically attractive. In an era of globalization, it is easy to emphasize the ubiquity of McDonalds and *Friends* and explain this phenomenon as the power of American culture. Certainly, soft power is borne by American trade and cultural output, and no other nation can compete with America's global reach through these mechanisms. However, Nye highlights the role of political values in "soft power": America's cultural appeal is, in part, rooted in values that underpin its culture and affluence, such as liberty and democracy.

Various terms have been used to describe the enormity of America's power in the world, including "hyperpower" and "hegemon". However, for much of the 1990s, debate raged as to how this power should be used. The collapse of the Soviet Union rendered the central organizing principle of US foreign policy, containment of the communist threat, obsolete. Even the nature of US interests in the world was unclear. The Clinton administration offered an emphasis on "engagement" and "enlargement," suggesting that the US should further the spread of liberal democracy. More liberal democracies would assist both America's security and her economic well-being. Bush's 2000 campaign suggested a change in direction, although not necessarily a radical one. Bush would focus directly upon the pursuit of US interests. He also spoke of a more "humble" attitude toward the world, implying a more restrained foreign policy. His pledge not to embroil the US in nation-building won particular attention as it suggested that the US would play a lesser role in international affairs. However, under Bush, US foreign policy has changed fundamentally. New principles underpin both the administration's attitude to the world and the resulting policies.

Principles

Two of Bush's core principles, a realist understanding of the world and an inclination to act unilaterally, were apparent before September 11, 2001.

Bush's team conceived the surrounding world in much more competitive terms than the preceding Clinton administration. The US would act as one power among rivals in an anarchic environment, expecting that each nation, including the US, would pursue its own interests. Bush seemed to see the world in terms of classic geopolitics, as best reflected in the early redesignation of China as a "strategic competitor." In this hostile world, the US would need to work to maintain its primacy in international affairs.

This brand of realism and the allied desire to maintain primacy were particularly evident in the administration's tendency to act unilaterally. The US showed little inclination to cooperate with the institutions that constituted the international order. US rejection of the Kyoto Protocol on Global Warming caused international consternation. The administration's desire to establish a National Missile Defense (NMD) system ended America's participation in the Anti-Ballistic Missile Treaty. The administration refused to accept a new protocol to the Biological Weapons Convention. Most of all, Bush refused to involve the US with the International Criminal Court (ICC), fearing that US troops could be tried as war criminals. Administration resistance to the ICC was extreme. Bush's team threatened to withdraw US foreign aid from other nations unless they signed bilateral agreements with the US that pledged not to handover US citizens to the ICC. Dozens of countries had US military aid withdrawn.

The administration's antipathy to multilateral organizations seemed to lie in their conception of those organizations' efficacy. Rather than seeing US interests as enhanced by multilateral agreements and organizations, members of the Bush administration appeared to consider the commitments to multilateral organizations as risky and constraining. First, there was doubt surrounding the worth of international treaties. Honorable countries might be restrained by treaties, but other nations might well sign an accord and then ignore its requirements. Treaties did not therefore guarantee security. Second, the multilateral order restricted the ability of the US to pursue its own interests. The international order brought US power under the control of a broader community of other nations and committed the US to a series of burdens. Kagan argues that the Bush administration chose to resist these restraints, allowing the US to pursue its interests more freely (Kagan, 2003). Under Bush, America would be able to pursue its interests "unbound" (Daalder and Lindsay, 2003).

After a decade of debate, the Al Qaeda terrorists restored security as the central organizing principle for US foreign policy-making in a matter of minutes. Within days of 9/11, Bush had declared a "War on Terror", pledging to bring those responsible for the attacks to justice. Bush's rhetoric focused upon the need to attack terrorist organizations of global reach to prevent further attacks upon the American people. Effectively, he promised the American people security at home. That promise would make great demands of US foreign policy.

The first form of assault against terrorists would be direct. Bush promised every effort to dismantle the financial networks used by terrorists. This attack would be matched by a military operation against Al Qaeda's camps in Afghanistan and their hosts, the Taliban regime. Bombing began on October 7, 2001, with US and British special forces already on the ground. Much of the initial war was fought by proxy: the US provided money and technological assistance to the Northern Alliance, which had long been resisting the Taliban regime. Despite some slow progress initially, the Alliance made quick advances aided by US support, taking Kabul on November 13. On December 22, a transitional government was sworn in. A stunning victory had been achieved.

Most regarded the war in Afghanistan as a necessary dismantling of Al Qaeda's organizational hub. However, the administration had a broader understanding of its "War on Terror." The principles under-pinning the new "War" became clearer in early 2002 as Bush emphasized the role of nation-states in terrorism. The administration's concern was two-fold. First, the administration believed terrorists needed a national base if they were to launch attacks on the scale of the September 11 operation. Hence, the administration wished to deny terrorists that base. Second, the administration feared that terrorists would obtain access to chemical, biological or nuclear weapons. Therefore, the administration focused sharply on nations that possessed, or aspired to attain, these weapons of mass destruction (WMD). The idea that irresponsible regimes might pass WMD to terrorists, for ideological or financial reasons, caused sleepless nights in Washington.

According to the Bush team, states sponsoring terrorism needed to change their ways. Bush declared that there was no scope for compromise:

> Every nation, in every region, now has a decision to make. Either you are with us, or you are with the terrorists. (Bush, 2001)

Bush's threat to those states "with" the terrorists won great attention. He promised to pursue "regime change" in these cases: nations that continued to support terrorists were likely to face American action. The US would interfere with the internal affairs of other states to change either the behavior of their governments or the governments themselves. The announcement of a doctrine of "pre-emption" in the 2002 National Security Strategy formalized and extended this new direction. The administration asserted its right to attack other states that threatened US security (National Security Council, 2002). Any idea of a community of nations coming to a consensus on the nature of a threat, and then agreeing to act in concert against this threat had been superceded by the preponderance of US power. The US could, and would, act alone. This "Bush Doctrine" amounted to a fundamental assault upon the international order. Since the 1648 Peace of Westphalia, international politics had relied upon the principle of the nation state's sovereignty. One nation's internal affairs were not to be disrupted by another nation, and any attempt to interfere could be considered an act of war. While the US had sometimes pursued regime change covertly in the past, it now claimed publicly the right to project its power anywhere in the world, ignoring both sovereignty and the immediacy of the military threat (Dumbrell, 2003). The concepts of "regime change" and "pre-emption" represented a major upheaval in US foreign policy.

Bush identified three regimes as potential threats to US security. In his famous "Axis of Evil" speech, Bush nominated Iraq, Iran and North Korea. However, the implications of Bush's words had far wider repercussions. In his commitment to stop nation states harboring or aiding terrorists, Bush might have mentioned a series of other nations, such as Syria, Libya or Pakistan. Equally, the commitment to keep WMD from terrorist hands must have alarmed the many nations outside the "Axis of Evil" which were known to hold chemical and biological weapons. Bush's words amounted to a pledge to pursue an aggressive anti-proliferation agenda. Given the location of such nations, Bush's commitments raised the Middle East to a new status in US foreign policy, and amounted to a set of demands of every Middle Eastern nation.

During his first year in office, Bush had transformed US foreign policy. Initially, he had delivered a new realism and an augmented unilateralism. Then, the attacks of September 11, 2001 had generated a re-conception of security. Bush's response amounted to a "rogue states" strategy. Regimes that had shunned the international order were targeted by the Bush administration, for anti-proliferation efforts and potentially for "pre-emption."

Many claimed that Bush was pursuing a neo-conservative agenda. While the label "neo-conservative" is not a precise one, it is often associated with a particular series of beliefs. Neo-conservatives believe in the primacy of US power, particularly military power, and the active application of that power to pursue US interests. Furthermore, neo-conservatives also tend to believe in an aggressive promotion of US values, notably democracy and free markets. Particularly, neo-conservative thinkers such as Paul Wolfowitz, Deputy Secretary of Defense, and Douglas Feith, Under-Secretary of Defense, believed that the peoples of the Middle East were yearning for modernity and democracy.

The principles in action: war in Iraq and anti-proliferation

Many had expected the war in Afghanistan to conclude direct military action in Bush's War on Terror. However, media coverage over the summer of 2002 portrayed a Bush foreign policy team riven by debate over whether to attack Iraq.

Evidence suggests that neo-conservative members of Bush's team advocated a "pre-emptive" war to overthrow Saddam Hussein and wished to connect the attacks of September 11 with Iraq. Richard A. Clarke, then Bush's counter-terrorism adviser on the National Security Council, recounts Defense Secretary Rumsfeld's insistence that the attacks should be blamed upon Iraq, and that Iraq should be the first target in a War on Terror (Clarke, 2004). Paul Wolfowitz also demanded action on Iraq. However, neo-conservatives confronted vigorous resistance from Secretary of State Colin Powell (Woodward, 2004). Initially, Powell argued that an Iraq war could be avoided by imposing new forms of targeted, or "smarter," sanctions. Powell feared both an international backlash and the stimulation of more fundamentalist terrorism if a unilateral attack was undertaken. He also worried about the stability of a future Iraq. However, during 2002 Powell realized that the Bush administration would launch an American attack upon Iraq. Accepting this inevitability, he argued that UN approval for an Iraq invasion should be sought to give international legitimacy and so to avoid the appearance of American imperialism. Of course, to bring the UN into the operation was an anathema to the neo-conservatives.

Initially, Powell won the argument. Bush spoke to the UN in September 2002, challenging the international community to enforce previous resolutions on Iraq. After the very public debate within the Bush administration, diplomats of many nations were greatly relieved that the US had chosen the multilateral route. On November 8, 2002, the UN Security Council adopted Resolution 1441, calling on Iraq to comply with its disarmament obligations. Weapons inspectors returned to Iraq within a week. However, over December and January, Iraq appeared to cheat the inspectors, providing inadequate information on weaponry and, according to the first report from the inspectors, providing less than full cooperation with the inspection team. Bush declared Iraq in material breach of UN resolutions, and demanded military action. Resolution 1441 had been ambiguous on the consequences of Iraqi noncompliance. The Americans argued that the previous resolutions amounted to an authorization of military action, but other nations disagreed. Although British Prime Minister Tony Blair helped to persuade Bush to go back to the UN for a second resolution on the need for military action, it quickly became clear that this second resolution would not pass. It foundered upon French,

Russian and Chinese opposition. US attempts to win international legitimacy for the conflict ceased. The US would invade Iraq without UN support, instead leading a "coalition of the willing" including Britain, Australia, Italy and Spain.

It is questionable whether Iraq stood out among the Arab nations as a particularly egregious proliferator or sponsor of terror. After the first Gulf War, its chemical and biological weapons stocks had been destroyed under the watchful eyes of UN inspectors. However, Iraq had expelled the inspectors in 1998, and despite international sanctions, intelligence estimates from numerous nations suggested that Iraq had attempted to restore its WMD capability. The Bush administration certainly trumpeted such intelligence as its principal *casus belli*, even if some evidence supporting their case later proved dubious. The administration also emphasized links between Iraq and the perpetrators of the September 11 attacks. Certainly, Iraq's behavior warranted concern, but Iran, known to hold WMD and to sponsor a range of terrorist organizations, struck many analysts as a greater threat.

Other interpretations of the administration's motivation abound. Some claim that Bush's interest in the Middle East reflected the continuing US need for oil. Others see the administration's actions as, primarily, an attempt to protect Israel, reflecting the powerful Jewish influence over American policy. Nonetheless, tangible evidence suggests that, behind the scenes, the neo-conservatives had won their policy battle. Arguably, some within the Bush administration had always intended to engineer an attack on Iraq and the September 11 attacks provided a suitable pretext.

Iraq, of course, represented only one third of the "Axis of Evil." If the administration aspired to keep WMD from terrorists, the issue of weapons proliferation in Iran and North Korea also required attention.

In many ways, the two regimes provided similar challenges. Each country had been developing a nuclear program. Each claimed that their program was for energy generation, not weapons development. Each was considered likely to spread nuclear technology: North Korea actively threatened to sell expertise and materials while Iran's support for terrorism has been well documented. Each was considered a threat to regional stability, particularly if they gained nuclear capabilities. Neighboring states seemed likely to develop nuclear weapons if North Korea and Iran established themselves as nuclear powers. The nuclearizing of both the Middle East and Pacific Rim could result. Each also had a record of deceit concerning their nuclear programs. Since accepting an "Agreed Framework" with the US in 1994, the Koreans have pursued a covert uranium enrichment program that the agreement had prohibited explicitly. The enrichment program was revealed in 2002. North Korea ejected independent UN inspectors and abandoned their membership of the

Non-Proliferation Treaty. Iran deceived inspectors for the best part of two decades before their uranium enrichment program was exposed, also in 2002.

The Bush administration's initial response to the anti-proliferation challenges was a blunt disengagement, particularly in the case of North Korea. The Clinton administration had been negotiating with the Koreans and, purportedly, had come close to a settlement which would have frozen North Korea's plutonium program. Bush's team cut off all further negotiations in March 2001, arguing that the North Korean dictatorship could not be trusted to abide by any agreement. Instead, the Bush team would wait for "regime change," perhaps assuming that suppressed North Koreans were on the brink of overthrowing their leadership. The policy towards Iran was equally uncommunicative. The Bush administration expressed its antipathy towards a regime that sponsored numerous terrorist groups and failed to recognize Israel's right to exist.

Successes and failures

Bush's new foreign policy can claim a number of successes. The quantum leap of a "War on Terror" involving more assertive US behavior might have been expected to disrupt relations with other major powers. However, Russia and China tolerated the change. Military campaigns in Afghanistan and Iraq were triumphs for US military power. Al Qaeda's base in Afghanistan was dismantled, and no additional major terrorist attacks on the US mainland had taken place by the end of 2005. However, there are also reasons to doubt the effectiveness of Bush's new direction. The conflicts in Iraq and Afghanistan are ongoing, and have not, yet, fulfilled neo-conservative expectations. Any assertion that the War on Terror is being won is highly questionable; substantial debates have developed both in the US and internationally on the nature and efficacy of Bush's "War". Proliferators have responded little to America's cajoling. The Bush administration has been forced to engage with the Israel–Palestine problem, but, like so many before, has struggled to make progress toward a resolution. The changes wrought by the Bush administration have not offered the expected achievements. Whether US power is suited to the tasks undertaken is in question. The "Bush Doctrine" has been poorly received by most of the international community, and America's diplomatic capital and soft power have been jeopardized. Arguably, US power has been damaged by the Bush administration's approach.

The war in Iraq provided a spectacular demonstration of US military power. The war began in March 2003, and Bush could, with credibility at the time, declare "Mission Accomplished" from an aircraft carrier off the US West Coast. The early triumph, though, was not matched by subsequent developments. Expecting a friendly welcome from liberated Iraqis, the administration undertook little planning for a post-invasion Iraq. The sense that Iraq's democratic future would be easily organized was reflected in a limited US troop commitment. The reality was far more harsh. The usurping of Saddam Hussein was received positively by the Iraqi people, but events that followed qualified that response. Law and order broke down quickly after the invasion and public services were undermined. Many areas, including Baghdad, found themselves without regular water or electricity. The invasion's popularity with the Iraqi public dropped quickly, and the US found itself responsible for Iraq's infrastructure. An organized resistance to the US presence emerged. Initially, the insurgency in Iraq was thought to consist of many fighters with Al Qaeda sympathies who had gone to Iraq to fight the US. However, the insurgency includes not just foreign *jihadis* but also many Sunnis, largely Iraqi nationalists who remain loyal to Saddam Hussein's Baath party or fear Shia or Kurd control of their nation. Areas of western Iraq remain outside US control. The insurgency targeted US troops, those attempting to participate in any rebuilding effort and the nascent Iraqi Security Forces. Iraqis have little personal security. The Americans continue with street patrols in Baghdad, and to attack groups of insurgents when they can be traced.

Despite his election pledge, Bush had led the US into a nation-building exercise far bigger than anything Clinton had contemplated. The invading force had to become an occupying force to control the insurgency. It quickly became clear that the US military was less than well-prepared for the task, incurring heavy losses and failing to establish order. As conditions worsened, the US looked to other nations and the UN for assistance. However, US appeals for help with the rebuilding elicited only a lukewarm response. Fewer than half of the countries approached offered support. Many others refused to make a serious commitment of aid or support for training. The US was left to resolve the Iraq problem.

If the administration's hopes were based on the neo-conservative vision of an Iraq awaiting liberation, they were dashed. The initial invasion did demonstrate the absolute superiority of US military technology, and seems to have had an initial "shock and awe" impact. However, in two senses, Iraq has left a question mark over US military power. First, that military power is now committed both in Iraq, to the tune of 138,000 soldiers in mid-2005, and in Afghanistan. Given the continuing campaigns, many other military operations cannot be undertaken. US threats of military action against other nations would sound hollow, limiting the effectiveness of this leverage over other countries. Second, it seems unlikely that an ultimate military victory will be achieved. The insurgency's success suggested that US military power is not necessarily applicable to the kind of task that Bush's conception of a War on Terror demands. In October 2005, the 2,000th American soldier died in Iraq with little sign that victory over the insurgency was close. The advanced technology that forged the route into Baghdad was not delivering a route out again.

The "War on Terror" has scored notable victories. The very concept earned some early diplomatic success. In the context of the international community's sympathetic response to the September 11 attacks, Bush's announcement that his administration would impose "regime change" in Afghanistan was widely supported. Indeed, the Afghanistan operation depended upon a degree of international cooperation. Most notably, Russia and China tolerated significant US military activity in their spheres of influence. The "War on Terror" played well with these powers as it allowed them to pursue their internal campaigns against nationalists with impunity. Russia could re-label its campaign in Chechnya as a "War on Terror." China could do the same in Tibet. Unquestionably, the "War" was also successful in its initial incarnation: the invasion of Afghanistan removed Al Qaeda's foundation. Although Osama bin Laden eluded capture, many other leaders of the movement were captured or killed. The organization, in its original form, lost effectiveness.

However, the Bush administration's approach to the "War" has triggered widespread debate. The administration considers terror a military problem to be addressed by regime change in rogue states. An alternative conceptualization suggests that terrorism is a problem rooted in the Arab–Israeli problem and poverty in the Middle East. These conditions provided the resentment of the West that could be tapped by Arab nationalists. Despite its professed religiosity, Al Qaeda could be interpreted as an organization exploiting anti-Western, ethnic and nationalist sentiment. Given this understanding of the terrorist problem, many looked upon the invasion of Iraq with chagrin. On leaving the Bush administration, Richard Clarke claimed that the Bush administration's approach to the "War," primarily attacking Iraq, was misguided as it fulfilled bin Laden's prediction that the US would attempt to dominate the Middle East. An American invasion merely reinforced the impression of a Western crusade to suppress the Arab peoples. The Iraqi campaign seemed likely to create new resentment, new martyrs and new financial and personnel support for terrorism, and thus to encourage further terrorist attacks. Clarke emphasized the likelihood that "second-generation" Al Qaeda, consisting of offshoots from the original organization but not under its command, would thrive on an image of US imperialism. Beating terrorist organizations needed to be undertaken not in terms of rogue states and military adventurism, but by cutting recruitment through addressing sources of Muslim resentment (Clarke, 2004). Terrorist attacks in Madrid, London and Sharm El Sheikh during 2004 and 2005 provided evidence to sustain that criticism. The identification of the London bombers as British citizens demonstrated the potential for Muslim communities within Europe to contribute to the development of "second-generation" organizations. To many, the administration's approach seemed flawed.

The administration's campaign to prevent the proliferation of WMD has clearly struggled. The proliferators proved unresponsive to America's aggressive posturing and disengagement. Furthermore, the uncovering of both Iran's and North Korea's uranium enrichment programs in 2002 emphasized the seriousness of the problem. The Bush administration's first response was to encourage the United Nations Security Council to impose tough sanctions on Iran. Russian, Chinese and Japanese interests in Iran meant that UN action was unlikely. America's disengagement looked like an ineffective approach to the problem. It appeared that the Bush administration could not prevent two of the most anti-American regimes from developing nuclear weapons. Indeed, a credible argument could be made that US posturing encouraged proliferators to strengthen their defenses. The cold shoulder shown North Korea and Iran, accompanied by the threat of military power in the doctrine of pre-emption, did not change those nations' behavior.

International and domestic reactions

The new direction in American foreign policy also generated a spectacular international reaction. The extraordinary sympathy toward the US generated by the September 11 attacks quickly dissipated as the full ramifications of a "War on Terror" were revealed. The US decision to act unilaterally in Iraq became the focus for international resentment, but in fact, the Iraq war acted as a symbol for numerous, broader concerns about US foreign policy. The war embodied a number of Bush's new principles. US allies loathed American presumptions about their role. The new realism of the administration, as revealed in US dealings with the UN, offended those that set store by the ideal of a community of nations. Both the military assertion of US primacy and the specific strategy of Bush's War on Terror caused much concern.

As neo-conservative members of the administration often stated, allies were expected to fall into line with US policy. Such declarations cast any ally as a junior partner in its diplomatic relationship with the US: America's allies would, eventually, have to follow the American lead, or could be safely ignored. The clear implication was that consultation with allies was a luxury generously offered to the junior partner, rather than an open negotiation over policy direction. Allies were skeptical about this approach. Fierce French and German opposition to the Iraq war has persisted. That opposition was compounded by the Bush administration's punishment of those nations refusing to cooperate over Iraq. For example, Donald Rumsfeld excluded the French from the 2003 and 2004 "Red Flag" military exercises.

From the perspective of many outside the US, the realist message sent by the administration's dealings with the UN was particularly insidious. In pursuing the first resolution, Bush appeared willing to embrace multi-lateralism and thus to respond to the concerns of others within the international community. In the context of the unilateral invasion that followed, though, pursuit of the first resolution appeared to be a political nicety undertaken by the administration for political convenience, rather than a consultation. Remaining true to its realist rhetoric, the administration appeared to believe in pursuing US interests through multilateral institutions when it was to America's advantage, but ignoring multilateral constraints when an advantage was not available. The double standard looked even more dramatic as the US expected other nations would respect multilateral rules. The US had, after all, complained to the UN that Iraq was obstructing the investigations of UN weapons inspectors sent by UN resolutions. The subsequent failure to uncover WMD merely compounded the sense that the international community had been deceived.

Furthermore, Bush's unilateralism did not account for others' under-standing of the terrorist threat. In common with Clarke, many outside the US did not regard the Iraqi war as a logical part of a War on Terror. Many Europeans regarded terrorism as a problem reflecting poverty in the Middle East and the tensions of the Israel–Palestine dispute, and so proposed longer-term solutions rather than military adventurism.

The Iraq war also represented the first highly controversial application of pre-emption. The doctrine drew great international criticism. The idea that the US reserved the right to intervene anywhere begged the question of when and where the US would stop. Observers questioned whether invasions of Iran and North Korea were imminent or if others, such as Axis of Evil "second string" nations like Cuba and Syria, were likely to face action. Many nations felt threatened by US power. American primacy seemed to be replaced by American empire, and looked like a threat rather than a protection. The need to restrain US power became a primary issue in international politics.

This hostile international reaction had tangible consequences. The US undermined its own diplomatic capital: its behavior made allies less willing to consider US interests. In each case in the face of American opposition, the Kyoto Protocol was ratified, European Union nations discussed lifting their arms embargo against the Chinese, and the European Union's Defence Pact developed planning arrangements outside the operations of NATO. In each case, US interests were jeopardized. A price was being exacted for America's unilateralism. The administration's tendency to act, "as if the world had entered a post-diplomatic age – where making speeches and issuing ultimatums took the place of give-and-take negotiations," reduced other countries' willingness to support US strategic interests (Daalder and Lindsay, 2003: 191).

Bush's foreign policy also damaged America's soft power. The publics of other nations were alienated from the US as well as leaders. Politicians wove anti-Americanism into political campaigns: Gerhard Schroeder rode a wave of anti-US sentiment back into office in Germany's 2002 election. Surveys showed populations across the world turning against the US (Pew Global Attitudes Project, 2005). As the polls reflected, the US had undermined its own legitimacy as bearer of key values such as liberty and justice. To Arab nations, the apparent imperialism of the Iraq conflict did not project America as the nation of liberty. To European nations, American unwillingness to participate in multilateral negotiations, the disdain for allies' opinions, and the refusal to acknowledge international law, smacked of bullying, and hardly reflected America as leader of the free world. US abuse of international law, most notably in the establishment of the Guantanamo Bay detention center, compromised any reputation for justice. The spectacle of Libya, in its role as Chair of the UN Commission on Human Rights, condemning the US for its human rights abuses, showed how little of the moral high ground the US could claim. The promotion of American values has, to some eyes, become an exercise in hypocrisy rather than the projection of freedom around the world. America's soft power has been diminished.

The change in foreign policy also had significant domestic repercussions. Public support for the Iraq war diminished sharply after the 2004 election. Media coverage changed as the insurgency continued, and descriptions of the US being in a "quagmire," a staple of Vietnam War reportage, emerged. By August 2005, 54% of the population considered the war a mistake (Gallup Organization, 2005). One observer considered public opinion to be at a key "tipping point" by mid-2005: the public would soon demand action from the Bush administration on its lack of progress in Iraq (Yankelovich, 2005). Congress also began to question the US commitment to Iraq. Democrats called for a timetable for withdrawal. Congressional opposition has been heightened by concern over the budgetary impact of the war. By August 2005, the war had cost the US over $200 billion. The administration was forced to mount a strong defense of the conflict. A "National Strategy for Victory in Iraq" was issued and Bush made public speeches to emphasize that the administration had a plan for disengagement (National Security Council, 2005). Public disapproval, congressional skepticism and budgetary pressure, in combination, could have significant repercussions for US foreign policy as they may restrain Bush's ability to employ US military force. The US might have power, but domestic opposition may prevent its use.

The basic neo-conservative paradigm, that America could shape the world through more assertive use of its power, had been called into question. Iraq had fallen into chaos. The War on Terror was achieving mixed results and international controversy. North Korea and Iran continued their pursuit of nuclear capabilities and the Israel–Palestine conflict festered. In each case, the US attempted to use its power, and found itself falling short of its goals. Military power was overwhelming, but proved inapplicable in key situations. The Bush administration's reliance upon US military power and unilateral action looked highly questionable. Many of Bush's innovations were based upon a misperception of that power's efficacy.

As the administration were discovering the limitations of power that could be exerted unilaterally, their policies were doing much to undermine America's powers that depended upon persuasion. The damage done to America's diplomatic capital reduced potential allies' willingness to cooperate. US soft power, dependent upon the image of the US in other nations, had been compromised by American conduct.

New directions

Commentators have suggested that Bush's second term has witnessed a softening of, even a sea-change in, administration policy. Changes in administration personnel, rhetoric and policy can be cited to support this argument.

The appointment of Condoleezza Rice as Secretary of State, replacing Colin Powell, was interpreted as indication of a new Bush approach. Many also noted departures of neo-conservatives from the State and Defense Departments. The nominations of Paul Wolfowitz and John Bolton, to act as President of the World Bank and US Ambassador to the UN respectively, caused concern, but their moves from Washington encouraged outsiders to believe they would have a lesser role in policy formulation.

In policy terms, as well as personnel, Bush's position appears less aggressive. First, Bush has not followed through the logic of pre-emption. Despite their identification within the "Axis of Evil," Iran and North Korea have not been invaded. Pre-emption is beginning to look like an

"Iraq-only" policy. Indeed, the US has adopted a far more conciliatory and flexible stance toward both nations, despite the proliferators' continuing nuclear programs and other provocations.

In the case of Iran, the lead has been taken by the British, French and Germans, who became known, in this context, as the E3. Fearing further US adventurism after the Iraq invasion, the E3 approached Iran to establish negotiations over its nuclear projects. Offers of trade perks and non-nuclear energy technology persuaded the Iranians to negotiate and to suspend uranium conversion in late 2004. Unusually, the US accepted, and even quietly encouraged, this multilateral approach. In 2005, and with American support, the Europeans offered an improved package to Iran detailing trade preferences, security guarantees, technology transfers and access to nuclear fuel. The last of these is particularly significant. By approving the new E3 package, the US has, for the first time, acknowledged that Iran could pursue a peaceful nuclear program, if under supervision. Rather than taking a hard-line position, the US has offered concessions.

Revelations concerning North Korea's uranium program also seemed to induce a change in the Bush approach. The Bush team declared their willingness to bargain with the North Koreans, in sharp contrast to their earlier belligerence. However, the US was reluctant to negotiate with the Koreans directly, believing that more pressure would be brought to bear if other regional powers would support the talks and demand action from the Koreans. Offers of energy support, and pressure from the Chinese persuaded North Korea to embark upon multilateral talks with South Korea, China, Russia, Japan and the US in April 2003. The talks have been marred by breakdowns, usually induced by Korean declarations of advances in their nuclear capability. However, all parties returned to the negotiating table during 2005 for further rounds of talks. The US has made a series of concessions to encourage this process. Bush's aggressive rhetoric toward the Korean regime has been toned down. The US has acknowledged that North Korea functions as a sovereign state, and has approved other countries' offers of energy, food aid, economic assistance and trade links to North Korea. Also, operating within the context of the six-party talks, the US has agreed to bilateral talks with North Korea. The US has embraced a new multilateralism and shows willingness to make concessions.

In both the Iranian and North Korean cases, the administration's strategy has had to adjust to the inability of the US to change other nations' behavior. Military strikes against either nation look a poor option. The location of any weapons program is unclear, which necessarily limits strikes' effectiveness. Strikes also risk inducing retaliation. The

North Koreans could destroy the South Korean capital of Seoul with conventional weaponry, while the Iranians could step up the activities of their proxies in Iraq or attack Israel. Unilateral US sanctions would have a limited impact upon either proliferator, but broader sanctions on the part of the international community have proved hard to achieve. Many developing countries are very reluctant to set a precedent of restricting allegedly peaceful nuclear programs. Instead, the US is attempting to coopt other nations' influence over the proliferators. Other powers, most notably China, have power over Iran and North Korea, through trade, aid and energy. China and Russia are keen to stop North Korea becoming a nuclear threat, so they have an interest in cooperating with the Americans at the six-nation talks. The multilateral route, though, has problems. First, proliferators may be playing for time by negotiating. Weapons programs may be completed over the years spent in negotiations, leaving the international community facing a *fait accompli*. Second, the US has to be tolerant of others' interests to coopt their power. The interests of Korea's neighbors may include a nonnuclear North Korea, but they also lie in trade and a good relationship with the communist dictatorship. Hence, the US must attempt to corral the power of the other nations involved in the talks, without taking positions that sacrifice their co-negotiators' assistance.

Ultimately, the Americans' aim has become to present proliferators with a choice. Either North Korea and Iran must negotiate, and sacrifice large parts of their nuclear program, or they must show commitment to that program and incur their neighbors' wrath. The US calculates that, if the negotiating process demonstrates the inherent unreliability of the proliferators, political support for further actions will grow.

As yet, the two series of talks have not yielded results. North Korea has agreed to give up the nuclear weapons it claims to have built, but the schedule for disarmament and Korea's receipt of the associated rewards is still under debate. Dealings with Iran have moved further down the route mapped out by US strategy. Iran's resistance to nuclear regulation increased in late 2005 and early 2006, as marked by Iran's resumption of both uranium gas production and research work on uranium enrichment. Effectively the E3 negotiations were terminated by the Iranian's determination to further their nuclear capabilities. Russia and China were disturbed by the Iranians' actions, which allowed the E3 and the US to refer the problem to the UN with some hope that political support for measures against Iran could be mustered in the Security Council. Whether this approach will dissuade Iran from becoming a nuclear power is not obvious. But in terms of US policy, it is clear that the US has adopted a more multilateral approach to its anti-proliferation efforts as a response to its limited direct leverage over the proliferators.

Democratizing the Middle East

Bush's rhetoric on foreign policy changed sharply as he started his second term. His second inaugural speech adopted a tone that contrasted with the previous swagger, instead echoing the earlier rhetoric of liberal internationalist Woodrow Wilson. He offered the expansion of freedom and democracy as means of achieving security for Americans:

> The survival of liberty in our land increasingly depends on the success of liberty in other lands. The best hope for peace in our world is the expansion of freedom in all the world ... So it is the policy of the United States to seek and support the growth of democratic movements and institutions in every nation and culture, with the ultimate goal of ending tyranny in our world. (Bush, 2005a)

Bush's terminology had moved from the realism of pursuing US security interests, to a much more idealist tone. The speech represented the completion of a change in the administration's public justification for the Iraq war. The conflict had been billed as a necessity to address the threat of WMD, to overthrow the tyranny of Saddam Hussein and to eliminate state support for Al Qaeda. As 2005 began, Bush fitted the conflict into a grand project of democratization in the Middle East. Bush advocated democracy for all Middle Eastern nations. It seemed that Bush had adopted the neo-conservative vision wholeheartedly: he appeared to promise the assertion of US values throughout the Middle East.

The neo-conservatives had suggested that any campaign of democratization should begin with an invasion of Iraq to overthrow Saddam Hussein and establish a democratic Iraq. Such actions were expected to unleash democratic movements across the Middle East. However, achieving a democratic Iraq remains a challenge for the administration. Confronted with the task of nation-building, the refusal of many other nations to contribute to that task, and the inability to defeat the insurgency by military means, the US has adjusted its approach significantly. The administration has focused on political reform, but this tactic has not proved straightforward. Acting as an occupying force and trying to win Iraqi support for democratic principles are not tasks that sit comfortably alongside one another. This challenge is especially difficult as Iraq is marked by deep sectarian conflict. Kurds in the north, Sunnis in the centre and Shia in the south are fighting to control the new Iraqi state. The tension between Shia and Sunnis is particularly deep, although there is also dispute within the factions. Amid such tensions, the administration has shaped a phased process for establishing a new political system: the January 2005 elections, in which an estimated 8.4 million voted, were seen as a triumph for the Bush administration and that process. Labyrinthine attempts to write a new constitution followed. The negotiation process, and the final constitution itself, revealed the problems inherent in the development of a democratic Iraq. Arguments over the role of Islam in the new Iraqi state, the dispersion of power within a federalist structure and the allocation of oil revenues shattered the committee designing the new document. The constitution was finally completed in August 2005, but it excluded many concerns of the Sunni population. The document, intended to underpin the new Iraqi state and to play a key role in undermining the insurgency, ignored the interests of a whole faction of Iraqis. Whether Sunnis can be dragged back into the political process, and thus undermine the insurgency, remains an open question. Sunnis voted in large numbers in the December 2005 general election, but the majority Shia population seem likely to dominate the new Iraqi parliament and government. Many experts predict that Iraq will effectively become, though formally united, three separate statelets in varying degrees of chaos. Political reform is proving a long-lasting, dangerous and expensive investment for the United States. With continuing economic problems and fragile political and security institutions, Iraq's future will remain in the balance for some time.

Any attempt to democratize the Middle East could not ignore the continuing machinations over the Palestinian problem. After the September 11 attacks, the administration recognized that action on the problem was necessary. Bush publicly declared the need for a Palestinian state in a late 2001 speech to the UN General Assembly. He also made a substantial foray into the peace process, offering a "road map" to peace. In February 2004, Israel announced a radical plan to withdraw Israeli forces and settlers from most of the Gaza Strip. This plan contradicted Bush's Road Map, and was regarded by many as part of a broader Israeli plan to decide the shape of the peace unilaterally. The administration was presented with a choice: defend the road map, or accept Israel's initiative. The administration chose the latter course, welcoming the 2005 withdrawal from Gaza as progress. The peace process has resumed, if in a low-key manner, with US Special Envoy James Wolfensohn acting as mediator. Progress has been made in allowing more freedom of movement for Palestinians to and from Gaza and allowing Palestinian produce into Israel. However the conflict remains a long way from a final peace, and Hamas' victory in the Palestinian elections of 2006 has complicated matters further. Both the US and Israel have refused to negotiate with an organization that does not recognize the right of Israel to exist.

The administration's campaign of democratization has not been limited to the two flashpoints of Iraq and Palestine. Bush has pursued democratic objectives across the Middle East. During the second term, it has even pursued this policy where it may risk US strategic interests. For example, Rice travelled to Cairo in June 2005 and gave an unabashed pro-democracy speech. The speech embarrassed her Egyptian hosts who have long been American allies. After the initial reluctance to embrace nation-building, the Bush administration has adopted, effectively, region building.

However, the neo-conservative vision of a democratic Middle East has not yet come to pass. Regimes in Iran and Syria maintain their overt hostility to the US and Iraq remains a running sore. However, neo-conservatives can claim some successes. Elections have taken place in Palestine and Afghanistan, even if under controversial circumstances. In the "Cedar Revolution," arguably encouraged by US actions nearby, the people of Lebanon forced Syria to withdraw its military presence. In Saudi Arabia and Egypt, tentative democratic reforms were undertaken. Even avowed enemies of the US responded. Libya's decision to abandon its pursuit of WMD was hailed as a triumph for US pressure.

These successes may, though, have come at a cost. In attempting to democratize the Middle East, the administration may have embarked upon a long-term gamble. Traditionally, the US has supported the stability of Middle Eastern regimes friendly to it. Now, instead of backing a number of autocracies, the US is threatening and cajoling these nations to encourage the establishment of democracy. As exemplified by Iraq, the removal of dictatorships can unleash factionalist forces, whether nationalist, tribal or sectarian. The administration is gambling that this factionalism can be managed, rather than states falling into disunity reminiscent of the former Yugoslavia during the 1990s. Even if these states survive the transition to democracy, the newly liberated peoples might choose to elect Muslim fundamentalist governments. Such results could seriously jeopardize US interests in the region. The Bush administration appears to have gambled upon the vicissitudes of local politics, tying its legacy to a series of factors it may prove unable to control. Academic debate rages as to how committed the Bush administration is to the promotion of democracy: some believe the rhetoric to reflect a genuine devotion that does involve the above risk, while others believe that the US will not jeopardize its strategic interests in the region for idealist goals.

A new multilateralism?

Clearly, the US has embarked upon a degree of engagement with other nations that would have been hard to predict before September 11. US involvement in multi-nation talks with Iran and North Korea, in the Middle East peace process, and in negotiations to reform the UN might be interpreted as representing a new American multilateralism. Simply the presence of US representatives at a series of negotiations has generated a sense of re-engagement among the diplomats of the international community. The administration's willingness to offer concessions in its dealings with Iran and North Korea has added to the impression of a superpower willing to understand others' interests.

Yet, the administration has not embraced the traditional understanding of multilateralism, that is, the process of working through a series of established institutions where a community of nations come together. The administration's attempts to reform the United Nations might be interpreted as a new US commitment to multilateralism, but in fact, seems to typify the more qualified Bush approach.

The administration identified six major objectives for UN reform including establishment of a peace-building commission and replacement of the United Nations Human Rights Commission, a new treaty opposing terrorism and the initiation of a UN Democracy Fund. It also assailed existing reform plans which focused on the ICC, the Kyoto Protocol and the Comprehensive Test Ban Treaty. These proposals reflected the commitments that realists in the US have always tried to avoid. The peace-building commission and democracy fund represented the US belief that it should not be nation-building, but giving that task to others. The anti-terrorism treaty clearly fitted into the aims of Bush's War on Terror. In taking these roles, the US hoped the UN would act as an adjunct to Bush's policy. The US would have been relieved of unwelcome burdens and have more scope to pursue its own interests.

The Bush administration has pursued similar "multilateral" diplomacy elsewhere. The administration negotiates agreements that do not divert US policy from the chosen route. The 2002 Moscow Treaty on arms control allowed the US to hold 2,200 strategic nuclear weapons by December 31, 2012, much as it had planned. The "Asia Pacific Partnership on Clean Development and Climate", an American-approved substitute for the Kyoto Protocol that was revealed in 2005, seems cut from the same cloth. It is notable for not being binding upon its signatories, allowing the US to decide when it will disregard the treaty's provisions.

The administration has toned down its aggressive unilateral rhetoric, but the apparent move toward multilateralism should not be over-stated. A distinctly American multilateralism has emerged. Standard multilateralism works through established institutions. Instead, the administration has constructed *ad hoc* coalitions to pursue specific aims. In this sense, the coalitions of the willing negotiating with Iran and North Korea are little different from the coalition that accompanied the US into Iraq. The administration's involvement with UN reform has been oriented toward increasing the UN's capacity to deliver American goals. Treaties may be negotiated, but only if they fail to restrict US aspirations. Across its first and second terms, the Bush administration maintains a more vigorous adherence to US interests when dealing with other nations. Multilateral institutions are to be exploited to further US interests. There is little to suggest increased US willingness to compromise over these goals: as Bush explained directly after his re-election, "I will reach out to others and explain why I make the decisions I make" (Bush, 2004a).

The return of geopolitics as usual

While the Bush administration has established the "War on Terror" as a new narrative in foreign policy, the challenges for US foreign policy do not all sit neatly within the administration's chosen paradigm. American interests are not all absorbed in the pursuit of security against fundamentalist terrorists. Two particular features of the international environment stand out as providing challenges for the administration during its second term, the increasing influence of China and the problem of international trade.

China's growth in economic and military power has been matched by energetic diplomacy, and has had both regional and global impacts. In dealing with China, the US faces a key decision. On the one hand, the US could regard China as an autocratic enemy to be condemned and isolated. On the other hand, the US could regard engagement with a rising and rapidly modernizing power as highly desirable. Initially, the Bush campaign's designation of China as a "strategic competitor" implied that the US regarded the Chinese with hostility. Tensions between the two nations developed over Taiwan and the landing of a US surveillance plane on the Chinese Hainan Island. Subsequently the US sponsored an attempt to censure China at the UN Human Rights Commission during 2004, and on a 2005 visit, Secretary Rice lectured Chinese dignitaries on their failings over human rights. The US has also confronted what it labels as unfair Chinese trade practices. While there is reason to believe that Chinese practices are in fact fair, the Bush administration has blocked unwelcome Chinese imports (Hughes, 2005). The US has also expressed concern about the modernization and expansion of the Chinese military (Department of Defense, 2005). Chinese willingness to sell arms to rogue states has also been criticized. Congress has contributed to the China-bashing, effectively blocking, on strategic grounds, the purchase of the US oil company Unocal by a Chinese government-owned company. Over a series of issues, Chinese and American interests differ and the US has shown hostility. Yet, the message from the US has not been consistent. China's extraordinary economic progress has made US companies very keen to exploit the vast Chinese market. In trade policy, textile imports excepted, the administration has maintained good relations with the Chinese, arguing that China should become a "responsible stakeholder" in the world economy (Zoellick, 2005). Furthermore, the US wants to tap both China's regional power in dealing with North Korea, and her economic power in pressuring Iran. Also, administration policy is probably influenced by Chinese leverage over the US economy. Due to an ever-expanding trade imbalance between the two countries, China now holds $750 billion of foreign currency reserves, much of it as US government debt. Hence, China holds power over the US economy: a release of currency reserves could undermine US financial stability.

The US faces dichotomous forces. There are many reasons to isolate China but her growing regional influence and economic power make it desirable to remain engaged. The Bush administration has often been undiplomatic in its approach to the Chinese, but it has remained involved. Over the next decade, future US governments seem likely to follow the same difficult path of selective condemnation alongside improved trade and diplomatic interactions.

The international trade system also presents a challenge to the Bush administration. The US economy depends upon trade, indeed, Clinton's commitment to globalization enhanced that dependency. However, tensions growing between developed and developing nations threaten the current international trade system's effectiveness.

The Bush administration has declared its support for free trade. Bush notched a significant victory in liberalizing trade by persuading Congress to ratify the Central American Free Trade Agreement during 2005. However, the administration has a blemished record in this area as represented by steel tariffs imposed in 2002, safeguard proceedings applied to Chinese textiles and increased farm subsidies. The last of these was especially significant as farm subsidies have become a major issue for developing nations. Many developing nations hold comparative advantage in producing agricultural goods, but developed world tariffs and subsidies prevent them from exploiting that advantage. The World Trade Organization (WTO) rules give developing nations substantial power, most importantly an effective veto over trade settlements. Hence, developing countries are now using the WTO to make the free-trade agenda apply to their goods, that is, to open up developed world markets by removing tariffs and subsidies. Such an opening could hurt a number of developed world industries, forcing major structural changes to the American, and other, economies. Developed and developing countries are at loggerheads over the issue. These tensions have been greatly evident during the current Doha round of trade negotiations. Most notably at the Cancun meeting of October 2003, the US and other developed nations refused to reduce farm subsidies despite pressure from the developing world. The disagreement threw the Doha round into crisis and, even after slightly more productive negotiations in Hong Kong during 2005, it is unclear how a settlement will be reached.

The US stands at a crossroads. The US could open up its markets and further the free trade agenda. Domestic political pressure to resist such a change would be substantial. The US Congress would be unlikely to pass the relevant legislation given the serious economic dislocation that would follow. Alternatively, the US, working with other developed nations, will have to satisfy developing nations through means other than free trade. If that satisfaction cannot be achieved, the Doha round might collapse. The credibility of the WTO would be damaged, and diminished trade could wreak economic havoc.

Conclusion

Even before September 11, 2001, the Bush administration had changed US foreign policy by instituting a new realism and heightened antipathy to multilateral institutions. However, after the terrorist attacks, these principles were attached to the radical rethinking of the US security agenda embodied in the "War on Terror" and the "Bush Doctrine." The administration established a new narrative in US foreign policy that demanded the division of the world into friend and foe, and global US engagement. Security would depend on the ability of the US to contain rogue states and prevent proliferation.

The new foreign policy was not, though, an unqualified success. While military victories were delivered in Afghanistan and Iraq, the latter turned into an extended occupation and anti-proliferation attempts went awry. Arab–Israeli tensions remained acute despite US re-engagement in the peace process. Clear limits to the reach of American power emerged. While US military prowess was compromised by the inability to nation-build, Bush's attempt to act "unbound" seemed to damage US diplomatic capital and soft power.

The administration does appear to have responded to its difficulties. It is more sympathetic to multilateral actions, as indicated by rhetoric and engagement with other nations over anti-proliferation. However, the core principle seems to remain intact: the US looks to mobilize bias within the multilateral system for US advantage, but to avoid burdens where few direct gains for the US can be identified. The rules of multilateral organizations are to be followed when they suit US needs, and contravened when they do not. In this sense, Bush is no more an idealist than in 2001.

The Bush attitude to multilateralism establishes a contradiction at the heart of US foreign policy. The pursuit of American security, as articulated by Bush after September 11, demands US engagement with virtually every nation in the world. Hence, Bush talks of every nation either being with the US or with the terrorists: this requirement amounts to a demand for commitments and cooperation from other nations. However, the desire for an America truly "unbound" demands that the US not be restricted by such engagements. This contradiction may suit the United States, but it places other nations in a position where their engagements with the US may involve a series of commitments, but there are limited guarantees of rewards.

The fundamental presumptions of Bush's War on Terror remain intact. His approach to foreign policy is still rooted in the concept of the nation-state and particularly in the control of rogue states. However, the democratization of the Middle East has also become a central pillar of the "War on Terror," replacing the doctrine of pre-emption. Arguably, the democratization project could even be considered a second "Bush doctrine." Bush is now evoking classic US values of liberty and democracy. This rhetorical shift toward idealism has been matched by some degree of action. Rice's direct and critical speeches pressing autocratic allies toward democratic reforms have been notable, both for their genuine strand of idealism, and for their delivery despite the harm that they might do to US strategic interests by weakening or alienating potential allies. In this respect, the blunt realism of Bush's first term appears to have receded.

The move to democratize the Middle East, though, relies on a grand strategic gamble. The Bush administration has begun a campaign that depends upon winning the hearts and minds of the region's peoples for democracy. The gamble suggests that democracy, combined with US support, will prevail over such forces of local politics as ethnic factionalism, religious fundamentalism and strident nationalism. Effectively, the Bush legacy in foreign policy is tied to a series of factors that will be extraordinarily difficult for the administration to control. If the gamble fails, the US could find itself confronting a series of hostile nuclear regimes in a region of key strategic importance.

Chapter 15

Governing the United States: From Consensus to Majoritarian Democracy?

B. Guy Peters

Even a cursory examination of American government presents any number of internal contradictions and paradoxes. A system designed to minimize executive power is often described as dominated by an "Imperial President." Likewise, a federal system designed to minimize the power of central government has become more dominated by that central government, despite numerous versions of "new federalism" that have attempted to return powers to the states. It is also a government that is often described as "weak" and very small compared to the public sector in other industrialized democracies, but also a government that can be extremely effective and powerful when confronted with the need to act decisively (see Van Waarden, 1995).

We could go on proliferating examples of the contradictions and paradoxes residing within American government. Many of these contradictions are related to the fundamental question of the capacity, and willingness, of this complex and highly fragmented political system to govern. When viewed strictly on paper, in its stark constitutional form, the government does appear difficult to manage internally, and also highly unlikely to be capable of providing effective steering for the economy and society. The framers of the Constitution were consciously concerned with limiting the capacity for rapid and arbitrary decisions by the federal government, and were successful in their design efforts. And yet the system has shown the capacity to be decisive when action is required, and arguably much of its apparent weakness on a daily basis is simply a response to many Americans' profound distrust of government. As Anthony King once wrote, American government is different because Americans want it to be different (King, 1973).

While the governance capacity of American government has always been somewhat suspect, that capacity can be argued to have waned, or at a minimum to be used even less than in the past, at the beginning of the twenty-first century. That loss of governing capacity may be absolute (assuming that we could specify an appropriate metric for governance), but it is certainly true relative to the challenges the system of government now confronts. Major problems such as an immense public deficit, the costs and inefficiency of health care (combined with the lack of insurance for over 40 million citizens), the potential bankruptcy of Social Security, and a range of other policy problems simply are being ignored. The inability of all levels of government to respond to the disaster created by Hurricane Katrina exposed this weakness in governance capacity for the whole world to see. At the same time as these general governance failures have occurred, government has responded with astounding speed and vigor to specific issues such as one woman dying in Florida, tragic though that event may be, or the use of performance-enhancing drugs by athletes, lamentable as that may be.

Again, some of the apparent decline in governance capacity in the federal government has happened by design. A conservative president, and a perhaps even more conservative Congress, have taken it upon themselves to reduce the size and influence of American government in many areas of public life, although paradoxically doing so by public action. By reducing taxes and increasing the public deficit to historic proportions these conservatives have placed a mortmain on the capacity of the federal government to engage in any programs that would require significant public funding – the strategy of "starve the beast" has been implemented rather explicitly. The assumption of some contemporary lawmaking in the federal government appears to be that indeed the market, or society, can and will have to take care of the major problems because government simply will not.

Despite the general conservative ideology of the leadership of the Republican Party, and the associated opposition to most government intervention in American life, the current majority, as has been noted in many of the chapters, has undertaken several programs that do require substantially greater involvement in the society. Notably, the No Child Left Behind program to evaluate all elementary and secondary schools and to punish "failing schools" has involved the federal government in the details of local education policy to an extent that had not been true before this presumably conservative administration. The contradiction of a conservative administration and Congress being so willing to intervene is even more apparent in social policy issues such as banning most stem-cell research, the Defense of Marriage Act (DOMA) 1996, and numerous other attempts to impose their own set of social and religious values on the remainder of society. And these interventions are in addition to the substantially greater powers assumed by the federal governing in the policing of terrorism.

Although many political practitioners have been attempting to reduce the governance capacity of government, and perhaps to eliminate the financial capacity of government to act for decades, some of the reduced governance capacity has resulted from attempts to reform the political system, and indeed from changes that have been assumed would *increase* the capacity to govern. Other challenges to the governance capacity of American government have resulted from social change and the shift from the "bread and butter" politics of the New Deal and the Great Society to a politics more driven by ideology and religious fundamentalism. In contemporary politics dominant economic concerns appear to have been supplanted, or at least complemented, by desires to pursue participation, personal fulfillment, and a host of other values through the political system. Perhaps more than anything else politics appears driven by the wish to impose individual values on the rest of society, and to reduce the pluralism that has characterized American social life. These changes have combined to pose serious questions about the ability of this political system to deliver the steering necessary in a complex and interdependent world.

Perhaps the fundamental paradox about governance in the United States is that the changes, made both consciously and unconsciously, have transformed the United States from a consensual democracy to a majoritarian democracy. Not only have the issues that divide Americans changed, the manner in which political elites work together (or now do not work together) to address those issues has changed as much or more. The argument that I will make here is that despite majoritarian institutions such as plurality elections for Congress and the Electoral College, the American political system was able to function because its essential style was consensual. This consensus model did not include the mechanisms for building societal consensus common in the smaller democracies of Europe (see Rokkan, 1967; Heisler, 1974) but did involve close and extensive cooperation among elites across partisan lines. Now that those partisan lines have become more solidified and intense, especially at the elite level, governing is becoming more difficult.

In his discussion of majoritarian and consensual democracies, Arend Lijphart (1990) argued that majoritarian government had the predominant trait of "winner take all," and hence alternation in control leading to relatively sharp differences between policies. There would be relatively little attempt on the part of the majority to accommodate the views of the minority, believing that the best way to run a democracy is to give voters clear evidence of the programs of the party in power and then let the voters respond to the perceived success and failure of those programs at the next election. American government to some extent appeared to fit this model, but the numerous checks and balances among the institutions, and even within the Congress itself, tended to produce a more consensual style. For example, the institutions of the filibuster and Senatorial courtesy within the upper chamber tended to minimize the capacity for majority domination. These institutions limit the capacity of the current majority to exercise their will, and hence the Senate reached an agreement on how to limit the use of filibusters against judicial appointments, crucial with then two vacancies on the Supreme Court and numerous vacancies on lower federal courts.

Thus American politics was largely majoritarian at the electoral stage, but was then capable of becoming consensual once the elections were over and the winners had to get down to the difficult task of governing. Ideologically the differences between the parties were minimal, and most politicians, and even fewer ordinary citizens, thought in ideological terms. This provided the capacity for the politicians to work across party lines to solve particular problems. There may not have been true consensus of issues (there certainly has not been in the consensual democracies in Lijphart's analysis) but there was an ability to build agreement on specific programs at specific times. The movement away from that style of governing must be seen in light of some conscious attempts to change American politics, presumably reforming it to perform more effectively as a political system.

Responsible governing in the United States

During the 1950s, and for years thereafter, one of the standard remedies for improving governance, and especially for improving democratic governance, in the United States was the creation of a responsible party system. The American Political Science Association (1950; see also Ranney and Kendall, 1956) was one of the sponsors of a report on political parties arguing that the inconsistencies and internal differences within American parties made it difficult for voters to make rational choices about which party to choose when they went to the polls. Further, once in office, the parties had little reason to pursue the policies that voters might have thought they were choosing at election time. The political leaders tended to consider themselves more as individual political entrepreneurs than as members of political parties that were meant to present coherent and meaningful programs to the public. In contrast, one of the conditions of party government advanced by Richard Rose was that the parties had to present voters with statements of means and ends that they could when deciding among the parties.

At the time that the proposals for reform of the American party system were made, American political parties were not really organizations in the sense of European political parties, or the models of the political science textbooks, but rather were loose coalitions of activists with more of a personal basis of support than a partisan or ideological foundation for collective action. To the extent that the parties were consistent in their policy stances and campaigning, there were in fact four parties and not two in the United States. There were two Democratic parties, one Southern and conservative (at least on race) and one Northern and liberal. There were also two Republican parties. The western Republicans were epitomized by Barry Goldwater of Arizona and Eastern Republicans by Nelson Rockefeller of New York, characterizations that are still used even if "Rockefeller Republicans" are an endangered species. In this setting political party was not a particularly important predictor of behavior in Congress, except perhaps on issues of organizing the houses, and on some social programs where Southern populists might cooperate with Northern liberals in the Democratic Party. James McGregor Burns (1963) described the four party system in the United States more in terms of differences between Congressional parties and Presidential parties, but in either case it was clear that American parties were not the unified actors that many scholars, and also many practitioners, considered essential for effective public governance.

These political parties were able to cooperate and negotiate effectively with one another in part because the political and economic orientations cross-cut rather than overlap, and therefore it was possible to build coalitions across party lines. For example, although Southern Democrats might disagree with their Northern brethren on issues of race, there were enough in the populist tradition who could cooperate on some social and economic policy issues. And both could work with Eastern Republicans who accepted a stronger role for government than members of their party from other parts of the country. Likewise, conservative Southern Democrats could cooperate with the Western Republicans who would be conservative on issues of race, and social issues more generally.

Although in this chapter I am concerned primarily with the governance and management capacity of the federal government, much of the justification for developing a more responsible party system was to enhance democracy within the American political system. If citizens are able to identify what the parties stand for, and can have some assurance that the parties will follow through on their programs if elected, then they will be able to make better choices when they vote. Given that enhanced knowledge about parties and their program, and the ability to avoid the confusion about what different versions of the parties mean, citizens also will be more likely to participate in politics and may have more positive orientations towards politics and political parties. This perspective on democracy is based on a somewhat negative view of voters and their ability to sort out differences among candidates and platforms (Key, 1966). The relatively low levels of turnout, and the generally negative view of politics in the United States, however, were taken as evidence of the consequences of these ill-defined party positions.

From the time that the APSA report on parties was written in the 1950s until the early 1990s, these internal divisions within the parties persisted. However, despite those divisions, the political system was able to govern, and often to govern effectively. In that era governing depended upon the capacity of presidents or powerful leaders in Congress to broker deals that brought together individuals from different parties and perhaps of different political persuasions to pass individual pieces of legislation. This mode of governance was far from elegant, and involved making significant side-payments to the parties involved in the form of "pork-barrel" projects or reciprocal votes on other pieces of legislation; but legislation did get passed. Indeed, some major pieces of legislation were enacted and American government moved forward in ways that often are forgotten or ignored (Polsby, 1983; Light, 2002).

The capacity of the system to govern was even more remarkable because of the continuing presence of "divided government" in the United States (Mayhew, 1991), with at least one house of Congress being controlled by a party other than the president's for 14 of the 56 years between 1948 and 2004. Just as it was assumed that the absence of responsible parties presented fundamental problems for American governance, so too it has been argued that divided government has been a barrier to effective policy-making. The assumption has been that divided government creates "gridlock" and an inability to cope with significant problems (Sundquist, 1995). Although there is some evidence to support that perspective, still the political system did appear to make and implement policy, and often major policy initiatives came from unlikely coalitions assembled for idiosyncratic reasons.

To some extent the partisan and institutional conflicts between Congress and the presidency can be conceptualized as analogous to Fritz Scharpf's (1988) analysis of the impact of territorial divisions in federal systems, with governance becoming a search for the lowest common denominator because no other types of decision would be possible. What made it possible for the American government to work, however, was that the system was rich and there was money available to use for "buying" the votes of potential coalition members with other programs that may benefit their supporters. Further, the actors were involved in an iterative game, so that cooperating on one piece of legislation now could be repaid by cooperation from others in the future on another piece of legislation.

Although divided government has been blamed for problems in legislating and in governing more generally, the evidence from this period is that it made little appreciable difference to the ability of government to produce legislation during that time, especially if the degree of polarization among the parties is taken into account. Even in the face of partisan differences the political system was able to make and implement legislation, and some of the most significant pieces of legislation were passed in circumstances that might have been expected to produce only gridlock and conflict. As noted, the absence of any internal consistency within the parties facilitated cooperation and coalition-building so that effective policy entrepreneurs and congressional leaders could bring together coalitions from across the two parties and find means of coping with the issues confronting the country.

In the first decade of the twenty-first century American government is now unified, and perhaps more unified than it has been since the New Deal and World War II. The Republican Party controls both houses of Congress with working majorities, as well as the White House. Further, political parties, and especially the Republican Party, have become more responsible. President Bush and his congressional allies are broadly in agreement on policy and share a common ideology about minimal government interference in the economy, but a strong role for government in imposing social values. They campaigned in much the same way in each part of the country and have attempted to implement their electoral agenda, and their espoused ideas about the role of government, once they have come to office.

The paradox is that they have not been more successful in governing than they have, and that they have not been able to impose as much of their agenda as might have been expected. The shift toward responsible parties, and more particularly toward ideological parties and ideological politicians, appears to have reduced the governance capacity of American government, rather than increasing it. While the old system of a *de facto* multi-party system, and of the importance of individual political entrepreneurs, in Washington may have appeared messy and irresponsible, in fact it provided a locus for bargaining and coalition-building. The absence of significant partisan or ideological constraints (except perhaps for the Southern conservatives on race) meant that effective politicians could begin to build a coalition with relatively few constraints. This was hard work, but it was possible. And the political system tended to identify people such as Lyndon Johnson who were more than capable of operating in that seemingly chaotic environment to produce results.

With the advent of more ideological and committed political parties the capacity to bargain and to build coalitions across partisan or ideological lines becomes more difficult. The members of the Republican Party in Congress have been elected using relatively similar campaign pledges and to some extent on the coattails of a president with a clear set of political values that appeared to be shared by those candidates. The Republican Party certainly has operated as a phalanx when dealing with organizational issues in Congress and for some (sometimes rather trivial or symbolic) legislation; but it does not seem capable yet of dealing with the real policy problems of government.

One of the reasons for this apparent governance failure is that the basis of the consensus and the ideology of the party has relatively little to do with the major governance challenges facing the country. The election of 2004 had little to do with privatizing Social Security, and nothing to do with the budget deficit, or with the looming crisis in energy policy. The social issues that were important for many voters could hardly be considered the crucial threats to the maintenance of the political economy of the United States, and in many ways represented reactions to the continuing modernization of the society. Terrorism also was important in voting decisions in 2004, but much of that discussion in the campaign appeared to be about the Vietnam War rather than the wars in Iraq and Afghanistan.

The Republican Party thus appeared to be united around a social agenda, but once other issues have become central to governance that unity is much less apparent. It also appears that some of the policy proposals of this party are not widely supported by the public, even by their own voters. One clear example of this has been the partial privatization of the Social Security system. Although this issue was put forward during the campaign, it did not apparently play a central role in public decisions. As President Bush began to press for this major policy change public reactions have been less than widely supportive, and important figures in Congress also began to express their own doubts (perhaps in response to the strong public skepticism). Similarly, some of the more extreme appointments to public office, e.g. John Bolton as Ambassador to the United Nations, have also divided the seemingly unified Republican Party.

This seeming discrepancy between the programs of the party elites and the mass supporters of the party is supported by individual survey evidence (Hetherington, 2001) particularly in the Republican Party. Those surveys indicate that the Party activists are more extreme, and more ideological, than are the rank-and-file members of the Party, and certainly more so than voters. Thus, while there has been some realignment among the public, the shifts in the political elites have been sharper, making compromise once in government that much more difficult to achieve. Further, this increasing ideological fervor would mean that if the logic of responsible parties is followed, the policies being produced would be more extreme than those preferred by voters.

The results of campaigns and subsequent attempts to govern represents what may be the worst possible outcome for American government. The parties have become divided and much less willing to cooperate than in the past. Any number of Op-Ed pieces in the *Washington Post* and *New York*

Times by current and former politicians have pointed to the loss of "comity" in Congress and the declining ability to compromise as in the past (see, for example, Danforth, 2005). The problem, however, is that the current dominant party in the federal government is unified on a range of issues that have little to do with the objective demands for governance in the contemporary era. The result seems to be the capacity on the part of groups within government to block policy proposals, but substantially less capacity to move policy forward. The United States now has responsible parties, and unified government, but yet appears unable to govern.

Changing political issues and values

As intimated above, a good deal of the problem in governance in the United States appears to be a function of the issues that have been at the core of political debate. A great deal of ink was spilled during and after the 2004 election campaign analyzing, praising and deploring the importance of values in that campaign. To some extent the same issues had been important in the 2000 campaign, but the excessive utilization of value issues in campaigning – especially among social conservatives – was perhaps unprecedented. Homosexuality, especially gay marriages, abortion, anything less than fervent patriotism, and even values such as environmentalism were used to characterize many Democrats and their supporters negatively, and to rally the faithful to the Republican cause. In the end what were styled as traditional values carried the day, and most candidates who could be made to appear "out of touch with the mainstream" were defeated. This is perhaps a rather simple story about the presidential campaign, but not too simple. For many voters these appear to have been the real issues in the campaign, while only the effete appeared worried about issues such as the deficit, health care, poverty and inequality.

These political successes of values issues in this campaign also have been described as fundamental shifts in the bases of politics in the United States, and perhaps the creation of a "permanent" Republican majority. In this view, the social conservatives will form a basis for a political coalition that can dominate American politics for the immediate future, if not longer. While these forecasts are themselves perhaps too pessimistic or optimistic, depending upon one's political persuasion, analytically it is interesting to relate these predictions to claims that have been made by political scientists about the changing social and ideological nature of politics – in the United States and in other advanced industrial democracies. As interesting as these predictions are, we can identify clear discrepancies between them and the predictions of the academic pundits who also had foreseen the emergence of cultural and value-based politics as a result of political and social change.

Two strands of academic writing about social and political change appear to require some rethinking in light of recent elections, especially that of 2004. First, by most objective indicators the United States has been moving even more clearly into the postindustrial era. The economy has continued to de-industrialize and to add employment in service industries, average levels of education have continued to increase, communications technology has enabled information to spread readily, and mass affluence has been achieved, if with high levels of inequality. These are the objective indicators that authors such as Daniel Bell (1960; 1973; see also Waxman, 1968) considered to characterize postindustrial society. The theorists of postindustrial society also assumed that politically the achievement of postindustrialism would be associated with lessening political tensions and a rationalistic form of governing based on a broad consensus about political values. Affluence would lessen the economic zero-sum game that had prevailed in politics prior to that time (see Rose and Peters, 1976) and enable governments to address objective social needs more effectively. One styling of this postindustrial version of politics was that "the administration of things will replace the governing of men," and with that change a new era of effective and efficient governance would emerge.

Samuel Huntington pointed to the less appealing possibilities of this version of the future as an Age of Aquarius in social and political life, even if the postindustrial society were achieved in objective terms. First, he assumed that political conflict would continue, and that it might become more intense and less tractable. The convenient thing about the issues involved in industrial politics was that they could be addressed by money, and therefore all government had to do was to identify an acceptable level of taxing and spending in order to be reasonably successful in governing. In the postindustrial world, however, the important political issues would not be about money but would be about values or status. Not only can these issues not be monetized easily, but they are more difficult to bargain about. If social equality is a goal then going 60 percent of the way there (assuming there is a means of measuring such progress), or even 90 percent, still does not really "solve" the problem—this is an absolute value. Further, positional goods (Hirsch, 1977) may be even scarcer than economic goods, so that the zero-sum nature of political choices becomes accentuated.

Huntington also understood that declining social forces in a postindustrial world might not give up their positions and their power as readily as some other theorists had assumed they might. As the American economy and society have changed, knowledge-based industries and their employees have tended to prosper while more traditional economic structures have continued to decline in importance. The semi-skilled and unskilled workers in manufacturing have been perhaps the hardest hit, with declining employment opportunities, declining relative and even real wages, and a quality of life that continues to worsen. What had been in many ways the backbone of the middle class in the United States has been becoming increasingly marginalized. While these changes may be a transition to a rosy future of postindustrial society, some members of the population may believe that they are bearing a disproportionate share of the costs of that transition.

The anti-tax message of the Republican party in the 2000 and 2004 campaigns were supported strongly by many in these marginalized groups who believe that their tax money is going to support welfare, foreign aid, and a host of other causes that they do not support. Further, they simply need all the money they can get to maintain their standard of living. This political issue is clearly about money, but other types of issues are becoming increasingly salient, and many of Huntington's conceptions about cultural politics and the continuing controversies within politics appear more prescient than the postindustrialist's optimistic predictions. Although the basic argument and ideas about the source of conflict are unrelated, it is interesting to note that much of Huntington's more recent work has focused on the "Clash of Civilizations", not dissimilar to this clash of cultures. The political conflicts that have been emerging as we move into the twenty-first century are very much about cultural values and ideologies, and the remaining economic issues to some extent appear closely related to the values questions as well.

Politics in the United States during the early twenty-first century to some extent remains about bread-and-butter issues, and there certainly have been redistributive choices about economic and social policy implemented by the administration of George W. Bush. Those redistributive policies, however, largely have been to take money away from the middle and working classes, and give benefits to the upper classes, and especially the very richest segments of society. The electoral support for tax cuts during the campaign came heavily from middle and low income earners, but the benefits did not flow that way, nor did support for other economic policies that might have improved their economic position.

The "NASCAR dads" who replaced the "soccer moms" as the symbols of politics in the 2004 election may be another of the symbols of the competition of rising and declining social forces in the United States. The soccer moms represented suburban, affluent America with children engaging in a sport that offered greater opportunities for both genders than most other sports, and represented some international influence in American life. Despite the widening appeal of stock-car racing in the United States, it still engages largely lower- and lower-middle-class men in the South and Midwest, just the segments of society that have been increasingly marginalized by globalization, and by the increasingly knowledge-based economy. These groups also espouse very traditional social values and hence were strongly attracted to the Republican Party and its appeals on these issues.

What is perhaps most interesting in the election of 2004 is that much of the Republican support came from groups that might well not have been natural supporters of George Bush and his fellow Republicans. As already noted, the anti-tax rhetoric of the campaign played well with lower-middle-class and working-class voters, although the evidence was clearly that the direct benefits of the tax cuts had gone, and probably would continue to go, to the most affluent in society. Likewise, the proposals for privatizing part of the Social Security system might well undermine the benefits of middle- and lower-income people who were less likely to be skillful investors than the more affluent. This list of disparities between apparent economic interests and voting behavior could be extended, but if the election had been about economic and class interests, the voting pattern should have been expected to be rather different from that observed.

In historical terms the contemporary political strength of these declining social forces can be compared to the rise of populism and agrarian movements responding to industrialization. While hardly so dramatic or organized as the populist movements in the nineteenth and twentieth centuries, the mobilization of segments of the population that perceived themselves under siege from social and economic change has had a significant influence on politics, and has offered an avenue for those segments of the society to attempt to recoup some of their losses. This conservative populism (see Taggart, 2003), based on the protection of traditional values, is of course significantly different from the more economically based populism encountered earlier. Again, however, when faced with the range of issues that now confront the federal government, those traditional values offer little guidance for policy-makers, and the dominant coalition appears less viable in the face of the policy challenges now confronting government.

Culture shift

The second strand of academic writing about social and value change was Ronald Inglehart's (1977; 1990) discussion of changing political values and the rise of "postmaterialism" in political life. These changes were hypothesized to be occuring, in the United States and in other affluent countries, and to represent a fundamental realignment of political cultures in these countries. Similar in some ways to the Huntington characterization of postindustrial politics, Inglehart's concept of postmaterialism assumed that increasing affluence would enable all or nearly all citizens to have "enough," that is, the question of economic satisfaction that had been the battleground of the materialist politics over the distribution of income, employment and basic issues of social class that had been typical of government for most of the twentieth century, and before. In the place of those materialist political issues, issues such as rights of effective participation, human rights, the environment, and forms of self-actualization would arise as the focus of political action. The burgeoning of peace movements, the environmental movement and the women's movement during the 1960s and 1970s were seen as clear evidence of this "culture shift" in politics.

The above having been said, however, much of the politics of the 2000 campaign, and particularly the 2004 electoral campaign, was about values rather than more substantive policy issues. Social Security, and the war in Iraq were discussed, and discussed in often heated terms, but much of the political discourse during the election was about social issues such as abortion, gay marriage, stem-cell research and prayer in the schools. Traditionalists in political and social life appear threatened by the changes they see in society, and have found political outlets for those concerns. Further, institutions associated with the traditional values, notably evangelical Protestant churches, also have mobilized and have become involved in politics in ways that previously might not have been thought to be appropriate

While the federal government may have substantial power, the campaign for the presidency often appeared to be as much about the presumed styles and values of the candidates as about substance. These style issues were certainly factors very different from the economic issues that had been central to politics in the past. The successful versions of those issues were certainly not, however, going in the ideological direction that Inglehart had anticipated. Indeed, support for the values that Inglehart – and many other people in the 1960s and 1970 s– considered the natural progression of political life tended to be taken as an indication of an absence of the proper values for a president. John Kerry (and even more Teresa Heinz Kerry) represented those values perhaps more than any candidate in American electoral history.

Political values and governance

Although any political group that is ideologically committed is likely to be intolerant of individuals with different views, the social conservatives that have become dominant in the Republican Party have demonstrated a marked unwillingness to compromise on policy. As well as having a political ideology, the link of that ideology with religious belief makes compromise difficult, and virtually immoral (Layman, 2000). The importance of these more extreme political activists has been accentuated by the replacement of political leadership in Washington and in state capitals. Many of the political elites who were more comfortable with the compromise and bargaining of the "old system" within Congress have left politics, some retiring early while expressing their disdain for the polarization of contemporary politics.

Divided government has been successful in the past in providing governance to the society, even when there were marked partisan differences. That degree of effective governance is less likely to happen any longer, given the level of politicization and polarization between the parties, and especially between the party elites (Jones, 2001). The majority party may be able to govern alone, but even in a party that has worked on building ideological consistency there will still be some internal differences. For example, although the Republican Party is in control of both Houses of Congress, in 2005 it was having difficulty in maintaining that majority to pass reforms of Social Security or even to get the president's appointments for executive offices or the judiciary through the Senate. Policy-making must still be conducted with some eye to the voters, and there is little evidence that the public is as interested as the elites about reforming pensions, or indeed many of the other changes proposed by the dominant party.

What the polarization of contemporary American politics may indicate is a significant disjuncture between the interests of rising and declining social forces in the society, and the temporary victory of some of the declining forces. The map of the 2004 election to some extent vividly demonstrates the sharp differences between segments of the society, and their potential role in the future, postindustrial society. Support for the Democratic Party came from the two coasts, generally more economically and intellectually progressive, while the red states in the middle of the country, and in the South, generally are much less in alignment with the forces and ideas identified as making up "postindustrial society."

The importance of terrorism as an issue for voters also to some extent has played out in contrast to the reality of the threat. The areas of the country that appeared most concerned about the terrorist threat were those least likely to actually be attacked, unless grain silos in the Dakotas suddenly take on the same appeal to terrorists as the twin towers of the World Trade Center. This emphasis on terrorism, often conceptualized as an issue of nationalism and patriotism, indicates again the importance of more traditional values in defining the political agenda. The use of Iraq as a political issue again often has been reduced to terms of patriotism and supporting the troops in the field, rather than as an important question of foreign policy and the use of armed force for national interests. Even those policy questions, as important as they are, would ignore the perhaps more fundamental question of the apparent use of deception concerning weapons of mass destruction to create the justification for entry into Iraq in the first place.

The triumph of the founders – the ability to block

Perhaps most fundamentally, the changes in American politics outlined above ultimately will test the capacity of the founding fathers to design a set of institutions that can slow, or even stop, what Tocqueville referred to as a "tyrannical majority". It is very clear that there is a majority in the Congress that wants to control government very closely and to impose its own agenda on the society. For one of the few times in the post-war period both Houses of Congress and the presidency are controlled by the same party. Further, that dominant party now has a clearer ideological stance and greater internal unity than has been true in the past, and there is less commitment at present to the consensual norms that had minimized more extreme action in past years.

The above having been said, the need to govern may demonstrate that the dominant party is not so unified as it appeared during the 2004 campaign. The social conservatives have been ascendant, but there are also some old-fashioned Goldwater conservatives left in the party who do not want government to tamper with the bedroom any more than it tampers with the boardroom. Further, this more traditional segment of the party is not as keen on the spend but not tax fiscal policy of the current administration, preferring neither spending nor taxing. Thus, although there has been unity in the party, that may be unraveling. The problem may be that neither of these segments of the party will find many allies on the other side of the aisle in Congress (save for some fiscal conservatives in the Democratic party) so that forming coalitions may be no easier.

The injection of religion and social values into a central position in American politics represents a fundamental challenge to the capacity of the political system to govern. These issues are less debatable and less amenable to bargaining than the issues that have characterized politics in the past and tend to divide political leaders, and their mass publics, more profoundly than did even issues of race and civil rights. The inability to bargain and to create temporary coalitions to pass legislation appears to be reducing the capacity of the system to govern effectively, and to confront the serious economic and social problems that now confront the nation.

More than in the past, therefore, the difficulty of making American government move forward in the face of numerous policy challenges is not being met.

If the above characterization of contemporary politics is accurate, and I obviously believe that it is, then what are the options available for governance in the United States? One option, implied in much of the continuing discussions over federalism, is to depend more on state and local government. Placing major responsibility on the states has been a conventional part of the conservative plan for governing the United States. To some extent, relying on the states is now a more viable alternative than in the past, given that this level of government has modernized its administration more than the federal government and is capable of providing efficient services. That efficiency, however, assumes adequate fiscal resources, but the combination of tax cuts and slow economic growth in many states does not provide those resources. The same lack of available resources is even more evident for most cities. The states have been, by necessity, much better financial managers than the federal government, however, and do not face either massive deficits or a large obligation for pensions. The states do have some fiscal problems, and although by no means as significant as the problems in Social Security, the states do have large unfunded pension liabilities that will impose fiscal burdens in the near future (Mitchell, 1998).

Not only do the states and cities lack adequate financial resources to address major policy issues, the dominant problems for the United States are very much national problems. The states can do some things by better management with health care costs, but that contribution to cost reductions would be marginal, and real answers must be national. Some states have taken it upon themselves to encourage energy conservation, but national policies reside at the heart of the current energy concerns. This list of major issues confronting the United States could be extended but it should be apparent that the major policy problems arise at the federal level, and that they also will have to be solved at the federal level.

The other alternative for governance would be to rely on the career bureaucracy. The United States does not have the bureaucratic elite that much of Continental Europe does, but it does have a cadre of excellent public managers. The problem is that the bureaucracy does not appear to be trusted by the current administration, and the structure of American government permits a large, and growing, number of political appointees in the executive branch to supervise the permanent public service. While the bureaucracy may be able to deal with day-to-day regulations and implementation, political officials retain control over policy and attempt to ensure that the bureaucracy does not exercise much discretion of its own. Although Katrina and other failures have highlighted some of the problems with political appointees in crucial positions, political control is not likely to be decreased.

Perhaps the final option for enhancing the governance capacity of American government is through learning, and regaining at least some of the previous capacity for compromise among the political elites. The failures of the current administration in Iraq and in coping with natural disasters, among others, may be sufficient to reduce the hubris and insulation that has dominated their governance style. Returning to a consensual style of governing may be difficult once the comity that had lubricated politics in Washington has been eroded. That having been said, the need to govern and to govern effectively, may provide sufficient incentive to return to a more cooperative and collaborative style.

Guide to Further Reading

Chapter 1 Introduction

Fiorina (2005) provides a stimulating overview of America's new democracy. King (2000) and (2005) looks at the role of immigration and national identity. Ahlstrom (2004), Eck (2002), Garber and Walkowitz (1999) and Wurthnow (2005) all examine aspects of contemporary religion. Bellah (1986) remains insightful. On ideology the evolution of the new right can be traced in Peele (1984), Hodgson (1996) and Blumenthal (1986). Olasky (2000) provides some insight into compassionate conservatism.

Chapter 2 Electoral Politics

The editors and staff of *Newsweek* were granted exclusive access to the Bush and Kerry campaigns for a book to be published after the election (see Thomas *et al.*, 2005). For early takes on the election by political scientists, see Nelson (2005) and Crotty (2005). Useful websites include the National Election Studies, which includes surveys of voters during all presidential and congressional elections since 1948. A useful summary of trends is at < www.umich.edu/~nes/nesguide/nesguide.htm >. For polling data during the campaign, see < www.pollingreport.com/2004.htm >. A basic summary of the 2004 election results is < www.cnn.com/ELECTION/2004/pages/results/ >. For information about campaign fundraising and spending, see < www.opensecrets.org > and < www.politicalmoneyline.com >. Project Vote-Smart has nonpartisan information about the candidates and their positions on issues < www.vote-smart.org/ >.

Chapter 3 Parties

Bibby (2002) provides a comprehensive introduction to political parties in the United States. Jewell and Morehouse (2001) is an invaluable resource to understanding state political systems and the linkages between state and national parties. Malbin (2006) provides up-to-date coverage of the impact of campaign finance regulations and how BCRA has impacted on parties and interest groups since its passage in 2002. A good place to look for the latest in campaign finance reform is the Campaign Finance Institute < www.cfinst.org/ >. For a comprehensive and well-organized source on research related to US political parties, the newsletters of the Political Organizations and Parties Section of the American Political Science Association < www.uakron.edu/bliss/VoxPop.php > from 1982 to the present are available on-line.

Chapter 4 Interest Groups

The best survey of academic research on interest groups is Baumgartner and Leech (1998). One of the dominant themes in the literature on interest groups is the power of business. David Vogel has written a series of books on business–government relations that command attention; see in particular his 1989 study of the political power of business. Smith (2000) has undertaken the most complete empirical examination of the power of business. The surprising success of public interest groups is best explored by Berry (1999). Goldstein (1999) provides a valuable study of the use of mass politics by interest groups.

Among websites the FEC website has a wealth of material < www.fec.gov >, while lobby registration reports can be found at < www.sopr.senate.gov/cgi-winm_opr_viewer.exe?DoFn = 0 >

Chapter 5 The Presidency

The literature on the presidency is huge and there are several outstanding collections of essays focusing on it. Particularly good recent ones are Pika and Maltese (2006) and Nelson (2006). Aberbach and Peterson (2005) provides an excellent analysis of the executive branch as a whole, as does Burke (2000). Neustadt (1960), Nathan (1986), Moe (1985), and Lowi (1985) offer important interpretations of the presidency, while Edwards (1983), Kernell (1997), and Tulis (1987) all focus on the public aspects. Edwards (1989) looks at the management of legislation while Rudalevige (2002) looks more broadly at managing the president's agenda. Mayer (2001) considers the role of executive orders and the power of the presidency. Edwards (2006) examines the Bush presidency in detail as does Greenstein (2003), Gregg and Rozell (2003), and Campbell and Rockman (2004) The journal *Presidential Studies Quarterly* is a useful source of scholarly material focused on the executive branch

Among relevant websites < www.presidentsusa.net/ > is a good resource for tracking down further information while the White House (< www.whitehouse.gov/ > itself has an excellent website for information about the current administration.

Chapter 6 Congress

Davidson and Oleszek (2005) and English (2003) are good introductions to Congress while Oleszek (2004) provides a definitive account of congressional procedures and processes. Dodd and Oppenheimer (2005) is an excellent collection of essays by leading congressional scholars. The evolution of Congress is examined in Zelizer (2004) and Polsby (2004). Up-to-date information on Congress can be obtained from Congressional websites: a useful gateway is < www.congresslink.org/ > while the Library of Congress is another invaluable source of information < www.thomas.loc.gov/ >.

Chapter 7 The Supreme Court

For a good overview of the Supreme Court, read Baum (2004) or O'Brien (2003). Keck (2004) argues that the Rehnquist Court has been the most "activist" in history, despite the fact that it has been conservative. For some empirical evidence on how justices vote (and why they do so) as well as how opinions are crafted, see Segal and Spaeth (2002) and Maltzman, Spriggs, and Wahlbeck (2000). Hammond, Bonneau, and Sheehan (2005) provide a comprehensive theoretical framework for how justices behave at each stage of the decision-making process. Finally, the text of Supreme Court decisions can be obtained through the Legal Information Institute at Cornell University Law School < www.law.cornell.edu/ > .

Chapter 8 Federalism and Intergovernmental Relations

The principal understandings of American Federalism are outlined in the thought of Morton Grodzins (1966). The best treatments of new developments in intergovernmental relations are found in yearly updates by *The Book of the States*, published by the Council on State Governments. Recent volumes include articles by Kincaid (2003), Wright (2003), and Zimmerman (2003) illustrating the changing dynamics of federal–state relations, while Zimmerman (2005) explores regulatory federalism and congressional pre-emption. Scheberle (2004) examines how environmental policy in the United States is shaped by federalism.

A number of websites are useful for the study of federalism. See especially the American Enterprise Institute's Federalism Project < www.federalismproject. org > . The Urban Institute provides useful material on assessing the new federalism, < www.urban.org/center/anf/ > . Temple University's Center for the Study of Federalism, < www.temple.edu/federalism/ > is an excellent resource for federalism and contains details of its flagship journal *Publius*.

Chapter 9 Minorities

Black and Black (2002) is a ground-breaking work that examines why race is the key to understanding the party realignment in the South, especially in congressional elections. Walton and Smith (2006) provides a thorough analysis of the role of African-Americans in the nation's political institutional history and McClain and Steward (2006) gives an overview of current minority politics concerning all major minority groups. Kousser (1999) is a well-written and thoroughly investigated case study of the impact of voting rights public policy on minorities' quest for justice. Swain (2002) gives an in-depth look at radical right-wing whites in contemporary US politics.

Chapter 10 The Media

Overholser and Jamieson (2005) is a helpful collection of essays examining historical, institutional, and normative dimensions of the press. Capella and

Jamieson (1997) presents the case that the way that journalists cover politics significantly contributes to public cynicism. On the basis of comparative research, Norris (2000) challenges the assumption of a connection between analytical journalism and political malaise. Sparrow (1999) thoughtfully places the news media within its institutional setting. There is a wide-ranging overview of the contemporary state of the media in the United States in Downie and Kaiser (2002). The Pew Research Center for the People and the Press has authoritative reports drawing on its surveys at < www.people-press.org > , as does the Pew Internet and American Life Project at < www.pewinternet.org > .

Chapter 11 Values, Lifestyles, and Politics

The classic exposition of "culture wars" is Hunter (1991). White (2003), Kaufman (2004), and Huntington (2004) offer more recent discussions of the effect that demographic changes have on politics. Fiorina *et al.* (2004) challenge the view that Americans are deeply divided over cultural issues. For a more general examination of the role of religion in American politics see Morone (2003) and Heineman (2005). The literature on abortion, homosexuality, and public health is extensive. Critchlow (2001) offers a good discussion of the politics of abortion. A recent study of gay politics is Hirsch (2005). Kluger (1997) offers a comprehensive study of tobacco control policy. Useful government websites include that of the US Census Bureau < www.census.gov > and the Centers for Disease Control < www.cdc.gov > . Both provide a wealth of data and information. All interest groups have websites that provide an indication of the intensity of the debate over values. People for the American Way < www.pfaw.org > is an example of a progressive group while Focus on the Family < www.family.org > is an example of a traditionalist group.

Chapter 12 Economic Policy

For up-to-date data on the US and other world economies, consult the latest edition of *The Economist's Pocket World in Figures*. A good source of data on-line is the *CIA World Factbook*, which can be accessed at < www.cia.gov/cia/publications/factbook > . Gallup < www.gallup.com > has excellent times-series data on attitudes toward economic performance. For the president's latest thinking and proposals on economic issues, see the *Annual Report of the Council of Economic Advisers* and *The Economic Report of the President*. The Congressional Budget Office also produces a range of informative economic reports, including the *Budget and Economic Outlook* each January

Chapter 13 Social Policy

Hacker (2002) offers a compelling explanation of the development of the American welfare state, particularly with regard to health care and pensions. Beland (2005)

analyzes the history of the Social Security programme and also discusses the contemporary arguments over the merits of reform. Weaver (2000) provides the best account of events leading up to the 1996 reform of welfare. For assessments of what has happened since 1996 and for ongoing debates about welfare reform and the nature of citizenship see Mead and Beem (2005). Black *et al.* (2004) provides an account of the Bush administration's faith-based initiative. For an array of data on poverty and health uninsurance see the US Census Bureau website: < www.census. gov/ > .

Chapter 14 Foreign Policy

For an intimate view of Bush's foreign policy-making, Bob Woodward's *Bush at War* (2002) and *Plan of Attack* (2004) are pretty much unparalleled. Woodward's phenomenal access to Bush administration members makes these compelling, but readers should be aware that Woodward is accused of being too charitable to his sources. The author of the other 'insider' volume, Richard A. Clarke, could not be accused of such charity: his *Against All Enemies* (2004) is highly critical of the strategy underpinning Bush's "War on Terror." For a broader view of US foreign policy, two works stand out. Daalder and Lindsay's *America Unbound* (2003) is incisive without being overbearing, while Halper and Clarke's *America Alone* (2004) provides an excellent introduction to the neo-conservative understanding of the world. Finally, Robert Kagan's short, and often blunt, *Paradise and Power* (2003) is a brilliant, if controversial, essay on US–European differences.

Chapter 15 Governance

Brady (2006) looks at gridlock in American politics and policy from the Carter period to the present. Donahue and Nye (2003) examines the problems of the public service. Hult and Walcott (2004) examines the role of the executive branch while Miller and Barnes (2004) looks more generally at lawmaking and the policy process. Wayne (2004) provides a critical review of American democracy.

Bibliography

Aberbach, Joel (2005a) "The Political Significance of the George W. Bush Administration," *Social Policy and Administration*, 39(2): 130–49.

Aberbach, Joel (2005b) "Transforming the Presidency: The Administration of Ronald Reagan" (paper delivered at the conference on the "United States in the 1980s: The Reagan Years," Oxford, November 2005).

Aberbach, Joel and Mark Peterson (2005) *The Executive Branch*, New York: Oxford University Press.

Aberbach, Joel and Bert A. Rockman (2000) *In the Web of Politics: Three Decades of the American Federal Executive*, Washington, DC: Brookings.

ADR (2005) "Divorce Rates," Americans for Divorce Reform, < www. divorcereform.org/rates > .

Ahlstrom, Sidney E. (2004) *A Religious History of the American People*, New Haven, CT: Yale University Press.

Aldrich, John H (2000) "Southern Parties in State and Nation," *Journal of Politics*, 62: 643–670.

Alexander, Herbert E. (2003) "The Political Process after the Bipartisan Campaign Reform Act of 2002," *Election Law Journal*, 2.

Allen, Mike (2005) "Conservative Groups' Steady Support," *Washington Post*, March 24, p. A1.

Alliance for Justice (2001) "14th Annual Report on the State of the Judiciary," Washington, DC.

Alterman, Eric (2003) *What Liberal Media? The Truth About Bias and the News*, New York: Basic Books.

Alvarez, R. Michael, D.E. Sinclair, and Catherine H. Wilson (2004) "Counting Ballots and the 2000 Election: What Went Wrong?" in Ann N. Crigler, Marion R. Just, and Wedward J. McCaffrey (eds), *Rethinking the Vote: The Politics and Prospects of Electoral Reform*, New York: Oxford University Press.

American Political Science Association (1950) *Toward a More Responsible Two-Party System*, New York: Rinehart.

ANR (2005) "Overview List – How many Smokefree Laws?," American Nonsmokers' Rights Foundation, < www.no-smoke.org > .

Apollonio, D.E. and Raymond J. La Raja (2004) "Who Gave Soft Money? The Effect of Interest Group Resources on Political Contributions," *Journal of Politics*, 66: 1134–54.

Auletta, Ken (2003) *Backstory: Inside the Business of News*, New York: Penguin.

Baer, K. (2000) *Reinventing Democrats: The Politics of Liberalism from Reagan to Clinton*, Lawrence, KS: University of Kansas Press.

Bai, Matt (2004) "The Multilevel Marketing of the President," *New York Times Magazine*, 25 April.

Barr, N. (2004) *Economics of the Welfare State*, Oxford: Oxford University Press.

Bartels, Larry M. (1988) *Presidential Primaries and the Dynamics of Public Choice*, Princeton: Princeton University Press.

Bartels, Larry M. (2000) "Partisanship and Voting Behavior, 1952–1966," *American Journal of Political Science*, 44: 35–50.

Bartels, Larry M. (2005) "Homer Gets a Tax Cut: Inequality and Public Policy in the American Mind," in *Perspectives on Politics*, 3: 15–31.

Bauer, Raymond, Ithiel de Sola Pool, and Lewis Anthony Dexter (1963) *American Business and Public Policy: The Politics of Foreign Trade*, New York: Atherton.

Baum, Lawrence (2004) *The Supreme Court*, 8th edn, Washington, DC: Congressional Quarterly Press.

Baumgartner, Frank and Beth Leech (1998) *Basic Interests: The Importance of Groups in Politics and Political Science*, Princeton: Princeton University Press.

Beckerman, Gal (2003) "Tripping Up Big Media," *Columbia Journalism Review*, November–December.

Beer, Samuel H. (1978) "Federalism, Nationalism, and Democracy in America," *American Political Science Review*, 72: 9–21.

Beland, D. (2005) *Social Security: History and Politics from the New Deal to the Privatization Debate*, Lawrence, Kansas: University of Kansas Press.

Bell, Daniel (1960) *The End of Ideology*, Glencoe, IL: Free Press.

Bell, Daniel (1973) *The Coming of Post-Industrial Society*, New York: Basic Books.

Bellah, Robert (1986) *Habits of the Heart: Individualism and Commitment in American Life*, New York: Harper and Row.

Bennett, Anthony J. (1996) *The President's Cabinet: From Kennedy to Bush*, Basingstoke: Macmillan.

Berger, R. (1974) *Executive Privilege: A Constitutional Myth*, Cambridge, MA: Harvard University Press.

Berger, R. (1981) *Impeachment: The Constitutional Problems*, Cambridge, MA: Harvard University Press.

Bernstein, Jonathan and Casey B. K. Dominguez (2003) "Candidates and Candidacies in the Expanded Party," *PS*, 36: 165–70.

Berry, Jeffrey M. (1999) *The New Liberalism: The Rising Power of Citizen Groups*, Washington, DC: Brookings.

Bibby, John F. (2003) *Politics, Parties and Elections in America*, 5th edn, Belmont, CA: Wadsworth Publishing.

Binder, Sarah and Steve Smith (1997) *Politics or Principle: Filibustering in the United States Senate*, Washington, DC: Brookings.

Black, A., D. Koopman, and D. K. Ryden, (2004) *Of Little Faith: The Politics of George W. Bush's Faith-Based Initiatives* Washington, DC: Georgetown University Press.

Black, Earl and Merle Black (2002) *The Rise of Southern Republicans*, Cambridge, MA: Harvard University Press.

Brady, David W. (2006) *Revolving Gridlock: Politics and Policy from Jimmy Carter to George W. Bush*, Boulder, CO: Westview.

Brady, Henry, Justin Buchler, Matthew Jarvis, and John McNulty (2001) *Counting All the Votes: The Performances of Voting Technology in the United States*, Available at < www.ucdata.berkeley.edu >.

Brandt, Allan M. (1990) "The Cigarette, Risk, and American Culture," *Daedalus*, Fall, 119: 155–76.

Brody, Richard and Catherine R. Shapiro (1989) "A Reconsideration of the Rally Phenomenon in Public Opinion," in Scott Long (ed.), *Political Behavior Annual vol. 2*, Boulder, CO: Westview Press.

Brookings Institution (1999) Presidential Appointees Initiative, Washington, DC, < www.appointee.brookings.edu > .

Brooks, David (2001) "One Nation, Slightly Divisible," *Atlantic Monthly* (December): 53–65.

Brown, Robert (2005) "Minority Politics in the 2004 Presidential Election," in Larry J. Sabato (ed.), *Get in the Booth: A Citizen's Guide to the 2004 Election*, New York: Pearson Education.

Burke, J. (2000) *The Institutional Presidency: Organizing and Managing the Presidency from FDR to Clinton*, Baltimore: Johns Hopkins Press.

Burkeman, Oliver (2004) "Religious Right Relishes Chance to Push Agenda," *The Guardian*, November 5: 18.

Burns, James McGregor (1963) *The Deadlock of Democracy*, Englewood Cliffs, NJ: Prentice-Hall.

Bush, George W. (2001), "Address to a Joint Session of Congress and the American People," Washington, DC: September 20.

Bush, George W. (2002) "President Promotes Compassionate Conservatism," April 30, < www.whitehouse.gov > .

Bush, George W. (2003) "President Applauds Congress for Partial-Birth Abortion Bill," October 21, < www.whitehouse.gov > .

Bush, George W. (2004a), "Presidential Press Conference," Washington, DC: November 4.

Bush, George W. (2004b) "President Calls for Constitutional Amendment Protecting Marriage," February 24, < www.whitehouse.gov > .

Bush, George W. (2005a) "Inaugural Address," Washington, DC: January 20.

Bush, George W. (2005b) "President Highlights Faith Based Initiative at Leadership Conference," March 1, < www.whitehouse.gov > .

Cain, Bruce (1995) "Racial and Ethnic Politics," in Gillian Peele, Christopher J. Bailey, Bruce Cain, and B. Guy Peters (eds), *Developments in American Politics 2*, Chatham, NJ: Chatham House.

Caldeira, Gregory A. and James L. Gibson (1992) "The Etiology of Public Support for the Supreme Court," *American Journal of Political Science*, 36: 635–64.

California Official Voter Information Guide: < www.voterguide.ss.ca.gov/ proposition/prop70–analysis.htm > .

Caltech-MIT Voting Project (2001) *Voting: What Is and What Can Be*, < www.vote.Caltech.edu/reports/2001report > .

Campbell, Colin (1986) *Managing the Presidency: Carter, Reagan and the Search for Executive Harmony*, Pittsburgh: University of Pittsburgh Press.

Campbell, Colin and Bert A. Rockman, (2003) *The Bush Presidency: Appraisals and Prospects*, Chatham, NJ: Chatham House.

Campbell, James E. (2000) *The American Campaign: US Presidential Campaigns and the National Vote*, College Station: Texas A&M Press.

Campbell, James E. (2005) "Introduction – the 2004 presidential election forecasts," *PS* 37(4): 733–5.

Campbell, James E. and S. J. Jurek (2003) "The Decline of Competition and Change in Congressional Elections," in S. Ahuja and R. Dewhirst (eds), *Congress Responds to the Twentieth Century*, Columbus, Ohio: Ohio University Press.

Cappella, Joseph N. and Kathleen Hall Jamieson (1997) *Spiral of Cynicism: The Press and the Public Good*, New York: Oxford University Press.

Carlson, Darren K. (2004) "Smoking: Personal Habits Meet Public Policy," Washington, DC: The Gallup Organization, July 27.

Carmines, Edward G. and James A. Stimson (1989) *Issue Evolution: Race and the Transformation of American Politics*, Princeton: Princeton University Press.

Carroll, Joseph (2005) "Party Lines Shape Views of What's Morally Acceptable," Washington, DC: The Gallup Organization, May 24.

CDC (2005) "The Burden of Tobacco Use," Centers for Disease Control, < www.cdc.gov/tobacco/overview/oshsummary2004 > .

Center for Arms Control and Non-Proliferation (2005), "US Military Spending vs. The World," < www.armscontrolcenter.org/archives/001221.php > , February 7.

CFABA (2005) "Belief and Mission Statement," Citizens for a Better America, < www.cfaba.org > .

Citizens Conference on State Legislatures (1971) *The Sometime Governments: A Critical Study of the 50 American Legislatures*, New York: Bantam Books.

Clarke, Richard A. (2004) *Against All Enemies: Inside America's War on Terror*, New York: The Free Press.

Clymer, Adam (2002) "Republican Party's 40 Years of Juggling on Race," *New York Times*, December 13th.

Coates, Ta-Nehisi (2004) "Running from Race," *The Village Voice*, February 11–17.

Collins, Scott (2004) *Crazy Like a Fox: The Inside Story of How Fox News Beat CNN*, New York: Portfolio.

Congressional Budget Office (2005) *Budget and Economic Outlook: Fiscal Years 2006 to 2015*, < www.cbo.gov > .

Connolly, Ceci, (2003) "Health Costs of Obesity Near Those of Smoking," *Washington Post*, May 14, p. A9.

Converse, Phillip (1964) "The Nature of Belief Systems in Mass Publics" in David E. Apter (ed.), *Ideology and Discontent*, New York: Free Press.

Cook Political Report (2005a) "2006 senate race ratings," < www.cookpolitical. com/races/report_pdfs/2006_sen_ratings_dec2.pdf > .

Cook Political Report. (2005b) "2006 house race ratings," < www.cookpolitical. com/races/report_pdfs/2006_house_comp_dec2.pdf > .

Cornfield, Michael (2004) *Politics Moves Online: Campaigning and the Internet*, New York: Century Foundation Press.

Corrado, Anthony (1997) "Party Soft Money," in Anthony Corrado, Thomas E. Mann, Daniel R. Ortiz, Trevor Potter and Frank J. Sorauf (eds), *Campaign Finance Reform: A Source Book*, Washington, DC: Brookings.

Corrado, Anthony and Thomas E. Mann (2004) "In the Wake of BCRA: An Early Report on Campaign Finance in the 2004 Elections," *The Forum* 2.

Cotter, Cornelius P., James L. Gibson, John F. Bibby, and Robert J. Huckshorn (1984) *Party Organizations in American Politics*, New York: Praeger.

Council of Economic Advisors (2005) *Annual Report of the Council of Economic Advisors*, Washington, DC: US Government Printing Office.

Council of Economic Advisors (2006) *Annual Report of the Council of Economic Advisors*, Washington, DC: US Government Printing Office.

Council of Europe (2003) *Demographic Year Book 2003*.

Critchlow, Donald T. (2001) *Intended Consequences: Birth Control, Abortion and the Federal Government in Modern America*, New York, NY: Oxford University Press.

Crotty, William (ed.) (2005) *A Defining Moment: The Presidential Election of 2004*, Armon, NY: M.E. Sharpe.

Daalder, Ivo H. and James M. Lindsay (2003) *America Unbound: The Bush Revolution in Foreign Policy*, Washington, DC: Brookings.

Dahl, Robert (1956) *Preface to Democratic Theory*, Chicago: University of Chicago Press.

Danforth, John (2005) "Onward, Moderate Christian Soldiers: Religion and American Politics," *New York Times*, June 23.

Davidson, Roger H. and Walter J. Oleszek (2005) *Congress and Its Members*, 10th edn, Washington, DC: Congressional Quarterly.

Davis, Richard (1999) "Electronic Lobbying," in Richard Davis (ed.), *The Web of Politics: The Internet's Impact on the American Political System*, New York: Oxford University Press.

Dean, John W. (2004) *Worse than Watergate: The Secret Presidency of George W. Bush*, New York: Little, Brown.

De Crèvecoeur, J. Hector St. John (1986, [1782]) *Letters from an American Farmer*, Harmondsworth, Middlesex: Penguin.

Department of Defense (2005) "Annual Report to Congress: The Military Power of the People's Republic of China, 2005," < www.defenselink.mil/news/Jul2005/d20050719china.pdf >, July 19.

Dickinson, Matthew J. (2005) "The Executive Office of the President: The Paradox of Politicization," in Joel D. Aberbach and Mark A. Peterson (eds), *The Executive Branch*, Oxford: Oxford University Press.

DiIulio, J. (2003) "A View from Within," in Fred Greenstein (ed.), *The George W. Bush Presidency: An Early Assessment*, Baltimore: The Johns Hopkins University Press.

Dodd, Lawrence C. and Bruce Oppenheimer (eds) (2005) *Congress Reconsidered*, 8th edn, Washington, DC: Congressional Quarterly Press.

Donahue, J.D. and J.S. Nye (2003) *For the People: Can We Fix the Public Service?*, Washington, DC: Brookings.

Downie, Leonard and Robery G. Kaiser (2002) *The News about the News: American Journalism in Peril*, New York: Knopf.

Dreyfuss, B. (2004) "Cheap Trick," *The American Prospect*, 9(15): 25–8.

Dumbrell, John (2003) "The Bush Doctrine," in Edwards, George C. and Philip John Davies, *New Challenges for the American Presidency*, New York: Pearson Longman.

Durr, Robert H., Andrew D. Martin, and Christina Wolbrecht (2000) "Ideological Divergence and Public Support for the Supreme Court," *American Journal of Political Science*, 44: 768–76.

Eck, Diana (2002) *A New Religious America*, New York: HarperCollins.

Edwards, George C. (1999) *At the Margins: Presidential Leadership of Congress*, New Haven, CT: Yale University Press.

Edwards, George C. (2006) *On Deaf Ears: the Limits of the Bully Pulpit* New Haven, CT: Yale University Press.

Edwards, George C. and Philip John Davies (2004) *New Challenges for the American Presidency*, New York: Pearson Longman.

Elazar, Daniel J. (1990) "Opening the Third Century of American Federalism: Issues and Prospects," *The Annals*, 509: 11–21.

English, Ross (2003) *The United States Congress*, Manchester: Manchester University Press.

Entman, Robert N. (1989) *Democracy Without Citizens: Media and the Decay of American Politics*, New York: Oxford University Press.

Eskridge, William N. (2002) *Equality Practice: Civil Unions and the Future of Gay Rights*, New York, NY: Routledge.

Esping-Andersen, G. (1990) *The Three Worlds of Welfare Capitalism*, Oxford: Polity.

Evans, D. (2004) *Greasing the Wheels: Using Pork Barrel Projects to Build Majority Coalitions in Congress*, Cambridge: Cambridge University Press.

Farmer, Rick and Rich Fender (2003) "Casting a Weak Net: Political Party Websites in 2000," in John C. Green and Rick Farmer (eds), *The State of the Parties*, New York: Rowman and Littlefield.

Fenno, Richard E. (1959) *The President's Cabinet: An Analysis of the Period from Wilson to Eisenhower*, Cambridge, MA: Harvard University Press.

Fenno, Richard E. (1973) *Congressmen in Committees*, Boston: Little, Brown.

Fenno, Richard E. (1997) *Learning to Govern: An Institutional View of the 104th Congress*, Washington, DC: Brookings Institution Press.

Fenton, Tom (2005) *Bad News: The Decline of Reporting, the Business of News, and the Danger to Us All*, New York: ReganBooks.

Fineman, H. (2003) "Bush and God," *Newsweek*.

Finkel, Steven E. (1993) "Reexamining the 'Minimal Effects' Model in Recent Presidential Campaigns," *Journal of Politics* 55: 1–31.

Fiorina, Morris P., Samuel J. Abrams, and Jeremy C. Pope (2004) *Culture War? The Myth of a Polarized America*, New York: Pearson Longman.

Fitzgerald, Faith (1996) "The Tyranny of Health," *New England Journal of Medicine*, 331: 196–8.

Fitzpatrick, Michael (2001) *The Tyranny of Health*, London: Routledge.

Fletcher, Michael A. (2005) "Bush is Keeping Cabinet Secretaries Close to Home' *Washington Post*, March 31.

Fortier, J. and N. Ornstein (2003) "President Bush: Legislative Strategist," in Fred Greenstein (ed.), *The George W. Bush Presidency: An Early Assessment*, Baltimore: The Johns Hopkins University Press.

Foust, Michael (2005) "A First: Federal judge strikes down Neb. Marriage Amendment," *Bpnews*, < www.bpnews.net >.

Fowler, Adam and Brian Levy (2005) "The Message Behind the Madness: The 2004 Presidential Email Campaign," Paper presented at the Annual Meeting of Western Political Science Association, Oakland, California.

Franck, Thomas and Edward Wesiband (1979) *Foreign Policy by Congress*, New York: Oxford University Press.

FRC (2005) "Justice Sunday: Stop the Filibuster Against People of Faith," Family Research Council, < www.frc.org >.

Frymer, Paul, Dara Z. Strolovich and Dorian T. Warren (2005) "Katrina's Political Roots and Divisions: Race, Class and Federalism in American Politics," in *Understanding Katrina: Perspectives from the Social Sciences*, < www.ssrc. org >.

Fukuyama, Francis (1993) *The End of History and the Last Man*, New York: Avon Books.

Gallup Organization (2005) "Moral Issues," < www.gallup.com >, May 16.

Gallup Organization (2005) "Iraq versus Vietnam: A Comparison of Public Opinion," < www.gallup.com > August 24.

Gernter, Jon (2004) "The Very, Very Personal Is the Political," *New York Times Magazine*, 15 February.

Gilbert, N. (2002) *Transformation of the Welfare State: The Silent Surrender of Public Responsibility'*, New York: Oxford University Press.

Gimpel, James G. (1999) *Separate Destinations: Migration, Immigration, and the Politics of Places*, Ann Arbor, MI: The University of Michigan Press.

Glasgow, Garrett (2002) "The Efficiency of Congressional Campaign Committee Contributions in House Elections," *Party Politics* 8: 657–632.

Goldberg, Bernard (2003) *Bias: A CBS Insider Exposes How the Media Distort the News*, Washington, DC: Regnery.

Goldberg-Hiller, Jonathon (2002) *The Limits to Union: Same-Sex Marriage and the Politics of Civil Rights*, Ann Arbour, MI: University of Michigan Press.

Goldstein Kenneth M. (1999) *Interest Groups, Lobbying and Participation in America* New York: Cambridge University Press.

Goldstein, Kenneth and Paul Freedman (2002) "Campaign Advertising and Voter Turnout: New Evidence for a Stimulation Effect," *Journal of Politics*, 64: 721–40.

Goodin, R., B. Headey, R. Muffels, and H. Dirven (1999) *The Real Worlds of Welfare Capitalism*, Cambridge: Cambridge University Press.

Green, Donald P. and Alan S. Gerber (2004) *Get Out the Vote!*, Washington, DC: Brookings.

Greenhouse, Linda (2004) "Same Justices, New Court," *Washington Post*, July 3.

Greenstein, Fred I. (2003) *The George W Bush Presidency: An Early Assessment*, Baltimore: The Johns Hopkins Press.

Greenstein, Fred I. (2004) *The Presidential Difference: Leadership Style from FDR to George W Bush*, 2nd edn, Princeton: Princeton University Press.

Greenstone, J. David (1969) *Labor in American Politics*, New York: Knopf.

Gregg, Gary and Mark Rozell (eds) (2003) *Considering the Bush Presidency*, New York: Oxford University Press.

Grodzins, Morton (1966) *The American System: A New View of Government in the United States*, Chicago: Rand McNally.

Gumbel, Andrew (2004) "The New Republican Reality: No Policy is Too Right-wing," *The Independent*, November 8.

Hacker, J. (2002) *The Divided Welfare State: The Battle Over Public and Private Social Benefits in the United States*, Cambridge: Cambridge University Press.

Hacker, J. and P. Pierson (2005) "Abandoning the Middle: The Bush Tax Cut and the Limits of Democratic Control," *Perspectives on Politics*, 13: 33–53.

Halper, Stefan and Jonathan Clarke (2004) *America Alone: The Neo-Conservatives and the Global Order*, Cambridge: Cambridge University Press.

Hammond, Thomas H., Chris W. Bonneau, and Reginald S. Sheehan (2005) *Strategic Behavior and Policy Choice on the US Supreme Court*, Palo Alto, CA: Stanford University Press.

Hansen, John Mark (1991) *Gaining Access: Congress and the Farm Lobby 1919–81*, Chicago: University of Chicago Press.

Haskins, R., I. Sawhill, and K. Weaver (2001) *Welfare Reform: An Overview of Effects to Date*, Washington, DC: Brookings.

Heclo, Hugh (1978) "Issue Networks and the Executive Establishment," in Anthony King (ed.), *The New American Political System*, Washington, DC: American Enterprise Institute.

Heineman, Kenneth J. (2005) *God is a Conservative*, New York: New York University Press.

Heisler, Martin O. (1974) *Politics in Europe: Structures and Processes in Some Post-Industrial Democracies*, New York: McKay.

Hetherington, Marc J. (2001) "Resurgent Mass Partisanship: The Role of Elite Polarization," *American Political Science Review*, 95: 619–32.

Hickey, Neil (2003) "FCC: Ready, Set, Consolidate," *Columbia Journalism Review*, July/August.

Hillygus, D. S. and T. Shields (2005) "Moral Issues and Voter Decision Making in the 2004 Presidential Election," *PS*, 38: 201–10.

Hirsch, Fred (1977) *The Social Limits to Growth*, London: Routledge.

Hirsch, H.N. (2005) *The Future of Gay Rights in America*, New York: Routledge.

Hodgson, Godfrey (1980) *All Things to All Men: The False Promise of the Modern Presidency*, New York: Simon & Schuster.

Howard, C. (2003) "Is the American Welfare State Unusually Small?," *PS*, 36: 411–16.

Howell, William G. (2005) "Unilateral Powers: A Brief Overview," *Presidential Studies Quarterly*, 35: 417–39.

Hughes, Neil C. (2005) "A Trade War with China?," *Foreign Affairs*, July/Aug.

Hult, K.M. (2003) "The Bush White House in Comparative Perspective," *Presidential Studies Quarterly*.

Hult, K.M. and C. E. Walcott (2004) *Empowering the White House*, Lawrence, KS: University Press of Kansas.

Hunter, James Davison (1991) *Culture Wars: The Struggle to Define America*, New York: Basic Books.

Huntington, Samuel P. (1974) "Post-Industrial Politics: How Benign Will It Be?," *Comparative Politics*, 6: 163–91.

Huntington, Samuel P. (2004) *Who Are We?*, New York: The Free Press.

Inglehart, Ronald (1977) *The Silent Revolution: Changing Values and Political Styles Among Western Publics*, Princeton: Princeton University Press.

Inglehart, Ronald (1990) *Culture Shift in Advanced Industrial Society*, Princeton: Princeton University Press.

Ivins, Molly and Lou Dubose (2000) *Shrub.The Short But Happy Life of George W Bush*. Thorndike, ME: Thorndike Press.

Ivins, Molly and Lou Dubose (2003) *Bushwhacked: Life in George Bush's America*, New York: Random House.

Jaenicke, Douglas and Alex Waddan (2005) "President Bush and Social Policy: The Strange Case of a Prescription Drug Benefit for Medicare," paper presented at the American Politics Group (PSA) conference, January.

Jackson, John S., Nathan S. Bigelow, and John C. Green (2003) "The State of Party Elites: National Convention Delegates, 1992–2000," in John C. Green and Rick Farmer (eds), *The State of the Parties*, New York: Rowman & Littlefield.

Jacobson, Gary C. (2001) "A House and Senate Divided: The Clinton Legacy and the Congressional Elections of 2000," *Political Science Quarterly*, 116: 5–27.

Jacobson, Gary C. (2003) "The Bush Presidency and the American Electorate," in Fred Greenstein (ed.), *The George W. Bush Presidency: An Early Assessment*, Baltimore: The Johns Hopkins University Press.

Jacobson, Gary C. (2004) *The Politics of Congressional Elections*, 6th edn, New York: Pearson Longman.

Jacobson, Gary C. (2005) "The Public, the President, and the War in Iraq," paper presented at the Annual Meeting of the Midwest Political Science Association, Chicago.

Jennings, James (1994) "Conclusion: Racial Hierarchy and Ethnic Conflict in the United States," in James Jennings (ed.), *Blacks, Hispanics, and Asians in Urban America*, Westport, CN: Praeger.

Jewell, Malcolm E. and Sarah M. Morehouse (2001) *Political Parties and Elections in American States*, Washington, DC: Congressional Quarterly Press.

Johnson, Steve (2003) "How Fox is Winning the War," *Chicago Tribune*, 4 April.

Jones, Charles O. (1999) *Separate but Equal: Congress and the Presidency*, 2nd edn, Chatham, NJ: Chatham House.

Jones, Charles O. (2005) *The Presidency in a Separated System*, Washington, DC: Brookings.

Jones, D.R. (2001) "Party Polarization and Legislative Gridlock," *Political Research Quarterly*, 54: 125–41.

Jost, Kenneth (2005) "School Desegregation," in *Issues in Race, Ethnicity and Gender*, 2nd edn, Washington, DC: Congressional Quarterly Press.

Judis, John B. (2005) "Money Train," *New Republic*, December 11.

Kagan, Robert (2003) *Paradise and Power: America and Europe in the New World Order*, London: Atlantic Press.

Kaufman, Eric P. (2004) *The Rise and Fall of Anglo-America*, Cambridge, MA: Harvard University Press.

Kaufman, K.M. and J.R. Petrocik (1999) "The Changing Politics of American Men: Understanding the Sources of the Gender Gap," *American Journal of Political Science*, 43: 864–87.

Kazin, M. (1998) *The Populist Persuasion: An American History*, Ithaca, NY: Cornell University Press.

Keck, Thomas M. (2004) *The Most Activist Supreme Court in History: The Road to Modern Judicial Conservatism*, Chicago: University of Chicago Press.

Keller, Bill (2003) "The Radical Presidency of George W Bush: Reagan's Son," *New York Times*, 26 January.

Keffer, Gerard T. (2003) "Federal Spending in the New Millennium," *The Book of the States*, 35: 38–46.

Kernell, Samuel (1997) *Going Public: New Strategies of Presidential Leadership*, 3rd edn, Washington, DC: Congressional Quarterly Press.

Kernell, Samuel and Samuel Popkin (1986) *Chief of Staff: Twenty Five Years of Managing the Presidency*, Berkeley, CA: University of California Press.

Kettl, Donald F. (2003) *Team Bush: Leadership Lessons from the Bush White House*, New York: McGraw-Hill.

Key, V. O. (1966) *The Responsible Electorate*, Cambridge, MA: Harvard University Press.

Kincaid, John (1990) "From Cooperative to Coercive Federalism," *The Annals*, 509: 139.

Kincaid, John (2003) "Trends in Federalism: Is Fiscal Federalism Fizzling?," *The Book of the States*, 35: 26–31.

Kinder, Donald R. and Lynn M. Sanders (1996) *Divided by Color: Racial Politics and Democratic Ideas*, Chicago: University of Chicago Press.

Kinder, Donald R. and David O. Sears (1981) "Prejudice and Politics: Symbolic Racism versus Racial Threats to the Good Life," *Journal of Personality and Social Psychology*, 40: 414–31.

King, Anthony (1973) "Ideas, Institutions and the Policies of Government: A Comparative Analysis," *British Journal of Political Science*, 2: 291–313, 409–23.

Kingdon, J. (1995) *Agendas, Alternatives and Public Policies*, 2nd edn, New York: HarperCollins.

Kluger, Richard (1997) *Ashes to Ashes*, New York: Vintage.

Kuhn, David Paul (2004) "Kerry's Communion Controversy," < www.cbsnews.com >, April 6.

Kumar, Martha and Terry Sullivan (eds) (2003) *The White House World: Transitions, Organizations and Office Operations*, College Station, Texas: Texas A &M University Press.

Ladd, Carl Everett (1994) *The American Ideology: An Exploration of the Origins, Meaning and Role of American Political Ideas*, Storrs, CN: The Roper Center for Public Opinion Research.

Layman, Geofrey C. (2000) *The Great Divide: Religious and Cultural Conflict in American Politics*, New York: Columbia University Press.

Layman Geoffrey C. and Thomas M. Carsey (2000) "Ideological Realignment in Contemporary American Politics: The Case of Party Activists," paper presented at the annual meeting of the Midwest Political Science Association.

Layman Geoffrey C. and Thomas M. Carsey (2002) "Party Polarization and 'Conflict Extension' in the American Electorate," *American Journal of Political Science* 46: 786–802.

Lazarsfeld, Paul F., Bernard Berelson and Hazel Gaudet (1948) *The People's Choice*, New York: Columbia University Press.

Leal, D. L., M. A. Barreto, J. Lee and R. O. de la Garza (2005) "The Latino Vote in the 2004 Election," *PS*, 38: 41–9.

Legal Information Institute: < www.law.cornell.edu/ > .

Lewis, David E. (2005) "Staffing Alone: Unilateral Action and the Politicization of the Executive Office of the President 1988–2004," *Presidential Studies Quarterly*, 35: 496–514.

Light, Paul (1995) *Thickening Government: Federal Hierarchy and Accountability*, Washington, DC: Brookings.

Light, Paul (2002) *Government's Greatest Achievements: From Civil Rights to Homeland Defense*, Washington, DC: Brookings.

Light, Paul (2004) "Bush's New Cabinet: Changes in Attitude," *Newsday*, November 21.

Lind (2003) *Made in Texas: George W. Bush and the Southern Takeover of American Politics*, New York: Basic Books.

Lijphart, Arend (1984) *Democracies: Patterns of Majoritarian and Consensus Government in Twenty-One Countries*, New Haven, CT: Yale University Press.

Lipset, Seymour Martin (1996) *American Exceptionalism*, New York: W.W. Norton.

Liu, Frederick and Stephen Macedo (2005) "The Federal Marriage Amendment and the Strange Evolution of the Conservative Case against Gay Marriage," *PS: Political Science and Politics*, 38: 2.

Lowi, Theodore (1969) *The End of Liberalism*, New York: Norton.

Lowi, Theodore (1985) *The Personal President*, Ithica, NY: Cornell University Press.

Mackenzie, G. Calvin (2002) "The Real Invisible Hand: Presidential Appointees in the Administration of George W. Bush," PSOnline < www.apsanet.org > , March.

Malbin, Michael J. (1980) *Money and Politics in the United States*, Washington, DC: American Enterprise Institute.

Malbin, Michael J. (2004) "Political Parties Under the Post-*McConnell* Bipartisan Campaign Reform Act," *Election Law Journal*, 3.

Malbin, Michael J *(ed) (2006) The Election after Reform: Money, Politics, and the Bipartisan Campaign Reform Act*, Lanham, MD: Rowman & Littlefield.

Maltzman, Forrest, James F. Spriggs II, and Paul J. Wahlbeck (2000) *Crafting Law on the Supreme Court: The Collegial Game*, New York: Cambridge University Press.

Mann, James (2004) *The Rise of the Vulcans: The History of Bush's War Cabinet*, London: Penguin Books.

Marshall J (2004) "Bush's Cabinet Moves are about Loyalty and Control," *The Hill*, November 18.

Mayer, Kenneth R. (2001) *With the Stroke of A Pen: Executive Orders and Presidential Power*, Princeton: Princeton University Press.

Mayhew, David R. (1991) *Divided We Govern: Party Control, Lawmaking and Investigations, 1946–1990*, New Haven, CT: Yale University Press.

McCarty, Nolan, Keith T. Poole and Howard Rosenthal (2001) "The Hunt for Party Discipline in Congress," *American Political Science Review*, 95: 673–88.

McCormick, Joseph and Charles E. Jones (1993) "The Conceptualization of Deracialization: Thinking Through the Dilemma," in Georgia A. Persons (ed.), *Dilemma of Black Politics: Issues of Leadership and Strategy*, New York: Harper Collins College Publishers.

McDonald, Michael P. and Samuel Popkin (2001) "The Myth of the Vanishing Voter," *American Political Science Review*, 95: 963–74.

McFarland, Andrew (1984) *Common Cause: Lobbying in the Public Interest*, Chatham, NJ: Chatham House.

MacKuen, Michael B., Robert S. Erikson and James A. Stimson (1992) "Peasants or Bankers: The American Electorate and the US Economy," *American Political Science Review*, 86: 597–611.

McMurray, Coleen (2004) "Public: Lifestyle, Not Disease, Causes Obesity," Washington, DC: The Gallup Organization, August 10.

McSweeney D. and J.E. Owens (eds) (1998) *The Republican Takeover of Congress*, London: Macmillan Press.

Mead, L. and C. Beem (eds) (2005) *Welfare Reform and Political Theory*, New York: Russell Sage Foundation.

Meffert, Michael F., Helmut Norpoth and Anirudh V.S. Ruhil (2001) "Realignment and Macropartisanship' *American Political Science Review*, 95: 619–32.

Meyer, Dick (2004) "The Anatomy of a Myth: How Did One Exit Poll Answer Become the Story of How Bush Won?," *Washington Post*, December 5, p. B1.

Miller, M.J. and J. Barnes (2004) *Making Policy, Making Law: An Inter-branch Perspective*, Washington, DC: Georgetown University Press.

Miller, Warren E. and J. Merrill Shanks (1996) *The New American Voter*, Cambridge, MA: Harvard University Press.

Minutaglio Bill (1999) *First Son: George W. Bush and the Bush Family Dynasty*, New York: Times Books.

Mishel, L., J. Bernstein and H. Boushey (2003) *The State of Working America 2002/2003*, Ithica, NY: An Economic Policy Institute Book.

Mitchell, O.S. (1998) *Public and Private Pension Plans*, Princeton, NJ: National Bureau of Economic Research.

Missouri School of Journalism (2005) "New Research Shows Americans' Love-Hate Relationship with Journalism," University of Missouri at Columbia, Press Release, April 27.

Moe, Terry M. (1985) "The Politicised Presidency," in John E. Chubb and Paul E. Peterson (eds), *The New Directions In American Politics*, Washington, DC: Brookings.

Mokdad, Ali H. *et al.* (2004) "Actual Causes of Death in the United States, 2000," *Journal of the American Medical Association*, 291: 1238–41.

Moon, Woojin (2004) "Party Activists, Campaign Resources and Candidate Position-Taking: Theory, Tests and Applications," *British Journal of Political Science*, 34: 611–33.

Mooney, Christopher Z. (ed.) (2001) *The Public Clash of Private Values: The Politics of Morality Policy*, New York, NY: Chatham House.

Moore, James and Wayne Slater (2003) *Bush's Brain: How Karl Rove Made George W. Bush Look Presidential*, New York: John Wiley.

Morone, James A. (2003) *Hellfire Nation*, New Haven, CT: Yale University Press.

Mucciaroni, Gary (1995) *Reversal of Fortune: Public Policy and Private Interests*, Washington, DC: Brookings.

Mullan, Fitzhugh (1989) *Plagues and Politics*, New York, NY: Basic Books.

Murdoch, Rupert (2005) Speech to the American Society of Newspaper Editors, News Corporation Press Release, April 13.

Nathan, Richard (1975) *The Plot that Failed: Richard Nixon and the Administrative Presidency*, New York: John Wiley.

Nathan, Richard (1986) *The Administrative Presidency*, New York: Macmillan.

National Security Council (2002) "The National Security Strategy of the United States of America," < www.whitehouse.gov/nsc/nss.pdf > , September 17.

National Security Council (2005) "National Strategy for Victory in Iraq," < www.whitehouse.gov/infocus/iraq/iraq_national_strategy_20051130.pdf > , November 30.

Nelson, Michael (ed.) (2005) *The Election of 2004*, Washington, DC: Congressional Quarterly Press.

Nelson, Michael (ed.) (2006) *The Presidency in the Political System*, 8th edn, Washington, DC: Congressional Quarterly Press.

Neustadt, Richard E. (1990) *Presidential Power and the Modern Presidents: The Politics of Leadership from Roosevelt to Reagan*, New York: The Free Press.

Neustadt, Richard E. (2001) "The Weakening White House," *British Journal of Political Science*, 31: 1–11.

Newport, Frank (2005) "Church Attendance and Party Identification," Washington, DC: The Gallup Organization, May 18.

Newsweek (2004) "Face to Face," 15 November.

Newsweek (2004) "Trench Warfare," 15 November.

Nicholls, J. (2004) *Dick: The Man who is President*, New York: The New Press.

Niemi, Richard G. and Paul S. Herrnson (2003) "Beyond the Butterfly: The Complexity of US Ballots," *Perspectives on Politics*, 2: 317–26.

Niemi, Richard G. and Herbert F. Weisberg (1976) "Are Parties Becoming Irrelevant," in Richard G. Niemi and Herbert F. Weisberg (eds), *Controversies in American Voting Behavior*, San Francisco: W.H. Freeman.

Nolan, James L. (1996) "Political Discourse in America's Culture Wars," in James L. Nolan (ed.), *The American Culture Wars*, Charlottesville, VA: University Press of Virginia.

Norris, Pippa (2000) *A Virtuous Circle: Political Communication in Post Industrial Societies*, Cambridge: Cambridge University Press.

NOW (2005) "NOW Leaders Meet Face-to-Face with Senators, Urge Them to Vote "NO" on Alito," < www.now.org/issues/judicial/supreme > , November 10.

Nye, Joseph S., Jr (2004) "The Decline of America's Soft Power," *Foreign Affairs*, May/June.

O'Brien, David M. (2003) *Storm Center: The Supreme Court in American Politics*, New York: Norton.

OECD (2003) "Health Data 03," Organization for Economic Cooperation and Development, Paris, < www.oecd/dataoecd/10/20/278977.pdf > .

OECD (2005) *Main Economic Indicators, May 2005* Paris: OECD Publishing.

Office of Management and Budget (2005) *Budget of the United States Government, Fiscal Year 2006*, < www.whitehouse.gov/omb/budget/fy2006/ > .

Oleszek, Walter J. (2004) *Congressional Procedures and the Policy Process*, Washington, DC: Congressional Quarterly Press.

Olson, Mancur (1968) *The Logic of Collective Action*, New York: Schocken Books.

OpenSecrets (2005) < www.opensecrets.org/pacs/industry >, May 31.

Ornstein, N. (2002) "Why Close Races Ruin Politics," *New York Times*, November 4.

Overholser, Geneva and Kathleen Hall Jamieson (eds) (2005) *The Press*, New York: Oxford University Press.

Patterson, Thomas E. (1993) *Out of Order*, New York: Knopf.

Peele, Gillian (1984) *Revival and Reaction*, Oxford: Oxford University Press.

Peele, Gillian (2005) "Electoral Politics, Ideology and American Social Policy' *Social Policy and Administration* 39: 150–65.

Perkins, Tony (2005) "Washington Update," Family Research Council, < www.frc.org >, January 25.

Petrocik, John R. (1996) "Issue Ownership in Presidential Elections, with a 1980 Case Study," *American Journal of Political Science*, 40: 825–50.

Pew Global Attitudes Project (2005), "US Image Up Slightly, But Still Negative," < www.pewglobal.org/reports/display.php?ReportID = 247 >, June 23.

Pew Research Center for People and the Press (2004) "Voters Impressed with Campaign But News Coverage Gets Lukewarm Ratings," October 24.

PFAW (2005a) "PFAW's Mission," People for the American Way, < www.pfaw.org >.

PFAW (2005b) "A Brief Summary of the Records of the Rejected Judicial Nominees," People for the American Way, < www.pfaw.org >.

Pierson, Paul. (2001) "Coping with Permanent Austerity" in Paul Pierson (ed.), *The New Politics of the Welfare State*, Oxford: Oxford University Press.

Pika, Joseph A. and John Anthony Maltese (eds) (2006) *The Politcs of the Presidency*, 6th edn, Washington, DC: Congressional Quarterly Press.

Plasser, Fritz (2001) "Parties' Diminishing Relevance for Campaign Professionals," *Harvard International Journal of Press/Politics*, 6: 44–60.

Polsby, Nelson W. (1963) *Community Power and Political Theory*, New Haven, CT: Yale University Press.

Polsby, Nelson W. (1983) *The Consequences of Party Reform*, New York: Oxford University Press.

Polsby, Nelson W. (2004) *How Congress Evolves: Social Bases of Institutional Change*, Oxford: Oxford University Press.

Pomper, Gerald M. (2003) "The Fate of Political Parties," *Election Law Journal*, 2.

Pomper, Gerald M. (2005) "The Presidential Election: The Ills of American Politics After 9/11," in Michael Nelson (ed.), *The Elections of 2004*, Washington, DC: C.Q. Press.

Program on International Policy Attitudes (PIPA)/Knowledge Networks (2003) "Misperceptions, the Media and the Iraq War," October 2.

Program on International Policy Attitudes (PIPA)/Knowledge Networks (2004) "Americans and Iraq on the Eve of the Presidential Election," October 28.

Rabkin, Jeremy A. (1996) "David Souter: Stealth Justice," *Reader's Digest*, February.

Raja, Raymond J. La (2004) "Breaking Up the Party: How *McConnell* Downsizes Partisan Campaigns," *Election Law Journal*, 3.

Ranney, Austin (1951) "'Toward a More Responsible Two-Party System': A Commentary," *American Political Science Review*, 45: 488–99.

Ranney, Austin (1954) *The Doctrine of Responsible Party Government*, Urbana: University of Illinois Press.

Ranney, Austin and W. Kendall (1956) *Democracy and the American Party System*, New York: Harcourt, Brace.

Rehnquist, William H. (2005) *2004 Year-End Report of the Federal Judiciary*, Washington, DC: US Supreme Court.

Renshon, Stanley A. (2004) *In His Father's Shadow: The Transformation of George W Bush*, Basingstoke: Palgrave.

Richardson, Jill Darling. (2003) "Poll Analysis: US Nowhere near Eliminating Racism, but Race-based Affirmative Action Not the Answer," *Los Angeles Times*, February 6.

Rimmerman, Craig A. (2002) *From Identity to Politics: The Lesbian and Gay Movements in the United States*, Philadelphia, PA: Temple University Press.

Roberts, John G. (2006) *2005 Year-End Report of the Federal Judiciary*, Supreme Court of the United States.

Rohde, D. W. (1991). *Parties and Leaders in the Postreform House*, Chicago: University of Chicago Press.

Rokkan, S. (1967) "Norway: Votes Count but Resources Decide," in Robert A. Dahl (ed.), *Political Opposition in Western Democracies*, New Haven, CT: Yale University Press.

Rose, Richard (1976) *The Problem of Party Government*, London: Macmillan.

Rose, Richard (1991) *The Postmodern President: George Bush Meets the World*, New Jersey: Chatham House.

Rose, Richard and B. Guy Peters (1976) *Can Government Go Bankrupt?*, New York: Basic Books.

Rosenstone, Steven J. and John Mark Hansen (1993) *Mobilization, Participation, and Democracy in America*, New York: Macmillan.

Ross, Fiona (2002) "Social Policy," in Gillian Peele, Christopher J. Bailey, Bruce Cain, and B. Guy Peters (eds), *Developments in American Politics 4*, Basingstoke: Palgrave.

Rozell, Mark J. (2002) "Executive Privilege Revived? Secrecy and Conflict During the Bush Presidency," *Duke Law Journal*, 52: 403–16, November.

Rudalevige, Andrew (2002) *Managing the President's Program: Presidential Leadership and Legislative Policy Formulation*, Princeton: Princeton University Press.

Saad, Lydia (2005a) "Americans Closely Divided Into Pro-Choice and Pro-Life Groups," Washington, DC: The Gallup Organization, May 12.

Saad, Lydia (2005b) "Gay Rights Attitudes a Mixed Bag," Washington, DC: The Gallup Organization, May 20.

Saletan, William (2004) *Bearing Right: How Conservatives Won the Abortion War*, Berkeley, CA: University of California Press.

Scharpf, F.W. (1988) "The Joint Decision Trap: Lessons from German Federalism and European Integration," *Public Administration*, 66: 239–78.

Schattschneider, E. E. (1960) *The Semisovereign People*, New York: Holt, Reinhart and Winston.

Schick, A. (2003) "Bush's Budget Problem," in Fred Greenstein (ed.), *The George W. Bush Presidency: An Early Assessment*, Baltimore: The Johns Hopkins University Press.

Schlesinger, Arthur M. (1973) *The Imperial Presidency*, Boston: Houghton Mifflin.

Schrag, Peter (1998) *Paradise Lost: California's Experience, America's Future*, New York: The New Press.

Schreckhise, William D., and Todd G. Shields (2003) "Ideological Realignment in the Contemporary US Electorate Revisited," *Social Science Quarterly*, 84.

Scotchie, J. (2002) *Revolt from the Heartland: The Struggle for an Authentic Conservatism*, New Brunswick, NJ: Transaction.

Segal, Jeffrey A. and Harold J. Spaeth (2002) *The Supreme Court and the Attitudinal Model Revisited*, New York: Cambridge University Press.

Serafini, M. (2002) "An Rx for the Democrats?," *National Journal*, June 22.

Sigelman, Lee and Emmett H. Buell (2004) "Avoidance or Engagement? Issue Convergence in US Presidential Campaigns, 1960–2000," *American Journal of Political Science*, 48(4): 650–61.

Silverstein, Ken (2002) "Bush's New Political Science," *Mother Jones*, November–December.

Simon, Mark (2003) "Indian Campaign Donations in the Spotlight: One Fifth of All Recall Money – $6.7 million – Has Come from Tribes," *San Francisco Chronicle*, September 24.

Smith, Mark A. (2000) *American Business and Political Power: Public Opinion, Elections, and Democracy*, Chicago: University of Chicago Press.

Snyder, James M. and Tim Groseclose (2001) "Estimating Party Influence on Roll Call Voting: Regression Coeffcients versus Classification Success," *American Political Science Review*, 95: 689–98.

Sparrow, Bartholomew H. (1999) *Uncertain Guardians: The News Media as a Political Institution*, Baltimore: Johns Hopkins University Press.

Stevenson, Richard and Elizabeth Bumiller (2005) "Cheney Exercising Muscle on Domestic Policies," *New York Times*, January 18.

Stigler, George (1975) *The Citizen and the State: Essays on Regulation*, Chicago: University of Chicago Press.

Stimson, James (2004) *Tides of Consent: How Public Opinion Shapes American Politics*, New York: Cambridge University Press.

Stone, P. (2002) "Peddling Prescription Plans," *National Journal*, July 13.

Sullum, Jacob (1998) *For Your Own Good: The Anti-Smoking Crusade and the Tyranny of Public Health*, New York: The Free Press.

Sundquist, James L. (1995) *Back to Gridlock? Governing in the Clinton Years*, Washington, DC: Brookings.

Swain, Carol M. (2002) *The New White Nationalism in America: Its Challenge to Integration*, New York: Cambridge University Press.

Taggart, P. A. (1996) *The New Populism and the New Politics*, New York: St. Martin's Press.

Taggart, P. A. (2003) *Populism*, Basingstoke: Palgrave.

Taskforce on Inequality and American Democracy (2004) *American Democracy in an Age of Rising Inequality*, Washington, DC: American Political Science Association.

Tessier Marie (2001) "Women's Appointments Plummet Under Bush," *Women's E News*, < www.womensenews.org/article.cfn.dyn/aid/600/ > , January 7.

Thomas, Evan, *et al.* (2005) *Election 2004*, New York: Public Affairs.

Tocqueville, Alexis de (2002) *Democracy in America*, New York: Penguin.

Trippi, Joe (2004) *The Revolution Will Not Be Televised: Democracy, the Internet, and the Overthrow of Everything*, New York: ReganBooks.

Truman, David B. (1971) *The Governmental Process*, 2nd edn, New York: Knopf.

Tulis, Jeffrey K. (1987) *The Rhetorical Presidency*, Princeton: Princeton University Press.

US Census Bureau (2004) *Statistical Abstract of the United States, 2004–2005*, Washington, DC: GPO.

US Census Bureau (2005) *Current Population Reports, P60–229, Income, Poverty, and Health Insurance Coverage in the United States: 2004*, Washington, DC: GPO.

US EPA (1992) *Respiratory Health Effects of Passive Smoking: Lung Cancer and Other Disorders*, US Environmental Protection Agency, Washington, DC: GPO.

US HEW (1964) *Smoking and Health: Report of the Advisory Committee to the Surgeon General of the Public Health Service*, Public Health Service, Washington, DC: GPO.

US HEW (1979) *Healthy People – The Surgeon General's Report on Health Promotion and Disease Prevention*, Public Health Service, Washington, DC: GPO.

US HHS (1986) *The Health Consequences of Involuntary Smoking: A Report of the Surgeon General*, Public Health Service, Washington, DC: GPO.

US HHS (1990) *Healthy People: National Health Promotion and Disease Prevention Objectives*, Public Health Service, Washington, DC: GPO.

US HHS (2000) *Healthy People 2010*, Office of Disease Prevention and Health Promotion, Washington, DC: GPO.

US HHS (2001) *The Surgeon General's Call to Action to Prevent and Decrease Overweight and Obesity 2001*, Public Health Service, Washington, DC: GPO.

US HHS (2003) *Prevention Makes Common Sense*, US Department of Health and Human Services, Public Health Service, September.

US HHS (2004) "Citing 'Dangerous Increase' in Deaths, HHS Launches New Strategies Against Overweight Epidemic," News Release, US Department of Health and Human Services, March 9.

US Surgeon General (2005) "Public Health Priorities," < www.surgeongeneral. gov/publichealthpriorities > .

Van Waarden, F. (1995) "Persistence of National Policy Styles," in B. Unger and F. van Waarden (eds), *Convergence or Diversity: Internationalization and Economic Policy Response*, Aldershot: Avebury.

Viguerie, Richard A. and David Franke (2004) *America's Right Turn: How Conservatives Used New and Alternative Media to Take Power*, Chicago: Bonus.

Waddan, Alex (2002) *Clinton's Legacy: A New Democrat in Governance*, Basingstoke: Palgrave.

Walcott, Charles E. and Karen M. Hult (2005) "White House Structure and Decision-Making: Elaborating the Standard Model," *Presidential Studies Quarterly*, 35: 303–18.

Walsh, Kenneth T. (2006) "White House Watch: Bartlett to Play Bigger Role in Bush Message," *US News and World Report*, January.

Wand, Jonathan N., Kenneth W. Shotts, Jasjeet S. Sekhon, Walter R. Mebane, Michael C. Herron and Henry E. Brady (2001) "The Butterfly Did It: The Aberrant Vote for Buchanan in Palm Beach County, Florida," *American Political Science Review*, 95: 793–810.

Warshaw, Shirley Anne (1996) *Power-sharing: White House Cabinet Relations in the Modern Presidency*, Albany, NY: State University of New York Press.

Waxman, C. (1968) *The End of Ideology Debate*, New York: Funk and Wagnalls.

Wayne, S.J. (2004) *Is This Any Way to Run a Democratic Government?* Washington, DC: Georgetown University Press.

Weaver, R.K. (2000) *Ending Welfare as We Know It* Washington, DC: The Brookings Institution.

Weaver, R. K., R. Shapiro, and L. Jacobs (1995) "The Polls-Trends: Welfare," *Public Opinion Quarterly*, 59: 606–27.

White, John Kenneth (2003) *The Values Divide*, New York: Chatham House.

Whorton, J. C. (1982) *Crusaders for Fitness: The History of American Health Reformers*, Princeton, NJ: Princeton University Press.

Wilcox, Clyde (2002) *New Interest Group Strategies*, Washington, DC: Campaign Finance Institute.

Wilson, Graham K. (1977) *Special Interests and Policymaking: The Politics of Subsidizing Agriculture in Britain and the United States*, Chichester: John Wiley.

Wilson, Graham K. (1979) *Unions in American National Elections*, London: Macmillan.

Wilson, Graham K. (1981) *Interest Groups in the United States*, Oxford: Clarendon Press.

Winant, Howard (2004) "Behind Blue Eyes: Whiteness and Contemporary US Racial Politics," in Michelle Fine, Lois Weis, Linda Powell Pruitt, and April Burns (eds), *Off White: Readings on Power, Privilege, and Resistance*, New York: Routledge.

Winn, Pete (2005) "Judge Strikes Down Nebraska DOMA," *Citizen Link*, < www.family.org > , May 12.

Winner, Langdon (2003) "The Internet and Dreams of Democratic Renewal," in David Anderson and Michael Cornfiled (eds), *The Civic Web: Online Politics and Democratic Values*, New York: Rowman & Littlefield.

Wolfe, A. M. and G. A. Colditz (1998) "Current Estimates of the Economic Cost of Obesity in the United States," *Obesity Research*, 6: 96–106.

Woodward, Bob (2002) *Bush At War*, London: Pocket Books.

Woodward, Bob (2004) *Plan Of Attack*, London: Pocket Books.

World Bank (2005), "World Development Indicators 2005," < www.worldbank. org/ > .

Wright, Deil S. (2003) "Federalism and Intergovernmental Relations: Traumas, Tensions, and Trends," *The Book of the States*, 35: 21–31.

Wright, John R. (1996) *Interest Groups and Congress: Lobbying, Contributions and Influence*, Needham Heights, MA: Allyn and Bacon.

Wuthnow, Robert (2005) *America and the Challenges of Religious Diversity*, Princeton: Princeton University Press.

Yankelovich, Daniel (2005) "Poll Positions," *Foreign Affairs*, Sept/Oct.

Zaller, John (2001) "Monica Lewinsky and the Mainsprings of American Politics," in W. Lance Bennett and Robert M. Entman (eds), *Mediated Politics: Communication in the Future of Democracy*, New York: Cambridge University Press.

Zelizer, J. E. (2004) *On Capitol Hill: The Struggle to Reform Congress and its Consequences 1948–2000*, Cambridge: Cambridge Univesrity Press.

Zimmerman, Joseph F. (2003) "Trends in Congressional Preemption," *The Book of the States*, 35: 32–7.

Zimmerman, Joseph F. (2005) "Congressional Preemption: Removal of State Regulatory Powers," *PS*, 38: 375–8.

Zoellick, Robert B. (2005) "Remarks to National Committee on US–China Relations," New York City, September 21.

Index